WILLIAM PENN AND THE
DUTCH QUAKER MIGRATION TO PENNSYLVANIA

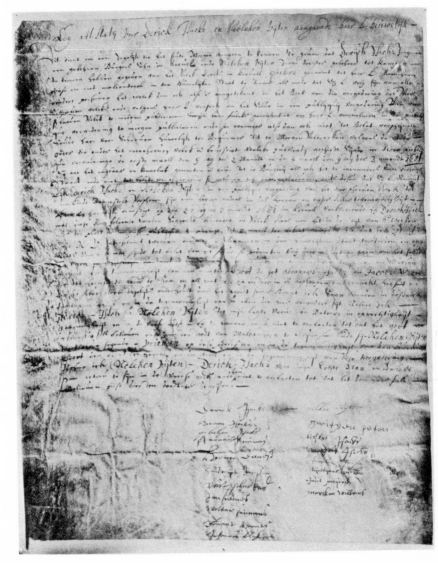

A Dutch Quaker Marriage-Certificate, Krefeld, 1681

WILLIAM PENN

and the

DUTCH QUAKER MIGRATION TO PENNSYLVANIA

BY

WILLIAM I. HULL, Ph. D., F. R. Hist. S.

HOWARD M. JENKINS RESEARCH PROFESSOR OF QUAKER HISTORY IN SWARTHMORE COLLEGE

Author of "The New Peace Movement" (1912), etc.

Baltimore

GENEALOGICAL PUBLISHING COMPANY

1970

Originally Published
Swarthmore, 1935
as *Swarthmore College Monographs on Quaker History*, Number 2
Under the Auspices of the
Howard M. Jenkins Research Professorship

Reprinted with permission and an added half-title
Genealogical Publishing Company
Baltimore, 1970

Library of Congress Catalog Card Number 79-112826
International Standard Book Number 0-8063-0432-4

Made in the United States of America

To

CHARLES FRANCIS JENKINS

President, Friends' Historical Association (Philadelphia)
Member of the Council, The Historical Society of Pennsylvania
Honorary President, The Germantown Historical Society
Vice President, The Genealogical Society of Pennsylvania
Former President, The Friends Historical Society (London)

Author of many helpful Writings in the Field of American and
Quaker History

Founder (in Memory of his distinguished Father) of the Professorship
under whose Auspices this Monograph is published

CONTENTS

ILLUSTRATIONS

Illustrations—*(Con't.)*

Page

PREFACE

The original purpose of this monograph was to tell the European half of the story of William Penn's relations with the Dutch Quakers who emigrated to Pennsylvania. But the predominance of the Dutch Quaker pioneers, as revealed by that story, in the settlement of Germantown made it desirable to follow them across the Atlantic and indicate the part which they played for at least a quarter-century in the affairs of the Quaker colony.

Hence the study comprises, first, Penn's efforts on his three journeys to Holland and Germany to convert to Quakerism the Labadists, Pietists and Quietists whom he found there; second, the way in which small Quaker communities on the Continent had prepared the way for these visits; and finally, the rise and progress of those congregations of Dutch and German Quakers who, fleeing from persecution, accepted Penn's invitation to settle in Pennsylvania.

The results of the study show, in the first place, that while Penn failed to bring many people on the Continent into the Quaker fold, he was extraordinarily successful in paving the way for a great exodus from it to the Promised Land beyond the Atlantic; and second, that the founding of Germantown which together with Philadelphia was the prime center and the original magnet of settlement in the Province, was due, not as historians have so interpreted it, to *German Mennonites,* but to *Dutch Quakers.*

That the pioneer "Germantown" was in reality "Dutch Town" and that it, like Philadelphia, was a Quaker town, is revealed by many facts which have emerged from the study of its European origins and of its local history. It lies outside the scope of this monograph to give all the details of its local history—a task which has been well accomplished by numerous authors; but enough of these details have been cited, it is believed, to complete the story which the European origins begin.

Since one important evidence of Dutch heredity is the original form of the names borne by the first settlers, care has been taken to de-Germanize and de-Anglicize all those which were derived from a Dutch ancestry. With this object in view, the text has been supplemented by two appendices which give the names of all the settlers in Germantown during the pioneer years between 1683 and 1709, at which latter date the great tide of German immigration set in.

As to the religious affiliations of the founders of Germantown, it should be recalled that membership in the Society of Friends was purposely left at first without hard and fast rules and in an elastic condition demanded by the rapid growth of Quakerism. No outward ceremonies of baptism, confirmation, and mutual participation in the Lord's Supper were recognized as constituting membership; while the acceptance of no creed was demanded; and "birthright membership", impossible at first, was not officially recognized until 1737.

But the forsaking of other religious services and regular attendance upon Friends' meetings for worship and "discipline"; contributions to the funds of the society; participation in such Quaker "testimonies" as simplicity or plainness of speech, dress and, conduct, opposition to oaths, war, etc.; practice of the Friends' customs relating to marriage, funerals, etc.; and above all, a share in the social obloquy, fines, imprisonment and exile which were visited upon Dutch and English Quakers alike: these were the distinguishing marks of a "Quaker" in the early days of a religious community which has always preferred to regard itself as a *society*, rather than as a *church*. And these were the marks, as will be seen, of the founders of Germantown and the early Dutch immigrants into Pennsylvania.

The task of inducing households in the civilized Old World to pull up stakes and emigrate to a barbarous New World was by no means an easy one, to be taken as a matter of course. The varied methods adopted by Penn and his associates to accomplish it make in themselves a story full of historical and personal significance. To do part justice to this story, the monograph portrays not only the efforts made by Penn himself, but revives those of his assistants, especially of Jacob Telner, Benjamin Furly and Roger Longworth. Biographical sketches (the only detailed ones which have hitherto been written) of Telner and Longworth are included in this monograph, while an extended biography of Furly is reserved for a later monograph in the series.

The primary source upon which the first three chapters of this monograph are based is Penn's own account of his "Travails in Holland and Germany, Anno MDCL XXVII". The original manuscript, written by Penn himself, and signed in five places with his initials and in four places with his full name, was preserved in the Collection of his grandson, Granville Penn (1761–1844). It was bought by Sotheby's, London, November 4, 1888, and sold by them to "an Irish Lady", in or after May, 1889; its next owner was an English Friend, Joseph J. Green, of Stansted, Essex, who bought it from "the Irish Lady" before January 2, 1890, and sold it to Charles Roberts, an American Friend, of 1716 Arch Street, Philadelphia. After the latter's death, it was sold by Mrs. Charles Roberts, July 16, 1914, to the Pennsylvania Historical Society, in whose library it has since been preserved.*

---

* Cf. the fly-leaves of the bound manuscript, and a letter from Joseph J. Green to *The Friend* (London), Vol. XXX (1890), p. 40. The large money-value which collectors have placed on even the printed copies of this book is indicated by the fact that a copy of its 1695 edition was sold in 1926 for £340. About one year earlier, the original MS. of Penn's first Charter to the People of Pennsylvania, April 25, 1682, was bought for $25,000.00 and presented to the Commonwealth of Pennsylvania, which preserves it among its state archives in Harrisburg.

It consists of 116 closely written quarto pages. It does not include the Preface which Penn wrote for the first printed edition (1694), but begins with his departure from Worminghurst, the 22nd. of 5th. Month (July), 1677, and ends with the letter which he wrote to the Countess of Hoorn on the eve of his re-embarking from Briel, the 20th. of 8th. Month (October), 1677. The differences between this original manuscript and its printed editions are not very numerous; but the helpful marginal details which are found in the manuscript have been incorporated in this book.

To the Historical Society of Pennsylvania, the author is indebted for access to this manuscript journal of Penn's "Travails", as well as to the Pemberton, Etting and Streper Manuscripts. From these, and from the various European archives mentioned in the preface to the first monograph in this series, and cited in the foot-notes of this one, the details of the story have been drawn.

For permission to use the Dutch Quaker Marriage-Certificate of Krefeld, 1681, which is reproduced in the frontispiece, and which is so important a link between the Dutch Quakers in the Valley of the Rhine and in the Valley of the Schuylkill, the author extends his special thanks to its present possessor, Mrs. Benjamin K. Kirk, of Drexel Hill, Pennsylvania, who traces her descent from several of the first settlers.

Although comparisons are said to be odious, and analogies are usually precarious, they are sometimes helpful in estimating the value of events which in themselves seem to be of slight or no historic importance. Perhaps, then, it may be of service to link Germantown and Philadelphia together in the founding of Pennsylvania, even as Plymouth and Boston are linked in the founding of Massachusetts, and to contemplate their small beginnings in the light of their great contributions to the growth and character of the American Republic.*

WILLIAM I. HULL.

Swarthmore College,
June 18, 1935.

---

* While Plymouth and Boston have grown to be cities of 13,000 and 780,000 people, Germantown and Philadelphia have grown to 100,000 and 2 millions respectively.

WILLIAM PENN AND THE
DUTCH QUAKER MIGRATION TO PENNSYLVANIA

William Penn and the Dutch Quaker Migration to Pennsylvania

CHAPTER I

PENN'S MISSION TO HOLLAND AND GERMANY

The connection of William Penn with Holland is believed by many of his biographers to have begun before he was born. His contemporary, the chronicler Samuel Pepys, writing under date of December 28, 1664, records: "To Sir W. Pen's to his Lady, who is a well-looked, fat, short, old Dutch woman; but one that hath been heretofore pretty handsome, and is now very discreet, and I believe, hath more wit than her husband." Lord Braybrooke, in his edition of Pepys's Diary (1825), adds the footnote, "Margaret, daughter of John Jasper, a merchant at Rotterdam." There are sundry other gossipy entries in Pepys's Diary relating to William Penn's mother, but no other clue to her origin.

Later research[1] appears to have established the fact that she was the daughter of John and Marie Jasper, who resided before 1641, at Ballycase, County Clare, Ireland. Whether her father was at any time "a merchant at Rotterdam", we are not informed. Margaret Penn's first husband was "Nicasius Vanderscure", who resided at the time of the marriage (1641) at Kilrush, County Clare, Ireland. The records of the Dutch Reformed Church of Austin Friars, London, reveal this fact, and thus connect him, as does his name, with Dutch ancestors. His widow, "Margaret Van der Schuren", married Captain William Penn, in 1643. It was perhaps this Dutch name of her first husband which she retained as a widow that caused Pepys to refer to her as a "Dutch woman"; while Lord Braybrooke's knowledge of the family of Jaspers in Rotterdam may have caused him to assign John Jasper to that city—although, of course, John

---

[1] Albert Cook Myers in *The Journal of the Friends' Historical Society*, Vol. V. (1908), p. 118.

Jasper of Ireland may have been at one time "a merchant at Rotterdam."

A careful search[2] in the Gereformeerde and Schotsche Trouw Registers and the Gereformeerde Doop and Begrafenis Registers, of Rotterdam, has revealed only the betrothals of Jan and Jacob Jasperszoon (1608); the baptism of Grietje, daughter of Willem Jasperse (1626); and the burial of Jan Jasperse's wife and of Jasper Janszoon (1609). But no trace has been found of Margaret, daughter of Jan.

These Rotterdam records reveal the names of sundry members of the family of Margaret Jasper's first husband, the Van der Scurens, in the first half of the Seventeenth Century. That her second husband, Sir William Penn, had important naval and military connections with Holland is inscribed in history; and tradition reports that a "Dutch Punch Bowl" made for him in Holland, in 1653, was possessed by W. Stuart, of Tempsford Hall, Sandy, in 1884.[3]

THE LABADISTS

William Penn's first authentic connection with the Continent dates from 1671 when, at the age of twenty-six, he went with Benjamin Furly of Rotterdam and Thomas Rudyard of London to try his hand at winning to Quakerism the sect of the Labadists. The latter were an interesting Protestant Community, some of whose superficial resemblances to the Quakers led the Quaker founders to hope that they might be induced to unite with Quakerism. Their leader was Jean de Labadie, a Frenchman, born in Guienne in 1610, and educated at Bordeaux, in a Jesuit college; falling into disfavor with the Jesuits, in Paris, he sided with the Jansenist party and, becoming a canon in Amiens, he preached and worked against the Romish tendency in the Gallican church; driven from this post by Jesuit hostility, he went to Port Royal des Champs, where he read Calvin's works and became a Protestant; appointed rector of the university at Montaubon, he filled this post for seven years, and then

---

[2] Made in 1905 and 1908 through the courtesy of that gentleman and scholar, Dr. E. Wiersum, the Archivist of Rotterdam.

[3] *The Pennsylvania Magazine*, Vol. 8 (1885), p. 362.

IOHANN de LABADIE

S.J.ARCHIFANATICUS.

ANNO MDCLXXIV.

Mort

went as professor to Geneva; here, he is said to have exerted a great influence and become "a second Calvin."

At the age of fifty, he received from the Walloon congregation in Middelburg a call to become its minister, and for seven years he served in that capacity, stirring up much opposition by refusing to subscribe to the Walloon confession of faith. Seven synods were held, between 1666 and 1669, to consider his "heresy", which consisted principally in his rejection of linguistic and classical knowledge alone for the interpretation of the Bible, and insisted on the light shed on the mind of the reader by the Holy Spirit. This "Light Within", as the Quakers called it, Labadie claimed to be as essential as the Bible itself; and it was this doctrine that drew the Quakers' attention to him. It was this doctrine, too, which led his opponents to class him as an "Archfanatic" and to associate him with Spinoza, Böhme and "Oxmann the Quaker and Anabaptist."

Withdrawing from the Reformed Church, and founding the first Reformed sectarian church in Holland, Labadie and his followers removed to Amsterdam in August, 1669. His fame as an eloquent and popular preacher had been established throughout Holland by his innumerable sermons, which he had delivered, like the contemporary Quakers, in village, town and city, on every opportunity, and in every possible place on land and canal.

The Labadists' doctrines were expounded in a French treatise by Jean Samuel (translated into Dutch by Samuel Schorel, and published in Amsterdam in 1669), and were similar to some of those which were taught by the Friends. For example, they renounced many of the traditional forms of worship, and coördinated with the Bible, or "exterior Word", as the source of religious truth, the "interior Word", or the direct illumination of the soul of man by the spirit of God through the Holy Ghost. These and other similarities between the Labadists and the Friends were to bring their leaders into contact at various times and places, and led the populace of Amsterdam to confuse the two sects and to denounce them indiscriminately as Quakers.

On Labadie's arrival in Amsterdam, he rented a house for himself and his assistants and began the holding of religious meetings. To him came a distinguished convert, Anna Maria van Schurman, of Utrecht,[4] her nephew—a boy of eleven— her friend, Anna de Veer, their two maids, two widows with their children, and two older girls, all of whom lived on the lower floor of De Labadie's house, while he and his assistants lived on the upper floor and the religious meetings were held in the large room on the floor between them. Some prominent Hollanders were converted to the Labadists' faith, among them being the three Van Sommelsdijk sisters, Anna, Maria, and Lucia, of Friesland;[5] Luise Huyghens, of Rijsbergen; Aemilie van der Haar, of The Hague; a preacher, Adrian van Herder, and Conrad van Beuningen, Burgomaster of Amsterdam. These successes, added to their being confused with the despised Quakers; the charge that De Labadie, like Penn, was a Jesuit spy; and some unfortunate occurrences at the Labadist house, caused the clergy, the populace, and finally the magistrates of the city to turn against them.

Some of the occurrences referred to above may be cited as illustrative of those incidents, the misinterpretation of which often led to religious persecution, in the seventeenth century in Holland and at many other times and places. One of the elderly widows who had come from Middelburg to live in the Labadist house at Amsterdam, died after a three weeks' illness, and her corpse was placed in a coffin beside the street-door; at this very time, the owner of the house sent some workmen to dig a drain in the back-garden, and the street urchins, associating the two facts and inferring a secret burial, raised the cry of "murder", and collected a mob, which stoned the house and any of its inmates who showed themselves; as a result, the Labadists were confined to their house for three days and nights, at the end of which time the widow's funeral had to be conducted under military escort. Again, one of the deacons, Ménuret by name, went insane, abused De Labadie violently, and finally died of brain fever, whereupon it was reported that De Labadie had kicked him to death; and although a public in-

[4] *Infra*, p. 10.

[5] These were the daughters of Cornelis van Aersens, Lord of Sommelsdijk, said to have been the richest man in Holland. See *infra*, pp. 10, 14.

vestigation resulted in De Labadie's acquittal, the incident was one more cause of popular indignation.

The Labadist deacons, too, in their zeal, attempted to make converts by participating in the meetings of the theosophist, Gichtel, who held large prayer-meetings at night in the fields outside of the city; and they attempted also to convert the followers of Antoinette Bourignon, who became notorious in Amsterdam by publishing there, in 1669, in a French version, her treatise entitled, "The Grave of the false Theology." Antoinette succeeded in collecting a large number of followers, who believed in her assumed power to heal the sick and cast out devils, and who followed her in 1671 to the island of North Strand, off the coast of Holstein.[6] The Labadists, however, were not so successful as some of the other "New Lights"; for as Anna Maria van Schurman complained: "We learned quickly enough how far our age had fallen from truth, for so few were willing to give themselves to Christ and to forego earthly comfort."

Within the Labadists' House in Amsterdam—"the Cloister", as it was styled, "of the Evangelical Church"— spiritual joy reigned supreme and made itself manifest by dancing, singing and sundry exuberances of an animated life; but the sect was far indeed from gaining in the city, or in the nation, the 60,000 converts whom Anna Maria van Schurman in her enthusiasm claimed for it at one time. Finally, its head and adherents were ordered by the Amsterdam magistrates to permit none but "house-mates" to attend their religious meetings. This order—a kind of Conventicle Act—came at the critical time when some of De Labadie's followers in Middelburg were about to join him in Amsterdam, and was the final cause of his accepting an invitation which had been extended by Anna Maria van Schurman's old friend and admirer, the Princess Elisabeth of the Palatinate, who was the Protestant Abbess of Herford, and who invited the Labadist community to settle upon her estates at the latter place.

Accordingly, in the Spring of 1671, De Labadie and four other pastors, with about fifty followers, and escorted to the quay by a throng of citizens, set sail from Amsterdam for

---

[6] *Infra*, pp. 19–21.

Bremen, whence they were to be conveyed by carriage to Herford. Here they were to be visited several times by Quaker missionaries; and even before they left Amsterdam an effort had been made to convert them to the Quaker faith.[7] A nucleus of twenty-eight members was left temporarily in Amsterdam, and an attempt at colonization was made, some years later, in what was supposed to be the Province of Pennsylvania; and in both the Old World and the New it was hoped for a time that these cousins-german of the Quakers would be united with the Society of Friends.

Gerard Croese records in his ''History of the Quakers''[8] that ''the first of the Quakers that came from Scotland to the Labadists in Amsterdam was George Keith, ... After him, comes out of England Robert Barclay, ... These men, one after the other, treat about this matter [union with the Quakers] with Labadie and the rest of them on whom the government of the society lay.'' If these visits really occurred,[9] in Amsterdam, they must have been made in 1669–70; and they may have inspired the visit which Penn made the next year to the Labadist community at Herford.

The modern Westphalian and Prussian city of Herford was called by Penn and his contemporaries Herwerden.[10]

---

[7] Cf. G. D. J. Schotel's „Anna Maria van Schurman", Utrecht, 1853, H. van Berkum's „De Labadie en de Labadisten", Sneek, 1851, and Una Birch's "Anna van Schurman", N. Y., 1909. Van Berkum's frontispiece is a portrait of De Labadie and a picture (a stone-cut by P. Blommers of The Hague) of the Labadists' departure from Amsterdam.

[8] Latin edition, 1695, Liber III, p. 515; English edition, 1696, II, 222.

[9] Croese is our only near-contemporary authority for them, except that Mosheim in his „Ketzergeschichte," 1746, cites in their support Mollerus (Moeller, or Moller), a Danish scholar, whose „Cimbria Literata" was published in Copenhagen in 1744. Mollerus cites as his authority "a manuscript journal" of 1717, extracts from which are given by J. F. Feller in his "Trimest. IX Monumentum ineditorum", sect. III. A. 1717, pp. 498–500. Willem Sewel does not refer to these visits, although in his brief references to Barclay he says that he "was well acquainted with him." The facts, however, that Barclay was well acquainted with the French language and people, and that his uncle was part owner of merchant-ships plying between England and the Continent, help to make a journey to Amsterdam in 1670 to visit the Labadists and their French leader at least possible and credible.

[10] Croese, in the Latin edition of his "Quaker History" (p. 517) calls it *Sylva Arausionensi*, which may have been the mediaeval Latin name for its abbey; the English edition of his book (Vol. II, p. 224) uses the form "the ——— Wood."

In the journal of his "Travails" in 1677, Penn gives the following account of his visit to the Labadists in 1671 when they were still living there:

"The Princess [Elizabeth of the Palatinate] giveth them an invitation [to settle in Herford], and they came and were protected by her; but since some miscarriages falling out in that place, she thereupon in good measure withdrew her Favour from them, and they removed into another place [Wieuwerd]. I was moved to Visit this Man and his Company [at Herford] six years ago, and did see him and his two great Disciples, but they would not suffer me to see the People which I laboured for. In that day I saw the airiness and unstableness of the man's spirit, and that a sect-master was his name. And it was upon me, both by word of mouth and writing, to let them know that the enemy would prevail against them to draw them into inconvenient things, if they came not to be stayed in the light of Jesus Christ, and to know the holy silence; and that at last they would come to fall out one with another, and moulder away; which is in some measure come to pass as I feared. For I clearly perceived, that though they had received some divine touches, there was a danger they would run out with them, and spend them like prodigals; not knowing then where to stay their minds for daily bread. Yea, though they were something angelical and like to the celestial bodies, yet if they kept not their station, they would prove fallen stars. They moved not in the motion of Him who visited them, but were filled with gross mixtures, and thereby brought forth mixed births, that is to say, things not natural but monstrous. In fine, they were shy of us, they knew us not; yet I believed well of some of the people, for a good thing was stirring in them."[11]

Gerard Croese, who may have seen a copy of Penn's "Travails" before his own book was published, reflects the Quaker attitude towards the Labadists as follows:[12] "But when the Quakers [i.e. Keith and Barclay] open'd their Mind briefly and in a common Style, they on the other hand

---

[11] Wm. Penn's "An Account of Travails in Holland and Germany, 1677", London, 1694; pp. 33–4 (London edition, 1714, pp. 29–30; Philadelphia edition 1878, pp. 34–5).

[12] English edition, II, 223.

us'd such deep and far fetch'd Speeches, and those so round about the bush, and turning and winding, and so much Eloquence, or endless Talkativeness, that the Quakers knew not what these Men would say, or how to know or find out and discern their Opinions, Institutions, and Intentions, or where to have them (which also had often happen'd to our People[13] enquiring of these Men about these things), and now began to suspect that they were not such a pure sort of People, and were either bordering upon some Errors, or privately entertain'd and bred some monstrous Opinion.''

Referring, apparently, to Penn's visit of 1671, Croese continues: ''And when the Quakers tried again at another time to see further if by any means they could bring things to a Consent and Agreement, and a conjunction together that they might act in common Concert, the Labadists not only drew back, but also resented it ill, and were so angry that they thought it would be to no purpose to try any farther Conclusions with them.'' Mosheim,[14] too, commenting upon De Labadie's refusal of Barclay's and Keith's invitation to join the Quakers, says that it was probably due to a principle of ambition and the desire of remaining head of a sect. But it would appear that one of the fundamental differences between the Labadists and the Quakers was that the former, like so many other Protestant sects, desired to reform only the church, while the latter desired to reform entire Christendom ''from the ground up and from within outward'', and, to accomplish this, to destroy the established church and all its ordinances.

The leading Labadists whom, besides the Princess Elisabeth and Labadie himself, Penn was most desirous of seeing were the two ministers Ivon and Du Lignon; Heinrich and Peter Schlüter and the latter's wife (née De Vries), from Wesel; Louisa Huygens of Rijnsburg; Juffrouw Wilhelmine of Buytendijk; the three sisters Van der Haar; Anna Maria van Schurman; and the sisters Anna, Maria and Lucia van Sommelsdyk. Nearly all of these came from Hol-

---

[13] Croese was a clergyman of the Dutch Reformed Church, and was well versed in the controversies between that church and De Labadie in the Sixteen-Sixties.

[14] *Op. cit.*

land, and nearly all lived in the same house. It was chiefly through the influence of Anna Maria van Schurman that the Labadists had received Elisabeth's invitation to settle at Herford; but Labadie's jealousy and influence with the two ladies prevented Penn in 1671 from seeing the Princess or even Anna Maria.

The people of Herford were bitterly opposed to the settlement of the Labadists among them, and persecuted them in various ways, including an attempt to starve them out by means of a food boycott. In spite of Elisabeth's continued favor, and during her absence in Berlin to make an appeal to the Elector in their behalf, the Labadist leaders decided to yield to the popular persecution and settle elsewhere. Starting forth in carriages, they withdrew "northward, not knowing their destination, but resigning themselves to the guidance of the Holy Spirit." Spending five months outside of Hamburg, during De Labadie's serious illness, they passed on to Altona, where De Labadie died in 1674. Altona was then in tolerant Denmark; but its king could not protect them against the popular prejudice, which persisted in classing them with the hated Quakers.

To disabuse the popular mind of this injustice, which had been visited upon them in Amsterdam and Herford as well, Labadie and four of his associates had written a pamphlet in French, which was translated into Dutch and published in Amsterdam in 1671. This was entitled "Disclosure or Revelation of the Purity of Sentiment in the Teaching and Belief of the Labadists." It indignantly denies that the Labadists had any connection with or real likeness to "Papists, Arrians, Nestorians, Eutycheans, Manichees, Pelagians, Socinians, Armenians, Quakers, or adherents to any other kind of foolishness whatsoever." To it, Anna Maria van Schurman added a postscript of seventeen lines (dated "In Erfurt den 14. February, 1671") which endorsed its claim for the Labadists to righteousness, sobriety, purity, etc.

The Quakers did not reply at this time to the Labadists' aspersions upon them, for they were still hopeful of achieving a union between the two peoples. In this hope, Penn made another visit to them, in 1677. By this time, they had

yielded again to popular prejudice and to rumors of war between Denmark and Sweden, and had removed to the little
village of Wieuwerd, in·the Dutch province of Friesland,
between Sneek and Leeuwarden. Three of their members,
the sisters Anna, Maria and Lucia van Sommelsdijk,[15] had
inherited from their mother, Lucia van Waltha, the estate
and castle of Thetinga-State, or Waltha House, just outside
of the village. Here about one hundred "brethren" and
"sisters", and two or three hundred "aspirants", settled
down in 1675 hoping at last for permanent peace and
comfort.

ANNA MARIA VAN SCHURMAN

After De Labadie's death, Anna Maria van Schurman
became until she died in 1678 the Labadists' spiritual leader.
The fame of this remarkable woman had endured into the
Nineteenth Century, although her rôle has become somewhat confused in the minds of English readers. For example, an article about her in the *Edinburgh Review* for
April, 1908, is entitled "A Dutch Bluestocking and Quaker
of the Seventeenth Century." A "Bluestocking" of a high
order she was, but not a Quaker. As an artist, scholar and
mystic, she attained considerable renown among her contemporaries.

Her art included painting (chiefly of miniature portraits),
etching, sketching, embroidery, wax-modelling, singing and
music. A rich collection of her handiwork is preserved in the
fine old town-hall at Franeker; and her musical talent was
such as to earn her the title of "the Dutch Sappho." Her
scholarship is said to have included some knowledge of
Hebrew, Syriac, Arabic, Chaldaean and Ethiopic; but she
was sufficiently modern and non-cloistral to become a leading advocate of "woman's rights". Her cultivation of what
has been called "the Tenth Muse", namely, the genius for
friendship, made friends of many of her eminent contemporaries. So wide-spreading was her fame that she was

[15] At Herford, the Labadists' vow of celibacy had been given up, and Maria
van Sommelsdijk had married one of the ministers, Yvon; and another minister, DuLignon, had married Magdalena van der Haar. Princess Elisabeth
denied that De Labadie had married another of the van Sommelsdijk sisters.

Photo: Hanfstaengl.   *Walker & Cockerell Ph. Sc.*

Anna Maria Van Schurman.
From the portrait by Jan Lievens in the National Gallery.

called also "the star of Utrecht", and became an object of pilgrimage and hero-worship to tourists from many lands.

Her mysticism appears to have developed rather late in life, after many years of religious experiments and controversies; and in 1677, at the age of seventy, she wrote a kind of spiritual autobiography, entitled "Eukleria". Ten years before this, as we have seen, she had come under the influence of Jean de Labadie and, together with her friend Anna de Veer and a dozen other relatives and dependents, became an inmate of the Labadists' House in Amsterdam.[16] She met with a torrent of abuse for taking this step, but turned it aside with the remark that "Religion changes people's nature and makes them care very little for the opinion of men, and very much for faithfulness to the light within."

Throughout her youth and middle age in Utrecht, Anna had been visited by many admirers of her artistic accomplishments and learning; and now in her old age, she continued to be visited by many besides the Quaker leaders who were impressed by her piety and her spiritual leadership of the Labadist community. A writer in *Onze Eeuw* remarks that William Penn as well as very many of his contemporaries came from Germany, France, England and Switzerland to this out-of-the-way village of Wieuwerd, to the small Separatist circle of Labadists, for the purpose of being strengthened in the faith, of receiving comfort, inspiration and uplift in the strife with the world and its enticements, and of learning to know the pure Zion on earth.[17] This may have been a partial result of Penn's visit to Wieuwerd, but it was hardly his purpose in making it. In the journal of his travels in 1677,[18] he says: "It was strong upon my Spirit .... to visit de Labadie's People, that they might know him in themselves, in whom their Salvation standeth; for these simple people are to be pittied."[19]

---

[16] For detailed accounts of this very interesting woman, see Van Berkum, Schotel and Birch, *op. cit.*

[17] J. Herman Riemersma, on „De Separatisten te Wieuwerd", in *Onze Eeuw*, June, 1908.

[18] 1694 edition, pp. 171–190.

[19] In his letter to Fraülein J. E. von Merlau (from Amsterdam, the 11th. of 7th. Month (September), 1677), he speaks of this intended visit, and uses the same words in regard to the Labadists.

Accompanied by Jan Claus, Penn went from Harlingen in Friesland, by way of Leeuwarden, and hired a wagon from that city to "Wiewart, the Mansion-house of the Family of the Somerdykes, where De Labadie's Company resideth." The two missionaries arrived on the 12th. of 7th. Month (September), about 5 P.M., and Penn inquired for "Ivon the Pastor and Anna Maria Schurmans." Ivon, and his Co-pastor (du Lignon) appeared, and received the visitors very civilly, but "seemed shy of letting me speak with A.M.S. objecting her Weakness, Age, taking Physick, &c." Penn reminded them, he says, "how unhandsomely I was used at Herwerden six years ago, by de Labadie their Father, who, though I came a great Journey to visit him and his People, suffered me not to speak with them." This time, the pastors were persuaded to arrange for an interview the next morning. The two travellers then walked "2 English Miles of unknown way" to their lodging (in the town of Wieuwerd), where Penn felt "a great weight" upon his Spirit; but his "Faith was in the power of God", and he had a plain sight that he should have a good service.

Arriving the next morning at the mansion, Penn and Claus were ushered into the chamber of Anna Maria van Schurman where they were met by her, one of the Van Sommelsdÿk sisters, the two pastors and a physician. Here, a long discourse was held on their respective reasons for becoming Labadists or Quakers, Penn illustrating finely his qualifications to be a Quaker ambassador to the simple and the sage alike. He concludes his account of the long interview with the remark: "So I left the blessing and peace of Jesus among them, departing in the love and peace of God; and I must needs say, they were beyond expectation tender and respectful to us; all of them coming with us but the ancient A.M.S. (Who is not able to walk) to the outward Door; giving us their hands in a friendly manner, expressing their great satisfaction in our Visit; and being come by the Porch, and meeting several persons of the Family, I was moved to turn about, and to exhort them, in the presence of the rest, to keep to Christ ..."

The senior pastor's parting injunction to Penn—whose Oxford training may have called it forth—was that since

ANNA MARIA von SCHURMANN
gebohren zu Cöln a. 1607 ſtarb unter: den
Labadiſten zu Wiewarden beÿ Leuwarden
in Weſtfriesland, a 1678 ält 72 Jahr.

the Truth had arisen first among "a poor, illiterate and simple sort of people", he should not let "the Learning of this World be used to defend that which the Spirit of God hath brought forth; for Scholars now coming among you, will be apt to mix School-learning amongst your simpler and purer Language, and thereby obscure the brightness of the Testimony." To this Penn replied: "I told him it was good for us all to have a care of our own Spirits, Words and Works, confessing what he said had weight in it; telling him, it was our care to write and speak according to the divine Sense, and no humane Invention." Willem Sewel, in his "History of the Quakers",[20] quotes Penn as replying also: "Yes, it is our comfort *(troost)* that we owe nothing of our doctrine to the learning of this world"; upon which reply, a modern Dutch scholar[21] comments that it reveals Penn as "full of pride *(vol trots)*."

A few months before Penn's visit to Anna Maria van Schurman, Robert Barclay had tried to gain an entrance for Quakerism with her and her fellow-Labadists by utilizing in a somewhat indirect fashion their mutual friend, the Princess Elisabeth. In one of his letters to Elisabeth, dated the 16th of March, 1677, from Aberdeen prison, Barclay wrote:[22] "I question not but thy old friend Anna Maria Shurman would be one [to rally to the Lord's standard of Simplicity and Truth] if yet in the body. O how hath my Soul compassionated her as well as the other simple hearts there with her in whom I have seen that the Simplicity is betrayed and they miserably misled, and a selfish Spirit mightily exalting itself among them under the specious pretence and notion of self denyall and mortification. . . . I have waited for a suitable opportunity in which I might write to her in particular and to the other honest hearted among them, but have feared my letters might be kept from them by those who dominate them, preaching self denyall and

---

[20] Dutch edition, p. 616.

[21] Hylkema „Reformateurs", I, 83. Penn's "No Cross, No Crown", with its broad erudition, had been published in its first English edition eight years before this visit, and it is possible that the Labadists had heard of it through Anna Maria van Schurman.

[22] "Reliquiae Barclaianae", p. 20.

mortification to others. Thou might assist me in the right
address of it. . . . Communicate to them some of our letters
to thee and Anna's, especially of the women's . . . from those
true Christians in Britain of whom thou formerly advised
Anna Maria Shurman . . . (not perhaps imagining that it
comes from the Quakers) and then afterwards when they
may come to understand from whom it is may . . . accept the
truth. I leave thee to do herein as the circumstances of the
case will bear."

There is no further reference to this appeal in the correspondence of Barclay with Elisabeth, and there is small
probability that the Princess used her influence with the
aged Labadist recluse. Anna Maria van Schurman died the
year after Barclay's letter and Penn's visit, and Ivon thirty
years later; the last of the Van Sommelsdyk sisters died in
1725, and her castle reverted to her family.

Gerard Croese, who states the resemblances of the Labadists and the Quakers, stressing the contempt of both sects
for the Reformed Church,[23] devotes a paragraph to the fate
of this last of the Van Sommelsdyk sisters as follows:

"Not long after this Society was dissolved and dispers'd
about, after the manner of the Primitive and most blessed
State of the Church, which a great many People presag'd
and foretold from the very first, and so all this expectation
was lost, and all those Treasures which several of the Society had contributed towards it, were turned into Ashes.
Now before this came to pass, this noble Maid, being now
stricken in years, and almost decripit, arriv'd at the end of
her Race, and Dying, was Cloth'd with Immortality: Happy
she, had she not in the very midst of her Glory turn'd aside
to this By-Way, and having run through part of her life, in
that very House, on which she had, with those prodigious
Endowments of Mind, bestow'd so much Cost, she was forsaken of all those that gap'd after her Estate, and all her
Family, and left all alone; but only not forsaken of God, or
abandoned to Desperation, and so in her mournful Seat she
breath'd out her Soul, when she had first recommended it
to God in Christ. Of this excellent Maid, (to add this by the
by) What was mortal and perishing was repos'd not in the

---

[23] "Historia Quakeriana", London ed., 1696, pp. 220-222.

Sepulcral Monument or Tomb belonging to the Family of the *Waltars,* erected in the Church, as it might have been; but without in the Church-yard, or Ground lying about it, in the common Earth, amongst the rest of her [Labadist] Brothers and Sisters, according to her own desire, leaving that Monument out of Modesty, that Familiarizer and Governess of all other Virtues, of which this Lady in her life-time was always the perfect Pattern.''

The Labadists in America

Croese devotes only a few lines to the visit of Penn to the Labadists, calling him ''that most famous *(electissimus)* Man amongst the Quakers: a Man of such Spirit and Wit, as was both willing and able to encounter with all their Adversaries; but'', he concludes, ''the result [of every effort] was the same *(sed fui eventus idem).*'' The result to Penn was doubtless to ease his mind of a duty performed; and although the Labadists did not exchange their religious leadership for that of Penn and Fox, Penn's colony of Pennsylvania was to profit by his labors among them. With the loss of their founders and leaders, and with financial losses due to missionary efforts abroad and to the influx of poor disciples on a communistic basis, the Labadist community dwindled and was dispersed, some of its members reverting to their former environments and faiths, others following in Penn's footsteps across the Atlantic.

Two years before this visit to the Labadists at Wieuwerd, Penn had begun his connection with American affairs in the characteristic rôle of friendly arbitrator. Having successfully arbitrated a dispute over lands in New Jersey, he himself became a trustee and the real founder of the colony of West New Jersey. For it, he drew up ''A Preamble of Concessions and Agreements'', which enthusiastic commentators have called ''the greatest code in popular government that has fallen from the pen of mortal man.'' Writing of it to his agent, Penn himself says: ''Therein we lay a foundation for after ages to understand their liberty as men and Christians, that they may not be brought in bondage, but by their own consent; for we put the *power in the people.*'' In an England which was bending under the tyranny of a

Stuart, and a Europe upon which the dawn of democracy
was to advance with such slow and halting steps during the
next two centuries, this charter of. government was indeed
a noteworthy advance in genuine statesmanship.

During the year following his visit to the Labadists in
1677, Penn actively furthered the colonization of West New
Jersey and was chiefly responsible for the settlement in it
(in 1677–78) of 800 European colonists, most of whom were
English Quakers. Meanwhile, the Labadist communities in
Zeeland, North Holland, South Holland, Utrecht and Friesland were undergoing persecution by the Dutch Reformed
clergy and were either conforming to the Dutch Reformed
Church or gradually emigrating to New York and West New
Jersey.[24] In 1679, two of their "speaking brothers", namely,
Pieter Sluyter and Jasper Dankers, who had doubtless been
among Penn's auditors and conferees, were sent from Wieuwerd to America to spy out the land for a Labadist settlement. They travelled through Long Island, up the Hudson
to Albany, thence eastward to Boston, and then through
New Jersey and along the Delaware into Maryland, which
last named colony they decided upon for the Labadist settlement. This was in Cecil County, on the manor (called "New
Bohemia") which they purchased from Augustine Hermans, whose son had been converted to Labadism in New
York. Not satisfied with the Labadists who were persuaded
to come to the colony from Wieuwerd and other places in
the Netherlands, the two missionaries proselyted and re-
cruited in New York, much to the disgust of the Dutch Reformed clergy in that place. Operating under the assumed
names of Dr. Vorstman (or Vosman) and Jasper Schilder,
they not only caused much concern in religious circles in
New York, but the former was denounced by his fellow-
medical practitioners for his malpractice.[25] Their disturbance continued as late as 1685, when a Dutch Reformed
clergyman of New York reported to the classis at Amsterdam, "concerning the Labadists—their blustering has

---

[24] "Ecclesiastical Records of the State of New York", 1901, pp. 656, 675–6,
746, 785, 830, 833, 856, 874–6, 906, 921, 1004–5, 1051–2, 1067, 1072–3, 1100,
1105–7.

[25] Ibid., pp. 830, 869–71.

mostly been quenched; but now, upon the arrival of some more from the house at Wiewarden, they again protrude their heads above the water. They have been reënforced also by Dutch Quakers, who have come to Long Island."[26]

By 1698, the same clergyman reported that the Labadists had had poor success in Maryland, and were divided among themselves. "In a few years", he writes,[27] "they will have turned to nothing"; and he adds the cheering note: "Neither has the Rev. Classis anything to fear from the Quakers here, who are little regarded and not worthy to be [noticed] in this country. A building of theirs, which has no connection with the Quakers as such, is now used for the Latin school. They too will vanish like smoke, and be scattered and driven away by the wind."

"The impudent head and teacher" of the Dutch Quakers in New York, as the reverend correspondent above quoted calls him, was Jacob Telner, who removed with some of his associates to Germantown, Pennsylvania. There he was visited by another Dutch Reformed pastor of New York, in 1690, who wrote an interesting miniature account of Penn's colony in that year.[28] But Sluyter and Dankers, although they too viewed the beauties of Penn's wood-lands, did not contribute many Labadist colonists to the Quaker colonies of Pennsylvania and New Jersey.[29] The settlement which they formed in "New Bohemia" on the Elk River, Maryland, was supposed for a time to be part of Penn's grant; but the line finally drawn between Pennsylvania and Maryland left it in the latter colony.

---

[26] *Ibid.*, p. 906.

[27] *Ibid.*, p. 1232.

[28] See *infra*, pp. 239–253, for Jacob Telner and Germantown.

[29] The Journal of their journey of 1679–80, was translated from the Dutch into English and published by the Long Island Historical Society in 1867. The Quaker poet, John G. Whittier, did not fail to introduce Sluyter into his narrative poem, "The Pennsylvania Pilgrim":

> "Or Sluyter, saintly familist, whose word
> "As law the Brethren of the Manor heard,
> "Announced the speedy terrors of the Lord,
> "And turned, like Lot at Sodom, from his race,
> "Above a wrecked world with complacent face,
> "Riding secure upon his plank of grace."

A glimpse of the Labadists in their American home comes to us from the Journal of Samuel Bownas, a Quaker minister from England, who visited them in the summer of 1702. "A Friend, my guide, went with me", Bownas writes,[30] "and brought me to a people called Labadies, where we were civilly entertained in their way. When supper came in, it was placed upon a long table in a large room, where, when all things were ready, came in, at a call, about twenty men or upwards, but no woman: we all sate down, they placing me and my companion near the head of the table, and having paused a short space, one pulled off his hat, but not the rest till a short space after, and then one after another they pulled all their hats off, and in that uncovered posture sat silent (uttering no words that we could hear) near half a quarter of an hour; and as they did not uncover at once, so neither did they cover themselves again at once; but as they put on their hats fell to eating, not regarding those who were still uncovered, so that it might be about two minutes time or more between the first and last putting of their hats. I afterwards queried with my companion concerning the reason of their conduct, and he gave this for answer, that they held it unlawful to pray till they felt some inward motion for the same; and that secret prayer was more acceptable than to utter words; and that it was most proper for every one to pray, as moved thereto by the spirit in their own minds.

"I likewise queried, if they had no women amongst them? He told me they had, but the women eat by themselves, and the men by themselves, having all things in common, respecting their household affairs, so that none could claim any more right than another to any part of their stock, whether in trade or husbandry; and if any had a mind to join with them, whether rich or poor, they must put what they had in the common stock, and if they afterwards had a mind to leave the society, they must likewise leave what they brought, and go out empty handed.

"They frequently expounded the scriptures among themselves, and being a very large family, in all upwards of a hundred men, women and children, carried on something of

---

[30] "The Life and Travels of Samuel Bownas", London, 1795, pp. 57-8.

the manufactory of linen, and had a very large plantation of corn, tobacco, flax, and hemp, together with cattle of several kinds. But at my last going there [in 1728], these people were all scattered and gone, and nothing of them remaining of a religious community in that shape."

ANTOINETTE BOURIGNON

Another sect similar to the Labadists were the followers of Antoinette Bourignon. This religious enthusiast was a native of Flanders and wrote her books in French; but she removed with some of her disciples to Amsterdam, and her writings (in nineteen volumes) were translated into Dutch and German. One of these, "The Grave of the False Theology", was published in Amsterdam, in French, in 1669, and caused her much notoriety. This was the year in which De Labadie settled in Amsterdam, and he made a strong effort to capture her and her followers for his own sect.

The Friends, too, looked upon them as promising converts to Quakerism, and Steven Crisp wrote a letter to them under date of Amsterdam, the 20th. of 3rd. Month, 1669. This letter and other attempts upon them failed; and when, two years later, one of Antoinette's disciples, Christiaan de Cort, "Director of the Island of North Strand", translated into Dutch her "Light of the World", and published it in Amsterdam, the Quakers made a more vigorous and none too amicable attack upon her doctrines. Benjamin Furly performed this service for the Friends in a Dutch pamphlet of some fifty pages which he bluntly entitled, "Anthoinette Bourignon Discovered, and her Spirit revealed in her Writings, plainly shown by her own Books not to be the Spirit of God."

Furly's pamphlet was published in Amsterdam in 1671, about the time of Penn's visit; but by this time Antoinette and her followers had left Amsterdam for their home in the island of North Strand, off the coast of Holstein. This was evidently too far afield from Herford for Penn to go in an attempt at a reconciliation between Antoinette and the Quakers; and by this time, the gulf between them was probably too wide to be bridged even by Penn's persuasive diplomacy. For Furly's sharp discussion of Antoinette's views had brought forth a sharp reply which was published, in Dutch, in Amsterdam in 1672. This was entitled, "Advertisement written by Anthoinette Bourignon to all whom it may concern against the Sect of the Quakers: in regard to their unfounded Arguments and Calumnies which they have endeavored to advance against her by Benjamin Furly and other Quakers." It was translated into English and published in London, in 1708, thirty-six years after its first appearance, and twenty-eight years after Antoinette's death. The Friends do not appear to have replied to it at all in Dutch, and not in English until its publication in that language, when Robert Barclay, son of the Apologist, published his "Modest and Serious Address to the well-meaning Followers of Antonia Bourignon."

The "Record Book of Friends att Urie"[31] has the following reference to this latter reply: "In the year 1708 one Garden[32] a learned and much followed preacher Att Aberdeen tainted with Bourigionism having in his writings inveighed against Friends principles Robert Barclay wrote a notable answer to it entitled *A Serious Address* to the well meaning followers of Antonia Boureignon which had so good an effect being printed and dispersed among a great many, that the Sect afterwards dwindled much away."

De Cort had died in 1669; and two years later, the year in which the Labadists left Amsterdam for Herford, Anthoinette and her followers left Amsterdam for Nord Strand. Here, she wrote and published her many books, selling them chiefly (when at all) at the annual fair held in the neighboring town of Husum. Removing later to Hamburg, where she led a very austere life under the guidance of "the light within", she died finally in 1680 at Franeker, and her followers also were dispersed.

So far from uniting with the Quakers, she turned the tables upon them and, according to one of her biographers,[33] "at Schleswig her company was increased by the arrival of

---

[31] *Journal of the Friends Historical Society*, London, Vol. VII (1910), p. 190.

[32] George Garden, D.D., author of "An Apology for M. Antonia Bourignon", 1699.

[33] Alex. R. Macewen, "Antoinette Bourignon, Quietist", London, 1910, p. 145.

M[r]. ANTOINETTE BOURIGNON born at Lile an[n] 1616 of Fransfort or Lyons an[n] 680 haveing written above 20 several Treatises

P.P. delineavit.   M. V[r] Gucht Sculp:

Christians I've sought from my Nativity:
I liv'd, I wrote, to shew how Such to be:
Convinc'd the World of errors, Sins, abuses;
All hate me for't, each one my *NAME* traduces.
To death they persecute me every where:
How should I other Lot than *JESUS* bear?

some twenty recruits, chiefly Quakers, Jansenists and Mennonites".

THE PRINCESS ELISABETH

The Labadists having departed from the Princess Elisabeth's estates at Herford, the Quaker leaders made strenuous efforts to bring her and her household within the Quaker fold.

Elisabeth was the daughter of the Electoral Prince Friedrich V. of the Palatinate and the Stuart princess Elizabeth, daughter of James I. of England. Born in 1618, at the beginning of the Thirty Years' War, in which her father tried vainly for a crown and lost temporarily his princely coronet, Elizabeth was taken by her parents in 1620 when they fled from the Palatinate to Holland. Here, in The Hague and in Rheine (near Utrecht), she was given an excellent education, far from the flattery of an obsequious court. Refusing the hand of King Ladislaus IV. of Poland, because she was unwilling to accept Catholicism even with a royal husband, she dedicated her life to piety and learning. She mingled in the Protestant and sectarian circles of her Netherlands home, and formed a warm friendship with Anna Maria van Schurman, her senior by eleven years, and with the Dutch Countess Anna Maria van Hoorn, who became her life-long companion. After the death of her father, and by the Peace of Westphalia in 1648, her brother Charles Louis was restored to his greatly diminished principality, and Elisabeth went to reside with him at Heidelberg.

Her childhood, youth and early womanhood had been passed in exile and sorrow. The downfall and death of her father; the drowning of one brother (Frederick Henry) in the Zuyder Zee; the death of another brother (Philip) in the Civil War in France, in 1653; the failure of her dashing brother Prince Rupert in his leadership of the royal cavalry in the Civil War in England; the execution of her uncle, Charles I; the acceptance of Catholicism by her brother Edward and her sister Louise; and the immorality at the court of her brother Charles Louis after his ,Restoration, all united to predispose her mind to seek consolation and guidance in true personal religion.

It is probable that she first heard of Quakerism as early as 1659, when William Ames paid a visit to the court of her brother at Heidelberg and was received with marked favor by him. Elisabeth was residing there at the time, and continued there and at Cassel until she became Abbess of Herford in 1667; so that for nearly a decade, she was in close proximity to the activities of the Quakers in the Rhineland and exposed at least to the echoes of the Quaker preachers following in the footsteps of William Ames.[34] Indeed, the report made by Ames and his successors of their kindly reception at the Palatinate court may have encouraged Robert Barclay and George Keith to try for the princess at Herford as well as for the Labadists, many of whom they must have found in the Rhineland, especially in the Palatinate in and near Krisheim.

ROBERT BARCLAY AND THE PRINCESS

Barclay and Keith may possibly have followed the Labadists to Herford, in 1670; and in 1676 Barclay did visit the princess, who was a distant relative of his mother.[35] Penn in his Journal of 1677, gives us the following brief reference to Barclay's visit: "About a year since R.B. and B.F. [Benjamin Furly] took that city [Herford] in the way of Frederickstadt to Amsterdam, and gave them [the Princess Elisabeth and the Countess of Hoorn] a Visit, in which they informed them somewhat of Friends Principles, and recommended the Testimony of Truth to them, as both a nearer and more certain thing than the utmost of De Labadie's doctrine. They left tender and loving."

Barclay's biographers give no details of this visit to Holland and Germany and merely stress the fact that he "had a satisfactory opportunity of conversing with the Princess on religious subjects." From his own pen, also, comes only the following faint echo of it. In a letter to Steven Crisp dated London, 3rd. of 5th. Mo. (July) 1676,[36] he refers to

---

[34] *Infra*, pp. 262–280.

[35] Katharine Gordon, of the ducal house of that name, and related to the Stuart kings and princes.

[36] Colchester MSS., No. 2.

Crisp's mention of the subject of the resurrection (which, Barclay says, he had "never meddled with") and then speaks of a Latin letter he had received from a schoolmaster in Oldeslow [Oldesloe]—"one of the Lutherans I told thee I met with." He sent with his letter to Crisp an English translation of this letter from the schoolmaster, Johannes Kember, by name, and from it we learn that Kember had met with Barclay and his companion, had heard them speak, had afterwards received a letter from Barclay, and various particulars as to Kember's own religious condition.[37]

In this letter also, he refers as follows to his efforts to secure the release of his father and other Friends from a Scottish prison: "I have at last, after long and tedious attendance, near finished my business; for the D. of Lauderdale told me yesterday he had received order to give me a letter to the Council for Scotland, in order to grant Friends their liberty; which he has promised to give me tomorrow: so that I purpose in two or three days to be going homewards."[38] This return to his home resulted, as will be seen, in his own imprisonment, in spite of ducal, princely and royal promises.

In view of the lack of biographical and autobiographical accounts of Barclay's communications with the Princess Elisabeth, we are fortunate to have preserved a score of letters which passed between them.[39]

The first of these is dated London, the 26th of 4th Mo. (June), 1676, and it refers to "the good opportunity which it pleased the Lord to minister unto us when together." After a long religious appeal, Barclay sends his "true and unfeigned love to the Countess of Hornes", and speaks with interest of her learning to read English; he states also that he had delivered the Princess' letter to her brother, Prince Rupert.

---

[37] *Infra*, p. 325.

[38] This portion of the letter is printed in "Letters, etc., of Early Friends", 1841, p. 202.

[39] "Reliquiae Barclaianae", lithographed copies of letters of various members of the Barclay Family, London, 1870, pp. 1–24, 28–35. Two of these letters are quoted from the M. Thirnbeck MSS. by Maria Webb in "The Fells of Swarthmoor Hall", London, 1865, pp. 327–30.

To this letter, the Princess replied, on July 21/31, 1676, as follows: "My dear Friend in our Saviour Jesus Christ, I have received your letter dated the 24th of June this day, and since I am pressed to take this opportunity to make a certain address unto your Brother Benjamin Furley, I must give you the abrupt Answer, your memory is dear unto me, and so are your lines and your exhortations very necessary. I confess myself still spiritually very poor and naked, all my happiness is, that I do know I am so,—and whatsoever I have seemed or studied heretofore, is but as dust in comparison to the true knowledge of Christ. I confess also my infidelity to this light, by suffering myself to be conducted by a false *politique* light; now that I have sometimes a small glimpse of the True Light, I do not attend to it as I should, being drawn away by the works of my calling, which must be done. Like your swift English hounds, I often overrun my scent,—being called back when it is too late. Let not this make you less earnest in your prayers for me,—you see I need them. Your letters will be always welcome, so shall your friends, if any please to visit me.

"I should admire God's providence, if my brother could be a means of releasing your father and the 40 more prisoners in Scotland. Having promised to do his best, I know he will perform it, he has always been true to his word; and you shall find me by the grace of the Lord a true friend.

Elizabeth.

"P.S. The Countess of Hornes sends her most hearty commendations, has not had time to learn English, having imployed it in more necessary work since God has visited this Family with many sick of small pox & contagious Feavers of which she has had a care not considering the Infection, amongst the rest there was a Servant of hers very desperately sick of whom she had ane especiall care deeming her to be also a Sister in Christ who did draw great comfort out of the Books you left here."

At the same time, the Countess of Hoorn wrote as follows: "Dear Friend, It was a real joy to me to receive your acceptable letter, which this morning awaited my hands by the post. It testifies your love and care for me who am unworthy

thereof. Therefore do I justly esteem it the more, being
heartily thankful that you remember me before the Lord,
who am waiting upon Him—oh that it might be truly in the
Spirit. I cannot but admire the wonderful providence of
God, which brought you hither, and raised such love mutu-
ally between us. I can in truth say that my heart went after
you in love, and hath been many a time in admiration of that
wonderful work of the Lord amongst us the last time we saw
each other. . . .

"That which now makes me fearful to receive anything
[I do not clearly see] to be the testimony of God, is, because
so many I perceive have deceived themselves, taking the
testimony of the flesh for the testimony of God; not that they
do it willingly, yet I must needs believe that they deceive
themselves therein. Yet this I see, that there must be a testimony of God in the soul . . . As the Lord gives you liberty,
sigh with me, and for me, for the arising of this witness. I
confess I am not worthy of such a favour, being an unfaith-
ful virgin, yet hope still for favour and mercy from Him
that calls me. . . . I could well desire with that lovely lady
(I mean the Lady Overkirk)[40] to be delivered from all these
opinions, and that I be no more of Paul's or Apollo's, but
only Christ's, and come into fellowship with those that have
the testimony of Jesus, by whatsoever name they are called.

"Satan pressed hard upon me some years ago, with most
of those temptations which now you tell me of. He came so
far as almost to make me believe there was no God; but my
faithful God, in whom my strength, and comfort, and joy
was, stood by me, and rebuked him, so that he became
silenced. . .

"Time permits me not at present to write more unto you,
only that I hope to do my best to learn English. A book that
may contribute to it will be very acceptable to me. When I
know the cost, I shall send it you, and I hope the Lord who
hath sent me in your letters so many good exhortations, will
cause them to live in my soul. I could very well read and
understand them all. I am glad to learn that on your return
home you found all there in a good state. I do thank you,
my beloved friend, for your faithful care of me, and that it

---

[40] *Infra*, pp. 99f.

extended so far as to inquire after my brother, who is now
before 'Mastwcht.'[41] May the Lord do with him what is good
in his eyes.

"Salute for me, I pray, all the lovers of the Cross of
Christ—all who fear the Lord in Spirit and in Truth. The
Lord bind us more and more in His pure love, in which I
remain your dearly loving friend,

Anna Maria''.

Barclay sent copies of the last two letters to the daughters
of Margaret Fell, writing them at the same time (27th of
10th mo. 1676, from Aberdeen Prison) as follows: "As I
intimated in my last, I do now send you a copy of the
Princess Elizabeth's first letter to me, and the Countess of
Horne's. I have since received letters again from both of
them, but they are not by me. You will by these perceive how
things stand with them, and I hope they will refresh you. I
send them to you with the greater confidence, that I know
you to be persons of such education as will use them with
discretion, and not trust them so as to come to the ears or
hands of any one who cannot so use them; knowing that
persons of their condition are apt to offend when their freedom is made public, and will thereby be straightened from
using the like hereafter.—But I fear not you in this particular."

Referring to the Countess of Horne's letter, Barclay
wrote the following postscript: "This was sent to Benjamin
Furley, and by him translated out of the Dutch. She is so
well advanced in the English, that she not only can understand what she reads, but she has translated out of English
into Dutch a book of Isaac Penington's.[42] Excuse the bad
ink. G. K. [George Keith] desires in particular to be minded
by you all."

Barclay's next letter to the Princess was dated Edinburgh 6 of September, 1676. He acknowledged the receipt,
the evening before, of her "acceptable letter", referred to

---

[41] Maastricht, Belgium, then in the hands of its French captors.

[42] This was entitled "The Way of Life and Death . . .," London, 1658; a
Dutch translation of it was published in Rotterdam, 1661, and a second
Dutch edition (probably by Benjamin Furly) in Rotterdam, 1675.

her brother and the persecution of the Friends in Scotland, and expressed his expectation of soon being himself in prison. Two months later, Elizabeth replied to Barclay's recommendations of "silent waiting" by saying that it "is no more in my power than flying through the air, since my calling gives me some diversions, I scarce have ane hour of the day to myself, the night is my best time in which I endeavour to practise your Lesson but cannot brag of much progress. The Countess of Hornes doth outgo me far, having stronger tyes and more Liberty, she hath sent to Benjamin Furly an essay of her translation out of English into Low Dutch, it is a treatise in which I have found great satisfaction. . . . I am sorry that my brother's affection and the king's order have both proved useless to you for the release of your Joyfull Prisoners. . . . P. S. Your Books have not yet come to my hands, but though I send [them] to the Elector of Brandenburg and my Brother-in-law I am certain neither of them both will vouchsaife to read it, but my Brother the Elector [of the Palatinate] will and perchance my Nephew the Duke of Hannover who is a Papist but curious of outward knowledge."

Barclay's "Books" here referred to may have been his "Theses Theologicae", which had been printed in Amsterdam in 1674 and 1675 in several Latin, Dutch and German editions.

Before the last letter was received, Barclay wrote again to the Princess under date of Urie, the 28th. of October, 1676, informing her that he had been in daily expectation of receiving a reply to his September letter—"Wherewith I also wrote one in French to Anna [the Countess]." "My mentioning of your condition," he continues, "to severall of my bretheren and Sisters did raise great love in their hearts towards you and frequent breathings for you . . . , among others one singular woman found herself drawn to write this foregoing [enclosed ?] Letter to Anna which I hope will be usefull to you both, she is a woman of great experience and tenderness of heart and who through great tribulations both of body and mind hath attained the earnest of the Kingdom. . . . Her husband and son-in-law are now in Prison."

The author of the "letter to Anna" was Lilias Skein (or Skene), wife of Alexander Skein, both prominent early Friends and sufferers in Aberdeen; and "the Friend from Amsterdam", to whom Barclay next refers, was Geertruid Deriks. Of her, he writes: "I was glad to hear of thy reception of our Friend from Amsterdam and owe thee so much the more love for it that meeting her at London I did much press upon her to make that visit."[43] William Penn says of this visit: "Gertrueydt Dircks and Elizabeth Hendricks from Amsterdam visited them, and obtained a Meeting with them, improving that little way God by his Providence had made more closely to press the Testimony, and though they, especially the Countess, made some Objections, in relation to the Ordinances and certain Practices of Friends, yet she seemed to receive at that time satisfaction from them."

Elisabeth replied to Barclay's October letter on the 1/11, December, 1676, acknowledging its receipt "and at the same time Information from Benjamin Furly that you have been clapt up though I am sure that the Captivers are more captive than you are being in the Company of him that admits no bonds & is able to break all bonds. . . . I have translated or rather read L.S. letter unto Anna for she is now able to translate any English into her native language but not to read ane English hand with abbreviations you will see by her answer (which perchance will need ane other Interpreter) what sence this letter raised in her." A copy of Barclay's own letter, the Princess stated, had been sent by Benjamin Furly to her nephew, Duke Ernest of Hanover.

From Aberdeen Prison, the 24 Xber (December) 1676, came Barclay's next letter to the Princess. It was a very long one, filled with earnest religious admonitions, and appeal. Its postscript said: "As for the sending of my books to those persons, I leave to do therein as thou shall find true liberty in the Lord. . . . I hope by now thou has received my last with that of our dear Sister [Lilias Skein] now very weak, to Anna." Elisabeth in her next letter (9/19, February,

---

[43] Another of Barclay's references to this visit is found in his letter to Steven Crisp, cited above, in which he says: "I have notice from some that have lately been with the Princess Elizabeth, that she speaks much to Friends' advantage, and saith that the Friends have been falsely reported of".

1677) acknowledged the receipt of Barclay's last two letters, and promised to write to Lady Lauderdale, wife of the
Governor-General of Scotland, in behalf of the Quakers.
She would do this, she said, "as you desire by the next
[post]though I have no kind of acquaintance with her and
as Helmont tells me her husband is no friend of my Brother's, therefore all which comes that way is like to want
effect."

In his efforts to persuade Elisabeth to accept Quakerism,
Barclay had referred to the example of Lady Conway, a
friend of Van Helmont, who had adopted the Quaker faith.
But Elisabeth was not to be moved by this, as she plainly
stated in her next letter, dated the 1/11 of March, 1677. In
this she wrote: "My breathings unto the Lord are both for
light and power to yield reall obedience unto that light which
he affords me, but I cannot submitt unto the oppinion and
practice of any others though I grant that they have more
light than myself. The Countess of Conoway doth well to go
on the way which she thinks best, but I should not do well
to follow her, unless I had the same conviction. . . . The 7th,
and 24th of Matthew are a great bar to all conformity which
comes by choise or perswasion." She then expresses her
gladness at the release of Barclay's father and Friends
from prison and says: "I do love the Duke of York the better for procuring of it." At the end of her letter she writes:
"I hope that my free confession may not deprive me of your
Prayer who am realy. Your Affectionate Friend Elisabeth."

Barclay evidently deemed it wise to refrain (in his next
letters, at least) from referring again to Lady Conway as
an example of faithfulness, and it was not until nearly ten
months later that he returned to the theme. Meanwhile, he
had written two letters from Aberdeen prison, on the 5th
and 16th of March, 1677—both dated before the receipt of
Elisabeth's letter of March 1/11. The first of these acknowledged her February letter and, in addition to a long religious discourse, sent Barclay's love to Anna and said that "G.
Keith my dear Brother and Fellow companion in bonds
salutes thee and Anna." In the second of these letters Barclay writes that he sends a letter to the Princess and
Countess which had been written by "a certain dear Sister

... wife to my dear Brother G. Keith and albeit but a young Woman, yet one who through great inward experiences and a sound work of Judgment in her heart, hath attained not only ane excellent understanding but also a good measure of discerning and a sound and steady place in the truth, she is also a Gentlewoman of good condition."

After further eulogy of Elizabeth Keith, and the plea in regard to Anna Maria van Schurman mentioned above, Barclay sends his "salutations to Anna and especially to the young Maid of whom I understand by Anna's letter to Lillias Skene that she is seriously seeking the Lord." A postscript to this letter states: "My dear Brother, G. Keith and husband to the Author of these Letters upon the seeing of thy last to me hath found in his heart to write a small Treatise for thine and Anna's sake of the discerning of what proceeds meerly from a naturall conviction or opinion and what from a principle of Faith, which because it would have swelled this Pacquet too great, is reserved for another occasion." This "Treatise" by George Keith was added to his "Way to the City of God", and printed in Holland in 1678; it figured later in his correspondence with Gerard Croese, in reference to the doctrines of Franciscus van Helmont, a friend of the Princess Elisabeth, but whether it was ever perused by the latter is not known—even from Penn's account of his and Keith's visit to her in 1677.

Before this visit, Barclay wrote again to Elisabeth (from London, the 15th of the month June 1677), telling her that he had been informed by Benjamin Furly (who was then in London) that he had missed one of her letters which had gone to Scotland. He told her that he had been released from [Aberdeen] prison, but that the persecution was still bitter [in Scotland]; that he had spoken to Lady Lauderdale, "who," he said, "is only like to return thee a court complement by convoyance of thy Brother; it troubles me for thy honour's sake, but take it patiently. . . G. Keith I hope will ere long be with thee and I understand from Scotland that his wife and L. S. who formerly writ to Anna have it in their hearts from the Lord to give thee a visit."

Elisabeth replied to this letter on the 6/16, of July 1677, stating that Benjamin Furly had forwarded to her Barclay's letter of June. She had no complaint to make, she said, about Lady Lauderdale's court complement; but she opposed Barclay's going back to Scotland to be jailed. Her "Sister of Osnabrugh", she said, "has much affection for Gertrude [Deriks] but the world and her husband do still possess her heart. God will in his due time touch us both, when your Friends come they shall be willingly received and lodged by Your true Friend, Elisabeth".

In anticipation of this visit, the Princess wrote also the same day to Benjamin Furly, to whom she said: "Dear Friend. I see by your last your happy return out of England and your design to come hither with G. Keith and his wife and L. S. they will be welcome but the great Assembly you propose will find more difficulty, because many are not resolved to go that way [to Quakerism]; though they seek God and approve many [Quaker] things, others are tyed to relations as Ernestus and the most part have ane aversion against all that relishes of a Sect since the 24th of Matthew makes them cautious. I have many servants in my house that seeks God heartily but will run away from me at the name of Quaker. I wish God would put it into your heart how to deal with them."

The "great Assembly" proposed by Furly was apparently designed to include not only the members of Elisabeth's household and the citizens of Herwerden, but also the Labadist community as well; for there are two inches left blank in this letter, with the comment: "As to the ———— they will be well bestowed if they serve the Friends"; and it is a reasonable conjecture that the Labadists were referred to. But, as will be seen in the sequel, Furly was to be disappointed of his "great Assembly", which he may have hoped would develop, as the contemporaneous meeting in Amsterdam did, into a Friends' Yearly or Quarterly Meeting.

Penn's references to Barclay's share in the visit to the Princess Elisabeth in 1677 are very few and brief; nor does Barclay himself give us more than a glimpse or two of it. On his return to England, he wrote a letter to Elisabeth dated "Theobalds near London 12th of 7/mo [September]: 1677", in which he says: "Dear Friend, By thy letter of the last of the month past I understand of the Friends being with thee, and was refreshed by the account they gave me of thy kind and Christian entertainment of them (they having overtaken me in Holland). God will not be wanting to reward thy love as well as to encrease the same.'' He then writes of his visit to London to ask the Duke of York to instruct Lauderdale to release the Quaker prisoners in Scotland in such terms as Lauderdale ''would take it seriously'', otherwise he would prefer that he should not write to him at all. The Duke replied that he would do so for Barclay and his father, but ''not for the generall.'' Reverting to the promotion of Quakerism in courtly circles, he tells the princess that on his return to Scotland he would stop at Ragly, the castle of the Countess of Conway; and he expresses pleasure at what the princess had written him about the ''Councellour [Chancellor] of the Electors and the other Preacher''; hopes she herself ''will come out of all that which cumbers'', sends his love to Anna and ''the French woman'' and his salutation to the Electors' Councellour.

In his next letter, dated Ury, 28 December, 1677, after long religious exhortations, he tells the princess that on his way home he had stopped at Ragly where, he says, ''I did find it to be the tryal of that truly noble and virtuous Lady the Vice Countess of Conoway who told me she had looked upon some things practised by us as so small and Inconsiderable that she was apt to believe either that there was not that weight in them . . . . but when she came to find it her place so to do then she saw there was a great deal more difficulty than she apprehended and could not have believed to have found in herself so strong wrestlings before she could give up to obey especially considering her circumstance who being constantly tied to her chamber was thereby delivered from many of those affronts which the like case might make others liable to.''

In this letter also, Barclay says: ''I was not a little refreshed to understand of the Second visit given thee by the Friends''; and in a postscript he acknowledges the receipt of Elisabeth's information in regard to Colonel Mollison's wife and children. This information had come in a letter from her dated ''Ruden, 25 of November, 1677'', which told of the death of Colonel Mollison and his two sons on the Continent. One of the latter, it said, had died on a journey with his mother to Duisburg, and "Colonel Melvill a Scotch man that is Governor of Cell [Celles, or Zell] in Lunenburg can give your brother-in-law details of Colonel Mollison's will". This Colonel Mollison appears to have been one of the sons of the prominent Scotch Quaker, Gilbert Molleson, "late Bailie of Aberdeen", whose daughter Christian Barclay had married in 1669.

More than a year elapses now before we have Barclay's next reference to the princess and countess. This was in a letter dated from Ury, the 27th of 8th mo. [Oct.-Nov.] 1678, addressed to the Fell sisters, and was as follows: "From Holland I had last night a letter that gave me much satisfaction, in which was one enclosed from Herwarden from Anna Van Horne (the Countess) to Lillia-Skeine, very loving; and a short postscript from Elizabeth (the Princess), in these words, 'Dear friend, I love your upright intention to travail in spirit for your friends, though unknown to you and doubt not it will prove efficacious to them in the Lord's due time; which is the wish of your loving friend, Elizabeth.' "

In Barclay's next and last extant letter to the princess, dated Rotterdam the 6th of the 5/mo: 1679, he writes: "Thy last came to me at a time when I was under great bodily weakness"—hence the long delay in this reply; "I choosed rather to be silent than forward. But being through a singular occasion come into this country[44] and not having access to make thee a visit I found a true liberty from the Lord in my spirit thus to salute thee. . . . I made mention in my last of the condition of that honourable Lady [Conway] who is now gone to her place not as if I proposed her practice for thee to imitate (but only I signified her condition as ane example) therefore in Judging so thou did mistake. . . . I never sought to gather thee nor others to myself but to the Lord, I pretend to be no sect master and disgust all such, my labour is only as ane Ambassadour to Instruct all to be reconciled to God."

---

[44] Cf. Monograph No. 5 ("Benjamin Furly and Quakerism in Rotterdam").

Having made this explanation or apology, Barclay proceeds to tell the princess of his efforts to procure the Scotch Quaker prisoners' release as follows: "Albeit I had no great expectation of success, I resolved once more to try thy cousin, the Duke of York. I told him that I understood from Scotland, notwithstanding Lauderdale was there, and had promised ere he went to do something, that our Friends' bonds were rather increased. I told him also that there was only one thing now to be done, and which was, to write effectually to the Duke of Lauderdale in that style wherein Lauderdale might understand he was serious in the business, and did really intend that the things he did write about should take effect; which I knew he might do, and if he would do, I must acknowledge as a great kindness. But if he did write, and not in this manner so that the other might not suppose him to be serious, I would rather he would excuse himself the trouble. Requesting, withal, that he would excuse my plain manner of dealing, as being different from the Court way of soliciting. All this he seemed to take in good part, and said he would so write as I desired for my father and me, but not for the general. So he hath give me a letter; whether it will prove effectual or not I cannot determine."

Elisabeth died the next year, but probably heard before her death of the immunity from persecution which the Quakers at last enjoyed in Scotland. This immunity was due to her cousin, James, Duke of York, who was made governor of Scotland in that year, and to the influence of Elisabeth, Penn and Barclay with him. Indeed, Barclay seems to have exerted a considerable influence upon James in favor of toleration (at least of the Quakers), both while he was Duke at Holyrood and King at Whitehall.

Barclay's own experiences both in prison and on the Continent doubtless impressed upon his mind the need of a place of refuge for his people. His interest and aid in Penn's "Holy Experiment" beyond the Atlantic may be estimated from the fact that in 1682 he was appointed Governor (in name, but with a deputy governor in residence) of the Province of East New Jersey. How much his writings and visits to the Continent may have contributed to the stream

of emigration to Pennsylvania and New Jersey can only be
surmised. It is evident that he retained his friendship with
some of the Dutch Quakers whom he had met. One of these
was his fellow-proprietor of East New Jersey, Arent Sonnemans, whom he was taking home from London to visit
him when highwaymen fell upon the party and fatally
wounded Sonnemans.[45]

As governor of East New Jersey, Barclay's chief efforts
seem to have been directed towards inducing the persecuted
Scotch Covenanters to emigrate thither as tolerated and
welcome colonists. James, while tolerating the Quakers in
Scotland, was very severe in his persecution of the Covenanters for a decade after 1679, especially in the "Killing
Time", the "Black Year" of 1685. Barclay died in 1690, at
a time when Penn's colonies were receiving many colonists
from the British Isles and the Continent. Thus, through the
compulsion of persecution and the persuasive eloquence and
probity of the Quaker leaders, was sifted the choice seed to
be sown in the wilderness.

George Fox and the Princess

George Fox did not visit Herford on his journey of 1677,
but during his stay in Amsterdam that year he wrote to the
Princess Elisabeth a long religious letter which, he says,
"Isabel Yeomans delivered to her when George Keith's
Wife and she went to visit her."[46] This letter was dated, Amsterdam, the 7th. of 6th. Month (August), 1677; so that it
was written about a fortnight before Penn and his companions arrived at Herford. Fox's postscript to the letter
says: "The bearer hereof is a Daughter-in-law of mine, that
comes with Gertrude Dirick Nieson and George Keith's
Wife, to give thee a Visit." When this visit was made, we
are not informed; but the Princess wrote a reply to Fox's
letter, dated, Hertfort, the 30th. of August, 1677, which is
quoted by Fox as follows: "Dear Friend; I cannot but have
a tender Love to those that love the *Lord Jesus Christ,* and

---

[45] See Monograph Number Five ("Benjamin Furly and Quakerism in Rotterdam").

[46] Fox's Journal, 1697 edition, p. 435.

to whom it is given not only to *believe* in him, but also to *suffer* for him: Therefore your Letter, and your *Friends Visit,* have been both very welcome to me. I shall follow their Counsel, as far as God will afford me *Light* and *Unction:* Remaining still

Your loving Friend,

Elizabeth.''

Presumably, the Friends' visit referred to in this reply was that of the three women Friends mentioned by Fox; but Penn does not refer to their visit, although he and his companions had been at Herford once in August and once in September. Fox's own letter begins: *"Princess Elizabeth:* I have heard of thy *Tenderness* towards the *Lord* and his holy *Truth,* by some *Friends* that have visited thee,[47] and also by some of thy *Letters,* which I have seen.''

Writing of this visit, Croese says: "Isabel Fell, Fox's Daughter in Law and Wife to Keith, together with a certain Dutch Woman, went from Amsterdam to Herward in Westphalia, there to speak with the Princess Elizabeth. . . . When these women came to the Princess' Court, and desired liberty to speak with her, she who was full of humanity and gentleness, and never disdained any tho never so mean and unequal to her Condition, that desired to apply themselves unto her, admits and hears them with chearful and favourable Countenance, being especially pleased with Isabells Discourse, who indeed had a curious voice and a freer way of delivering herself, and having heard what they had to say, dismist them with a short and pithy answer, and having afterward opened and read Fox's Epistle; She takes care to deliver unto them her own Letter, writ in the same Language he had done, to wit, English, that they might give it to Fox.''[48]

---

[47] These were probably Robert Barclay and Benjamin Furly, and Gertrud Deriks and Elisabeth Hendricks (cf. Monograph Number Six: "Dutch Quaker Leaders, 1668–1800").

[48] Isabel Fell was not "Fox's Daughter in Law and Wife to Keith", as Croese appears to state. She was the daughter of Margaret Fell (later Fox's wife) and the wife (first) of William Yeamans and (in 1689) of Abraham Morrice. Her companions on this visit were the "Wife to [George] Keith" and "a certain Dutch woman", namely, Geertruid Deriks of Amsterdam. (Cf. Monograph Number Four: "The Rise of Quakerism in Amsterdam").

"Fox", he writes further, "who thought that the Fame of his Name was no less known to this Princess, than it was in *England,* his Native Country, delivers these Women a Letter for them to carry in his Name to the Princess, that they might, by that means, have easier access unto her, and their Discourses be of more weight with her; in which Epistle *Fox* addressed himself unto her in a little more neat and civil manner, than he was wont to do, laying aside that fusty harshness and Rusticity he was accustom'd to, whereby he made no distinction between Persons of High Birth and Quality, and the meanest Car-men and Porters, but now he caresses and saluteth the Princess in the most engaging manner, and highly extolls her Piety and Modesty, as being Vertues worthy of a Princess, and sets forth how much all mankind at this time receed from these offices and duties incumbent upon them, and as the State of the Church stood at this present time, there was more need than ever to keep fast to them, and at last exhorts the Princess that as she had been engaged in the work, she should go on more and more." In introducing his account, Croese had himself praised Elizabeth as "a lady truly renowned and famous for her wit, Learning and Piety, and if so be the endowments of the mind are to be looked upon and esteemed of themselves without the goods of Fortune, a Princess the most happy and famous of any of her Age."

PENN AND THE PRINCESS

Such was the notably large correspondence which led up to the visit of Penn and his companions to Elisabeth in the autumn of 1677. The letters were shared by Penn, who gives his estimate of the opportunity for the extension of Quakerism into Germany's princely circles as follows: "In this also was the Countess [Princess] commendable in that she left all to have joyned with a People [the Labadists] that has a Pretence at least to more Spirituality and Self-denial than was found in the National Religion she was bred up in; For God had reached her, as she told me, about Nine Years ago, and that by an extraordinary way. Now, it seemed great Pity to us [the English Friends] that Persons of their Quality in the World should so willingly expose themselves for the *false Quaker*, the reprobate *Silver*, the *Mixtures*, and they should not be acquainted with the Life and Testimony of the *True Quakers.*''

Penn took up the work of ''convincing'' the princess in 1677. The year before, he had paved the way for his visit by writing a long letter to her. The editor of Penn's ''Works'' (Joseph Besse, 1726) relates under the year 1676 that ''about this time it pleased God to inspire the hearts of two Protestant Ladies of great quality in Germany with a sense of the follies and vanities of the world and to excite them to an earnest enquiry after the knowledge of himself. The one was the Princess Elizabeth . . . ; the other Anna Maria de Hornes, Countess of Hornes, a familiar acquaintance of the said Princess. The report of their religious inclination coming to our author's ears, who gladly embraced every opportunity of watering the growing seeds of virtue, he sent them a letter of encouragement and consolation, exhorting those noble women to a constancy and a perseverance in that Holy Way which the Lord had directed their feet into. The Letter itself, tho' large, deserving the reader's perusal, we insert in the Appendix.''

The letter was indeed a ''large'' one (of 25 folio pages) and could have been written and read, even though by William Penn to a Princess and Countess, only in that era of unlimited leisure and patience. Addressing them as ''noble of this world, but more noble for your enquiry after the Truth and love to it, the fame whereof hath sounded to the ears of some of us in this Island,'' Penn tells them that he has had them often in his remembrance and has had a clear prospect of the difficulties and temptations that beset them. He then proceeds to give them an account of the rise of Quakerism in England, rather fiercely denouncing the persecutions it had encountered, but ending with a note of triumph for its survival and victory, and with a fervent appeal to the two women to hold fast to the Truth they had acquired and to seek steadfastly for more. He explains that 'something had arisen in his Heart to write of his own Convincement' and of the trials attending it, which 'though inferiour to their [the princess' and countess'] Quality, might not be ungrateful or unserviceable to them'. He hints that he had a message to be given to them in person, but that his visit was 'not to be this season.'

This letter was probably delivered by Barclay and Furly in 1676. Speaking of it and its predecessors, Penn says: "By them the Princess and Countess have been brought nearer into a waiting Frame, by those Heavenly Directions they have frequently received by Way of Epistles from several of us. In answer to Two of mine, the Princess sent me the following Letter, which being short, I insert it here:

"Herford, May 2, 1677.

"This, Friend, will tell you that both your Letters were very acceptable, together with your Wishes for my obtaining those Virtues which may make me a worthy Follower of our Great King and Saviour Jesus Christ. What I have done for his True Disciples is not so much as a Cup of cold Water; it affords them no Refreshment; neither did I expect any Fruit of my Letter to the Dutchess of L. [Lauderdale] as I have expressed at the same Time unto B.F. [Benjamin Furly]. But since R. B. [Robert Barclay] desired I should write it, I could not refuse him, nor omit to do any Thing that was judged conducing to his Liberty, tho' it should expose me to the Derision of the World. But this a meer moral Man can reach at; the True inward Graces are yet wanting in

Your affectionate Friend,

Elizabeth.''

Of Penn's own motives in visiting the Princess and of the dramatic character of their meeting, an impartial commentator writes as follows:[49]

"Elizabeth having afforded shelter to the much-persecuted flock of Labadists, kept her protecting hand over them in spite of the outcry raised by the clergy, the protest of the civil magistrates, and even in the face of an imperial edict, issued from the Chancery Court at Spires, Oct. 20, 1671 [demanding that she expel the Labadists, on pain of losing

---

[49] Oswald Seidensticker, in *The Pennsylvania Magazine of History and Biography*, Vol. II (1878), pp. 249, 257–8.

her imperial privileges as abbess].[50] So much interest bestowed upon a kindred sect, coupled with firmness of character, made Elizabeth, in the eyes of the Friends, a very important personage for the prospective planting of their principles on the soil of Germany. If she, the scion of the royal house of England, the sister of a reigning sovereign (Charles Louis), and the cousin of the great Elector of Brandenburg (Frederick William), could be 'convinced,' the despised sect of the Quakers would have cast an anchor in Germany, not easily dragged from its moorings. . . . .

"Penn, at the age of 33 years, in the flush of manly beauty, blending all the graces of the courtly gentleman with the fire of the religious enthusiast, looking back upon a strangely checkered life, that had led him from the lawns of Oxford to the prison walls of Newgate, the determined champion of religious liberty, and dreaming, perhaps, of a distant domain, that should be blessed with it; opposite to him Elizabeth, who was then in her 60th year, the granddaughter of a king, and who herself might have been a queen, an adept in philosophy, the friend of the sages of her time, still seeking an answer to life's enigmas, which science did not give, in religious experience, in an inward revelation, such as the ministry of Labadie had led her to hope for. And now the young Quaker stood before the old Princess, to teach, to convince, to inspire her."

After these extensive preparations, Penn's visit to them was resolved upon in 1677 by the Quaker leaders at Amsterdam. After the General Meeting held in that city, Penn, George Keith, Robert Barclay and Benjamin Furly journeyed by way of Osnabrück to Herford, arriving on the

---

[50] An Imperial Edict, issued upon the representation of the magistrates of Herford, is thus headed: "An earnest edict of his Roman Imperial Majesty to the Abbess of Herford, to remove, and no longer to tolerate the Anabaptists, new Fanatics, and Sectaries, as Jean Labadie, Peter Ivon, Peter de Lignon, Henry and Peter Schlüter, and other dangerous and restless spirits." In the text, the Labadists are styled Quakers and Anabaptists. Before this, the people of Herford had appealed to Elisabeth's suzerain, the Elector of Brandenburg, against the Labadists as Quakers; but the Elector's commission of inquiry reported that the Labadists were harmless, and that even the Quakers should be tolerated by the Reformed Church; which did not pretend to uniformity.

Elisabeth Princess Palatine
from a painting by Gerard Honthorst

evening of Thursday, the 19th. of 6th. Month (August). The next day, the travelling Friends held two religious meetings with the Princess Elisabeth, the Countess of Hoorn, and the members of their family.[51] The first of these meetings lasted from 7 until 11 A. M., and the second from 2 until 7 P. M.: but neither the visitors nor the visited having been satisfied with these somewhat extended opportunities, another meeting was held on the morning of the next day, when Penn addressed "the more inferiour Servants of the House, who would have been Bashful to have presented themselves before the Princess." While Penn was thus engaged, Barclay discussed religious matters with the Princess, the Countess having arranged the meeting with the servants for Penn. "We were all sweetly tender'd and broken together," writes Penn, "and the Life of our God was shed abroad amongst us as a Sweet Savour; For which their Souls bowed before the Lord, and confess'd to our Testimony. Which did not a little please that Noble Young Woman, to find her own Report of us and her great Care of them so effectually answered."[52]

The morning meeting having lasted from about 8:30 until noon, the visitors again declined the pressing invitation of the Princess to dine with her, but returned at three in the afternoon. On this occasion, Penn complied with a promise he had made in one of his letters to the Princess and Countess to tell them of his "first Convincement, and of those Tribulations and Consolations which I had met withal in

[51] The "family" included, besides the Princess and the Countess of Hoorn, another "Countess, sister to the Countess," Penn calls her, "who had then come in to visit her, and a *French* Woman of Quality; the first behaving herself very decently and the last often deeply broken; And from a light, and slightly carriage towards the very Name of a *Quaker*, she became very intimately and affectionately kind and respectful to us."
This "French Woman of Quality" was Mlle. de Reneval, who was at that time betrothed and later married to Reiner Copper (1645–1693), who had been Elizabeth's court-preacher from 1674 to 1677, and was to meet Penn at Mülheim-on-the Ruhr soon after his visit to Herford. The "Countess, sister to the Countess" was the Princess Elisabeth's "Sister of Osnabrugh", as Elisabeth had called her in a letter to Barclay, quoted above.
[52] The Countess, Penn says, "took hold of the Opportunity [while Barclay was discoursing with the Princess], and whispered me to withdraw to get a Meeting for the more inferior Servants."

this way of the Kingdom." His story was interrupted by supper, to which the Friends accepted an invitation to remain; and after supper, Penn continued his narrative until 11 o'clock. An engagement was then made for a public meeting the next afternoon (Sunday), which was duly held, after the Friends had held a private meeting of their own in the morning at their inn.

In the morning meeting they had felt, Penn says, "a great Travail upon our Spirits, that the Lord would stand by us that day and magnifie the Testimony of his own Truth by us, that he might have a Seed and People in that place to lift up a Standard for his Name." The afternoon meeting appears to have been a very impressive one, the Princess in particular being deeply affected. At its close, the Friends declined another invitation to supper, preferring "a bit of her Bread and a glass of her Wine if she pleased in the Chamber where we were." She complied with their desire, and left them with the Countess and several others of her ladies, while she returned immediately after supper to take a very friendly leave of her unusual visitors and to urge them to stop to see her again on their return from Frankfurt.

The next morning (at seven o'clock!),[53] after another religious meeting at their inn, (which was attended by one of the Princess' courtiers and one of the townsmen), the party left Herford, Penn, Keith and Furly going on to Frankfurt and the Palatinate, and Barclay returning to Amsterdam. While Penn was at Krisheim, on this visit, he wrote a long letter of admonition and encouragement to the Princess and Countess; and at Mannheim, one to their relative, the Elec-

---

[53] The early hours kept by Penn's contemporaries in Holland are reflected in the lines well known in olden times, as follows:

Dit zij uw les:	This be your text:
Sta op ten zes,	Arise at six,
En eet ten tienen:	Eat at twice five:
Dat zal u dienen;	So shall you thrive;
En weer ten zes	Again at six
Zoo trek uw mes	Draw forth your knife;
En slaap ten tienen:	To bed at ten:
Dat zal u dienen.	Enjoy your life.

(Quoted from Herman van Lil „Het Leven, de Gevoelens en Lotgevallen van William Penn", Amsterdam, 2 Vols., 1821, 1825.)

toral Prince of the Palatinate, whom Penn and his companions were unable to visit, because of his absence in Heidelberg and because of a religious meeting they had appointed in Krisheim.

After a long journey in the Rhineland and to Bremen, Penn, Keith and Furly arrived in Herford again on the 22nd. of 7th. Month (September). Calling in the morning at the Court of the Princess to know when they could be received, they were told that business of government would prevent a meeting until two o'clock in the afternoon. At that hour, the Friends returned, and the afternoon was spent in talking with the Princess, the Countess and "the French-woman"[54] about the journey of the past month, and in holding "a precious little meeting." Again an urgent invitation to stay to supper was accepted, "the house being clear of Strangers," and the meal itself proved "a blessed Meeting", the "Power of the Lord coming" upon Penn, and "the hidden Manna was manifested amongst us." This visit lasted until 10 P. M. and ended with a promise to return the next morning at seven. The next day being Sunday, a religious meeting was held for the court and the townspeople, which lasted from 8 until 11; and at 2 in the afternoon another meeting of the same kind began at the abbey. At supper that evening, Penn was moved to speak of "the Covenant of Light" and "the Followers of the Light", as he had done the night before; and until 10 P. M., the time was spent "in holy silence or discourse."

The next morning at 8, the Friends were again at court, and engaged with the Princess and Countess "in very serious Conference", concerning the "affairs, practice and sufferings of Friends in England", until 11 o'clock, when the "ratling of a Coach" interrupted them. The coach contained, the Countess of Hoorn reported—"with a countenance somewhat uneasie"—"the young Princes, Nephews to the Princess and the Graef of Donaw [Count of Donau]". Penn thereupon announced that he and his friends would

---

[54] Penn says that she was "greatly improved, both in her Love and Understanding; yea, she was very zealous and very broken, and was always with us on these Occasions."

withdraw to their inn; the Princess agreed to this, but told them that her visitors would stay only for dinner, and invited them to return in the late afternoon for a farewell visit. Immediately after dining at their inn, the Friends received a message from the Princess requesting them to come to her at once, as the Count "had a great desire to see us, and to speak with us." The message interrupted Penn as he sat down in his bed-room to finish writing an appeal "to the Professors of that Country"; but he set this task aside, and obeyed the Princess' summons,—although it "brought a fresh Weight and Exercise upon us; but, committing all to the Lord, and casting our care upon him, we went."

The Count addressed them in French, and "at first took no great notice of our inceremonious behaviour, but proceeded to inquire of us our success in our Journey." A long conversation followed on religion in general and the practices and beliefs of the Quakers in particular, the Count objecting especially to the Friendly custom of not removing the hat to superiors. Penn's argument in defence of this custom was based, not directly on Democracy, but on that interpretation of Christianity which necessitates a democratic and brotherly regard for all men. It is improbable that the Count was convinced by the argument; but he took his leave of the Princess and the Friends "with great civility." This dinner-conversation à propos of heretics and heresy is reminiscent of a recent one which had occurred at the same dinner-table between the Princess and her sister, the Duchess Sophia, wife of Bishop Ernst August of Osnabrück, in which the Labadists had been attacked and defended with much animation. Elisabeth was the champion of the attacked in both instances.

After the Count's departure, the Princess and her household took part in a deeply religious and quite emotional meeting, in which Penn stressed the temptations and victory of Jesus, and the parable of the Ten Virgins. The farewells were of an intimate and affectionate character, and the Princess, Countess, their household and the visitors were all alike deeply affected.

Writing of Elisabeth in his "No Cross, No Crown", Penn says: "Being in some agony of spirit, after a religious meeting we had in her own chamber, she said: 'It is an hard thing to be faithful to what one knows. Oh the way is strait! I am afraid I am not weighty enough in my spirit to walk in it.' ... I cannot forget her last words when I took my leave of her: 'Let me desire you to remember me, though I live at this distance, and that you should never see me more. I thank you for this good time; and know, and be assured, though my condition subjects me to divers temptations, yet my soul hath strong desires after the best things.' "

This passage probably refers to an incident which occurred on Penn's visit to the Princess in August, 1677. Of this he writes in his Journal:[55] "As soon as the Meeting was done, the Princess came to me and took me by the Hand (which she usually did to us all coming and going) and went to speak to me of the Sense she had of that Power and Presence of God that was amongst us, but was stop'd. And turning herself to the Window, brake forth in an extraordinary Passion, crying out, *I cannot speak to you, my Heart is full;* clapping her Hands upon her Breast. It melted me into a deep and calm Tenderness, in which I was moved to Minister a few Words softly to her, and after some Time of Silence she recovered herself."

Having supped at their inn, "clear'd the House, exhorted the Family and left Books", the travellers left by the Post-Waggon for Wesel, 200 English miles distant, and reached it after "three Nights and Days without lying down on a Bed, or sleeping, otherwise than in the Waggon, which was only covered with an old ragged Sheet." Surely, the vicissitudes and contrasts in the lives of "the travelling ministers" were as great abroad as they were in their own English home.

On his arrival in Amsterdam, after his second long journey through the Rhineland, Penn wrote the Countess another long letter,[56] giving her a narrative of the journey. And it was probably at the same place and time that he wrote a

---

[55] "Works", 1726, Vol. I, p. 63.
[56] *Ibid.*, Vol. I, pp. 101–108.

very long letter to the Princess, practically beseeching her to become a Friend. Parts of this letter are as follows:[57]

"My dearly Respected ffriend

"Great & notable is ye day of ye Lord wch is now dawning upon ye inhabitants of ye Earth a day of sore tryal & deep distress shall it be. . . .

"O Dear Princess this is thy day; ye Lord God allmighty, y^t called out Abraham from ye Land of Idolatry, in which he lived, hath visited thy court, & hath called thee by his eternal word & power out of ye nature, spirit, life & inventions of ye world. Yea, & I testify thou hast given him Audience in thy heart; & thou hast been sensibly struck with his presence, & livingly been affected with his appearance: & imortality hath taken hold of thee, & heavenly desires hath he kindled in thy soul after him: And I am satisfyed, ye Spirit is willing, though ye flesh be weak.

"Now give up, o give up thy all, that thou mayst inherit eternal life: follow him: for he is worthy forever. Consult not away thy convictions; stifle not thy tender breathings by letting in, & entertaining ye politique Spirit of this world, ye prudence & discretion of man, that never did god's will, nor never can. . . .

"O Dear ffriend, gods candle is lighted in thee; sweap thy house, & seek ye Kingdom, & thou shaft find it. For ye Kingdom of god is within: yea, in thee is his holy day dawned. Therefore o search, o trye, & watch. . . .

"Dear Princess; O come, & let ye prince of this world be judged in thee; ye false power, righteousnes, church, Authority, Inventions & buildings, which stand not in gods covenant, in his wisdom, wch is Christ Jesus. O is it ye earnest supplication of thy spirit to feel him, see him, love him, & possess him; & wouldst thou inherit that peace, & joy that he giveth them; Castaway all that is not of him. Love his likenes; embrace his holy example; be faithful to ye manifestations of his light, & that daily; & thou wilt be re-

---

[57] The letter is not printed in Penn's "Travails," or "Works", but is preserved in MS. in the Gulielma M. Howard Collection in Haverford College. It is printed in the *Bulletin* of the Friends' Historical Society of Philadelphia, Vol. IV (1912), pp. 86–97, and is said to be "an autograph copy, in the earlier style of William Penn's handwriting, and may be the original from which the copy was made for the Princess" (Amelia M. Gummere, *ibid.*, p. 82).

deem'd out of that, to wch god revealeth his judg^{mts} ag^t ye world. For I must testify to thee, & y^t in god's fear & counsil, thou canst never see, know & taste that, which thou desirest after till thou hast deserted & relinquisht, w^t grieveth him. This is gods way.

"Therefore dally not; but let it all go for ye sake of ye Joy and glory that is set before thee. O that thou hadst but once broke through ye Impediments I see before thee! & truly, faithfulnes quickly doth it.

"Bear with me my Dear ffriend; for my soul is deeply affected with thy condition. I love thee, I honour thee; but I must be plain with thee. I confess I have been rejoyced in ye visits I have made thee, yea, abundantly comforted from ye Lord: for his power hath been with us, & ye hearts have been sensible of it; & that is our great reward: Because it's our meat and drink to do his will that sent us. And I must say y^t I left you all both times with dear love & great pleasure, & ye blessings of ye allmighty upon thee & thy house. Yet before I had been 3 hours in ye waggon, that weight, burden, & exercise fell upon me, wch I remember not that I ever felt śince I knew ye Lord. My spirits sad, my poor soul exceeding heavy: all comfort seemed to leave me, & joy to fly from me. I was as man drunk with sorrows, & I did even sweat with pains. My brethren took notice of a great weight upon me; but I kept my troubles to myself; & hid my travails in my own bosom.

"This remain'd many hours upon me: I cryed: O Lord, w^t have I done? w^t have I left undone? why is this heaviness befallen me? o my god, stay my soul in thy word; & show me ye end of this bitter cup; that if thou hast any work for me to do, thou wouldst be pleased to shew it me: & be but with me, & I will go with chearfulness, let w^t will come of me.

"Then ye Lord open'd his will in this exercise unto me, & I clearly saw, ye cause & end of y^{tt}, great weight, y^t lay upon my soul, was, that nothing might be lost that I left behind me; & that you might never go back, nor ye enemy by his subtile temptations shipwreck any of y^t love & faith, y^t god's divine word had quickened in your hearts. I beheld Satan as lightning descending in divers shapes & appearances; sometimes as religious, sometimes prudent, to insinuate, captivate & deceive you; who is that Spiritual Herod, that would murder that, which is born of god; that dragon, who would devour it; yea, ye sense of his designs & workings ag^t that life, that god hath begotten in you; & ye holy fear y^t seized my soul, lest he should be permitted to prevail, & any of you loose that tender love & sense, wch we left you in, cast me into such an Agony, that this know, o Princess, if ever my mother was in pain for me, then was my soul in deep distress for you. O ye beating of my heart, & wrestlings of my bowels! & ye earnest & strong crys of my life to god through him, that sweat drops of blood for me, that all ye devices of ye evil one might be discovered, & all his darts quenched by ye true light of Jesus in al y^r consciences (ye holy blessed armour of ye saints of old.) Then did ye Lord distinctly show me y^r states & conditions how it stood with you, & how & where he would assault you; wch increased my holy care, concerns & Travail for you. I wished in my soul, o that I had I but enjoyed one day more with you! but gods time is not our time, & to his providence I submit; whose I am in the service of an everlasting gospel.

"By this time we were got well to Wesel, & my soul was somew^t dased, yet it lay upon me to write to thee, & declare, w^t the Lord had give me to understand of thy present condition; & w^t counsel he had give me in charge for thee, as thy case stood separate, & distinct from ye rest, with respect to thy worldly circumstances: wch with unfeigned respect, holy love, & Christian faithfulness I here present unto thee: intreating thee, that it would please thee to read it & weigh it in ye tender, lowly & sensible frame of spirit, in wch I left thee.

"Consider with X^{ts} light, & lay to heart, O princess, as thou wouldst give an Accompt with joy to god at ye great day of his terrible tribunal, who will not be mocked; but judge all ye people according to ye deeds done in ye body, If thy present publique station & capacity in ye world be altogether in ye way of god, & to be found & justifyed in & by ye light & ye truth of Christ. Hath it gods institution, or X^{ts} ordination? For all true & just power cometh from god & X^t, to whom all power in heaven & earth is given; I speak now to those things, about which we discourst ye evening we left thee. For seriously weigh, who was ye Author of ye Invention of Abbess; whose child it is; whom it resembleth;

whose mark it beareth, & ye end of it? at best it is a complex of civil & ecclesiastical power not to be found in Scripture, nor pure tradition; ye offspring of a dark Apostasy. 'Tis true, ye protestants have rendered it more civil then it was; yet still it standeth on ye old foot too much, & is perplext with a religious power; & that more monstrous, then in ye days of popory. For then it signified only a feminine over-seer of priests & people of one religion, a sort of spiritual pastoress, yet endowed with temporal privileges & dignity; but now a pastoress or overseer of divers, yea opposite, & contrary religions. And which is yet most of all strang, ye Abbess herself hath no opinion of ye religious part of her own institution: She alloweth it to be popish; & Anti-christian; a limb of ye beast; & declareth, she believeth none of those priests to be truly sent, deputed or spirited by X^t Jesus, ye great prophet & high priest of Christians; neither can she have intimate Communion with them.

"O Dear Princess, Consider, how canst thou then chuse, appoint, or place such priests or ministers, as thou canst not hear, or have fellowship with; especially, when thou knowest in thy Conscience, that ye poor people at ye same time receive them as Gospel ministers, & ye Apostles successors; *now* it is a crime in them greatly punishable, to say ye contrary. O how canst thou employ a power, thou condemnest ye very institution of; or appoint, or consent, that ye blind should lead ye blind? Remember, w^t is not of faith, is sin.

"But consider; if this doth not break ye 3^d Commandment. Thou shalt not take ye name of ye Lord thy god in vain. For thou stampst an Authority upon such priests & ministers, as thou knowest, call God & Jesus *lord* by ye holy ghost; but are vain & lifeles, yea bablers, & some of them Idolaters. And 'tis ye highest breach of that Commandment to take gods name into their mouths without gods power, life & spirit. Yet under a pretense of being his ministers, though never sent by him but made by men, not knowing ye tribulations, of ye new birth. Next, it is expressly s^d, that Idolaters cannot inherit ye Kingdom. if not, how can thou place Idolatrous priests or authorise their exercising of a Idolatrous office; yea blasphemous, viz: to make their god of a wafer; then worship him; and lastly eat him; cum multis alys: o sad! . . . .

"Dear Princess, The hour of gods judg^{mt} upon all these things is come, & coming. Wherefore prepare to meet thy Lord; & See that thou hast on ye wedding garment, which never waxeth old.

"But further I beseech thee to consider, What a Coercion & Persecution thy Conscience lieth under, since thou art forc'd to chuse & place priests at all, as well as that thou must chuse such, as thou hast no spiritual fellowship with: yea, such as thou utterly disownest in thy own Judg^{mt}: . . .

"To which let me add, that ye necessity of having a Chaplin is another Evil Burden, that attendeth ye place. For w^t is a Chaplin? No creature of gods making; look from Genesis to ye Revelations. But a certain sort of a thing gotten in popish times betwixt Laziness & grandures, when people grew to sluggish or great to pray for themselves; then came up Chaplins for to pray for them; which is worshipping God by proxy. But is this according to ye example of holy Abraham, or Joshuah, or David, that taught their familys themselves? or suitable to the tenure of ye new & everlasting Covenant, that god would write his law in the hearts of men & women, & put his Spirit into their Inward parts, that all should know him from ye least to ye greatest.

"Tell me Dear Princess, how can any mans Conscience be at anothers Dispose? That is, to speak, pray, say grace etc. at ye Appointment of any Creature living: yet thou knowest this is ye duty & practice of every chaplin. O how hath Cerimony & formality prevailed ast true & spiritual worship! Consider, if god requireth not other things from thee. Remember ye Elect Lady John writ to, that was come to ye holy unction, that teacheth all truth: take her for thy example.

"But then last of all to receive money for exhibiting such Warrants, Licenses or Authoritys for a work confest to be a Limb of ye beast: to a princess of a less generous, free, & religious disposition than thyself, I should have called it ye Wages of unrighteousness: but I will leave the now, O Princess, to give it a name thyself. . . .

"O how doth my Soul bow before ye god of ye whole Earth, who is ffather of lights & Spirits, & that daily, that he would more & more give unto thee ye revelation of ye

Knowledge of all that is not of him: & that by his divine
power he would keep thee sensible of his pure & blessed
word in thy Soul, that with a noble & truly princely resolution, thou mayst cast away this offspring of ye night, & become a princely pattern of true disdain of ye Worlds vain
glory, & a Noble Example of Antient Christian Resignation; that it may appear, thou art not one of the beasts followers, but ye Lambs; not inhabitant of Babilon, but a retired Traveller towards Zion ye City of gods Solemnity with
thy face directed that way, walking in ye light of him, that
is ye life, light, truth, way, & salvation of all nations.

"Ah! help ye Lamb ag^t ye mighty, for his day is come:
his trumpet has sounded, & is daily sounding a visitation to
all before ye great & notable day of final Judg^{mt}. ffear O
princess, & obey; & thou shalt have eternal life. And put not
off thy counsel, nor thy own soul with other excuses, then w^t
thou canst use with boldness before ye Lord of heaven &
earth at his great Judg^{mt}; & then I am sure, this letter will
be justifyed. And know, thy faithfulness herein will be a
great stroke to ye beasts & false prophets power; yea, a
forerunning of their downfall: which I testify from ye Lord,
is begun & will in a little time be accomplisht.

"Yet mistake me not; I am not striking at ye civil power
of thy office; that is independent upon ye Ecclesiastical constitution, by no means: for 'tis my present Judg^{mt}, that thou
shouldst double thy diligence therein & employ it for god:
that is to say; to be a terrour to Evil doers, & a praise to
them that do well. That ye righteousness of true Magistracy
may shine before ye World in thy diligent & just administration. Nay, thus far I could yet go with relation to the
Charge of Abbess: They instituted it superstitiously: I
would use it Christianly. That is; when ye priests come I
would interrogate them if they were true Christian Priests,
regenerated & annointed to preach ye Gospel? if they had
rec^d gods living word, as ye prophets & Apostles did? &
call for a proof. If ignorant hereof (as no doubt thou wilt
find them) declare, that in conscience thou canst not give
any consent, that such unqualifyed persons should exercise
ye office of ministers & priests: but if the people would chuse
them they had their Liberty. This would preach, yea greatly.

"Next suffer none to swear; for Christ forbiddeth it, Matth. 5 & Sam. 5. . . .

"Neither let any kneel before thee for that is only done to god: it is ye worship of ye body to him; & therefore not to be given to any mortal. Nor suffer them to give thee those titles that belong to god & not to ye nature of thy office & capacity.

"These things I write, that thou mayst not shun ye cross in thy employment either by continuing it in ye present extent of it, or casting it entirely off. Renounce w^t is not practicable in ye clearness of ye truth of god in thy heart; & use ye rest to good ends & purposes; that thou mayst become a pattern to other potentates, not so much to desert their power, as to convert it to righteous ends. And this I know, that thou wilt find more peace, & in ye end obtain a more glorious recompense, then can be expected from a private Retreat, & voluntary Sequestration.

"Dear Princess, though ye cup may be bitter in ye mouth, yet is it sweet in ye belly. Be faithful to ye manifestation of ye Light of Jesus in thy heart, that is not of ye World, but leadeth out of ye Nature & Customes of it all those, that receive it in ye love of it, & bear ye reproach of his holy cross without ye camp of this world.

"And if for thy tender & conscientious forbearance to practise or indulge any such unchristlike things thou art affronted or displeased, O rejoice; for great shall be thy reward in ye Kingdom of ye ffather.

"And this I press ye more earnestly, that it may appear to all, thou hast not deserted De Labadie & his people, to sit down short of their Attainments: but for ye love of a more excellent way, testimony, & service. . . .

"Well, I leave this Letter to thy Serious consideration in all ye parts of it; be cool & still in thy mind; & a plain way will be opend in thee, in which thou shalt meet with wisdom, strength & refreshment. And truly, till thou hast begun to discharge thy conscience in these matters, this was ye word of ye Lord God to me in my deep Travail for thee, that ye comfort, peace, & life thou desirest, & my soul so earnestly supplicated on thy accompt, would be hid from thee.

"And this I *must* do; 'tis God's certain way: I never rec'd life or comfort, or assurance any other way. . . .

"Thus have I open'd my heart, & unbosom'd my very soul to thee in that true love, & with that holy respect, wch all words are much too short to express: & god alone knoweth how it is with me on thy behalf. With that humility & tender spirit it pleas'd thee to receive & entertain us, accept this epistle; & with it my unfeigned & endeared Salutations; & please to assure thyself that in w^t Country or Region soever god shall order me, thou hast of me in ye holy truth, that abideth forever,

A ffaithful, Constant
& Ready ffriend,

My Brethren   W P.
G.F. G.K. & B.F.
present thee
with their
Christian Salu-
    tations.''

This letter is replete with interest, not only because of its forthright condemnation of a "hireling" ministry, but chiefly because of the views of civil government which its author was so soon to translate into action within his own princely domain.

The night before Fox and Penn and their companions left Briel on their return to England, in October, 1677, Penn wrote again to the Princess and Countess.[58] In these letters, he made another fervent appeal to the Princess to become a Friend: "My Soul most earnestly desireth thy Temporal and Eternal Felicity, which standeth in thy doing the Will of God now on Earth. . . . *O, Dear Princess,* do it! Say the Word once in Truth and Righteousness, *Not my Will, but Thine be done, O God!* Thy days are few, and then thou must go to *Judgment.*[59] . . . I could not leave this Country, and

---

[58] Penn's "Works", 1726, Vol. I, pp. 111–113.
[59] The editor of Penn's "Works", adds a marginal note to this, namely: "She died about four years after."

not testifie the Resentments[60] I bear in my Mind of that *Humble* [humbling ?] and Tender Entertainment thou gavest us at thy Court. . . . Thy Business I shall follow with all the Diligence and Discretion I can, and by the first give thee an Account, after it shall please the Lord to bring me safe to London. . . . Thou hast taught me to forget thou art a Princess, and therefore I use this Freedom; and to that of God in thee am I manifest; and I know my Integrity. . . . Accept what I say, I intreat thee, in that Pure and Heavenly Love and Respect in which I write so plainly to thee. . . . I am more than I can say, Thy Great Lover and Respectful Friend, William Penn.''

Penn's letter to the Countess was enclosed in that to the Princess, to whom he wrote: ''Give, if thou pleasest, the Salutation of my dear Love to A.M. de Hornes, with the inclos'd. Dear Princess, do not hinder, but help her: That may be required of her which (considering thy Circumstances) may not yet be required of thee. Let her stand *Free,* and her Freedom will make the Passage easier unto thee.'' His letter was addressed ''For Anna Maria de Hornes, stiled Countess of Horns.'' Most of it is a rhapsody on the Love of God, which ''transcendeth the Friendship of the World and the vainglorious Honour of the Courts of this World.'' He refers to his ''last long Letter''[61] to her, and says that he had ''hoped not to have been so quick [with this one] upon it; but God's pure Love . . . moved fervently upon my Spirit to visit thee once more before I leave this land. I referred it to this Extremity [the eve of his departure for England], and being not clear to go hence, I send thee my *Christian* Salutation, in this pure Love that many Waters cannot quench, Distance cannot make it forget, nor can Time wear it out.'' He then gives her a brief account of his visit in Holland; requests her to ''Salute me to my French Friend, bid her be Constant''; commends her to God, her *Pavilion, Shield, Rock* and *Sanctuary* for *Ever;* bids her twice *Farewell,* and signs himself ''Thy friend and the Lord's Servant, W.P.''

---

[60] This word is now obsolete in English. It should be resentiments, and was used in the 17th. Century as equivalent to the French *ressentiments* (deep feelings).

[61] It was written from Amsterdam, the 10th. of the 8th. Month, 1677.

After his arrival in London, he received from Elisabeth a letter, dated Herford, the 29th. of October 1677,[62] replying briefly to his long letter appealing to her to become a Friend. "Dear Friend," she wrote,[63] "Your tender Care of my Eternal well-being doth oblige me much, and I will weigh every article of your Counsel to follow as much as lies in Me, but God's Grace must be assistant; as you say your self, he accepts nothing that does not come from Him: If I had made me bare of all Worldly Goods, and left undone what he requires most, I mean to do all In, and By his Son, I shall be in no better Condition than this present. Let me feel him first governing in my Heart, then do what He requires of me; but I am not able to teach others, being not taught of God my self. Remember my Love to G.F. [George Fox] B.F. [Benjamin Furly] G.K. [George Keith] and dear Gertruick [Gertrud Deriks]. If you write no worse than your Postscript, I can make a shift to read it. Do not think I go from what I spoke to you the last Evening, I only stay to do it in a way that is answerable before God and Man. I can say no more now, but recommend to your Prayers,

Your true Friend,
Elizabeth."

Another letter from the Princess to Penn, which he calls a third one, was dated November 17, 1677, and was in reply to his letter from Briel. It reads as follows: "Dear Friend, I have received a Letter from you, that seemeth to have been written at your Passage into England, which I wish may be prosperous, without date, but not without vertue, to spur me on, to do and suffer the will of our God. I can say in Sincerity and Truth, thy will be done, O God, because I wish it heartily; but I cannot speak in Righteousness, until I possess that Righteousness which is acceptable unto him. My house and my Heart shall be always open to those that love him. Gichtel has been well satisfied with the Confer-

---

[62] Penn calls it "a second Letter" which had come "to Hand" from her ("Works", 1726, Vol. I, p. 115; and "Journal," pp. 267-8. This A. L. S. letter is in the Granville Penn Collection of the Pa. Hist. Soc.); and after the receipt of a third letter from her, which he quotes, he (or his editor) adds (*Ibid.*, p. 116; and "Journal", pp. 269-70): "There are more of this Nature from her and divers other Persons of Eminence in those Parts, but not immediately relating to the Journal, are therefore not published."

[63] This letter is printed in his "Travails".

ences between you.[64] As for my Business, it will go as the Lord pleaseth, and remain in him.

Your Affectionate
Friend,
Elizabeth.''

This sowing of the seed in the courtly circle of Herford, did not result in the "convincement" of any of its members, as far as formal membership in the Society of Friends was concerned; but it may well have strengthened the piety and morality for which the court of the Princess Elizabeth was so favorably known, and stimulated among the common people of its vicinity a desire to participate in Penn's experiment in colonization a few years later.

Sewel devotes two pages of his "History" to these visits of 1677, and three pages to the correspondence connected with them.[65] Croese devotes a page and a half of his "History" to the story,[66] but devotes it chiefly to Fox.

William Penn's visit to the princess in 1677, Croese dismissed in one short paragraph ("that I may not multiply many words"), and says that "he did so far prevail by his polite Eloquence, and Approbation of the Auditors, that the Princess declared that she had been always intent upon the Duty *Penn* spoke off, and did not yet cease to go on the same Work and Duty, with which answer those Men departed.''

PENN AND THE PRINCESS MARY

In compensation for his brief reference to Penn's visit to this princess, Croese narrates his alleged visit to another princess, who is evidently the Princess Mary, wife and later queen of William III of Holland and England. Following his reference of a few lines to Penn's visit of 1677 to the Labadists at Wieuwerd, Croese says:[67] "I will add this Relation, that *William Penn* at this time being so near the ——— Wood, the Summer Residence of that Illustrious

---

[64] *Infra*, p. 87.

[65] The New York edition, 1844 (Vol. II, pp. 249–52, 256, 258–261). In his Dutch edition, he does not include Elizabeth's two letters to Penn (in October and November, 1677), or his letter to her (in October, from Briel).

[66] English edition, II, 236–8.

[67] *Ibid.*, II, 224–5.

Lady, the Princess of ———— of whom, as indeed she was, and is a Princess who has a peculiar Talent of Wisdom, and Piety, and Greatness of Soul, in asserting and promoting the Interest of Religion, he had heard much talk, and this Princess being now there present, it comes in his mind, and he intreats it as an extraordinary Favour, that he may have the Liberty of Access to wait upon her Highness. And she her self too having heard much of *Penn*, admits him; but so, as what she had heard many say, runs in her highness's mind, that *Penn* was not the Man that he desired to be taken for, but was either a Jesuit, or else an Emissary of his King's sent to sound the minds of the People and Grandees of this Country, and therefore she forearmes her self against him. But when this Princess had admitted *Penn* to her Speech; and he composes his Speech not with those Artificial Elegancies and courtly Niceties, which his former Inclination, Education, and Customs had enabled him to; but with the highest gravity, and as far as Religion would permit, in the most exquisite terms he could devise; and thinking this discourse might not be displeasing to the Princess, at the end of it, he begs leave to make a Sermon before her Highness. To which the Princess, to make short with him, Answers, that she had very good Preachers of her own, whom he might hear; and she had not far off *David Flud a Giffen,* a Preacher worthy of such a Princess; as who besides his natural parts, Learning, and sweetness of Conversation, Joyn'd with Probity of Life, and endued with a singular gift in Preaching, was now the worthy pastor of the Church at *Dort,* a Man to us well known and our very great friend, Which Answer *Penn* taking in the stead of a civil Refusal, with a chearful Countenance and in kind terms asks her Highness, if in any other respect he might be serviceable to her; and so takes his leave of her Highness.''

This rather curious story is not authenticated elsewhere than in Croese, so far as this present author is aware; but it is not in itself impossible. Mary, the daughter of Penn's close friend, James, Duke of York, later King James II, was married to William III, Prince of Orange, in November, 1677, and may well have been preparing for that event at her summer palace in September, when Penn was at Wieuwerd.

CHAPTER II

PENN IN THE NETHERLANDS

Of Penn's first journey to the Continent in 1671, but very little is known, and but few traces of his presence are found in that year in the centers of Quakerism in Holland. The pioneer period of planting the faith, which had begun sixteen years before, was nearly ended and the period of conservation and organization well started; in the latter work Penn performed a leading part, while at the same time he paved the way for the colonization of Pennsylvania.

Before the founding of his colony, Penn made another visit to the Continent, in 1677; and nine years later, after having seen in person the auspicious beginnings of Pennsylvania, he made a third and final visit to his Dutch and German Friends and prospective colonists.

PENN'S JOURNEY, 1671

Just before making his first visit, in August, 1671, he saw George Fox and his companions off from Gravesend on their voyage to America, and then came direct to Rotterdam. Here, Benjamin Furly joined him and his companion, Thomas Rudyard, and the party probably went thence to Amsterdam. In his journal of 1677, Penn writes that he went that year by boat to Naarden and thence by "the common Post-waggon to Osnaburg [Osnabrück[68]]"; and then he adds: "We past through a very dark Country to that place, yet I felt not so great a weight and suffering in my Spirit as Six Years ago, when I went through the same places."

His destination in 1671 was the court of the Princess Elizabeth and the Labadists at Herwerden, or Herford; and on his return to Amsterdam, he stopped at Emden.[69] Of his stay in Amsterdam, we know only that he wrote there

---

[68] In the margin of his journal, the name is given as *Osnabrug*: "An Account of W. Penn's Travails in Holland and Germany. Anno M D C L XXVII", London, 1694, p. 31.

[69] Cf. *infra*, p. 172, and Monograph Number Seven ("The Persecution of the Quakers in the Netherlands and Western Germany").

(or perhaps in Rotterdam) a broadside entitled, "A Trumpet Blown in the Ears of the Inhabitants of High and Low Germany, of whatever State, Principality, Quality, Sect, or Nation they may be." This was translated into Dutch by Benjamin Furly and published in broadside without place or date. In 1671, it was added to a second (English) edition of Penn's "Truth Exalted" (London, 1668); and four years later, it was reprinted in the Dutch, in Amsterdam, together with a Postscript by Benjamin Furly, and as part of a Dutch version of "Truth Exalted."[70] Furly's Postscript states that the "Trumpet" was "written in Holland about September, 1671"; and this is the only evidence from Dutch sources of Penn's visit in that year.

Penn had written, also, while in Newgate Prison, "A Warning to the English Nation"; this was dated the 7th. of the 2nd. Month [April], 1671, and was added to the English edition of "Truth Exalted", in 1671. The next year, he wrote a "Missive or Warning to the Netherlands Nation", under date of the 14th. of the 4th. Month [June], 1672, which was also translated and published by Furly in broadside and forwarded, he says in his Postscript, "to the heads of the Netherlands nation."[71] This summed up Penn's impressions gained during his visit and admonished the Dutch people as follows:

"The dark and gloomy day of the visitation of the hand of the Lord god Almighty is upon you, therefore abide the judgment and search out that accursed thing amongst you which provokes the Lord; for god is risen in his terrible displeasure to lay you utterly wast, unless you repent of the evill of your wayes, and humbly calling to mind your former low state, *return unto the Lord whom ye have grown too high, too rich, and too proud for.* And count this triall more precious to you than all your stately habitations, great wealth and trade in this changeable world; for it is the mind of the lord god eternall (and his word to you all, from one

---

[70] The Dutch translation of "Truth Exalted" was also made by Benjamin Furly, who supplied it with a Dutch Preface.

[71] It, too, was included in the 1675 Dutch edition of "Truth Exalted", together with a Postscript for the "Missive" which stated how Furly had disposed of the broadside editions of the "Trumpet" and the "Missive."

of his remnant who hath measured you in the ballance of the light and sanctuary of god) that ye should be awakened out of your earthly security *and know a staining and a withering of all visible empire, trade, and treasure,* that so you may all come to know his blessed seed and witnes raised and quickened in every one of you, to the laiing judgment to the line and righteousness to the Plummett, yt ye may know a cleansing from the evill of your waies. O! build not upon the justice of your cause, as you conceive, neither let your expectations be from your navies, horses, chariots and mighty men of war; nor glory in the wisedom of your counsellors; *but awake, awake you sleepy, earthly inhabitants of the land, and let your eye be to the Lord god alone in the lowness of your spirits, and be ye resigned to his al wise disposall*: for I testify from the god that made heaven and earth, *if you make man your refuge, and put your confidence in the stratagems of men, god will confound you for ever and give you up as a prey into the hands of your cruellest adversaries.* Neither cry you, we are betraied, and men have dealt treacherously with us; for god hath suffered these things to come upon you that ye may be humbled thereby, and *weaned from the covetous pursuits of this fading world,* and learn to do justice and love mercy, and to walk humbly with the Lord; wch ye can never do *till you come out of all your emty professions, and meer formalities in Religion and worship, and sweep your streets of all lewdness and your trade and government of oppression, and bow unto gods righteous appearance by his pure light and spirit in everymans heart and conscience,* for in obedience thereunto (which leads into a cross to all the lusts of the flesh) true peace consists. This is Christianity indeed, and *the blood that cleanseth, ransometh and saveth from sin here and wrath to come, is only witnessed in being led and guided in and by that pure light of god with which he hath enlightened every man that comes into the world.*

  "This lay upon me in the deep and weighty love and councell of god to send amongst you in this hour of your great tryall, who about ten months since (being amongst you) and burthened in spirit with your glory, pride, earthly-mind-ness, oppression and forgetfulness of god that made and raised you, did then from a clear sight, warn you of this very day that is come like a deluge upon you, as such of you who have read my trumpet and allarm to the high and low dutch nation may call to mind.

"I am at peace with all men. W. P."

These messages of Penn to the people of Germany and the Netherlands were religious and moral admonitions; but he gave them an ultra-international touch by signing himself, "I am not of this World, but seek a Country Eternal in the Heavens, William Penn." The opportunity which he seized for impressing them was the threat of French invasion and conquest. Louis XIV's first war of aggression against the Netherlands had ended in 1668; but a new war was launched by him against Holland in 1672, which lasted until the Peace of Nymwegen, a half-dozen years later.

Another echo of this first visit of Penn to Holland is found in a letter which he wrote to "My Dearly beloved ffriends J[saac] and G[ertrud] Jacobs, Peter and Eli[zabeth] Hen⁸ [Hendricks]." This letter has no place or date of writing; but from internal evidence is seen to have been written some time during or before the year 1673.[72] After its long, religious salutation, it continues: "And Dear friends, my heart is melted in dear and heavenly love towards you, by which you are deeply engraven in my remembrance, and often in our holy assemblys I feel the interceeding spirit of the Lord for your support and assistance under all your great and (to many) unknown exercises. And lett the living seed arise: O lett the powr have its way and be bold and vallient for god and stop not our testemony, surely testimonys must arise for the good old way off everlasting life, faine would I be with you; but cannot, and when to see you I know not, but it is much desired by me, for my heart cleaves towards you. I have been sometimes a little troubl'd not to hear from you, so much as of the receipt of severall letters I have written to you, specially one containing 2 of

---

[72] Roberts Collection, Haverford College; it is printed [for the first time?] in the *Bulletin of the Friends' Historical Society of Philadelphia*, Vol. IV (1911), pp. 2–4.

G ffoxes letters from Barbadoes,[73] I long to understand how
it is with you. . . . . I am your endeared friend and
Brother Wm. Penn. . . . . Salute me dearly to all friends of
yr Generall meeting; if my letters already writt be not lost
keep them till I come or send me copys P[er] post; forgett
me not to Jo. Lodge and honest John claws.''

One of the ''severall letters'' referred to in this letter
may have been a ''general epistle'' dated ''From my House
at Rickmersworth, in the Nation of England, the 4th of the
10th Month S.V. 1673.''[74] It is addressed ''To the Little
Flock and Family of God, the People whom He hath called
and gathered to the Knowledge and Belief of His Everlasting Way to Life and Salvation. Of God beloved, but of Men
traduced and spoken Evil of. As also such as have of late
any Desires begotten in them after His Eternal Truth, now
residing in the United Provinces. . . . .'' It is signed: ''I am
your Sensible, Tender and Sincere Friend and Brother in
the Everlasting Truth, to serve you to the utmost of my
Ability therein, W.P.''

It begins by sending them his ''True and Tender Love in
God our Life''; compares God to ''an Everlasting Fountain'' from whom issue ''Living Chrystal Streams'' of consolation for their refreshment; reminds them ''That as you
once bore the Earthly Image and wore the Beasts Seal in
your Foreheads, so now you may daily Witness the Renew-
ing of the Heavenly Image upon you by the Power of the
Lord, inwardly felt, and a Wearing of the Lamb's Seal in
your Foreheads by the Spirit of our God;'' and warns them
against being ''scattered from this blessed Hope'' either by
''the Bawlings of some Thick, Carnal, Headwise Opposers,
who are more in Word than in Deed and only skill'd in
Science falsly so called (for it is filled with endless Jangles
and Debates),'' or by the ''Reproaches of the Prophane, the
cruel Sufferings of Some Persecuting Pharisees, or the
falling-away and Treacherous Apostacy of any Judas,

---

[73] George Fox arrived in Barbados on the 3rd. of 8th. Month (Oct.), 1671,
and wrote a letter to "Deare ffrends" from that island on the 1st. of 10th.
Month (Dec.), 1671; he left Barbados on the 8th. of 11th. Month, 1671, (18th.
of January 1672).

[74] Penn's "Works", 1726, Vol. I, pp. 162–3.

Demas or Alexander the Coppersmith; but as Pilgrims, estranged from the Life and Spirit of this World, who are embarked for a more durable Country and Building that is Eternal in the Heavens, pass away your sojourning here below in Fear and Trembling, in Diligence and Godly Conversation. . . .''

One year later (12th of 10th Month, 1674), Penn addressed another letter from London to "The Friends of God in the Netherlands and severall Partes of Germany," which was so highly regarded by its recipients that they reprinted it in Dutch translation in "Ancient Truth Revealed" (*De Oude Waarheid Ontdekt*, Rotterdam, 1684).

His first-hand experiences with the persecution of the Quakers in Emden, on his visit there, led Penn to write a letter on "Christian Liberty" to the city's Consuls and Senate. This was written in Latin, and appears to have been published first in that language in Holland in 1672; if such be the case, it too was probably written in Amsterdam or Rotterdam on his return from Emden in 1671.[75] Furly translated it into Dutch, "at the request of the Author", and published it in Rotterdam under the date of the 18th. of the 2nd. Month (February), 1675; he supplied it with a preface of four pages, and at the same time appears to have procured its publication at Rotterdam in a German version.

When Penn learned in England of the persecution of the Quakers in Danzig, in December, 1674, he had copies of his letter to the Emden magistrates published in Latin (at Rotterdam) and in German (at Amsterdam) and sent to the magistrates of Danzig also. The letter expostulated with the rulers of the two cities "upon Occasion of their late Severity to several of their Inhabitants, meerly for their Different Perswasion and Practice in Point of Faith and Worship towards God".[76] Thus, on his first visit to the Continent, Penn struck the three-fold note of his life's mission, namely, the spread of Quakerism, the establishment of religious toleration, and the founding of a community dedi-

---

[75] An English version, dated London, the 14th. of 10th. Month [December], 1674, was published in London in 1674/75, and a Latin version of the same date was published in Rotterdam in 1675.

[76] Cf. Monograph Number Seven ("Persecution of the Quakers").

cated to the Kingdom of God on earth. The thought of a colony somewhere in the Old World or New already lay germinating within him.

PENN'S JOURNEY, 1677

Six years now elapsed before his second visit to the Netherlands. In preparation for it, there was published in Rotterdam, in 1677, a Dutch translation (doubtless by Benjamin Furly) of a letter which he had written in Carberry, County Cork, Ireland, under date of the 19th. of the 12th. Month, 1669 (February, 1670). It was entitled, "A Letter of Love to the Young convinced of that blessed everlasting Way of Truth and Righteousness." A young man of twenty-five when it was written, Penn was still in his early thirties when he made his second journey to the Continent and heralded his arrival by this plea to the "young convinced": "Let us no more look back upon our ancient pastimes and delights, but with holy resolution press on, press on".

At the Yearly Meeting in London, in 1677, there were present "many Friends from most parts of England, and some out of Scotland, Holland, &c." The Dutch Friends present doubtless made a strong plea that the English Quaker leaders should visit the Friends of Holland and organize the society there. Accordingly, after "very glorious meetings" in London, the Holland visit was determined on. First, however, Penn, Fox and John Burnyeat spent three weeks at Penn's home in Worminghurst, Sussex, chiefly for the purpose of writing a reply to "a very wicked and envious book, which Roger Williams, a priest of New-England (or some colony thereabouts) had written against truth and friends.'"[77]

After "setting things in order", the Quaker leaders started from London for Holland by way of Colchester and Harwich. The party included Fox, Penn, Barclay, George Keith and his wife Elizabeth, John Furly (the second), William Tallcoat, George Watts, and Isabel Yeomans (a daugh-

---

[77] Fox's "Journal". The reply was published in London, 1678, under the title, "A New-England Fire-Brand Quenched", and was in answer to a book by Roger Williams, entitled "George Fox Digg'd out of his Burrowes", Boston, 1676.

ter of Margaret Fell Fox), and "two of our Servants". This was a company noteworthy in Quaker annuals. Fox was still in the prime of life, at the age of fifty-three; Keith in the late, and Penn in the early thirties; and Barclay twenty-nine, but already author of the famous "Apology" for the Quakers, which had been published in Latin, the year before, in London, Rotterdam, Frankfurt, and "certain other places".

At Colchester, the party's hosts were Steven Crisp, another famous Quaker leader, who had many links with the Friends of Holland, and John Furly, the father of Benjamin of Rotterdam. At Harwich, the travellers lodged at the home of John Vandewall, whose Dutch name prevents his English birth and parentage from obscuring the probability that some of his ancestors had come from Holland, perhaps in Elizabeth's time.

From Harwich, the party of missionaries took ship for Holland. Both Fox (in his "Journal" and in "Haistwell's Diary") and Penn have left a record of this journey to the Netherlands and western Germany which, while they omit many details, are nevertheless thankfully used two and a half centuries later.

Penn's account of these "Travails" of 1677 was written, he says in his Preface to the first printed edition[78] "for my own and some Relations, and perticular Friends Satisfaction, as the long time it hath lain silent doth show: But a Copy that was found amongst the late Countess of Connaway's Papers, falling into the Hands of a Person that much frequented that Family,[79] he was earnest with me, both by himself and others, to have leave to Publish it for a Common Good: which upon perusal, I have found a willingness to comply with, hoping that the Lord will make the Reading

---

[78] First edition, London, 1694. The original manuscript is preserved in the Pennsylvania Historical Society Collection. The author is indebted to that Society for the photographs of the first and next to the last pages of the manuscript, and to the Friends Historical Library of Swarthmore College for the photograph of the title-page of the first edition. See *supra*, p. XII; and Monograph Number Three ("Eight First Biographies of William Penn").

[79] This was Franciscus Mercurius van Helmont; see Monograph Number Six ("Dutch Quaker Leaders"). Lady Conway died in 1679, which was still fifteen years before the journal was published.

of it Effectual to some into whose Hands it may Fall. . . .
Oh, that the Nations would hear him, their only Saving
Health, and Israel's great Shepherd! . . . who hath sent and
is sending forth his Servants to gather home the Sheep that
are gone astray in all Nations, that so there may be but One
Shepherd and one Sheepfold.''

These high religious aspirations for all the world were
fully shared by his companions on this journey, and they
found expression even during the two days' voyage from
Harwich to Briel. "We had good Service", Penn writes,
"those two daies in the Ship with several Passengers
French and Dutch, and though they seemed at first to be
Shy of us, and to Slight us, yet at last their Hearts were
much Opened in kindness towards us, and the universal
Principle had place." Quakerism was still in its springtime,
in this 5th. Month, 1677, and its adherents were confident
that it would some time grow to include all humanity.

Briel

The voyage across the North Sea was an uneventful one.
A partial explanation of its comfort is given by Penn, who
says: "The best accommodation was given us by special
favour of the master (he having formerly served under my
father)." "A fine passage we had", writes Fox; "I was
very well this voyage, but some of the Friends were sea-
sick." At the end of the voyage, occurred an interesting
episode which Penn omits from his journal, but which is
given by Fox's amanuensis, Edward Haistwell, as follows:[80]
"There was a fair fresh Gaile, wch carried the packett Boat
to within one League of ye shoar, and then It was calme ag^n
so they cast Anchor y^t night; and they lett down A little
boat; & two men wch belonged to ye^e shipp carryed W Penn,

---

[80] "The Haistwell Diary", one of George Fox's Itinerary Journals, edited
by Norman Penney, Cambridge, 1925, p. 237. Haistwell was evidently one of
the "two servants".

Haistwell records a similar experience which came a few weeks later to
Fox and three companions on their return by boat from Harlingen to Amsterdam. They arrived, Haistwell says, "about the first hour in ye night: but
ye Gates being shutt ffr^{ds} lay on board till ye morning."

1677.

The 11th day of ye 5th month, 1677, being ye
First day of ye week I left my dear wife & family at worming-
ing [in] love & fear of God, & came well to London
that night.

The next day I employed myself on Friends
behalf, that were in suffering, till ye evening; & then I
went to my own mother in Essex.

The next morning I took my journey to Colchester & met George Watts upon ye way; who returned with
me & came well to ye town ye evening. We lodged
at John Furley's (ye Elder); but had a blessed meeting
at Jonathan Furley's house that night.

The next morning early I left Colchester, &
came to Harwich with about noon; accompanied
with G. Watts, & John Furley ye Elder, Wm. Talcoke,
& G. Whiterly of Colchester; where we found dear
G.F. at John Vandewall's house, with many more
Friends.

After dinner we went all to ye meeting, where
ye Lord gave us a blessed earnest of his love & presence, that should be with us in this voyage.
For his holy overcoming refreshing power fell upon
all our hearts, & many of our mouths in ministry,
prayer & praises, to ye magnifying of his own name,
& truth in that place.

The meeting done, we returned to John
Vandewall's house, where we took our leave
of Friends, that is to say, of ye Friends of that
place, ~~E. Camedister, Edward G. Whiterly,
J. Stockin, & J. Stocker~~, with others, that came with
us or met us there; & so went on board ye [packet]

William Penn's "Travails," 1677

& R.B: to shoar, and so they went to y⁰ Citty of Briell[81] but It being in y⁰ night the Gates were shutt, y^t they could not gett in: and there being no houses wth out y⁰ Gate they went to a fish^rs Boat and layd there till y⁰ morning and they went into y⁰ Citty.''

Benjamin Furly and two other Rotterdam Friends, Arent Sonnemans and Sijmon Jansz Vettekeuken,[82] met Penn and Barclay on their arrival, and ''three young men y^t Lives wth B ff:'' went in ''a pleasure boat to fetch G ff and ffr^ds to Shoar,'' and thence to ''the Briel where Friends received us with great gladness.''

Briel, a seaport in the province of South Holland at the mouth of the Rhine, or as it is named there, the Maas River, was variously called by the English Brielle, The Brill, The Bril and The Briell. It saw numerous Quaker missionaries, among countless other travellers enter its gates; but in recent years, it has been practically abandoned as a seaport in favor of the new channel from the Hook of Holland to Rotterdam.

Fifteen years before Fox and Penn arrived, the advent of Quakers had aroused public attention in the city; for in 1662 (from the 4th. to the 13th. of July), the Particular Synod of South Holland was held there and adopted an article (the VIII) which urged upon the presbyteries the duty of eradicating the Quakers, Socinians, and the Collegiants of Rijnsburg, and promised the assistance of the synodal deputies in this work whenever such assistance was asked for.[83] On this occasion, however, the Friends were not molested; and after they had spent two hours in refreshing themselves, took boat for Rotterdam.

Three months later, having cleared, as Fox explained, ''our spirits of the service which the Lord had given us to

---

[81] Fox in his large Journal says that Penn and Barclay, "understanding that Benjamin Furly was come from Rotterdam to the Briel to meet us, got two of the boatmen to let down a small boat", etc.

[82] Penn calls them "A. Sonnemann' and J. Johnson, Yetterkeuken". See Monograph Number Five ("Benjamin Furly and the Rise of Quakerism in Rotterdam").

[83] See Monograph Number Seven ("The Persecution of the Quakers in the Netherlands and Western Germany").

do in Holland", the party of English Friends again arrived in Briel en route for home. They were accompanied by a number of Friends from Amsterdam and Rotterdam, one of whose families (Gertrud Deriks's) went on to England with them. The "Pacquet-boat" not having arrived, the party spent the night at Briel, and Penn spent the evening hours in writing letters to the Princess Elisabeth and Countess of Hoorn.

Sailing for Harwich the next day, the voyagers did not reach their destination until two and a half days later, and were badly storm-tossed on the way. Nevertheless, on the evening of their arrival, Fox wrote before he went to bed an Epistle to the Friends of Holland; while Penn arose early the next morning to ride eighteen English miles on horseback and hold a Friends' meeting in Colchester. But before starting on this journey Penn took time to write a long farewell letter, of love and counsel to Friends in Holland and Germany! In this, he gave the following account of the voyage: "We got well last night about Seven to Harwich, being three days and two Nights at Sea: Most part of the time was a great storm of Wind, and Rain, and Hail, the Weather was against us, and the Vessel so leaky, that two Pumps went night and day, or we had perisht, 'tis believed that they pumpt twice more water out than the Vessel could contain, but our peace was as a River, and our joy full. The Seas had like to have washt some of the Seamen overboard, but the great God preserved all well. Frights were among the People, and Despondencies in some, . . . we were mightily throng'd, which made it the more troublesome." Fox adds in his journal: "And ffr^{ds} had a fine time on shipp board, wth a Collon [colonel] and severall Eminent *psons* who were very kind and Lovinge". But Penn's comment is: "It is observable that though the Lord so wonderfully delivered us, yet some vain People soon forgot it, and returned quickly to their wanton Talk and Conversation, not abiding in the sense of that hand which had delivered them."

In Fox's letter, dated "harag 23 day 8 mo. 1677",[84] occurs

---

[84] The original of this letter in George Fox's own hand is preserved in the Friends Reference Library, London; it was published *verbatim et literatim* in the *Bulletin of the Friends' Historical Association*, Philadelphia, Vol. 13 (1924), pp. 88–89.

the following account of the voyage. In it he refers also to another episode concerning Penn, which Penn omits, and which was later crossed over in Fox's letter. "Now con saring paseges," Fox writes, "it is like wilam pen hath given you an acount but this j doe say that it was the lordes pouer that did presuerfe us & it was a mirkell for wee had a great storme & ouer ship was soe leake that boeth the pompes could not hardly aneser & the master stoped som leakes in the day time but in the night the stormes was soe great & the ship soe leake [& the pasangeres all soe sicke][85] that the pomp went all night & j had such a travell on my spirit consaring the ship & the people for j saw the people as thof the [though they] had ben all sunke in the seay & the people was in a petefull feare & j deserd the lord god of heaven for his name & truth sake whoe had the windes in his hands & the seay in the holow of his hands whoe could stope the waves [or leakes][85] & the seay at his pleasher & the lord god did aneser mee & his pouer went over all & his glory did shine over all [& j did her the pompes suck][85] & the wind came mor fare for us & soe wee cam all safe to hareg abought 7 ouer the 23 day 8 mo: 1677 & in the midest of the storme j was over all in the life thof j felt j could a sueferd with the people but still j was over all in the glorues pouer & life in my walking.

"& ther came such a great forceable waveses of the seases up on the deecke that j was a feard [or *scard*] that som of the seamen had been washd over borde for the all did worke for ther liveses but the lord god did presuerfe all soe to his glory thankes & prase be it & ther was a meny pasengers & great parsones [& a lady & a cornall] & w p & j spake to them & the was loving & j spake to the people alsoe in publicke & all touke it well & was loving [& cartrit [Gertrud Deriks] was very sicke & wilam pen soe that hee vmotd blood] but all is well blessed be the lord for ever amen."

Such was the end of Penn's second journey to the Continent, his account of which he closes with thanks to God and the reflection, "I can say truly blessed are they, who can chearfully give up to serve the Lord: Great shall be the en-

---

[85] These words in brackets are crossed through in the original,—the first and the third heavily crossed; indeed, all of the letter quoted here was crossed through and not included in Fox's Journal.

crease and growth of their Treasure, which shall never end.'' His service of the Lord in the Netherlands on this visit (besides his long journey in western Germany) had taken him to Rotterdam, The Hague, Leiden, Noordwyk, Haarlem, Amsterdam, Hoorn, Enkhuisen, Workum, Harlingen, Leeuwarden, Wieuwerd, Lippenhuizen, Groningen, Delfzyl, Nÿmegen, Utrecht and Naarden.

ROTTERDAM

In Rotterdam, by this time, Quakerism was well established;[86] and ''many Friends came to see us'', Penn says in his journal, ''among whom we were comforted.'' The memory of his maternal grandfather, ''Jan Jasper, merchant of Rotterdam'', and of his mother's first husband, Nicasius Vanderscure, may have added a touch of personal interest to Penn's eager promotion of Quakerism in the city.

The day after their arrival being First-day, or Sunday, the Friends improved the opportunity by holding two meetings for public worship, to which resorted, says Penn, ''a great Company of People, some of them being of the considerablest Note of that City''; and Fox records more specifically: ''Many of the townspeople and some officers came, all were civil, and they heard the truth declared peaceably. Benjamin Furly or John Claus interpreted when any Friend declared.''[87] These meetings were both held in Benjamin Furly's second Rotterdam home, on the Wijnstraat; and from them it is believed that Egbert van Heemskerk derived his data for his well-known painting, De Quakers Vergadering. The portraits of Fox, Penn and Furly (also Barclay and Keith?) are believed to appear in the painting, and it would be very interesting if an artist of Van Heemskerk's ability has preserved for posterity the representations from life of these leading Friends and great men, as well as the meetings which they held and the interior of the house itself.[88]

---

[86] See Monograph Number Five (''Benjamin Furly and the Rise of Quakerism in Rotterdam'').

[87] Penn writes with marked enthusiasm of these meetings. ''The Gospel was Preached, the Dead was Raised, and the Living Comforted, and God even our God bore Heavenly Record to his only begotten Son in us.''

[88] Cf. *infra*, p.   , and Monograph Number Five.

This second home of Furly and his subsequent ones are of historic interest on other accounts; for in them, its hospitable and learned owner entertained Jean Leclerc, the Amsterdam professor and journalist; Philippus van Limborch, the Amsterdam theologian and historian; John Locke, Algernon Sydney, and the third Earl of Shaftesbury, all of whom resided for a time in Holland; and other distinguished contemporaries who were his friends and correspondents. In them, too, was gathered together that fine collection of books,—especially rich in Seventeenth Century literature,—the catalogue of which was published in Rotterdam, in 1714, under the title of *Bibliotheca Furliana.* Furly's home on the Wynstraat was also the lodging-place of Fox and the headquarters of the other visiting Friends, although they did not all lodge there, but were distributed among the other Friends' homes,—"in several quarters of the city", says Penn.[89]

The next day (Monday) was spent by Fox and his party in "visiting Friends from House to House, not in one Company, but in several small ones". In the evening of that day, Penn continues, "several of us dined and supped at two great men's houses, where we had blessed opportunities". These "opportunities" were religious ones,[90] which Penn and his companions utilized to the best of their ability. "All our Visits were Precious Meetings," he says, "for indeed, for that end God brought us into this Land. Several of us Dined and Supped that day at two great Men's Houses, where we had blessed Opportunities to make known unto them what was the Hope of our Glory . . . Truth is honourable in the Eyes of several of that place." The part which Rotterdam and its people were to play in assisting Penn's "holy experiment" in Pennsylvania a few years later, also was partially, even though unconsciously, prepared for by these opportunities.

The next morning, five of the party,—Fox, Penn, Tallcoat, John Furly and Isabel Yeomans,—breakfasted at Arent Sonnemans', and then set out with most of the others by trekschuit for Amsterdam. Jan Roelofs van der Werf and

---

[89] Cf. Monograph Number Five ("Benjamin Furly and Quakerism in Rotterdam").

[90] Haistwell's Diary calls them "good oppertunities for ye service of truth."

Jan Claus of Amsterdam and Jacob Arents of Oudesluis[91] had come to meet the party at Rotterdam, and went with them to Amsterdam. Robert Barclay and George Keith and his wife remained in Rotterdam to attend the regular Fourth-day (Wednesday) meeting of the Friends, and went to Amsterdam in time for "the general Meeting of Friends in this country," which was held on "Fifth-day (Thursday), the 2nd. of 6th. Month (August)". A number of the Rotterdam Friends also went to attend that exceptionally important meeting.

HAARLEM

Walking through Delft, the party took another boat to Leiden, where they lodged at an inn that night, and went on by boat the next day to Haarlem. Quakerism had been known in the latter city for a score of years, and its adherents had suffered some persecution.[92] The local Friends' meeting was loosely organized, and had had to deal with some recalcitrant members. The arrival of the travellers caused much excitement among them, and much interest in the city. Penn writes that on the party's arrival, about eleven o'clock, they "went to the House of a good Old Man, that had long waited for, and is now come to behold the Consolation and Salvation of Israel.[93] After we had a little refresht ourselves, we went to the Meeting, where the Lord gave us a blessed Opportunity, not only with respect to Friends, but many sober Baptists [Mennonites] and Professors [Dutch Reformed] that came in, and abode in the Meeting to the End."

Both Fox and Penn preached at this meeting, their interpreters being Jan Claus and Benjamin Furly. Fox called it "a very large meeting, to which came many of the towns-

---

[91] These names are given in Penn's printed Journal as "J. Bocliffs, J. Arents and J. Claus"; in the MS. Journal as "J. Roeloffs and Jo. Claus". Haistwell mentions Jn° Roeloffs and Jan. Claus.

[92] See Monograph Number Seven ("The Persecution of the Quakers in the Netherlands and Western Germany").

[93] Haistwell's Diary gives the name of this Friend as Dirk Klasen. He may have been one of the Klasen or Klaasz brothers who had been imprisoned several times in Haarlem for their opposition to war and military training. See Monograph Number Seven.

people and two of their preachers." One of the Haarlem
families who heard Penn on that occasion was that of Jan
Willemsz Boekenoogen, a cooper, and the son of Willem the
elder.[94] Seven years later, Jan and his family followed Penn
to Pennsylvania.

AMSTERDAM

Friends from Amsterdam, Alkmaar and Emden had come
to Haarlem to meet the English travellers; and they, with
other Friends from Haarlem, went on after the public meeting to Amsterdam. Here, the travellers lodged in the spa-
cious house of Gertrud Deriks (or Getrueydt Dircks, as
Penn calls her), and held a series of meetings for worship
and discipline, which resulted in the organization of the
Friends of the Netherlands and Germany into ten local
monthly meetings, with a quarterly and a yearly meeting to
be held at Amsterdam.

Fox, Penn, Barclay and Keith were the chief leaders in
this work of preaching and organization, Claus and Furly in-
terpreting for them. The form of society and the rules of
discipline which had been adopted in England were successfully transplanted to the Netherlands.[95] Letters came, also,
to the Amsterdam meeting from the Friends of Danzig,
"complaining", Penn says, "of their heavy Sufferings they
underwent, informing us also that the King of Poland was
there, asking advice about an Address to Him."[96] It fell
upon Penn, he continues, to write the letter to the king; and
in doing so, he doubtless utilized his "Letter to the Consuls
and Senate of Dantzic", published (in Latin) two years before in Rotterdam.

Having accomplished this task, and visited some Friends
of Amsterdam in their homes, Penn, Keith, Barclay and
Furly made preparations for a long journey into Germany.
First, however, they participated on the Sunday in a *five
hours* public meeting for worship (From 11 A. M. to 4
P. M.), which was attended, Penn says, by "a mighty Con-

---

[94] See Monograph Number Seven.
[95] See Monograph Number Eight ("The Friesland Monthly Meeting of the
Society of Friends").
[96] See Monograph Number Seven.

course of People from several places of this Country, and that of several Perswasions, Baptists [Mennonites], Presbyterians [Reformed], Socinians, Seekers, &c.''[97] The next day, Penn and his three companions set forth by boat to Naarden where, ''after having Eaten'', they took leave of the Amsterdam Friends who had accompanied them that far on their long journey, and went on by ''Post-waggon'' to Osnabrück and many other places in western Germany.[98]

NIJMEGEN

After three weeks of strenuous labors in Germany, Penn and his companions came down the Rhineland from Kleef to Nijmegen. Nijmegen (Nimeguen) was one of the imperial seats of Charlemagne, is now the capital of the Netherlands province of Gelderland, and stands like a miniature Rome upon its seven hills beside the River Waal. It is noted in history chiefly for the treaty of peace negotiated there in 1678, which put a temporary check upon the aggressive warfare of Louis XIV. It was the year before the peace, in September, 1677, that Penn first arrived in the city. He came again, one month later; but on both occasions, ''immediately took Waggon for Utrecht''.

ROBERT BARCLAY AND THE PEACE OF NŸMEGEN

Robert Barclay had left Penn, Keith and Furly at Herwerden, after their visit to the Princess Elizabeth, and returned by way of Amsterdam to England and Scotland, while Jan Claus joined the others in Barclay's stead. The latter was much absorbed at this time in seeking the release of Quaker prisoners in Scotland; but, although he did not go to Nijmegen in 1677, he did what he could to procure the establishment of a permanent peace when the ambassadors of thirteen of the warring European powers were negoti-

---

[97] Fox adds to this list, "Brownists, and some of the Collegians."

[98] The terrible massacre perpetrated in Naarden by Catholic soldiers, about one century before, appears to have suggested no opportunity to these or subsequent Quaker missionaries to propagate their faith in the city. Neither Penn's party in 1677, nor Kendall, Brown and Neal in 1752, nor Grellet and Allen in 1832, all of whom passed through on their missionary journeys, attempted to hold meetings in it.

ating the treaty there the next year. Hoping to impress upon them the Quaker principles of international peace and religious toleration, he wrote them an open letter in Latin, had it printed, and sent to each of the ambassadors and to each of their sovereigns a copy of his letter, together with a copy of his famous exposition of Quakerism, the "Apology for the True Christian Theology."[99]

Gerard Croese, commenting upon visits of English Quaker preachers to the Netherlands, says that "there was nothing worth remembering done by these Men; save that Barclay at such time, as the Ambassadors of several Kings and Princes were met together at Nimeguen to Treat about a general Peace; he also interceeds to procure a Peace for all their Churches, and delivers a Letter therupon to each of these Gentlemen, and withall certain Theological Theses, containing the Heads of their Doctrines, and afterwards affixes them to the Doors of a certain University and submits them to the Examination of all Men."

Copies of the letter and book were delivered at Nijmegen on February 24, 1678. The letter was entitled "AN EPISTLE OF LOVE AND FRIENDLY ADVICE," and was as follows:

"*To the* Ambassadors *and* Deputies *of the* Christian Princes *and* States *met at* Nimeguen, *to Consult the Peace of* Christendom, R. B. *a Servant of* Jesus Christ, *and hearty Well-wisher to the* Christian World, *Wishes Increase of Grace and Peace, and the Spirit of sound Judgment, with Hearts inclined and willing to Receive and Obey the Counsel of* GOD,

"Let it not seem strange unto you, who are Men Chosen and Authorized by the Great Monarchs and States of *Europe* to find out a speedy Remedy for the present great Trouble (under which many of her Inhabitants do groan) as such, whose Wisdom and Prudence, and Abilities have so recommended them to the World, as to be judged fit for so Great and Difficult a Work, To be Addressed unto by one, who by the World may be esteemed Weak and Foolish; whose Advice is not Ushered unto you by the Commission of

---

[99] This was the first, Latin, edition, published in Amsterdam, 1676. His letter was printed in Rotterdam, 1678.

any of the Princes of this World, nor Seconded by the Recommendation of any Earthly State: For since your Work is
that which concerns all Christians; why may not every
Christian, who feels himself stir'd up of the Lord thereunto,
contribute therein? And if they have Place to be heard in
this Affair, who come in the Name of *Kings* and *Princes*;
let it not seem heavy unto you to hear him, that comes in
the Name of the *Lord Jesus Christ* ...

"Know then, *My Friends*, that many and often times my
Soul has been deeply bowed down under the Weighty Sense
of the present State of Christendom; and in secret before
the Lord I have mourned, and bitterly lamented because
thereof. And as I was Crossing the Sea, and being the last
Summer in *Holland*, and some Parts of *Germany*, the
Burthen thereof fell often upon me, and it several Times
came before me to write unto you, what I then saw and felt
from God of these Things, while I was in those Parts. But
I waited, and was not willing to be Hasty; and now being
returned to my own Country, and at my own Home, I chearfully accept the fit Season, which the Lord has put in my
Hand, and called me to therein...

"The *Chief Ground, Cause* and *Root* then of all this Misery among all those called *Christians*, is, Because they are
only such in Name, and not in Nature, having only a Form
and Profession of Christianity in Shew and Words, but are
still Strangers, yea, and Enemies to the Life and Virtue of
it; owning *God* and *Christ* in Words, but denying them in
Works; And therefore the Lord Jesus Christ will not own
them as his Children, nor Disciples. For while they say,
they are his *Followers*; while they Preach and exalt his Precepts; while they Extol his Life, Patience and Meekness,
his Self-denying, perfect Resignation and Obedience to the
Will of his Father; yet themselves are out of it: And so
bring Shame and Reproach to that Honourable Name, which
they assume to themselves in the Face of the Nations, and
give an Occasion for Infidels (*Turks, Jews* and *Atheists*)
to Profane and Blaspheme the Holy Name of *Jesus*. Is it
not so?... While upon every slender Praetext, such as *Their
own small Discontents, or That they judge, the present
Peace they have with their Neighbour, cannot suit with their*

Grandeur and Worldly Glory, They sheath their Swords in one another's Bowels; Ruine, waste and destroy whole Countreys; Expose to the greatest Misery many Thousand Families; Make Thousands of Widows, and Ten Thousands of Orphans; ... And all this while they pretend to be *Followers of the Lamb-like Jesus;* who *came not to destroy Men's Lives, but to save them;* The Song of whose Appearance to the World was, *Glory to God in the Highest, and Good Will and Peace to all Men;* Not to Kill, Murther and Destroy Men; not to hire and force poor Men to run upon and murther one another, meerly to satisfy the Lust and Ambition of Great Men; they being often-times Ignorant of the Ground of the Quarrel, and not having the least Occasion of Evil Will or Prejudice against those their *Fellow-Christians,* whom they thus Kill; amongst whom not one of a Thousand perhaps ever saw one another before. Yea, is it not so, that there is only a *Name,* and *nothing of the True Nature* of Christians especially manifest in the *Clergy,* who pretend not only to be *Professors,* but *Preachers, Promoters* and *Exhorters* of others to Christianity, who for the most Part are the greatest Promoters and Advancers of those Wars; and by whom upon all such Occasions the Name of God and Jesus Christ is most horribly abused, prophaned and blasphemed, While they dare *Pray to God, and Thank him for the Destruction of their Brethren Christians,* and that for and against, according to the Changeable Wills of their several Princes: Yea, so that some will join in their Prayers with and for the *Prosperity* of such, as their *Profession* obliges them to believe to be *Heretical* and *Antichristian;* and for the Destruction of those, whom the same *Profession* acknowledges to be *Good* and *Orthodox Christians.* Thus the *French,* both *Papists* and *Protestants, Join in their Prayers and Rejoice for the Destruction of the* Spanish Papists *and* Dutch Protestants. *The like may be said of the* Danish, Swedish *and* German Protestants, *as respectively concerned in this Matter.* Yea, which is yet more strange, if either Constraint or Interest do engage any Prince or State to change his Party, while the same War and Cause remains; then will the Clergy presently accommodate their Prayers to the Case, *In Praying for Prosperity to those, to whom instantly before they wished Ruine;* and so on the contrary; As in this present War, in the Case of the *Bishop of Munster* is manifest. Was there ever, or can there be any more horrible Profanation of the Holy and Pure Name of *God*, especially to be done by those, who pretend to be Worshippers of the true God, and Disciples of *Jesus Christ?* This not only Equals, but far Exceeds the Wickedness of the *Heathens;* For they only Prayed such Gods to their Assistance, as they fancied allowed their Ambition, and accounted their Warring a Virtue; whom they judged Changeable like themselves, and subject to such Quarrels among themselves, as they that are their Worshippers; But for those to be found in these Things, who believe, there is but *One only God*, and have, or at least profess to have such Notions of his Justice, Equity and Mercy, and of the Certainty of his Punishing the Transgressors of his Law, is so horrible and abominable, as cannot sufficiently be neither said, nor written.

"The *Ground* then of all this is the Want of *True Christianity*, because the Nature of it is not begotten, nor brought forth in those called *Christians;* as therefore they bear not the Image, nor bring not forth the Fruits of it. For albeit they have the Name, yet the Nature they are Strangers to; The Lamb's Nature is not in them, but the Doggish Nature, the Wolfish Nature, that will still be quarrelling and destroying; the Cunning, Serpentine, Subtle Nature, and the Proud, Ambitious Luciferian Nature, that sets Princes and States a work to contrive and foment Wars, and engages People to fight together, some for Ambition and vain Glory; and some for Covetousness and Hope of Gain: And the same Cause doth move the Clergy to concur with their Share in Making their Prayers Turn and Twine; and so all are here out from the State of True Christianity. And as they keep the Name of being Christians; so also upon the same Pretext each will pretend to be for Peace, while their Fruits manifestly declare the Contrary. And how . . . doth Experience daily discover this Deceit! For how is Peace brought about? Is it not, when the Weaker is forced to give way to the Stronger, without Respect to the Equity of the Cause? Is it not just so, as among the wild and devouring Beasts? Who when they Fight together, the Weaker is forced to give way to the Stronger and so desist, until another Occasion offer? So who are found Weakest, who are least capable to hold out, they must bear the Inconveniency; and he gets the most Advantage, however frivolous, yea, unjust his Pre-tence be, who is most able to vindicate his Claim, and pre-serve it not by Equity, but Force of Arms; So that the Peace-Contrivers Rule is not the Equity of the Cause, but the Power of the Parties. Is not this known and manifest in many, if not most of the Pacifications, that have been made in Christendom? . . .

"Try and Examine your selves therefore seriously in the Sight of God, whether you be Led, Acted and Influenced in your present Negotiation by the Wisdom of this World . . . or by the *Heavenly* and *Pure Wisdom* of *God.* . . If the Warring Part be removed out of you. . . then are you fit to consult and bring about the Peace of Christendom, . . . Whereof, and of all those that Profess the Name of Christ I am,

A True Friend, and
Hearty Well wisher,
ROBERT BARCLAY.

"This came upon me from the Lord to write unto You at Ury, *in my Native Country of* Scotland, *the Second of the Month called* November, 1677."

George Fox also wrote a letter "for the embassadors that are met to treat for peace at the city of Nimeguen in the States dominions." This letter was dated at Amsterdam, the 21st. of 7th. mo. [October 1], 1677; it was translated into Latin, printed (probably at Rotterdam), and a copy of it delivered, together with Barclay's missives, to each of the ambassadors on the 23rd. or 24th. of February, 1678.

It is not apparent that these Quaker admonitions to the ambassadors to exemplify the principles of peace had any influence on the treaty which was actually adopted in the course of the year; but it is certain that the Quaker message left no tangible impression upon the people of Nijmegen. One century later, in April, 1788, Robert and Sarah Grubb, George and Sarah Dillwyn, and Mary Dudley passed through the town, in the course of their missionary journey of 2,500 miles, but held no meeting and heard no echo of a

Quaker message in it. The memory and message of Fox, Penn and Barclay had faded away as completely as that of the ancient Druids, whose shrine once hallowed the Valkhof.

UTRECHT

From Nijmegen, Penn went to Utrecht on his first visit, arriving there at ten o'clock in the morning of September 17, 1677, after a fifteen hours' drive in a wagon. "We hear there is a People in that City", Penn writes, "but had not now time to visit them, referring it to another opportunity." The people thus mentioned were doubtless those pioneer "Pietists" who had been influenced by Jean de Labadie in his visits to Utrecht in and after 1666, and those who had taken part in the controversy between "the Cocceians", led by Johannes Kok of Leiden and "the Voetsians", led by Gijsbert Voet of Utrecht. The Van Schurman brother and sister, Godschalk and Anna Maria, had been especially active in procuring adherents in Utrecht to the Labadists. That the latter had made a considerable stir in the city is evidenced by the fact that a professor of theology in the university, Andreas Essenius, wrote a treatise in Latin, German and Dutch against them (1671).

Penn was evidently desirous of making an appeal to these Labadists and near-Labadists; but on this visit to the city, after only a three hours' stay, Keith and Furly went to Rotterdam, while Penn and Claus hurried on first to Amsterdam, and then to Harlingen to help establish the Friesland Monthly Meeting.[100]

One month later, in October, 1677, after another strenuous effort with the Labadists at Wieuwerd and the court of the Princess Elizabeth at Herford, Penn and Claus came again by way of the Rhineland to Utrecht; but again "way did not open" for missionary effort in that city. Arriving from Nimeguen at evening, the two travellers took the night-boat for Amsterdam, "because," Penn explains, "of a pressure upon my Spirit to be next day [Sunday] at the Meeting, and the rather having intimated as much from Ceulen [Cologne]."

Although Penn's labors in behalf of Quakerism met with

---

[100] See Monograph Number Eight ("The Friesland Monthly Meeting").

no tangible results in Utrecht, the Quaker colony which he founded a half dozen years after his visit had an irresistible attraction for some of Utrecht's citizens and impelled them to leave the fatherland and seek new homes across the seas. One of these was Gharret van Hassen who, on reaching manhood's estate, prepared to set out for America. He was taken ill before the time set for his departure, and the ship upon which he had intended to sail was sunk in the Atlantic, with all on board. This escape, which he deemed providential, made a deep impression on his mind, and he became a member and "traveling minister" in the Society of which Penn had been a minister. He did not carry out his intention of going to America, nor did he preach the Quaker message in his native land; but, settling in England, he devoted his life from his fortieth year to visiting the families of Friends and preaching in their meetings throughout the British Isles.

To another native of Utrecht, Gerard Honthorst, we owe the earliest portrait of George Fox. This is attributed to the year 1654, when Fox was in the thirtieth, and Honthorst in the sixty-second, year of his age. Honthorst, like Van Hassen, spent part of his life in England; but, although he returned to his native land and died at The Hague in 1660, he does not appear to have had any other connection with Quakerism on either side of the Channel.

AMSTERDAM

Coming to Amsterdam from Utrecht, in September 1677, for the second time that year, Penn "found Friends generally well," he says, "though it is a sickly time in this Country. The Meeting-house is much enlarged, and there is a fresh enquiry among many people after Truth, and great desires to hear the Testimony and Declaration of it." The next morning, "being the first day of the week", Penn continues, "we had a blessed and large Meeting, larger than ordinary, because of a great addition of room since our Journey into Germany; indeed there was a great appearance of sober professing people, yea several of the chief of the Baptists [Mennonites], as Galenus [Abrahamsz] and Companions the Lord's heavenly power was over all, and the Meeting blessedly ended about the fourth hour [P. M.]".

HOORN

To take part in the organizing work at Harlingen, Penn was obliged to leave Amsterdam that same day; but first, he took leave after supper "in a sweet little Meeting among Friends," and then went by boat to Hoorn. He was accompanied this time by Pieter Hendricks of Amsterdam, and arrived after a sail of six hours at the North Holland city. Quakerism had been brought to Hoorn by Hendricks as early as 1661;[101] and the Quakers gathered in that place had suffered persecution until 1666.[102] George Fox and Jan Claus came there en route for Friesland, in August of 1677, but hurried on, after only one night's stay, without attempting any "service"; and Penn and Hendricks, one month later, spent only four hours there resting from two to six o'clock A. M., and then "took Waggon for Enckhuysen."

WORKUM

In Enckhuysen, too, Fox and Claus, and Penn and Hendricks, spent only a few hours before setting sail across the Zuyder Zee to the Friesland port of Workum. Six years before, William Caton and Hendricks had made a perilous voyage in the reverse direction across the Zee, and had had some service in Workum before embarking;[103] but the travellers of 1677 hastened on by wagon to Harlingen. Here, meetings for worship and propagandism were held, and monthly meetings for the men and women Friends were established.[104]

LEEUWARDEN

The next morning, Fox and Hendricks left Harlingen for Amsterdam, while Penn and Claus went to Leeuwarden. Penn must have arisen at a very early hour, for he started for Leeuwarden at four o'clock that morning; and the night before, apparently after ten o'clock, he had written a long

---

[101] See Monograph Number Six ("Dutch Quaker Leaders").
[102] See Monograph Number Seven ("Persecution of the Quakers").
[103] See Monograph Number Six.
[104] See Monograph Number Eight ("The Friesland Monthly Meeting").

letter (of nearly five printed pages) to "the noble young Woman, Joanna Eleanora Marlane [von Merlau], at Franckfort."

Leeuwarden was the capital of the province of Friesland; and, as Harlingen was the chief center of Quaker effort and achievement in the province, so Leeuwarden was its chief center of Quaker persecution and suppression.[105] This persecution had begun in 1661, and lasted into the 1680's; but Penn and Claus held the public meeting which they had "appointed" from Harlingen, "with peace and refreshment", Penn says, "several being there (as in other places) that were never at a Meeting before. The Meeting being done, and having refreshed our selves with food, we took Waggon for Wiewart [Wieuwerd], the Mansion-house of the Family of the Somerdykes, where De Labadie's Company resideth, it being strong upon my Spirit to give them a visit."[106]

LIPPENHUYSEN

From Leeuwarden, the two travellers journeyed on to Lippenhuysen, or Lippenhusen, as Penn calls it, and found there "a little Meeting of Friends." This Friesland village lies in the district which the Friends spoke of in their Monthly Meeting minutes as "the Woude"; and the members of the meeting who lived there played an interesting part in its activities.[107] Penn and Claus arrived there, after a drive of twenty-five English miles from Wieuwerd, at ten o'clock in the evening, and "the next morning," Penn records, "we had a blessed Meeting among Friends, many of the World came in, were very serious and well-affected; one whereof was a Magistrate of the Place: The Lord pleads his own Cause, and crowns his own Testimony with his own Power." In his manuscript (and first printed edition, 1694) of his Travails, Penn adds the optimistic sentence:[108] "There is like to be a fine gathering in that place." This optimistic prophecy was not fulfilled, as far as the Friends'

---

[105] See Monograph Number Seven.

[106] Cf. *supra*, p. 12.

[107] See Monograph Number Eight.

[108] It does not occur in its appropriate place in the edition of his "Works", 1726, Vol. I, p. 94.

meeting was concerned; for, within a score of years after Penn's visit, the meeting came to an end. Doubtless, Penn's words and personality were long discussed in this remote rural neighborhood; and it, too, made its contribution to the stream of colonists settling in Pennsylvania.

Groningen

From Lippenhuyzen, Penn and Claus drove on, "twenty-five English miles", to the university city of Groningen. Here, too, the Quakers had been known and ridiculed in student-songs for a dozen years or so, had suffered some persecution at the hands of the magistrates, and had been championed by Steven Crisp.[109] The month before Penn and Claus came to the city, Fox and Claus had visited the Friends there and had held "a good meeting, whithʳ Resorted severall professoʳs who were very peaceable and attentive." Penn and Claus, after spending the night, held a meeting the next morning, Penn writes, "among Friends of that City, whither resorted both Collegiant and Calvinist Students who behaved themselves soberly; the Lord's Power was over all, and his Testimony stands. When the Meeting was ended, they went out; and as I was concluding an Exhortation to Friends, came in a flock of Students to have had some Conference with us; but having set the time of our leaving the City, we recommended them to the Universal Love of God, promising them some Books of our Principles; with which they exprest themselves satisfied, and civilly parted from us." We are not told definitely that Penn kept his promise in regard to the "Books of our Principles"; but it is an interesting possibility that some of the Quaker tracts which are still preserved in the fine library of Groningen University may have come from this chance meeting of the great scholar of Oxford with the students of Groningen.

Ten years after Penn's visit to the city, Willem Sewel accompanied Richard Hoskins of Barbadoes there and interpreted the latter's message of Quakerism to "a large body of people, far beyond our expectation." Of this and

---

[109] See Monographs Numbers Six and Seven.

other matters concerning the city, Sewel wrote to Penn in his Latin letters of 1686 and 1687;[110] by which time, "Groninger Land" had begun its contribution also to Penn's colony beyond the Atlantic.

DELFZYL

After dinner in Groningen, Penn's story continues, "we took Boat for Delfzyl, and came there about six at night." This small town in the province of Groningen lies just across the River Ems from the city of Emden, and it became a frequent refuge for the Quakers fleeing from persecution in the latter city.[111] A few years before Penn's visit to it, an opponent of Quakerism published a story that a preacher in the Friends' meeting in Delfzyl persuaded six of the Friends to walk through the river "as a sign", and that three of them were drowned, while the other three waded in up to their knees and then turned back. Steven Crisp denied this and similar fabrications in a vigorous pamphlet; but Penn leaves no echo of Quaker affairs in the town. Before Penn's visit, Fox and Jan Claus with several other Friends had been in it twice, en route to and from Emden; but the only incident recorded of their visit is the fact that "yᵉ Souldiers examined G ff: and then had him up to yᵉ maine Guard and after they had examined him wee went to an Inn." From this, it would appear that Fox's soldier-like appearance impressed the military in Holland as well as in England.

AMSTERDAM

After making another tour into western Germany by way of Emden, and another visit to the Princess Elizabeth and the Rhineland, Penn came for the third time that year to Amsterdam. Here, he writes, "we found our dear Friends generally well, the City much Alarm'd [by the military successes of the French in the southern Netherlands], and great Curiosity in some, and Desires in others to come to the Meeting." This curiosity about Quakerism both he and

---

[110] See *infra*, p. 122, and Monograph Number Six.
[111] See Monograph Number Seven.

Fox strove to satisfy by the written and printed, as well as the spoken, word. Penn speaks of spending time "in divers Affairs relating to the Truth," among which was the writing of four pamphlets, as follows: "A Call to Christendom";[112] "A Tender Visitation in the Love of God ... to all People in the High and Low-Dutch Nations";[113] "To all those Professors of Christianity, that are Externally separated from the visible Sects ...";[114] and "To all those who are sensible ... wherever scattered throughout the World, but more especially in the High and Low-Dutch Nations."[115]

With the memory of their recent work in Germany fresh in mind, Fox and Penn wrote numerous pamphlets in Amsterdam for the benefit of their German hearers and readers. All four of Penn's pamphlets just cited were translated into German and published, probably in Rotterdam, in 1678; and Fox wrote at least a dozen addresses and appeals which were printed and distributed in German or Dutch or both.

Among Fox's visitors in Amsterdam were "a great high Priest", as Haistwell calls him, "who had belonged to ye Emperor of Germany, and anoth[r] Germã Priest: so after they had spoke wth him hee declared ye truth unto them (and they were tender) opening unto them how they might know God and Christ, & his Law & Gospell: and shewing them that they should never know It by Studying, nor by philosophy, but by Revelation, and Stillness in their minds by y[e]

---

[112] This was written in Amsterdam, the 20th [10th.] of 8th. Month [October], and left in Rotterdam on his way to England "to be Translated [into Dutch] and Printed" (doubtless by Benjamin Furly), and published in Dutch in Rotterdam, 1678; a Dutch reprint was included in the 1684 collection „De Oude Waarheid Ontdekt" ("Ancient Truth Revealed"). Penn said that it was "likely to be printed hereafter in English", so did not include it in his "Travails"; but its first English edition did not appear until 1694.

[113] and [114] These were published for the first time in English in the third edition of Penn's "Travels", London, 1714. Their Dutch editions were probably published for the first time in Rotterdam, 1678, and they were reprinted in „De Oude Waarheid Ontdekt", 1684.

[115] This was published for the first time in English in London, in 1695; its Dutch edition in Rotterdam, 1678, with a reprint in „De Oude Waarheid Ontdekt", 1684. For an edition of the four pamphlets in German, see *infra*, p. 309.

spirit of God: and they were well satisfyed, & so passed away.''

The identity of these German ''priests'' may be revealed in a postscript to a letter which Penn wrote to the Princess Elizabeth from Briel, ''Seventh-day, the 20th. of 8th. Month'', which reads as follows: ''We visited Gilrall and Hooftman, and they us, they were at one or two of the Meetings at Amsterdam.'' The first of these is evidently the Pietist, Johann Georg Gichtel, an eminent disciple of the mystic, Jacob Böhme, whose works he edited, and whose own disciples were known as Gichtelians, or Angelic Brethren (*Engelsbrüder*); and the second may have been Moritz Hoffmann, father or son, of Altdorf, Baden, who shared a belief in the Christ Within. In a letter from Elizabeth to Penn dated 17. Nov. 1677, is the sentence: ''Gichtel has been well satisfied with the Conference between you''. This satisfaction, however, did not lead to a union of the Gichtelians with the Quakers, in spite of at least one fundamental agreement between the two sects. This was the belief in ''that of God within us'', which Gichtel regarded as being the quintessence of all life of faith. Especially after the persecutions which he suffered in many places in Germany, and after his settlement in Amsterdam in 1668, he ranked the Light Within above all else,—Bible, church and sacraments.

At one time, Gichtel prepared to emigrate to America, together with Baron Justinianus Ernst von Weltz; but at the last moment, he decided to continue to prosecute his work in Europe. He died in Amsterdam in 1710.

Fox and Penn were keen to promote Quakerism by the spoken word also in Amsterdam at this time, and they held several public meetings for that purpose. Of one of these, Penn writes: ''We had a very great Meeting, and many People of note resorted. God's Gospel Bell was rung, the great Day of the great God sounded, and the Dead was raised, and much tenderness appeared in several. O blessed be the Name of the Lord, whose Work and Testimony prospereth.''

On the following Wednesday, another meeting was held, to which, Fox writes, ''there resorted many hundreds of

people, some of high rank in the worlds account. An Earl, &
a Lord, & many Eminent persons, who were very Loving
(and a Brother of one of yᵉ Lords of yᵉ states, Invited G ff
to dinner, and hee had good service with them)[116] and yᵉ ffrᵈˢ
afore-mentioned declared in yᵉ Meeting & B.F. & J: C: did
Interprett and all was quiett till W P had ended yᵉ Meeting,
& then there were some priests yᵗ made an opposition, but
W P. understanding stood up again, and answered them, to
yᵉ great satisfaction of yᵉ people: who were much affected
wᵗʰ yᵉ severall Testimonies, yᵗ they had heard declared.''

Penn's account of this meeting and its incidents is from a
letter which he wrote in Amsterdam, ''Fourth-day the 10th.
of 8th. Month'', but which is marked over in his Manuscript
Journal. It is as follows: ''The next day (which is this day)
we had a blessed publique meeting never to be forgotten: O
the majesty, glory and life that the Lord attended us with!
Our hearts were deeply affected with his presence.'' In a
letter from the Briel, dated ten days later, which is also
marked over in the Manuscript Journal, Penn makes this
reference to the same meeting: ''Since my last we had a
blessed meeting at Amsterdam, being the next day after the
date of my last: great reverence and brokenness were over
the meeting, more than I had seen. The meeting ended, we
were opposed by a preacher who was closely pursued by
several merchants, etc. (not of us) that cryed out he was
rude and ignorant: and offered to dispute in our defense.
But the priest run away: they followed him till they hous'd
him.''[117] The tables had surely been turned since a score of
years before, when Quaker preachers endeavored to participate in the religious exercises conducted by the
''priests'' of Amsterdam, and were chased and housed for
their pains!

GALENUS ABRAHAMSZ

Public debate was also a favorite means, then as now, for
the defense and promotion of Quaker principles; and it was
equally favored by the Collegiants of Amsterdam. Hence it

---

[116] This parenthetical statement is made in Haistwell's Journal.

[117] Penn's ''Works'', 1726, Vol. I, p. 108, gives this passage, and adds: ''What
followed, I know not.''

we arrived early morning at Amsterdam,
where we found our dear friends generally
well; ye city much allarmed, & great Curiosity
in some, & desired in others to come to ye moe-
ting: we had a very great meeting, & many
people of note resorted. God Gospel-bell was
rung: (ye great day of ye great god saund &, &
ye dead was raised; & much tenderness appeared
in general. & blessed be ye name of ye Lord,
whose work & testimony prospereth.

The next day was spent in divers affaires
relating to ye truth.

The day following we had a meeting w
Galenus Abrahams (ye great father of ye Socinian — mennists in these parts) accompanyed with several preachers, & others of his
Congregation; divers of our friends were also
present. It continued about 5 hours: the
affirmed in opposition to us, That there was
no Christian Church, ministry, or commission
apostolical now in ye world: But ye Lord
assisted us with his wisdom & strength to
confound his attempts. [Here followeth...]

The next day (w is this day) we had a blessed publique meeting never to be forgotten:
ye majesty, glory & life, that ye Lord attended
us with! our heads were deeply affected w
his presence. Tomorrow we have another
meeting with Galen & his company; for
they are ye most virulent & obstinate opposers of truth in this land.

(Thus much out of a letter from Amster,
I am, dated ye 6e 1o -Amo. — followeth
part of a letter from Briell,
dated ye 1o o 1677. viz:)
since my... we had a blessed meeting
at

Penn's Debate with Galenus Abrahamsz

is in character to find a debate among Penn's activities in the city. Penn's account of this famous discussion was a brief one, as follows: "The Day following we had a meeting wth Galenus Abrahams (ye Great ffather of ye Socinian Mennists in these parts) accompanyed with several preachers and others of his Congregation, divers of our ffriends were also present. It continued about 5 hours: He affirmed in opposition to us, That *there was no Christian Church, Ministry, or Comission Apostolical now in ye World*: But ye Lord assisted us with his wisdom and strength to confound his Attempts."

Fox's brief account of the debate was as follows: "After some time George Keith and William Penn came back from Germany to Amsterdam and had a dispute with one Galenus Abrahams (one of the most noted Baptists in Holland), at which many professors were present; but not having time to finish the dispute then, they met again two days after, and the Baptists was much confounded and the Truth gained ground."

Haistwell's Diary, referring to Penn's second meeting with "one Gollanus, who is ye greatest Baptist in all Holland", says: "On ye 11: day of ye 8: month W Penn, and G. Keith had a dispute again with Gollanus Abrahams, at Corneliss Roeloffs house, and G ff was there, and many ffriends & professors: and Gollanus was much confounded, so after ye dispute ffr^ds Returned to Gertruyd Dirknieson's, and ye most of ffriends in ye Citty came thither, and G ff: and W P: took their Leave with them."

This second meeting with Abrahamsz Penn refers to in a letter which is marked over in the manuscript journal of his "Travails". The letter was written to the Countess of Hoorn and dated from Amsterdam, the 10th. of 8th. Month, and says: "Tomorrow we have another meeting with Galens and his company; for they are the most virulent and obstinate opposers of Truth in this land." In another letter to the Countess, dated from the Brielle, ten days later, Penn says: "Since my last (being the next day after the Date thereof) we had a meeting with Galenus Abrahams and his Company (for they are the most virulent and obstinate Op-

posers of Truth in that Land)[118] the success thou mayest
perhaps see suddenly in Print, and therefore I may defer
the Narrative, only in general our Dear Lord, our Staff and
Strength was with us, and Truth reigned over all.''
  In the 1694 edition of his ''Travails'', Penn writes, under
the date of 4th. Day, the 10th. of 8th. Month: ''It was upon
me this day to engage Galenus Abrahams to a second Conference, that we might more fully debate and confute his
grand Objections against the present Dispensation of Truth,
and the heavenly Ministry witnessed among Friends: he
refused not my offer of a second Meeting; but sent me word,
his Business would not give him leave to let it be any time
this day, upon which the next was fixt for the Conference to
begin at Eight, which accordingly it did, and held till One.
The most impartial account of both these Conferences that
I am briefly able to give followeth.''[119]
  The substance of Penn's contribution to this debate may
have appeared in the pamphlet he wrote in Frankfurt, entitled ''To the Churches of Jesus throughout the World'',
which is included in the 1694 edition of his ''Travails''. But
the ''impartial account'' of it which he promised is not
forthcoming. The more important, or more pressing, affairs
in which he was soon afterwards engaged probably prevented the fulfilment of his promise.
  Nor do we have Abrahamsz' version of the debate. Two
historians of Holland, however, have left brief accounts of
it. The first of these, Gerard Croese, gives us the version of
a Dutch Reformed clergyman, who may be regarded as impartial, or as equally hostile, towards both Collegiant and
Quaker. Croese writes:[120] ''At several times there went
through these Countries [the Netherlands] to visit their
Friends, Fox, Barclay, Penn, Keith and others. But there
was nothing worth remembering done by these Men; save

[118] This parenthesis was probably quoted, by Penn's editor of 1694, from
the letter cited above which was marked over in his manuscript journal.
  [119] The editor of Penn's ''Works'', 1726 (Vol. I, p. 108) adds to this paragraph
the words: ''The Account of both the Conferences is not yet found, but with
the latter [conference] some of his own Friends seemed better satisfied, and
it ended very comfortably to us, because to a General Satisfaction.''
  [120] *Historia Quakeriana*, English edition, London, 1696, Book II, pp. 215–6;
Latin edition, Amsterdam, 1696, pp. 507–8.

that Barclay at such time, as the Ambassadors of several Kings and Princes were met together at Nimequen to Treat about a general Peace; .... And also, that William Penn and Galen Abraham a Physician, and also a Preacher amongst those Mennonites, which we account all, or for the most part of them at least, to be Socinians: At the same time almost [as the Peace Congress at Nimwegen] at Amsterdam disputed in a private House, of the signs of the New Church, and extraordinary Call of Ministers, and that after such a manner, as Penn who, after the manner of his Nation, spake nothing but in a premeditated and set form of speech; shew'd upon this occasion that when he had a mind to it, he was not wanting in the faculty of answering Extempore, to the suddain and large Discourses of others; but the other so abounded in multitudes of words, as he never came at the stress of the matter where the cause lay: And where he could not tell how to bring close Arguments to the purpose, he either very ingeniously put of [off] giving an answer at all, or turn'd it into Joke and Banter, and so it ended after the same rate as Disputations most commonly do.''

It will be observed that Croese mentions in this account only William Penn as being engaged on the side of the Friends: that Penn uses the impersonal "we"; and that Fox mentions both Penn and Keith. The second Dutch historian who refers to the debate,—Willem Sewel,—mentions Fox himself in an interesting way.[121] "Here [in Amsterdam]", Sewel writes, "Penn and Fox held a debate (*reedenstryd*) with Dr. Galenus Abrahamsz and some of his society. Galenus asserted, *That no one now-a-days could be accepted as a messenger of God, unless he confirmed his teaching by miracles.* Penn did not want for arguments to oppose to this assertion, since the Christian religion had been once already confirmed by miracles, and therefore such things were now needless among Christians. Fox also interjected a few remarks by means of an interpreter; but being very short of breath (*kortborstig*: suffering from asthma), he went away now and then: which

---

[121] Dutch edition of Sewel's "History of the Quakers", Amsterdam, 1717, pp. 617–18.

circumstance some ascribed to his shortness of temper
(*driftigheyd*) : but I know well that they were mistaken.
This dispute was on the whole very troublesome, because it
was necessary for the participants on both sides to speak
through interpreters, which was done so imperfectly that
the discussion was finally ended, without an agreement having been arrived at, although there were many arguments,
and those of the weightiest, advanced against the proposition.'' Sewel here devotes a page to his own arguments,
drawn chiefly from the Bible, against the proposition of
Galenus, and finally concludes: ''I deem this sufficient to
show that the thesis of Dr. Galenus could not stand the test;
but whatever was objected against it, he clung to his
opinion.''

JESKE CLAES

Abrahamsz' demand of the Friends for miracles as a
proof of their divine calling was based, not only upon historic precedent, but also upon an incident which had recently occurred in Amsterdam. This incident had been
heralded as a miracle and printed in detail in a pamphlet
just issued in the city. It was the alleged remarkable cure of
Jeske Claes, wife of Rinck Abbis, boatman, residing on the
Princes Island, in Amsterdam harbor. Jeske had been a
semi-helpless cripple for fourteen years; but on the night
of the 13th. of October, 1676, ''Light'' had been given her
to see very plainly the Christ-child, and by this she had been
immediately and entirely cured.

Among the Colchester MSS.,[122] there is a summary of
Jeske's story, translated from the pamphlet or leaflet
(printed on ''New Bridge Street, Amsterdam, 1677''),
which reads as follows: ''For fourteen years she had been a
cripple, in one leg no feeling, no strength in the other,
forced to creep on the floor, be drawn in a little waggon, or
carried in arms like a child. On the night between the 13th
and 14th of October, 1676, she heard the clock strike, and the
rattle watch cry out one o'clock. She lay on her side and

---

[122] Colchester MSS. No. 67; see C. Fell Smith's ''Steven Crisp'', London,
1892, p. 35.

dozed, but felt something grasp her right wrist three times, and a voice said, 'Thy goings shall be restored to thee again.' She sate up on end, and cried, 'Shall I, sinful creature, be so happy as to have my going restored?' and the answer came, 'It shall be so, but keep it private at present.' Then she cried still more loudly (so that the neighbours overhead heard her), 'Lord, had I but light to see what happens to me!' and, taking hold of her husband, sought to wake him, but in vain.

"Then the voice said, 'Light shall be given thee,' and immediately a brightness shone through the chamber, and she saw as plain as one can see another, a little lad of about the size of ten years, with yellow, curled hair, short like the hair of the blacks, and a white garment down to his feet, with another white garment, which hung in flat pleats above the first. He took two steps towards her, and then, neither of them having breathed a word, vanished. Then she cried, 'Lord, am I but to enjoy thy light for so short a time?' And next, she felt like a stream of luke-warm water, in her right hip and toe, and exclaimed, 'I have life where I had none before.'

"As soon as her husband was gone, she rose up and thought to stand, but alas! she could not, and in her despair, she wept, until the neighbours wondered. Now, two days after, she sat in her kitchen, trying to boil some fish and sour soup for her husband's mother, who lay sick, when again the voice said, 'Thy going is given thee, go and meet thy husband.' Which doing, he was amazed, and affrighted, and said, 'Thou are not she,' thinking it were a spirit, and retreated before her, until she clasped her hands about his neck. In the meantime, there entered her daughter, bearing a candle, and stood speechless, not knowing what this should mean. Upon which, her husband cried, 'Is this thy mother?' 'Yea, father,' she faltered. He, with much doubting, stretched out his hand, saying, 'if thou beest my wife, I give thee my hand in God's name.'

"Whosoever desires further satisfaction herein, may have the account from her own mouth, as long as it please God she lives."

This was the woman evidently referred to in Haistwell's

Diary under date of the 10th. of 8th. month (the day before the debate), as follows :[123] "And y^t day there was A Woman at ye Meeting, who had gone: 14: Yeares on her hands, & her knees, and thorow ye wonderfull hand & Arm of ye Lord was this year[124] Restored to her strength again, and can go very well: & It being such a miracle, y^t many people goes to see her: and after ye Meeting shee came to G ff: and since her Recovery, so many people going to se her, and shee not keeping Low in her mind, and in ye fear of ye Lord, was much runn into words, so G ff spoke much to her, Exhorting her to fear ye Lord, and telling her y^t if shee did not keep Low and humble before ye Lord, y^t shee would bee worse then ever shee had been, and ye woman was much tendered, & confessed to ye truth."

Fox and Abrahamsz, 1684

The last echo of the debate with Abrahamsz and his companions comes from Fox's Journal, in which an account is given of his visit to Amsterdam in June, 1684. "Before I left Amsterdam", Fox writes, "I went to visit Galenus Abrahams, a teacher of chief note among the Mennonites, or Baptists. I had been with him about seven years before; and William Penn and George Keith had disputes with him. He was then very high and very shy, so that he would not let me touch him, nor look upon him (by his good will), but bid me 'Keep my eyes off him; for', he said, 'they pierced him.' But now he was very loving and tender, and confessed in some measure to Truth. His wife also and daughter were tender and kind, and we parted from them very lovingly."

Leiden

Having finished their tasks in Amsterdam, and taken "a solemn leave of our dear Friends" in the city, Penn, Fox and Furly went on to Leiden. Quakerism had found its way thither about twenty years before, and had had a picturesque, painful, and none too successful career in this city of the Pilgrims and the great university.[125] On their first ar-

---

[123] This passage was omitted from the previous editions of Fox's Journal.
[124] The words "this year" are crossed through.
[125] See Monograph Number Six ("Dutch Quaker Leaders").

rival in the city, July 31, 1677, Fox, Penn and their Dutch and English companions had spent only one night, en route to Haarlem and Amsterdam; but now, three months later, the three travellers "staid a day or two", says Fox, "seeking out and visiting some tender people that we heard of there. We met with a German[126] who was partly convinced. He informed us of an eminent man who was inquiring after truth.[127] Some sought him out and visited him, and found him a serious man. I also spoke to him and he owned the truth. William Penn and Benjamin Furly went to visit another great man, that lived a little out of Leyden, who, they said, had been general to the King of Denmark's forces. He and his wife were very loving to them and heard the Truth with joy."

Penn gives some further details of this visit, as follows: "Coming to Leyden late at night, we forbore to inquire after any worthy in that place. But the next morning we found out two, one a German of or near Darmstad, who expressed much love to Friends and told us of a retired person of great quality that liveth about two hours back again towards Amsterdam at a village called Nortwyck." Penn could not act upon his impulse at this time and return to Noordwijk to visit the person referred to, for he had still work in Leiden and The Hague to perform. Their German friend took the party, Penn continues, "to the house of one who had formerly been a Doctor in the University [Abraham Heydanis ?], of a sweet, yet quick, wise, yet very loving and tender spirit." Fox and Penn were both "more than ordinarily open" in this interview; the ex-professor "assented to every Thing we said: And truly his Understanding was very clear and open to the Things that lay upon us to declare; and he expressed his firm belief in great revelations [or Revolutions] at hand and that they should terminate in the setting up of the glorious Kingdom of Christ in the world. What shall I say," Penn continues; "the Man felt our Spirits, and therefore loved us, and in the fresh

---

[126] Was this Henry Lampe, M.D., a student at the University of Leiden, 1676-? See Lampe's Autobiography, edited, with Introduction, by Joseph J. Green, 1895.

[127] Possibly Dr. Abraham Heydanis, who had retired from his professorship the year before; see Monograph Number Six.

Sense of that Love writ a Letter to a retired Person at
the Hague, like himself: Which in several Places of
Germany was the Way whereby we found out most of the
Retired People we visited.''

After a two hours' interview wth the professor, and
''leaving the Peace of God upon him'', the three Friends
went on by wagon to The Hague. A week or so later, Penn
returned from Rotterdam to Leiden, with three companions; thence, accompanied also by their German acquaintance of Leiden, he went to Noordwijk to visit the ''retired
person of great quality'' of whom the German had told him;
but no stay seems to have been made in Leiden at this time.

NOORDWYK

While in Rotterdam, Penn says, ''the sense of the serious
retreat of this great Man we heard of at *Leiden* was so
strong upon me, that I could not see my self clear to leave
the Country, before I had given him a Visit. I purposed
therefore the next Morning to set forward to the *Hague,*
from thence to *Leiden,* and so to *Nortwyck.*

''I arrived there in the Evening with *B.F. A Sonnemans*
and *M Sonnemans,* and immediately made known our coming, and the end of it to him and his Wife, by the means of
the young *German,* who was got thither before us to visit
them. An invitation came to us all at our Inn, and immediately we repaired to his House, which was very stately,
and yet plain; he presently came to us, took us by the hand,
and bid us heartily welcome. We immediately sate down,
and after some time of retirement, I spoke something of
what was upon me, yet not before he had given us a sober
and pathetical Account of his Life, and of the present frame
and disposition of his Spirit. All this was in the absence of
his Wife; but so soon as I had finisht what was then upon
me to speak of the Witness of God, and of its Work in Man,
upon the occasion of the History he gave us of his Life; he
led us into another Room, where his Wife was, he told her
here were some Christian Friends come to visit her, she
saluted us very kindly.

''We all sat down, and after some silence, the heavenly
Power of God did in a living and tender manner open their

States and Conditions to me, and opened my Mouth to them;
. . . . directing them to the blessed Principle of Light and
Truth and Grace, which God had shed abroad in our hearts.
I declared the nature and manner of the appearing and
operating of this Principle, and appealed to their own Consciences for the truth of what was said: And I can truly say
the holy Life of Jesus was revealed amongst us, and like
Oil swom at the top of all: In this I was moved to kneel down
and pray, great brokenness fell upon all, and that, that was
before the World began, was richly manifested in us and
amongst us. The Meeting done, the great Man and his Wife
blest us, and the work of God in our hands, saying, with
tears in his eyes, *My house is blessed for your sakes, and
blessed be God that I ever lived to see you.*

"And thus we left them, though with much difficulty, for
they prest us with great earnestness both to eat and to
lodge with them, and were hard to bear our refusal. They
said it was a Scandal to their house, that they should let
such good people as we were to go out of it; or suffer us to
lodge in any other place: But we declared our preengage-
ment elsewhere, and that it was not for want of true kindness towards them. One passage I had almost forgot to
mention, I was (*said he*) once at table with the Duke of *Hol-
steyn* at *Frederickstadt,* when the Magistrates came to com-
plain against a people called *Quakers* in that City. The Duke
was ready to be prejudiced against them, but at the very
naming of them I conceived a more than ordinary kindness
in my mind towards them. I askt the Magistrate what they
were for a People, he told me that they would not pull off
their hats to their Superiors; I askt him whether they would
pull off their hats to God, he said, yes; said I, that may be
the reason why they will not pull them off to Man. Do they
live peaceably? Yes, Do they pay their Taxes? Yes, Do they
rub their hats in your eyes? No, Do they do any harm with
them? No, Why what is your Quarrel then; they meet in
silence, and they will not speak or pray unless they be moved
by the Spirit; why, that is according to the Doctrine of
Scripture: If this be to be a Quaker, I would I were a
Quaker too, but, said he, I never saw one before, but I bless
God I see you now. He very much inveighed against the

false Christianity that is in the World, and greatly magnified a tender, mortified and retired Estate. I have great hopes he and his Wife will eye the truth. We returned to our Inn to supper, and to bed.''

THE HAGUE

Quakerism had left but few vestiges in The Hague before the visit of Fox, Penn and Furly in 1677; and even these energetic missionaries made but small effort there. On their first arrival, en route from Rotterdam to Amsterdam, they did not stop at all, but went direct by boat from Delft to Leiden. On their return from their three months' journey, they did make a brief stop, which is described as follows in Fox's Journal: "From Leyden we went to the Hage, where the Prince of Orange kept his court, and visited one of the judges of Holland, with whom we had much discourse. He was a wise, tender man, and put many objections and queries to us; which when we had answered, he was satisfied, and parted with us in much love.'' Penn calls this man "a judge of the Supreme Court'', and says that they had with him a long conversation, replete with questions and answers. "He received us with great respect,'' Penn continues, "and more than ordinary Desire to know the Truth of our Faith and Principles. We declared of the Things most surely believed amongst us, in the Power and Love of God. He made his Observations, Objections and Queries upon several Things we spoke, to whom we replied, and explained all Matters in Question; insomuch as he declared himself satisfied in our Confessions, and his Good Belief of us and our Principles. We took a Solemn and Sensible Leave of him, and we felt the Witness of God reach'd in him, and his Spirit tendred, which filled our Hearts with dear Love to him: He brought us to his Street-door, and there we parted.''

Even though this member of Holland's supreme court might not become a member of the Society of Friends in Holland, Penn and Fox must have felt that their visit had made a sympathetic friend in the seats of the mighty, and that persecutions of the Dutch Quakers might be thereby prevented or mitigated. A few years later, indeed, Benjamin

Furly doubtless utilized this high connection among others in behalf of some Quaker testimonies which he went to The Hague to defend.[128]

The "retired person", to whom the Leiden University professor had given them a letter, was not at home when they arrived at his house; but Penn took his companions to call on another promising prospect. On his visit a few weeks before to Anna Maria van Schurman and the Labadists at "Wiewart, the mansion house of the family of the Somerdykes, where De Labadie's company resideth", he had met with one of the three Sommelsdÿk sisters, "who are daughters of a nobleman at The Hague, people of great breeding and inheritance"; and in a letter from Amsterdam to the Countess of Hoorn, he spoke of his intention to pay "a Visit at the Hague to the Lady Overkirks, Sister of the Somerdikes, and some others that have sober Characters of Truth and Friends." He went accordingly to visit this "retired and religious character, separated from the public worship." But, his naive account continues, her husband, "a great man of the army, of another disposition and way of living, was at home and prevented access to her."

Fox's account of this visit in The Hague mentions only the last of these three calls;[129] nor does it refer to another fact which is stated only in the manuscript version of Penn's Journal. The original manuscript, immediately after mentioning the arrival of the party at The Hague, contains the words: "Where also we had a little meeting. O the lust and pride of that place." Why this significant statement was omitted from the printed versions of his Journal is not clear: whether because of the condemnation uttered against The Hague,— which may possibly be regarded as one reason why the Quaker missionaries were relatively so neglectful of the city; or because it was supposed by his editor that Penn had made a mistake in saying that a meeting had been held there. The improbability of the latter explanation is shown by the fact that a few days after leaving The Hague,

---

[128] See Monograph Number Five ("Benjamin Furly").

[129] Haistwell's Diary does add the few words: "and then they went to speak wth some other sober people, but they did not meet wth them: so ffr[ds] took Wagon and passed to Delf Citty."

Penn wrote a letter from Rotterdam to the Countess of
Hoorn, in which, describing this trip in Holland, he said:
"From Leyden we went next day to The Hague, where also
we had a little meeting. O the lust and pride of that place;
thou camest into my mind as I walked in the streets, and I
said in myself, Well, she hath chosen the better part. O be
faithful and the Lord will give thee an eternal recompense."

We know nothing of the time, place or circumstances of
this meeting, who composed it, who addressed it, in what
language, or by what interpreter. It may, of course, have
been only a religious service on the part of the three travellers; but the way in which Penn speaks of it, coupled with
the condemnation of the lust and pride of the city, would
seem to imply that it was, or was designed to be, a public
meeting, and was attended by disappointingly few of the
townspeople. If it really was a public meeting, addressed by
Fox or Penn or both, it is an extremely interesting fact; for
it would have been the only Friends' meeting actually recorded to have been held in The Hague between the time of
William Caton (1657) and William Allen and Elizabeth Fry
(1816).[130]

Penn does not appear to have stopped at The Hague on
his return trip from Rotterdam to Noordwyck; but he did so
when he went back to Rotterdam. This time, he met with
Docenius, the "resident" of the King of Denmark, who had
come from Keulen [Cologne] to have another interview with
him; had "some service with a lawyer"; called upon Lady
Overkirk again, but was again prevented by her husband
from seeing her; again failed to find at home the retired
gentleman to whom he had a letter of introduction; and was
prevented from seeing the judge who "had a great cause
pending."

Only five years before the Quaker leaders visited The
Hague, there had occurred in the city a dark and bloody
deed which still invests with historic interest the prison of
the Gevangenpoort. A Quaker letter-writer in London, John
Rous, wrote of this event to Margaret Fell, under date of

---

[130] See Monograph Number Nine ("Jean Etienne Mollet and the Aftermath
of Quakerism in Holland").

the 24th. of 6th. Month, 1672, as follows:[131] "Here is very strange news from holland, wch thou may see at Large in the Gazet, but least thou should not meet with it I may give thee a short acc^t thereof the 20th. instant their stile, Cornelius de wit for suspitition of having a designe to murther the Prince of Orange was banished the province of holland on paine of death, & his brother ye pentionarie John de wit going to see him & being in the prison, upon some disatisfaction among the burgers & common people they forced the prison doors open, some fired on y^m & some runne y^m & being dead tramplet on y^m, haled y^m to ye gallowes where they striped y^m starke naked cut of their fingers & toes & flesh of their bodies & sold them at several prizes, wch many bought untill neer their whole bodies were Consumed, & this was done in the face of the Burgers & Magistrates at ye Hague & noëbody asked why they did soe, I hear ye commonality threaten in divers places if their Magistrates will not agree to their tearmes, they will deale with y^m as wth the de wits.''

This Quaker version of one of the darkest and most cruel incidents in the history of The Hague gives a vivid idea of the dangerous environment and inflammable materials amidst which the Sowers of Quakerism sowed their seed in the Netherlands.[132] It was doubtless fresh in the minds of George Fox, William Penn and their companions,—as in that of all the world besides,—when they came to The Hague in 1677.

Before Penn came to The Hague again, he had become the hero of a very different historic event which occurred in the New World, namely, the founding of Pennsylvania. His old fellow-missionary, Benjamin Furly, had become his agent for selling land and securing colonists in the Netherlands for the Quaker colony beyond the Atlantic; and in fulfilment of this important function we find him publishing, in 1684, at The Hague a pamphlet designed to portray the ad-

[131] Thirnbeck MSS. (transcriptions in Friends Library, London; originals in the possession of Wilfrid Grace, of Bristol, England).

[132] For another Quaker reference to this historic event, Cf. the use made of it by Steven Crisp in a pamphlet written by him in Rotterdam, the same summer (Monograph Number Seven: "The Persecution of the Quakers, etc.").

vantages of Pennsylvania as a home. It is now a rare and costly pamphlet, its title being: Recueil de Diverses pieces Concernant la Pensylvanie. A la Haye, Chez Abraham Troyel, Marchand Libraire, dans la Grand Sale de la Cour, M. D. C. LXXXIV.[133]

ROTTERDAM

In Rotterdam, as Penn had written the Countess of Hoorn from Amsterdam, he had "much to do, both with Respect to Meetings and the Press." Benjamin Furly had met Penn and Fox in Amsterdam and escorted them to his home in Rotterdam, where they arrived October 22, 1677, at eight o'clock in the evening. After supper, Penn went to lodge at Arent Sonnemans's house; and the next day they visited "Friends and the friendly People in that place," Penn records, "among whom were several Persons of worldly Note."

"The next day being the first Day of the Week [Sunday]," he continues, "we had a large and blessed Meeting, wherein the deep Mysteries of the Kingdom of Christ and Antichrist were declared in the power of an endless Life. Several of divers Religions were there, but no Disturbance and Contradiction, but a profound Silence and reverent Attention were over the Meeting. That Night I had a blessed Meeting at my Lodging with those Persons of Note, that at sometimes visited our publick Meetings, as at [the one held] that day, and have a Convincement upon them: The Lord's Love, Truth and Life preciously reached towards them, and they were very sweetly affected."

On his return from Noordwyck to Rotterdam, Penn says "it was my desire to have been the next day at a Meeting at Dort, but it seems that Way that we hoped had been open for us was shut, insomuch that we were prevented of that service." Dort, or Dordrecht, long famous as an artistic and ecclesiastical center in the Netherlands, was one of the places where Quakerism struggled vainly, from about 1660 for a score of years, to strike in its roots. It is doubtful if Penn could have availed much for Quakerism in that strong-

---

[133] *Infra*, p. 313.

hold of Calvinists and Mennonites. But two of its citizens (and perhaps three), namely, Isaac and Harmen Karsdorp, and the latter's wife, became within a few years among the early settlers of Germantown, Pennsylvania; and it may have been through their agency and that of Benjamin Furly that the effort was made to "open the way" for a visit from Penn himself.

Instead, therefore, of going to Dort, Penn says "I applied my self to the perfecting of what yet wanted to be compleated in those Writings I left behind me to be printed"; and Haistwell's Diary adds, regarding the evening of that day: "and on ye 18: day at night W:P: came to G ff: there [at Benjamin Furly's], and ye King of Denmarks Resident [Docenius, of Cologne] came along wth him, W:P: had visited him in Germany, so hee hearing that W P was at Rotterdam, came to see him, being Convinced."

The next day, Penn records, "we had a very blessed publick Meeting, taking therein our leave of the Country; and after that was done we had another amongst Friends, recommending to them the *Peaceable, Tender, Righteous* Truth, desiring that they might live and grow in it, and be a People to the Lord's praise; so should his Work prosper, his Dominion enlarge and encrease among them. In the Evening I had also a Meeting at my Lodging among the great People of that place, of which I have before made mention, and magnified be the Name of the Lord, his Power did so sweetly visit them, and effectually reach them, that at their departure some of them fell upon our Necks, and with Tears of Love prayed that they might be remembered by us, and that they might have strength to answer our great Travel for them. We recommended them unto the Lord, and the pure Word of his Grace in their hearts."

Haistwell's Diary refers to only the first two of these meetings, as follows: "And on y^e: 19: day G: F: and W P: & G K: [George Keith] and Geertruyd Dirknieson [Deriks] were at a large Meeting at B: ff^s where there was many ffriends, as also a great concourse of people; and all was peaceable. And after ye Meeting was done ffriends had a perticular Meeting."

It was apparently the third meeting mentioned by Penn to

which Frans Kuyper refers in his ''Philosophical and Historical Proof that there are Devils.''[134] Kuyper was a
prominent Collegiant of Amsterdam and Rotterdam, and a
persistent opponent of the Quakers. His attacks upon them
in print were replied to by Furly, and these two arranged
the debate with the Quaker leaders. Of it, Kuyper writes: ''I
shall add here one of their [the Quakers'] contentions,—
which I never knew they had,—as proof of the greatness of
their blindness and perverseness, namely, that it would be
impossible for God to hear our prayers or know our
thoughts, if he were not within us, and that in reality
(*weezentlijck*). George Keith taught and tried to prove this
in the presence of George Fox, William Penn, Geertruid
Kitsken [Deriks] and many other Quakers, on the 28th. of
October, 1677, at Rotterdam, at the house, and in the presence, of Benjamin Furly; and the same was heard by me
[Kuyper], Jan Hartichfelt, Barent Stol, Paulus Breeden-
burg and many others.''

Such pamphlets and charges as Kuyper's were not precisely the response to his ''great travail'' which Penn might
have had the right to expect; but we learn from them at
least the identity of some of those who were present at his
meetings; and we learn, also, that George Keith had followed Fox and Penn from Amsterdam to Rotterdam, in
time to participate in the last meetings in the latter city.

During the next decade, Penn was supremely busy with
another of ''God's holy errands'', namely, the founding of
a Quaker commonwealth as a ''holy experiment'' beyond
the Atlantic. But he was not unmindful of the friends he had
made in Holland; on the contrary, it is evident from his correspondence during these years that their religious welfare
was much upon his heart, and that he relied largely upon
them after 1682 to send him colonists for Pennsylvania.

Two letters which he wrote in November and December,
1677, to Pieter Hendricks and Friends in Holland, are filled
with echoes of his recent visit. These were in reply to letters

---

[134] Part two, chapter four, of his „Korte Verhandeling van de Duyvelen",
Rotterdam, 1676; part two was published in Rotterdam, 1678. See Monograph
Number Five (''Benjamin Furly'').

he had received from Hendricks, and in one of them he writes :[135] "O my soul remembers with pure prayers the time of the Lord that was with us in your lands and countrys. What ever comes of the work gods day is sounded and the lords controversy is declared, and all shall work together for good to them that keep their eye to the lord." In the other, occurs the passage: "Read my love in the eternal truth wch time cannot ware out, distance forgett, nor many waters quench."

In 1678 and 1679, also, Penn wrote letters "To the Friends of God in Holland and Germany,"[136] and to P. Hendricks & J. Claus.[137] The first of these was written jointly with Thomas Green, and published (in Dutch translation) in "Ancient Truth Revealed."[138] It was dated from Worminghurst, the 2nd. of 6th. Month, 1678, and began: "Dearly Beloved Friends: My very dear and faithfull love salutes you and ye dear Remnant of God in Holland and thos parts adjacent." Then, after very tender and loving exhortations, he concludes: "And friends, wait degr [wade deep?] to the riseing of the powr of God, that instruments you may be in the hand of the lord to proclaim the acceptible year and time of deliverance, wch the lords powr will bring to pass."

The second letter was more personal, but bears Penn's characteristic touch of religious sensibility. "It is long," he says, "since I heard from you, and longer I believe since you heard from me, but surely our love remains in that which noe distance or time can extinguish or ware out; and I know not that I have ever been drawn forth of God in prayer in publiq that you have not been brought liveingly to my remembrance and indeed you are as an epistle writt upon my soul and tenderness often overtakes my soul in secret that truth may spring among you, O the precious meetings that we have had together lett my soul never forget the goodness of the Lord." After speaking of "the sickness" in London, of the Popish and Monmouth's plots, Penn

---

[135] Haverford College MSS.
[136] *Ibid.*
[137] *Ibid.*
[138] „De Oude Waarheyd Ontdekt", Rotterdam, 1684.

concludes: "No more, but that I should rejoice to hear from you of your wellfair and truths prosperity who am Your faithful Frd. and Bro. Wm. Penn."

PENN'S JOURNEY, 1686

The years 1679 and 1680 were crowded for Penn with work in behalf of religious toleration in England and abroad; and with 1680 began the series of events which led up to his grant of Pennsylvania. The coöperation of the Friends of Holland and Germany with him in this great enterprise will be treated in subsequent chapters. George Fox made a second visit to the Continent in 1684; but Penn did not accompany him, for he had not returned from his first memorable journey to Pennsylvania. His next and last visit to the Continent occurred in 1686, in the full course of his colonizing efforts, and was motivated by a three-fold desire to seek support for these efforts, to further the interests of Quakerism, and to promote religious toleration. He did not, alas, keep a diary of this visit, as he did of his journey in 1677, and all too few details are known of it.

In Quaker circles, his coming was heralded by a letter from Pieter Hendricks to Roger Longworth, dated Amsterdam the 18th. of 6th. Month (June), 1686, which says:[139] ". . . this necks week at ouwer Yearly Meeting which will bee 12 days hens . . . nouw wee expeckt dear Roger hadock and will: peen at our Yearly Meeting the Lord willing or permitting. we had expected deare will: pen before this time. wel thay will be wirry welkom." Eleven weeks later, the 3rd. of 9th. Month (September), 1686, Hendricks wrote to Longworth:[140] "Dear William penn has also been hier and wÿ have had such great meetings as never bevoor."

A few other references to this visit come to us from Quaker sources. Roger Longworth was at this time preparing for a trip to America, and he could not respond to Hendricks's pressing invitation to attend Amsterdam Yearly Meeting also. Roger Haydock, however, an intimate mutual friend, did go to Amsterdam at this time, and in ad-

---

[139] Pemberton MSS., II, 22.
[140] *Ibid.*, II, 67.

dition to Hendricks's brief references to his visit there are extant three of Haydock's letters in regard to it. He had been imprisoned for his religion's sake in Lancaster Gaol from December, 1684, to March, 1686; but soon after his release, he sailed for Holland, attended the Yearly Meeting in Amsterdam, and spent six weeks visiting Friends in the Netherlands and Germany. In one of his letters, addressed to Phineas Pemberton and dated, Warrington, the 20th. of 6th. Month, 1686,[141] he says that he had "newly returned" from his travels; that he had been "released from prison by the King's free pardon", and had then travelled through Western England, to London Yearly Meeting and Holland, "where I had the desirable company of your[142] Governour deare w: p: with whom I had free and open discourse of thee & some others to my great satisfaction. the esteem he hath for thee pleased me well, & to him in freeness I could speake a little concerning thee, of whom I had good experience though at London we were together yet his passing by Callis [Calais] Dunkirke & soe thro Flanders, we onely met againe at Amsterdam, now nigh a week together & had several heavenly sweet seasons, it being the time of the Yearly Meeting there; hee passed from Holland up the Ryn I travelled into Lower Saxony, was at Bremen, Hamborg, Frederickstatt, so back to Emden & thro Friesland, so to Holland which I left this day was a month."

A letter from George Fox to Roger Longworth, dated, London, the 15th. of 7th. Month, 1686,[143] says: "Wm. Pen was with me this morning lately come from Holland & Germany & he gives account of the great openness that is among people and magistrates." It was doubtless of this visit of 1686, also, that Joseph Pike, an Irish Friend, writes in his Journal as follows:[144] "In 1687, I went several times to England, and twice to Holland, on account of trade. On one of these occasions, I accompanied our beloved Friend W. Penn, who went to the Yearly Meeting at Amsterdam, where we met Roger Haydock, George Watts of London, and other

---

[141] Pemberton Papers, II, 21.
[142] The Pembertons had settled in Pennsylvania.
[143] Etting MSS., 64.
[144] London, 1837, p. 366.

Friends in the ministry. Great numbers attended, amongst whom were several Englishmen of considerable note, who fled from the country, having been suspected of, or charged with, being concerned in a plot. After the meeting was over I left William Penn, who travelled through Germany, and I returned home.''

It would thus appear that Penn, after attending London Yearly Meeting in 1686, set out for Holland in company with Joseph Pike and probably also with Jan Claus, who attended the Yearly Meeting that year, and went by way of Calais and Dunkirk to the Netherlands. He certainly visited Amsterdam, The Hague, Rotterdam, and Sneek in Friesland, before going up the Rhine; but details of his journey are very few and fragmentary. Roger Haydock, in the letter last quoted, also says : "hee [Penn] passed from Holland up the Ryn"; and in a letter to Longworth, dated Warrington the 28th. of 7th. Month (September-October), 1686,[145] Haydock says : "Wy : P. had a meeting at Sneak in yᵗ province [Friesland].''

REINER JANSEN OF SNEEK AND PENNSYLVANIA

The town of Sneek in Friesland, renowned for its butter and cheese, had known Quakerism for a score of years before Penn's visit, and had contributed a few members to the Friesland Monthly Meeting. Penn doubtless went to the province both to aid the growth of Quakerism and to procure colonists for Pennsylvania. He appears to have succeeded in the latter object, Reyner Jansen and his family leaving Sneek before the end of the century for Germantown and becoming influential citizens of that place and Philadelphia.

Jansen's name first appears among those of the twenty-seven Friends of Holland who, in 1676, addressed to the Friends of England a letter relating to aid extended to Quaker sufferers on the Continent. This document he signed, "Reyner Jansen vetermaker (lace-maker)," and he is usually referred to in the records in this way.

When the Friesland Monthly Meeting was organized in

---

145 Pemberton MSS., II, 3.

1677, he at once became one of its most active members.[146]
He was appointed one of the meeting's first two treasurers,
and presented his accounts from time to time. The receipt
and distribution of Quaker literature, sent out from Amsterdam, was entrusted to him, in 1678; and in that year, he
went with Auke Gerrits and Elizabeth Hendricks to Emden,
to hold Friends' meetings in defiance of the recent law
against them, and to visit the Quakers who had been imprisoned. Here, he shared the ten days' imprisonment of his
companions,—"on dry bread and water,"—was expelled
from the city under penalty of flogging if he returned, and
had his cloak taken from him in payment of "the costs" of
his treatment.

A good deal of the disciplinary action taken by the Friesland Monthly Meeting fell to him, often in association with
Jan Jansen and Willem Koenes, all three of them acting
apparently as "elders", as well as members of special com-
mittees. Beginning with Joannes Clasen of Deinum, in 1677,
we find him serving in this capacity on the cases of Tryntie
Jilles of Groningen in 1678, Popke Koerts of Groningen in
1679, Brucht Taekes of Lippenhuizen in 1680, and Lutske
Sibles of Lippenhuizen in 1685, his signature ("Reyner
Jansen lace-maker") being on the "certificate of disownment," issued against the last-named, in 1686.

Friendly affairs in "the Woude" were placed almost in-
variably in his hands. For example, in 1679, his advice was
decisive against removing "the Friends' bed" (an endowed
lodging) from Groningen to Gorredýk; in 1683, he represented Friends in the Woude in deciding on the times and
places of holding the Friesland Monthly Meeting; in 1685,
he was appointed to investigate the financial affairs of the
meetings in Gorredýk and Lippenhuizen, and to pay the
debts incurred by them.

On one occasion, in 1684, Reyner was himself reported to
the monthly meeting as having "behaved badly, to the
shame and dishonor of Friends", by having interrupted the
preacher's sermon in the Jan-Jacobs Mennonite meeting in
the Knýpe. A committee of four Friends was appointed by

---

[146] For details of Jansen's activities as a member of Friesland Monthly
Meeting between 1677 and 1698, see Monograph Number Eight.

the monthly meeting to investigate the report, and it was learned that Reyner had merely asked permission to say a few words in the Mennonite meeting, and when this was refused, he "was thereby satisfied and relieved of his concern." The monthly meeting thereupon declared that it too was satisfied with Reyner's conduct, and that "Friends have nothing against the same, since it does not redound to the detriment or dishonor of the precious Truth."

In this year, 1684, Reyner's friend and neighbor, Cornelis Siverts of Slooten, removed with his family to Pennsylvania; and from this time Reyner's spirit was restless, until he too removed to the trans-Atlantic land of promise. The manufacture and sale of lace was probably becoming less profitable in these years of almost incessant warfare, and the peaceful pursuit of farming appealed more and more strongly to him. Under the date of the 4th. of 12th. Month, 1687, the minutes of the Friesland Monthly Meeting record that "Reyner Jansen laid before this Meeting the information that he has had inclinations from time to time to be released, were it possible, from the occupation of a merchant and to betake himself to a country life and to bring up his children therein." The number of his children had increased, he said, but no suitable opportunity for the change had occurred. He therefore inquired of the meeting its judgment on his settling on a farm near Sneek.

Sneek was then, as now, the center of a flourishing butter and cheese country; but the meeting's judgment, arrived at after mature deliberation was "unitedly, as one man" against the dubious change from lace-making to dairying. It therefore "felt and advised" him to "come to Harlingen to give satisfaction to Friends and people."

No further reference to this matter is found in the minutes, and we are left in ignorance as to just what "satisfaction" the meeting desired or received. That it did receive some satisfaction, at least, is evident from the fact that Reyner continued to be a member in good standing. Two years later, for example, he served on a committee to inquire as to any "hindrance" to the marriage of Jakob Bruns and Martien Ales, Friends in the Knÿpe.

The next year, however, in May, 1690, the minutes record: "We are requested by some Friends to give a certificate to

Trynte Hedsers, the wife of Ryender Jansen, which was accordingly done."

This would appear to have been a "certificate of removal", and that Reyner had decided against the judgment of the meeting to give up his lace-making and retire to some rural home; if so, the usual certificate of removal would not have been asked for or received by him, while the certificate issued to his wife could not have been justly withheld. By this time, the Friends were having trouble with her because she was giving evidence of a desire to revert from Quakerism to her original Mennonite church. At least this would seem to explain an obscure reference in a letter from Pieter Hendricks to Steven Crisp.[147]

This letter was written in 1692, and its writer says that "Reyner Jans" came late to the Yearly Meeting held in Amsterdam in 1691, "supposing that he had waited until the women Friends had gone upstairs, but found that they were still with us." Again, in 1692, Hendricks continues, he "finally arrived at the Yearly Meeting more than two hours after the appointed time, so that he might be certain that the women Friends had left us and gone upstairs,—as was indeed the case,—so that he might not meet with such deep grief (*Hartzeer*) as last year;" for, Hendricks explains, "he does not expect to find any woman who has more (not even so much, perhaps, if he durst admit it) ability and virtues than his wife; hence, to refuse to admit such a one to such a meeting, where there are present some who, he happens to know (*hy altemets weet te noemen*), have so much of weakness, etc.,—he cannot get over it, but his hard feelings appear to increase the more on that account."

To bring him to a right frame of mind concerning the matter, Hendricks continues, six leading Friends of Amsterdam considered "whether a stop should be put to the affair by permitting the woman to come to the [next Yearly] meeting." They decided not to do so, however, for the reason, chiefly,—which was to be stated to Reyner and his wife, —that "only a few weeks ago she had again partaken of the Lord's Supper (*het Nachtmaal*) with the Mennonites."

It would seem that Reyner's wife was indeed the Cristijne

---

[147] Colchester MSS., 18.

Righaars, alias Stijntje Haasen, or Trijntije Hedsers, whose alleged mistreatment by the Friends of Amsterdam had been denounced by one of their opponents, J. R. Markon. If so, the trouble with her was of long standing, dating from 1684, in which year even George Fox is said to have participated in "dealing with" her for too conspicuous conduct in meetings and for having left her husband,—apparently to attend the Mennonites' meetings.[148] She was partially restored to good standing among Friends, a few years later; for in 1690, as has been seen, the Women's Monthly Meeting of Friesland "at the request of some Friends" gave a certificate of removal "to Trijntje Hedsers, the wife of Ryender Jansen." With this certificate, she accompanied her husband to Alkmaar; but she did not go with him to Pennsylvania in 1698, and probably died before that date.

Reyner's loyalty to his wife and her possible longings for her girlhood pursuits in the country may have led him to remove from the Knype to Alkmaar, then as now a great center (even more than Sneek) for the products of the dairy. To Alkmaar, at all events, Reyner removed his family, some time in the 1690's. But this move was evidently only preliminary to a longer journey to the land of rural peace and freedom beyond the Atlantic. His friend, Cornelis Siverts of Slooten, now well settled in Germantown, doubtless continued to correspond with him and to portray the advantages of Pennsylvania. In May, 1698, Siverts made out a power of attorney for "Reynier Jansen, lace-maker at Alkmaer" to act for him in reference to some land which he had inherited in Friesland.

It was evidently about this time that Reyner himself decided to remove to Pennsylvania, and that he received a

---

[148] Cf. Monograph Number Six ("Dutch Quaker Leaders, 1665-1685). Steven Crisp also remonstrated with Stijntje, in 1685, and it would appear to be a coincident that Jan Roelofs, writing to him (in a letter with no date, but apparently in 1670) says that "Stijnter" feels Crisp's words to her to be sound and good, and that he may expect a letter from her. Roelofs also says that he has just received through Stijnter a deal of books, to be perused, which having done, he finds them to be in that spirit of keeping on the hat in prayer, and that he intends to burn them in the fire. (Colchester MSS., No. 41.)

power of attorney from Benjamin Furly to act as the latter's agent in the sale of Pennsylvania land. Furly made out this power "to my loving friend Reynier Jansen;" but two years later (April 23, 1700), Furly substituted the Falkner brothers as his Pennsylvania agents in place of Jansen, who had by this time become deeply immersed in his own affairs. It was during the summer or autumn of 1698, then, that Reyner and his family made the American voyage. On November 29 of that year, he bought twenty acres of land in Germantown; and two months later, the Germantown court conferred the status of citizenship upon "Reynier Jansen, lace-maker."

Meanwhile, events had occurred which led up to Jansen's becoming the first official printer of the Society of Friends in America. William Bradford, formerly of London and an apprentice and son-in-law of the Quaker publisher, Andrew Sowle, had set up a printing-press in Philadelphia in 1685. He too was a Quaker and printed for the Friends until 1693, when he removed to New York; but although he thus became the first printer in the Middle Colonies, he was not the official printer for the Quakers of Pennsylvania, and he fell into numerous difficulties with both the meeting and the government. These difficulties were increased by his taking sides in the religious quarrel with George Keith, and he decided to withdraw from Philadelphia to New York.

This left the Quakers without a printer, official or unofficial; hence, in 1696, the Monthly Meeting of Philadelphia proposed to establish a printing-press of its own. The Yearly Meeting approved of the plan, and the sum of £30 was sent in 1697 to London to purchase "a press and letters or such things thereunto belonging as cannot be gotten here." The press did not arrive until late in 1698; but by this time "Daniel Pastorius of Germantown", who had previously said "he was willing and thought he may be capable of managing the same", withdrew from the undertaking. The Monthly Meeting, therefore, on the 30th. of 10th. Month [December], 1698, appointed a committee of four of its members "to agree with a printer, if any is to be found, to manage the press, and to see for a convenient place to set it up and to provide materials to set it to work."

To the meeting held the next month [February, 1699], the committee reported "that they have spoken with Reinier Jansen, who hath undertaken to print for Friends, and likewise have taken a house of David Lloyd to perform said work in."

This house was in Philadelphia, and Jansen set up his printing-press in that city. A deed of December 23, 1699, describes him as "a merchant of Philadelphia"; but he may have retained his residence in Germantown, for that deed conveys to him seventy-five more acres in the latter place. His merchandizing may have included lace as well as books; but since lace was not too much in vogue among the Germantown and Philadelphia Quakers at that time, he was doubtless glad to turn his hand to printing, which had become very much in demand among them.

Where he learned the trade of printing is not certain. He could not have done so with Bradford, who left Philadelphia five years before Jansen's arrival. It may be conjectured that his father was Reyner Jansen of Amsterdam, who published in that city, in 1662, a Dutch translation of Marmaduke Stephenson's "A Call from Death to Life" (London, 1660); if so, he doubtless learned printing when a youth in his father's shop.[149]

An ex-lace-maker and ex-Hollander, his printing ability in English was naturally quite restricted, and his press and type facilities were evidently crude. As Friend Caleb Pusey says in his behalf, in one of the books which Jansen published in 1700 ("Satan's Harbinger Encountered"): "the printer being a man of another nation and language, as also not bred to that employment is consequently something unexpert both in language and calling".

Besides numerous broadsides and papers which he printed during the half-dozen years between 1699 and 1706,

---

[149] Against this conjecture is the fact that it was the usual custom in Holland for the son to take as his last name the first name of his father; and this would have made him, not Reynier Jansen, but Jan Reyners. This custom, too, was followed by Reynier Jansen's sons, who were known as Tiberius and Josephus Reyniers. But exceptions to the custom were occasionally made; hence it is possible that Reynier Jansen was the son of that Reyner Jansen by whom Stephenson's book had been printed in 1662 (or, as it is stated on the Dutch title-page, *gedrukt voor Reyner Jansen*).

there are extant four of his imprints with the date 1699, two with that of 1700, and a half-dozen more. Among those of 1699, was an English version of Gertrud Deriks's "Epistle to be communicated to Friends", which had been dated in Colchester, translated into English by William Caton, and probably first printed in English (in London) in 1677. It would be an interesting fact if the very first book which appeared from the press of this Dutch-American-Quaker printer were this pamphlet written by one of his Dutch-Quaker contemporaries. Another of his imprints of 1699 was that rare and famous book, Jonathan Dickenson's "God's Protecting Providence." Benjamin Franklin was the illustrious successor of Jansen who published the second American edition of it in 1735; and a half-dozen more reprints of it appeared in London within the century.

Quaker literature was the chief product of his press; but he was the official publisher for the province as well, and we owe to him the 1700 and perhaps a few later versions of its laws. His brief printing career was ended by death, in the year 1706. His will was recorded in the Pennsylvania archives,[150] and shows an estate in personal property amounting to £226, 1 s. 8 d., and including "a p'cell of books from Wm. Bradford [his printer-predecessor] £4, 2 s. 6 d."[151]

Reyner Jansen's wife appears to have died in Holland before his departure for Pennsylvania; and he left established in Amsterdam as a printer one son, Stephen. Two other sons, Tiberius and Josephus, and two daughters, Alice and Imity (Jannety?) came with him to Pennsylvania and became the ancestors of a numerous family, some of whom took the name of Reyners, and others that of Jansen. The father lived long enough to witness the marriage of his daughter Alice, in 1704, and to sign her wedding-certificate; while his sons, Tiberius and Josephus "Reyners", were associated with his printing business and appear to have carried it on for a time after his death.

---

[150] It was witnessed, among others, by Thomas Story.

[151] S. W. Pennypacker, "The Settlement of Germantown", in the *Pennsylvania Magazine*, Vol. IV (1880), p. 36; and J. W. Wallace, "Early Printing in Philadelphia" (*Ibid.*, p. 432).

Reyner Jansen's acquaintance with William Penn doubtless dated from the Amsterdam General Meeting in 1677,
and was extended to include a first-hand account of Pennsylvania affairs when Penn visited Sneek in 1686.

OUDESLUIS

From Amsterdam, Penn appears to have gone to nearer
places than the towns of Friesland, persuaded to do so by
the rural Friends returning to their homes from Amsterdam Yearly Meeting. Among these places, were Alkmaar
and the neighboring village of Oudesluis in the Zijpe, where
dwelt a prominent Friend, named Jacob Arentsz or
Adriaensz. Jan Claus, in a letter to Steven Crisp, dated
Amsterdam, the 3rd. of 10th. Month, 1687, gives an account
of a trip which he had just made from Alkmaar to Hoorn,
and remarks parenthetically that "W:W: [Willem Willemsz Boekenoogen] was obliged to go with the farmers to
the Zijp (where not much opportunity has offered since the
visit of W:P:)."

ROTTERDAM

That Penn visited the Friends of Rotterdam is learned
from two widely different sources. Roger Longworth, in a
letter to Pieter Hendricks, dated, Dublin, the 21st. of 6th.
Month, 1686,[152] refers to a letter he had received from
Hendricks, dated the 18th. of the 6th. Month, in which
Hendricks had spoken of "Thomas Green being with" the
Dutch Friends, and of their "expectation of deare will: penn
& Roger Haydock all which J was verie glad to heare of,
that you might be refreshed togaither in the Lord." Six
days after this letter was written, "Joane Cooke" wrote another to Roger Longworth, which was dated, Cork, the 27th.
of 6th. Month, 1686,[153] and which included the following
sentences: "I heard from my dear Thomas [Green, "Joane
Cooke's" husband] 2 weeks since, & he was near ready to go
then to London Dear will: Penn was returned out of the con-
trey & was then very well & had had good meetings there

---

[152] Pemberton MSS., II, 20.
[153] Ibid., II, 14.

my husband writt me, he was gonn to Rotterdam bud did intend to return againe [to England] I know [not] but my husband may gett his company [en route to London] I harttly wish it might be soe ordered.''

It is not known that Thomas Green accompanied Penn to Rotterdam, as his wife so ''harttly'' wished; but that Penn visited that city soon after these letters were written, and preached a sermon there, is evident from the following statement of Dr. John Northleigh, a medical student, or embryo physician, of London, who was visiting the Netherlands and Rotterdam at that time. ''The Toleration and Liberty of Religion in Rotterdam,'' says Northleigh,[154] ''is as open as their Ports; tho' an Amsterdam of Religion has been used proverbially by way of Reproach; but I cannot see how 't is possible for such a Trading People to support their Traffick, unless they grant the same Freedoms in Opinion, that they do in their Trade. We have English and Scots enough there to make two considerable Churches; and by consequence other Nations have the same of Natives as their own. Quakers they are not without, no more than we; which I had occasion more than ordinary to observe seeing and hearing one there, the most Eminent of ours here, so noted both for Parts and Politicks, that I need not name him, preach a good Ingenious English Sermon, to his Dutch Congregation; which at first seem'd to me a little surprising, and almost as preposterous as Prayers in Public in an unknown Tongue. But the dexterity of his Interpreter was such, who being elevated with him, and standing by his side, by Paragraph translated his English to his Dutch Auditors, without the least hesitation: some seriously look'd upon the Preacher to come to propagate the Gospel that was here planted among that odd sort of Christians; Other Waggs more witty, thought his coming was only to get some more Proselytes or Planters for his large Plantations in America.''

Dr. Northleigh's last phrase leaves no doubt as to the identity of ''the most Eminent'' of English Quakers, whose ''Politicks'', or close relations with James II., are slyly

---

[154] See Northleigh's ''Topographical Description, etc.,'' London, 1702; reprinted in the *Pennsylvania Magazine*, XXII, 128-29.

hinted at by the Whiggish writer, and whose "good Ingenious English Sermon" in Rotterdam, and its translation,
he was privileged to hear. As to the identity of the dex-
terous interpreter, we can only suppose it to be Penn's old-
time friend, interpreter and agent, Benjamin Furly. Furly's
activities in behalf of Pennsylvania would alone have induced Penn to stay for a time at his home in Rotterdam.[155]

THE HAGUE

Another prime object of his visit to the Netherlands in
1686 was to influence William, Prince of Orange, to give his
support to religious toleration in England. The London
Yearly Meeting of this year was a memorable one because of
the fact that nearly thirteen hundred Friends had just been
released from English jails by James II's general pardon,
and many of these attended the meeting, some of them after
an absence of twelve or fifteen years during which they had
been imprisoned for religion's sake. Penn had published a
few months before his "Perswasive to Moderation", which
was widely read and had much influence in procuring from
the king his edict of toleration.

Among the arguments which Penn advanced in this
treatise, in favor of religious liberty, was the example of
Holland. "Holland", he wrote, "that bog of the world,
neither sea nor dry land, now the rival of the tallest monarchs, not by conquests, marriage or accession of royal blood,
the usual way to empire, but by her own superlative clem-
ency and industry, for the one was the effect of the other;
she cherished her people, whatsoever were their *opinions,* as
the reasonable stock of the country, the heads and hands of
her trade and wealth, and making them easy on the main
point, their conscience, she became great by them; this made
her fill up with people, and they filled her with riches and
strength."

Penn, as an intimate friend of James II, was close to
James's son-in-law, William III, Prince of Orange, and husband of the heir-presumptive of England's crown. As part
of the general plan of toleration, James sent a written or

---

[155] *Infra,* pp. 328–345.

oral message to William and asked Penn to deliver it. This may have been the immediate object of his visit at this time to the Netherlands.

Arriving at The Hague, he had several interviews with William, who agreed that toleration of faith and worship was the right policy for England, but he was opposed to the annulment of the Test and Corporation Acts which excluded dissenters from parliament and public office. He adhered to this policy in the Toleration Act, which was passed after the Revolution which placed him on England's throne.[156]

BISHOP BURNET

At The Hague, Penn met among other Scotch opponents of James, the well-known historian, Bishop Gilbert Burnet, who was in exile from Stuart England at the time, but high in favor with William. In his "History of My Own Times" (London, 1724–34), Burnet speaks of Penn's mission and of Penn himself as follows: "The King [James II] was very sensible how much it would promote his designs to have the concurrence of two such persons [William and Mary] so nearly related to the Crown, and so much concerned in the affairs of England; and therefore he sent over Penn the Quaker, a great favorite as being the Vice-Admiral's son, and suspected to be a concealed Papist, because he was much with Father Petre,[157] and particularly trusted by the Earl of Sunderland. He was a vain, talking man, and had such an opinion of his faculty of persuasion that he thought none could stand before it, though in that opinion he was singular, for his tedious and affected manner was not so apt to overcome a man's reason as to tire his patience. He undertook, however, to persuade the Prince to come into the King's measures of repealing the Tests and a general Toleration and had two or three long audiences of him upon the subject, and left nothing unsaid that might move him to comply in point of interest. The toleration of Papists, as well as

---

[156] Croese may have confused this visit with one which he says Penn made to the Princess Mary at her summer residence at Oranjewoud (*supra*, p. 56).

[157] James II's father-confessor, whom he admitted to the Privy Council in July, 1687.

Dissenters, the Prince was not averse to (for he thought that conscience was only subject to God), provided it was proposed and passed in Parliament; but he looked upon the Tests as such a real security, and indeed the only one, when the King was of another religion, that he would join in no councils with those who intended to repeal the laws that enacted them; and the King, being resolved to have all or nothing, Penn's negotiation with the Prince had no effect.'' From the above, it is evident that the bishop, a political and ecclesiastical opponent, was in sympathy neither with Penn's mission, nor with his character or manners as a man and a Quaker.[158]

PENN THE PACIFIST

Had Bishop Burnet been himself a seer and a statesman, he would have looked upon William Penn in The Hague that summer with far kindlier and more admiring eyes; for he would have seen in him the precursor and the prophet of international peace. He did not even appreciate the significance of the peace experiment which Penn had entered upon, four years before, in the forests and fields of Pennsylvania. Indeed from the days when Penn as a young man of high social rank laid aside his sword which he had been bidden by Fox to ''wear as long as thou *canst*,''[159] to the days when he practised his peace principles amidst the Indian tribes of Pennsylvania, and the year (1693) when he preached these principles to the warring nations of Europe in his famous ''Essay,'' he was a shining exemplar of the second, positive half of the Quaker philosophy of peace, which substitutes judicial settlement for the repudiated method of war.

The Hague was famous even in William Penn's time as ''le plus beau et le premier village du monde.''[160] It was called a *village*, rather than a *ville*, or town, simply because it was not protected by fortified walls, which fact may be regarded as an interesting premonition of The Hague Peace

---

[158] Cf. Monograph Number One (''Willem Sewel of Amsterdam'', pp. 30, 87f.)
[159] Cf. Penn's ''portrait in armor'' (Monograph Number Three).
[160] J. F. Reynard, 1681.

Conferences of 1899 and 1907, and the great work accomplished by them in the protection of unfortified towns and the creation of judicial means of settling disputes. A traveller of 1688,[161] contemporary with the early Quakers in Holland, singles out the great Hall of the Knights, in which the Second Peace Conference accomplished its tasks, for enthusiastic description, dwelling upon "the many hundreds of colors [banners] hung up in trophy, taken from the Emperor, Spaniards and other potentates with whom they have waged war." He too caught no prophetic vision, in the midst of these emblems of warfare, of the era of peace to be ushered in within those military feudal environments. Nor did the Quakers, despairing of establishing their Society within The Hague, dream of the crown which the nations assembled there were to place upon the peace principles which it was a fundamental duty of their religion to proclaim and exemplify.[162]

From Holland, Penn made a journey into the Rhineland, and may have spent the month of July there in propagating and recruiting for his Quaker faith and colony; but that he was back again in Holland early in August appears from the letter quoted above from Joan Cooke Green to Longworth. By the first half of September, Penn was back in England, as appears by the letter from Fox to Longworth, dated London the 15th. of 7th. Month (September), 1686,[163] which has been quoted above.

WILLEM SEWEL

During his visit to the Continent, Penn made his customary use of the press for spreading a knowledge both of the Truth and of Pennsylvania. His stay in Amsterdam was devoted partly to consultations with Willem Sewel in regard

---

[161] John Ker, "Memoirs and Secret Negotiations, 1688", London, 1726.

[162] It may be of interest to note that Sir Edward Fry, the head of the British delegation to the Conference of 1907, was an English Quaker, and that Wm. Penn's plan of an International Court was referred to in the Conference on several noteworthy occasions. Edward Fry was especially influential in persuading the conference to apply Penn's plan of a court in the creation of the International Court of Prize.

[163] Etting MSS., 64.

to the latter's Dutch translation of "No Cross, no Crown", which was published from the press of Jacob Claus the next year.[164] On his return to England, Penn wrote under the title of "Good Advice" an argument in favor of the repeal of the Test and other penal acts; and this too was translated into Dutch by Sewel and published in Amsterdam, in 1687.[165] His experiences at The Hague had accentuated the necessity of such an argument; and its burden may well have been talked over with Sewel, his warm friend, translator and correspondent. From Jacob Claus's press, in 1686 also, appeared a Dutch version (also by Willem Sewel) of Penn's "Further Account of . . . Pennsylvania"; from another Amsterdam press appeared at the same time a Dutch version of "Information and Direction to such Persons as are inclined to . . . Pennsylvania", the original of which has been ascribed to Penn, but was written chiefly by Robert Webb.[166]

After this visit to Holland, as after his other two visits, Penn kept in touch with the Dutch Friends by means of correspondence. A letter dated at "Windsor Castle 11th 6 mo. 87", to Jan Claus and Pieter Hendricks, bears a message of love and encouragement to them, to Jacob Claus, Willem Sewel and others. His correspondence in subsequent years with Sewel has been cited *in extenso* elsewhere.[167] Some replies to these letters (besides the many that Sewel wrote) are extant from individual Friends in Holland and from Friesland Monthly Meeting, the latter commending to his care and to that of Philadelphia Friends the members of the meeting who were about to remove to Pennsylvania.[168]

---

[164] See Monograph Number One ("Willem Sewel of Amsterdam").
[165] *Ibid.*
[166] *Infra*, p. 314.
[167] Monograph Number One.
[168] *Infra*, p. 316.

Chapter III

PENN IN THE RHINELAND

The first introduction of William Penn to Germany occurred, as has been seen, in 1671, when he visited the Labadists at Herford.[169] Six years later, in August, 1677, Penn, Barclay, Keith and Furly left Fox and other English Friends in Amsterdam, and went by boat to Naarden and thence by "common Post-waggon" to Osnabrück. This wagon-journey lasted two days and traversed, Penn says, "a very dark Country." Whether this darkness was due to the domination of the Teutoburg Forest with its tragic history, or to the prevalence of Roman Catholicism, Penn does not explain.

Osnabrück

Osnabrück itself (or, as it is variously spelled in Penn's writings Osnabrug and Osenburg) had at least one building which should have appealed to Penn's love of peace, namely, the *Rathhaus*, or Town Hall, in which were conducted the prolonged negotiations lasting from 1643 to 1648 and leading to the Peace of Westphalia which put an end to the exceptionally bloody and barbarous Thirty Years' War. Among its inhabitants at the time of Penn's visit were some of strong Pietistic and Quietistic leanings, and the keeper of the inn where the party lodged one night was evidently one of these; for Penn records that he had "a little time" with him . . . and left him several good books of Friends in the Low and High Dutch Tongues to Read and to dispose of." Thus casually may have been sown the seed which gave rise to a movement which the Amsterdam Yearly Meeting's Epistle in 1740 referred to as follows: "The Lord hath begun a work in Germany, particularly at Ceulen [Cologne] and Osnabrugh . . where the people are turning against outward Worship and toward the inward Christ." It was this good news which incited the London

---

[169] *Supra*, pp. 2–9.

Friends to arrange for the translation and publication of Willem Sewel's "History of the Quakers" in German,[170] and to publish in German, in a single volume, the four pamphlets which Penn wrote in Amsterdam in 1677.[171]

A Quaker meeting grew out of this movement; and by 1752, the Amsterdam Meeting's Epistle of that year reports: "The Clergy of Osnabrugh are inclined to make a stir against the meeting of those who hold to Truth."

To the aid and encouragement of the Osnabrück Friends, William Brown of America, Samuel Neale of Ireland, and John Kendall of England, went in 1752 to Amsterdam and thence to Osnabrück, where they "visited Friends." Although the Journals of these visitors are thus concise, we have a glimpse of the Osnabrück Friends from another source. This is the correspondence in 1751 and 1752 of G. R. Abeken of "Osnabrug" with Jan Vanderwerf of Amsterdam. Three of Abeken's letters were translated into English by Vanderwerf and the translation was sent to the London Friends, who endorsed them "Copy of three Letters wrote by G. R. Abeken at Osnabrug to Jan Vanderwerf of amsterdam." The manuscript book of "Epistles Received" by London Yearly Meeting (1752: pp. 295–297) gives these letters as follows:

"The First Letter dated, 3 July 1751.

"As to the meetings here, I acquaint thee that not only in this City but also in the outparts, in mine & some other gardens, several meet together in the drawings of Love & tender visitation of the Lord, among them are Six Friends who suffer much, one of them is my Brother in Law, there are others who as yet have not Resolution, come privately, the Lord knows his own. there are many things removed which in the beginning made an appearance among us, We hope the Lord will more & more enable and strengthen us, to bear the Difficulties we may meet with, discover all hypocrisie & unite us to himself.

"On the second Day in the Whitsun week, above one Hun-

---

[170] See Monograph Number One ("Willem Sewel of Amsterdam", pp. 188-9).

[171] *Supra*, p. 86. The German edition was supplied with a preface by "S. W." (Simeon Warner?).

dred Persons were gathered together mostly Husbandmen, at a small village called Buuren about two hours walk from hence, Situate in the King of Prussia's Dominions, where I met with great Opposition from some Person, as also I have done at this Place, which hath Troubled me much, nevertheless the Lord's will be Done. I intend to go there tomorrow, with another friend, named Hirzeg, they much long to See Us, as we do them, may the Lord remove all Opposition, and by his Shepherd's Crook gather us unto his Fold, and in the unity of the Spirit Love him above all.

"Since We have held meetings here, & visited the Friends at Buuren, we have been, not only from the Pulpit, but throughout the Town, Rediculed, Slandered and Belyed, and it is Currently reported, that the magistrates will make an Enquiry about us, We Endeavour as much as Possible to avoid giving any Occasion of Offence, so that things are yet quiet; the Lord carry on his Work, to the Honour of his great Name, & our Souls everlasting Welfare.

"I must further mention, that among the Friends at Buuren, who are a Poor harmless People, I find the Witness of Truth among them as Clear, as if they had lived, and Assembled with friends of amsterdam & Twisk many years, tho' they have not been instructed by men or writings, which was Cause of admiration, and was made to rejoyce when I was there the first time, and found great Love & Unity among them, and it also rejoyced them exceedingly when they were informed, that the Principle of Truth held by Friends in Holland, was the same with them, of whom they had never heard before.

"The Second Letter dated 24th, July 1751.

"I have been Examined by our Magistrates in the City Hall, respecting Sundry things also about Religion and Truth, which was taken down by the Secretary, and the Report is, that I am to be Expelled the Town, I must wait the Event.—as to my Suffering I am easy under the same, and hope the Lord will enable me to bear my present Affliction, hitherto have cause to praise him for his aid & assistance. Praying, Lord thy Kingdom Come, and thy, name be exalted to all Eternity. Amen.

"I heartily greet thee and all Dear Friends, Divers of the

Friends at Buuren and Branshe have desired me to remember their kind Love to you when opportunity offered,—Desiring that in the Unity of the One Spirit we may be Established in the One Truth and bound up together in Love to the Honour of God.

"The Third Letter dated 24th January 1752.

"It is not well with friends here, the Priests have gone from house to house, by which means divers are fallen back, and others stay at home & do not meet as heretofore; A Priest came to my house, and forbid my giving R: Barclay's Apology to Others, nor keep Meetings in my House, nor associate with Others. and also refrain from going to the Meeting at Buuren; To which I answered, that the Truths declared in R: Barclay's Apologie, might be against his Profession, they were not against the holy Scripture, nor against what the ancients Witnessed, nor against the Light in every Conscience, and therefore I Esteemed it my Duty to Spread the Truth to all mankind, either by these Books or others that declare the same, as likewise by Word & Conversation, as the Lord may please to open my way, and not to hide it as it were under a Cover, but put it on a Candlestick to Enlighten every one that comes near; to Do Contrary, I should hazard the welfare of my Soul, which would be an irreparable Loss; But I trust the Lord will preserve & Support me in times of Weakness; that this was an instigation of Satan, who would prevent my meeting with the Lord's innocent children, who meet in his Fear, to be made partakers in their measure of his Life giving Presence, be it in what Place it may;

"After his threatening, I said, I must waite for what it may please the Lord to Lay upon me, knowing that without him I can do nothing, but with him all things.—

"In the Conclusion he repeated twice, that an Heretick should be shunned; I asked him what he meant by Hereticks, because I was an enemy to all Heresie, nor had I found an Heretick among all my friends at Buuren, nor here, neither in R. Barclay's Apologie,—then He rose & went away without answering, altho' I requested him twice, yet he kept Silence;

"My Wife asked him if it was permitted to frequent Musick & Dancing houses, and if it was not more commendable and better to Convers with one another of the Lord & his Truth, but he gave no answer thereto.—

"The Lord be with us, and Lead me by his Power, that all my thoughts, Words & Actions may tend to the honour of his holy name, and my never dying Soul's Peace, Remember me before the Lord when it is well with you.

Farewell./."

Had Friend Abeken been living in Osnabrück at the time of Penn's visit, it is evident from these letters that they would have recognized in each other kindred spirits; and it is an interesting reflection that the seed sown by Penn and his companions may have grown, all forgetful of its sowers, in the hearts of these simple German peasants of two generations later.

The Princess Elizabeth's sister Sophia was living in Osnabrück at the time of Penn's visit; for Elizabeth wrote him after his return to London as follows: "I almost forgot to tell you that my Sister writes me word, she had been glad you had taken your Journey by Osenburg to return to Amsterdam: There is also a Drossard [steward, or bailiff] of Limburg near this place, (to whom I gave an Exemplar of R. B. Apology) very Desirous to speak with some of the Friends."

Limburg is far to the south of Osnabrück; but the Drossard who came from there may have been the steward of one of Elizabeth's or her sister's estates near Osnabrück. Penn must have regretted missing these two influential people at the time of his visit, especially since he would have been recommended to them by the Princess and by her gift of Barclay's "Apology".[172] It would be of interest to find connecting links between this steward, or Penn's "keeper of the inn", and G. R. Abeken, the writer of the letters seventy-five years later.

---

[172] *Supra*, pp. 43–4. The conversation at Elisabeth's dinner-table between the two sisters anent the Labadists may have been responsible for Sophia's interest in the Quakers; and it was probably Sophia's son with whom Penn had discoursed after dinner at the same hospitable and liberal board.

PADERBORN

From Osnabrück, Penn and his companions went to Herford to make Penn's first visit to the Princess Elizabeth. After four days of religious meetings and conversations at the princess' court, Penn, Keith and Furly went towards the Rhineland, while Barclay returned to Amsterdam. Before they parted, Penn records, "we had a little time together in the Morning in our Chamber [in the Herford inn]; whither came one of the Princess's Family, and one of the Town. The Lord moved me to call upon his great Name, that he would be with them that stayed, and with them that returned also, and with us that went forward in wild and untrodden places."

The first of these "wild" places was Paderborn, to which Penn refers as "a dark Popish Town, and under the Government of a Bishop of that Religion. Howbeit, the Woman where we lodged was an Ancient, Grave and Serious Person; to whom we declared the Testimony of the Light, shewing her the difference betwixt an outside and an inside Religion, which she received with much kindness. We left some Books with her; which she took readily.

"There was also with us at Supper a *Lutheran* that was a Lawyer, with whom I had very good Service in opening to him the great loss of the power of Godliness, as well among them who separated from *Rome,* as in the *Roman* Church: Which he confessed. I directed him to the Principle of Light in his Conscience, that let him see the lifeless State of the false Christians: And if he turned his mind to that Principle and waited there for Power, he would receive Power to Rule and Govern himself according to true Godliness, and that it was the loss of *Christendom* that they went from this Principle, in which the Power standeth, that conformeth the Soul to the Image and Likeness of the dear Son of God; and thither they must come again, if ever they will have the true knowledge of God, and enjoy Life and Salvation; with much more to that purpose, all which he received lovingly."

This characteristic appeal from Lutheran Protestantism to Protestant Sectarianism was a key-note often struck by Penn in his Rhineland journeys, and it found its response later in the migration of thousands of German Sectarians to Pennsylvania.

CASSEL AND JOHN DURIE

Penn's journey of about sixty miles from Paderborn to Cassel required nearly a day and a half of steady driving, because it was made "through great foulness of Ways and Weather", with "only naked Carts to ride in, the Waters being also High with the Rains." It is small wonder that the travellers were "wearied with the foulness of the Ways and Weather", and that they "made little inquiry that Night." But the next day, Penn continues, "we made our usual Inquiry, *viz.* who was worthy in the City? And found some that tenderly and lovingly received us; to whom we declared the Visitation of the Light and Love of God. Among the rest was *Dureus* our Countryman, a Man of Seventy Seven Years of Age, who had learned in good Measure to forget his Learning, School-Divinity, and Priest's Craft, and for his approaches towards an inward Principle is reproachfully saluted by some with the honest Title of *Quaker.* 'Tis much better than *Papist, Lutheran* or *Calvinist,* who are not only ignorant of, but Enemies to Quaking and Trembling at the Word of the Lord, as *Moses* and others did."

"Our Countryman, Dureus", referred to by Penn in this passage, was John Durie, born in Edinburgh in 1596;[173] educated for the Anglican Church in Sedan (where his cousin, Andrew Melville, lived), at Leiden (where his father had settled), and at Oxford; a minister to the English merchants in Elbing, East Prussia, and Rotterdam, and chaplain and tutor to Mary, Princess of Orange, at The Hague; a member of the Westminster Assembly; and especially noted for his advocacy of "the union of all Evangelical churches", which he worked for incessantly during a half-century after 1630. In behalf of this cause, he travelled throughout western Europe, making Amsterdam his headquarters for a few years before 1658, and Cassel from 1662 to the end of his life.

---

[173] Hence eighty-one, and not "Seventy-Seven Years of Age", when Penn met him.

William Caton, writing from Rotterdam to Margaret Fell, the 7th. of 5th. Month, 1661, gives us the following glimpse of Dury:[174] "yesterday priest Durry was with mee, & the cheife Occation of his comeing to me was (as appeared from his owne words) that J should Acquaint him where Giffrey Ellitson lodged soe J brought him to his Lodgeing, G :E. is exceeding much possessed with A spirit of prejudice & enmitie against yᵉ Truth, with which spirit the universalitie of them that are fled from England are Leauened, so that it is exceeding hard for the Truth to get any enterance in their harts."

This prejudice of the "Commonwealthmen" and English exiles against the Quakers may have been shared by "priest Durry" also, despite his devoted work for "evangelical" union. In pursuit of this work, he published four dozen scholarly treatises, engaged in innumerable conferences, and carried on endless correspondence; but he confessed the failure of his life's mission in the words: "The only fruit which I have reaped by all my toils is that I see the miserable condition of Christianity, and that I have no other comfort than the testimony of my conscience."

It was in this humbled condition that Penn found him in Cassel, where he died three years later. The Princess Elizabeth, writing to Penn in reply to a letter telling of his visit to Cassel, says: "Nothing surprized me there but the Good Old Dury, in whom I did not expect so much Ingenuity [Disingenuousness? he] having lately Writ a Book, Intitled, *Le Veritable Chretien,* that doth speak in another way." This book had been published the year before Penn's visit, and was a far cry from union with Quakerism; but two years before that he had published a remarkable treatise on the Book of Revelation, in which he had advocated a union of all Protestant and Roman Catholic churches. The fact that "his approaches towards an inward Principle" caused him to be "reproachfully saluted by some with the honest title of Quaker", evidently gave Penn some hope of his uniting at least with the Quakers; and Mosheim goes so far as to say that "Quakerus ille fuit ante Quakeros"! In

---

[174] Swarthmore MSS., I, 446.

addition, his life-long work for church unity may have greatly strengthened Penn's own views on this subject and impelled him to write an appeal in its behalf a few days later at Frankfurt.

It is possible that Durie had already associated his plan for church unity with those of the English "Philadelphians", who were represented on the Continent by Francis Lee with headquarters in Leiden, and by the writings of Jane Leade which were circulated in Dutch and German. The Philadelphians had been organized in London, in 1670, and it is probable that Penn knew them in England; although it is not certain whether the name of Pennsylvania's capital city was suggested indirectly by them, or directly by the reference in the third chapter (verses 7 to 13) of the Book of Revelation, of which John Durie made so much.

DURIE AND ROBERT BARCLAY

Among the Letters of the Barclay Family ("Reliquiae Barclaianae", pp. 35–42), are two letters from Durie to Robert Barclay the Apologist, the first of which is dated Cassel, the 25th November, 1677. Barclay's letters to Durie are not extant, but in this letter Durie says: "I have received yours of the first of this month yesterday"; and it appears probable that Penn reported to Barclay his visit with Durie in Cassel and suggested that Barclay might induce him to join with the Friends. At all events, Durie continues: "It is a joy that you accept the offer of communication which I made by the friend B.F. [Benjamin Furly] without scrupulosity, testifying the impartiall universall aim which I have had in mind many years ago although to avoid the prejudices of narrow hearted spirits I have not made it known till of late. . . . . I have accepted the offer of some godly Lutherans for the removing of scandals upon the profession of the Gospels." After commenting upon a paper he had written on the 3rd and 4th chapters of Zecharia and the 11th chapter of Revelation [concerning "the two Witnesses"], he continues: "This paper is to the truly godly; I do not desire it to go under my name, and have not imparted it to any in Germany, but to a Prince whom I think

is Godly. . . . . You are the first to whom it is sent abroad
when the way of our correspondence is settled. . . . May it
be God's will in thy heart to comment on it.

Thy truly affectionate Friend, John Durie."
Then follows a postscript replying to Barclay's request for
information as to the state of Protestantism in Austria,
Hungary and Eastern Europe, and one page relating to his
own uncomfortable and precarious position in Germany.

Durie's next letter was dated from Cassell the 17/27 day
2/mo called February, 1678. Again Durie informs Barclay:
"I received yesterday thy large letter in answer to mine of
25 November which hath given me matter of Joy." Commenting on Barclay's "two witnesses", namely, "the inward, immediate revelation of the Spirit, and the univer-
sality of the light and seed of the Kingdom", Durie entered
on a long denunciation of "the Scandals of the Protestant
ministers." Becoming more personal, he says: "I have a
purpose to answer Benjamin Furly and Edward Richardson who have written to me thy single hearted and plain
declaration whereby thou dost purpose to awaken the Protestants to intend and endeavour a more reall and perfect
reformation in that I do close with thee fully . . . . for almost
these fifty years have been directed singly by me to awaken
all. . . . . I beseech you continue in that affection for me,
and more particularly that I may find a free and fit place
to act more publicly than now I can do here."

Durie died in 1680, too soon and at too advanced an age
after his acquaintance with Penn and Barclay for their
mutual designs to come to fruition.

FRANKFURT-AM-MAIN

One week after leaving Herford, Penn and his companions
arrived in Frankfurt-am-Main; and, having announced their
plan to go there from Cassel, they were met on the road
"about half a German Mile from the City", by "two considerable Persons". One of these two was a merchant of
Frankfurt named Jacobus Vandewalle, a relative of John
Vandewall of Harwich, at whose hospitable home Penn and
his companions lodged on their way to and from Holland.
Jacobus may have been a first cousin of John, and the son of

the Jacob van de Wall who had aided in the establishment, in 1661, of the faience industry in Frankfurt. Not only was he of much service to Penn in his visit to that city in 1677, but we find him visiting the small community of Friends in the Dutch town of Moordrecht, the next year, and writing a letter about them to Steven Crisp, while in 1683 and subsequent years he became one of the first members of the Frankfort Company and its chief owner of lands in Pennsylvania.

When Penn met Vandewall outside of Frankfurt in 1677, he told him of "the end of our coming" and expressed a desire to hold a meeting with the "several well-affected" people in the city whom Vandewall mentioned. The meeting was held in Vandewall's house in the afternoon, and to it resorted, Penn records, "People of considerable Note, both of *Calvinists* and *Lutherans;* and we can say, they received us with gladness of Heart, and embraced our Testimony with a broken and reverent Spirit, thanking God for our coming amongst them, and praying that he would prosper his work in our Hands.

"This ingaged our hearts to make some longer stay in this City. We therefore desired another Meeting the next day, which they cheerfully consented to, where several came that were not with us the day before, and the Lord that sent us into the Land was with us, and by his Power reached to them, insomuch that they confessed to the Truth of our Testimony."

JOHANNA ELEANORA VON MERLAU

Among those who were most deeply moved at the meetings, Penn singles out "two Women, one a Virgin, the other a Widow, both Noble of Birth, who had a deep Sense of that power and presence of God that accompanied our Testimony, and their hearts yearned strongly towards us; the Virgin giving us a particular invitation to her House the next Morning, where we had the most blessed Opportunity of the three, for the Lord's power so eminently appeared, that not only those that had been with us before were most effectually reacht, but a certain Student residing in the House of a *Lutheran* Minister (sent for by that Young

Woman) was broken to pieces, and magnified that blessed
power which appeared. Also there accidentally came in a
Doctor of *Physick,* who unexpectedly was affected, and
confessed to the Truth, praying God to prosper us. This
was the blessed Issue of our Visit to *Franckfort.*''

The ''Virgin'' thus prominently mentioned by Penn was a
German noblewoman, Johanna Eleanora von Merlau. She
was of the same age as Penn (thirty-three years) and
shared fully his religious enthusiasm. She had been for
several years a lady-in-waiting at the court of the Duchess
of Holstein, but had reacted against the frivolities of aristo-
cratic life, broken her engagement with an army officer, and
retired to the home of a friend in Frankfurt. The latter
was the ''Widow'' referred to by Penn, namely, Frau (or
Mevrouw) Juliane Baur van Eysseneck, whose husband,
M. J. Baur van Eysseneck, was apparently of Dutch birth
or ancestry. The two women were near of an age, and resided together in the widow's home in Frankfurt from 1674
to 1680. Before Penn's arrival, they had become deeply interested in the circle of Pietists who centered around John
Jacob Spener's ''Collegia Pietatis'' at the old Carolingian
palace of the Saalhof. The ''Doctor of Physick'' who ''unexpectedly was affected'', was probably Dr. Wilhelm Petersen, a prolific writer of Pietistical books, who married
Fräulein von Merlau in 1680.

Joanna von Merlau and her friend, the Widow Baur van
Eysseneck, had not sympathized with the more timid or conservative Pietists of Frankfurt who, as Penn says, had
''Inclinations after God'', but possessed also ''a fearful
Spirit together with the shame of the Cross''. On the contrary, when Penn's testimony struck in part against this
spirit, he ''took Notice it was as Life to these noble Women,
for that was it as they told us, which had long opprest them,
and obstructed the work of the Lord amongst them. Therefore, said the Young Virgin, *Our Quarters are free for you,
let all come that will come, and lift up your Voices without
fear, for (said she) it will never be well with us till Persecution come, and some of us be lodged in the Stadthouse,*
That is the Prison.''

Joanna von Merlau's religious enthusiasm and courage appealed strongly to Penn, and a fortnight later, in Harlingen, he wrote her a long letter[175] of seven or eight printed pages. About half of this tells of his journey after leaving Frankfurt, and the rest is a fervent appeal to her and her friends to remain faithful to the faith that makes faithful. "My dear and tender Love", he writes, "which God hath raised in my Heart by his living Word to all Mankind, (but more especially unto those in whom he hath begotten an holy hunger and thirst after him) saluteth thee: And amongst those of that place where thou livest, the remembrance of thee, with thy Companion, is most particularly and eminently at this time brought before me: And the sense of your open-heartedness, simplicity and sincere love to the Testimony of Jesus, that by us was delivered unto you, hath deeply engaged my Heart towards you, and often raised in my Soul heavenly breathings to the God of my Life, that he would keep you in the daily sense of that Divine Life, which then affected you. For this know, it was the Life in your selves, that so sweetly visited you by the Ministry of Life through us.

"Wherefore, love the Divine Life and Light in your selves: Be retired and still . . . . . . And what I say unto one, I say unto all that received our Testimony in that City, to whom thou mayest give, if thou pleasest, the remembrance of my dear Love; . . . . . Particularly salute me the young Woman, that met with us at thy Lodging."

The hope of Penn that Joanna and her friends would withdraw entirely from the Pietist circle and form a Friends' Meeting in Frankfurt was destined not to be fulfilled. Three years later (September 7, 1680), Joanna was married by J. J. Spener to Dr. Wilhelm Petersen, and together they developed along Pietistic lines their own views of what constitutes God's kingdom here and hereafter. They encountered many vicissitudes in their subsequent lives, but Joanna survived until 1724, full four score years, and her husband until three years later.

---

[175] Addressed, in the printed edition, to "Joanna Eleanora Marlane, the Noble Young Woman at Franckfort."

The Pietists

Spener himself had been much influenced by the doctrines of De Labadie and his Pietistic leanings drew him strongly towards Quakerism; but even more than Galenus Abrahamsz of Amsterdam, he shied off from actual contact with the Quaker leaders, and neither listened to nor debated personally with them. In 1667, he had preached a powerful sermon against both Calvinism and Quakerism,—a sermon which he is said to have regretted on his death-bed, in 1705. At the time of Penn's visit, he was being attacked with unusual severity by the Lutherans and Reformed, and had just published two treatises defining and defending his views. Already taunted as "the Frankfurt Quaker", his failure to attend Penn's meetings may have been due to a desire to add no further fuel to the fire. The failure of his immediate followers to emigrate later to Pennsylvania was probably due partly to this disinclination to be absorbed and subordinated in Quakerism, as well as to reluctance to leave the fatherland and to an interval of comparative freedom from religious persecution in their German homes. But the very considerable aid, other than that of emigration in person, which the Frankfurt Pietists gave to Penn's colony will be seen in the sequel.[176]

Although Penn and his companions remained only two days in Frankfurt on this first visit, he found time to write a long "Epistle to the Churches of Jesus throughout the World." This fills twenty-eight pages of his printed Journal, and is chiefly an appeal to all Christian churches to be "gathered and settled in God's eternal light, power and spirit, to be one holy flock, family and household to the Lord." Besides the religious or ecclesiastical statesmanship that inspired it, there is in it the vision of a land and people that might well be drawn upon for aid in the "holy experiment" in the New World which was growing steadily in Penn's mind. The mingling of his ideals for church and state is shown in the following passages of the "Epistle":

"And now, Friends, as I have been travelling in this dark and solitary Land, the great Work of the Lord in the Earth

---

[176] *Infra*, p. 324.

has been often presented unto my view, and the Day of the Lord hath been deeply upon me, and my Soul and Spirit hath frequently been possessed with an holy and weighty Concern for the Glory of the Name of the Lord, and the spreading of his Everlasting Truth, and the Prosperity of it through all Nations; that the very Ends of the Earth may look to him, and may know Christ the Light to be given to them for their Salvation. . . .

"For, my Friends and Brethren, God hath laid upon us (whom he hath honoured with the beginning of his great Work in the World) the Care both of this Age, and of the Ages to come; that they may walk, as they have us for Examples: yea, the Lord God hath chosen you to place his Name in you; the Lord hath entrusted you with his Glory, that you might hold it forth to all Nations; and that the Generations unborn may call you Blessed. . . .

"Wherefore, Friends, redeem the Time, because the Days are Evil; God hath given you to see they are so: And be ye separated more and more, yea, perfectly disentangled from the Cares of this World. . . .

"For this I have to tell you in the Vision of the Almighty, that the Day of the breaking up of the Nations about you, and of the sounding of the Gospel-Trumpet unto the Inhabitants of the Earth, is just at the Door: And they that are worthy, who have kept their Habitation from the beginning, and have dwelt in the Unity of the Faith that overcometh the World, and have kept the Bond of Peace: The Lord God will impower and spirit you to go forth with his Everlasting Word and Testament to awaken, and gather Kindreds, Languages, and People to the Glory of the rising of the Gentiles Light; who is God's Salvation unto the Ends of the Earth.

"And I must tell you, that there is a Breathing, Hungering, Seeking People, solitarily scattered up and down this great Land of Germany, where the Lord hath sent me; and I believe it is the like in other Nations. And as the Lord hath Laid it upon me, with my Companions, to seek some of them out, so have we found several in divers places. And we have had many blessed Opportunities amongst them, wherein our Hearts have greatly rejoiced; having been made deeply sensible of the Love of God towards them, and of the great openness and tenderness of Spirit in them, to receive the Testimony of Light and Life through us. And we have a steadfast belief, that the Lord will carry on his Work in this Land effectually; and that he will raise up those, that shall be as Ministers of his eternal Testament amongst them. And O! our desire is, that God would put it into the Hearts of many of his faithful Witnesses, to visit the Inhabitants of this Country, where God hath a great Seed of People to be gathered; that his Work may go on in the Earth, till the whole Earth be filled with his Glory.

"And it is under the deep and weighty Sense of this approaching Work, that the Lord God hath laid it upon me, to write to you. . . . .

"Wherefore rejoice, O thou little Hill of God, and clap thy Hands for Joy; for he that is Faithful and True, Just and Righteous, and able to deliver thee, dwells in the midst of thee: Who will cause thee to grow and increase, till thou becomest a great Mountain, till thou becomest the Praise of the whole Earth, and the whole Earth be filled with thy Glory."

In a postscript to this Epistle, Penn says that he and his companions had "passed through several Cities of Germany, and are now at Franckfort, where the Lord hath given us Three blessed Opportunities with a serious and seeking People; whereof, as in other places of this Country, many of them are Persons of great Worldly Quality. Blessed be the Name of the Lord, to whom be Glory for ever."

Leaving Frankfurt for a journey farther up the Rhineland, Penn returned six days later to Frankfurt, where, he says, "we presently informed some of those People that had received us the Time before, of our return to that City, with desires that we might have a Meeting that Afternoon; which was readily granted us by the Noble Women, at whose House we met, whither resorted some that we had not seen before. And the Lord did, after a living manner, open our Hearts and Mouths amongst them, which was received by them as a farther confirmation of the coming of the Day of the Lord unto them; yea, with much joy and kindness they received us.

"The Meeting held till the ninth Hour at Night; they constrained us to stay and eat with them, which was also a blessed Meeting to them. Before we parted, we desired a select Meeting the next Morning at the same Place, of those that we felt more inwardly affected with Truth's Testimony, and that were nearest unto the State of a silent Meeting; which they joyfully assented to.

"We went to our Lodging, and the next Morning we returned unto them, with whom we had a blessed and heavenly Opportunity, for we had room for our Life amongst them: It was as among faithful Friends; Life ran as Oil, and swom a-top of all.

"We recommended a silent Meeting unto them, that they might grow into an holy Silence unto themselves; that the Mouth that calls God *Father,* that is not of his own Birth, may be stop'd, and all Images confounded, that they may hear the soft Voice of Jesus to instruct them, and receive his sweet Life to feed them and to build them up.

"About the ninth Hour we departed from that Place, and went to *Vander Walls,* where the Meeting was the Time before, and there we had a more publick Meeting of all that pleased to come. The Lord did so abundantly appear amongst us, that they were more broken than we had seen them at any time; yea they were exceeding tender and low, and the Love of God was much raised in their Hearts to the Testimony. In this sensible frame we left them, and the Blessings and Peace of our Lord Jesus Christ with and among them.

"And after having refresh'd ourselves at our Inn, we took Boat down the *Main* to *Mentz.*"

Frankfurt's "Mass or great Fair", as Penn calls it, which had existed four and a half centuries and was still of wide renown, was in preparation at the time of his visit, but evidently had no charms for him; on the contrary, it interfered with the success of his mission in the Rhineland, especially at Mainz.

WILLIAM CATON AND FRANKFURT

William Caton had been in Frankfurt, sixteen years before Penn's visit, but had received a hostile reception from its Christian inhabitants and had no success with its Jews.

The account he gives in his Journal of this visit points a
contrast between the characters and methods of William
Penn and William Caton. He writes: "I was also at Frankfort, and endeavoured to get some book or books printed
there, but could not prevail with the stationers; for the
books that were to be printed there, were first to be viewed
by some of the clergy. When I saw I could not prevail there,
I went (with a Friend) to another city called Hannau
[Hanau], where we got our business done; and afterwards
returned again to Frankfort, one of the chief (if not the
chiefest) city in Germany. And upon a certain time, I went
into their chief monastery or temple, where the emperors
are usually crowned;[177] and the priests were gathering to
their devotion; they were exceedingly offended with me, because I did not stand uncovered in that (they call) sacred,
(though it be an idolatrous) place. Some of the priests did
speak to me, and one especially was exceedingly angry; and
when we had spoke but a little together in Latin, he turned
from me in a fury, and another that was with him fell upon
me, and did beat me sorely, and there he left me bleeding in
the temple, where I left pretty much of my blood behind me,
as a testimony against the idolatry of that idolatrous place.

"I was also in the synagogue of the Jews of that city,
where I reasoned pretty much with them, and had a good
opportunity to bear a faithful testimony of the eternal
truth; though they could apprehend little of it with their
dark minds, which were blinded with the god of this world,
like as their forefathers were. I had also some books to dispose of among them, which for novelty's sake they coveted
much after: and when I had cleared myself of them, I left
them; and in due time returned again into the Palz."

In his letter "to Friends at London", dated "Cresheim
near Worms in Germany, the 30th. of the 11th. Month, 1661,
Caton refers to his experience with the Jesuits and Jews of
Frankfurt as follows:[178]

"But the Lord knows, and you know also, that our send-

---

[177] This was the old Cathedral in which, at the high-altar, the Elector of
Mainz solemnized the coronation of the emperors. In the neighboring Saalhof,
there is a chapel in which the Pietists held their meetings; but a local legend
that Penn and Fox(!) preached in it is not authentic.

[178] Besse's "Sufferings", London, 1753, Vol. II, p. 454.

ing was not by them [the Jesuits], and their shedding my Blood in their great idolatrous Cathedral, the Place where their Emperor was crowned at *Francfort*, did also demonstrate that I was not of them, for if I had been of them, or sent by them, they would not then and there in that desperate Manner have spilt so much of my Blood, who manifested themselves to be much more brutish and bloody-minded than the *Jews* were towards me, who that very Day had suffered me freely to dispute with them and among them in their Synagogues.

"There are also very many *Jews* in this Country, and pretty many of the Baptized People, and many of them have heard the Sound and Report of the Truth, though little Entrance as yet is to be got among any of them, and therefore is my Suffering the greater, as I believe you will feel: Yet am I satisfied in the Will of the Lord, and shall be hereafter, if others may but see and reap the Fruit of what hath been already sown in this Country. Some Books and Papers we have got translated and printed here in this Language, and Diligence is given that they may be dispersed and spread in the Wisdom of God, to the spreading of the Truth abroad, for I know it is your Desire, even as ours, that the Borders of the Lord may be enlarged, and that the Outcasts of *Israel* might be brought in, and therefore, I suppose, are you made so much the willinger to minister your Assistance for the Furtherance of this glorious Work, the Benefit and Fruit of which I have tasted of with others of the travelling Brethren beyond the Seas, and as certain, as I am assured, that we shall not lose our Reward, who are made willing thus to hazard our Lives on Truth's Behalf, so certain am I, that your Assistance by your Free-will Offerings are truly accepted of the Lord, and of his Chosen.

"I might oftner impart Passages to you in the General, but I hope some of the Brethren at *London* take Care to extract the remarkable Passages in brief out of our Letters, to the End that you may know how it is with us, and how the Lord is pleased to work by us, that so you may not only sufferingly travel with us in the Spirit, but that you also may some Time have Joy and Refreshment through us in the Lord, even as we have through your Faithfulness, though I am as alone, yet thus I can write as in the Behalf of the

Brethren, who I know are one with me in what I here
write.''

Thus, at Frankfurt and at many other places, the gracious
and heroic personality of William Caton was a precursor of
William Penn and his appeal in behalf of Quakerism.[179]

WORMS

Penn and his party had passed through Worms on their
way from Frankfurt to Krisheim, but they made no stay
there at that time. At one of the meetings in Krisheim, Penn
states, ''a Coach-full from Worms made a part, amongst
whom was a Governour of that Country, and one of the
chief Lutheran Priests.'' Again, on the 25th. of August,
they left Krisheim by way of Frankenthal for Mannheim
to see the Electoral Prince; but he having gone to Heidelberg, they failed to see him, and Penn wrote him the letter
from Mannheim which is quoted below.[180] Returning by way
of Worms (where they spent the night only) to Krisheim,
they bade a final farewell to the latter place, and on the
morning of August 27, they were accompanied by several of
the Krisheim Friends to Worms. Here, Penn says, ''having
refresh'd our selves, we went to visit the Lutheran Priest,
that was at the Meeting the sixth Day before at *Crisheim*;
he received us very kindly, and his Wife, not without some
sense of our Testimony. After we had discours'd about an
Hour with him of the true and heavenly Ministry and Worship, and in what they stood, and what all People must
come unto if ever they will know how to worship God aright,
we departed, and immediately sent them several good Books
of Friends in *High-Dutch*.''

Caton had visited Worms in 1661–62, and of his visit there
he writes in his Journal: ''I was also at the city of Worms;
and it was upon me to go to the Jesuits' college, to reason
with them, or some of them, concerning the truth of God,
and their traditions, which accordingly I did. And when I

---

[179] Cf. Monograph Number Four ("The Rise of Quakerism in Amsterdam").

[180] Penn called this place "Manheim alias Frederisbourg", and the Princess
in a letter to him wrote: "I wish to know what Reception you have had at
Fredisbourg."

came there, one that was eminent among them did soon enter into discourse with me, and spoke very feignedly [sic] to me for some time; for at the first he seemed to have hopes (as it appeared to me) to have won or gained me to his religion; and therefore did he seem to be the more ready and willing to resolve me in whatsoever I propounded, so far as (I believe) he well could. But when he saw I did notwithstanding lay open their apostacy, and boldly gave my testimony against their inventions, superstitions, and traditions, he could scarcely contain himself from breaking out into a passion. I had spent some hours in dispute with him, in the presence of several that belonged to the college, for whom he was as the mouth for the whole. When I had cleared my conscience, and borne a faithful testimony unto the truth among them, I left them, and returned again to Kreisheim, where our Friends inhabited; for sometimes I was there, sometimes at Heidleberg, and sometimes elsewhere, where I saw the Lord had a service for me.''[181]

Penn and Caton had no more success in converting their Lutheran and Jesuit listeners than did Luther in convincing the Emperor at the Diet of Worms; and there appears to have been no influx of the citizens of that town into either Quakerism or Pennsylvania.

MAINZ AND DOWN THE RHINE

The next place visited by Penn and his party was Mainz, which they found also to be too difficult. They came to it from Worms by an overnight boat down the Rhine, and on their arrival at five o'clock in the morning "took an open Chariot for Frankfort." After their visit there, they went by boat down the Main to "Mentz" which, Penn says, "is a great City, but a dark and superstitious Place, according to the Popish Way, and is under the Government of a Popish Bishop." Spending only half an hour in Mainz,

---

[181] It is an interesting possibility that this colloquy may have resulted in an attack upon the Quakers by a Jesuit of the Rhineland, Theodor Rhay by name, who wrote (in German) a book entitled "The Tremblers' or Quakers' confused Confession of Faith" (Confusa Confessio Trementium seu Quackerorum, das ist: Der Quaker verwirrte Glaubens Bekäntniss . . .), Cologne, 1666.

while their boat was getting ready, the party sailed down the Rhine by way of "Hampack" (Hambach, or Heimbach), where they stayed the night; thence "by Bacherach, Coblentz, and other places upon the Rhine, to Tresy that night, being about eleven German Miles."

Penn had naturally no premonition of the importance to our century of the Saar Valley, through which this journey led him; nor does he deign to pay any word of tribute to the beauty of the Rhine. Intent upon his religious mission, he pushed on without stopping, or perhaps without thinking much about his picturesque and historic environments. He stopped for the night at "Tresy", which was probably a suburb of Coblenz, under the shadow of Ehrenbreitstein, "the Gibraltar of the Rhine";[182] and if he could have foreseen the tragic events of subsequent years connected with these localities, he would have been greatly strengthened in his plea of 1693 for an international court to take the place of war.

COLOGNE

Another day spent upon the Rhine brought the party to "Cullen" (Köln, Cologne), "a great Popish City." Of their visit here, Penn gives the following account: "We gave notice to a sober Merchant in that Town, a serious Seeker after God, that we were there arrived; who presently came to us. We sate down, and had a living and precious Opportunity with him; opening to him the Way of the Lord, as *it had been manifested to us*; intreating him, if he knew any in that City, who had desires after the Lord, or that were willing to come to a Meeting, that he would please to inform them of our being here, and of our desire to meet with them. He answered, That he would readily do it.

"This night, when we were in Bed, came the Resident of several Princes (a serious and tender Man) to find us out: We had some discourse with him, but, being late, he promised to see us the next Day.

---

[182] "Tresy" could not have been *Treis*, which lies 25 miles up the *Moselle* from Coblenz, still less *Trèves*, which lies nearly 50 miles farther up the Moselle. It may have been *Breisig*, a short distance down the Rhine from Coblenz.

"The next Morning came the aforesaid Merchant, informing us that it was a busy Time, several preparing for the Mass or great Fair at *Frankfort*; yet some would come, and he desired it might be at his House about Three in the Afternoon.

"In the Morning we went to visit that Resident, whom we met coming to see us; but he returned and brought us to his House. We had a good Time with him; for the Man is an antient Seeker, opprest with the Cares of this World, and he may be truly said to mourn under them: His Heart was opened to us, and he blessed God *that he had lived to see us*. We gave him an Account how the Lord had appeared in the Land of our Nativity, and how he had dealt with us; which was as the cool and gentle Showers upon the dry and scorched Desart. About Noon we returned Home, and after we had eaten, we went to the Merchant's House to the Meeting; where came four Persons, one of which was the Presbyterian Priest, who preach'd in private to the Protestants of that Place, for they are no ways publickly allowed in that City. Surely the true Day and Power of the Lord made known it self to the Consciences of them present: Yea, they felt that we were such as had been with Jesus, and that had obtained our Testimony through the Sufferings and Travels of the Cross. They were tender: The Resident and Merchant conducted us to our Inn, and from thence to the Boat, being about seven at Night."

Penn in his subsequent letter from Amsterdam to Joanna Eleanora von Merlau says that they had had good service by the way: "For at Cullen we had a pretious Meeting, and were received with much gladness of Heart." One month later, Penn was again in Cologne where, he says, "we had a good opportunity with Van Dinando and Docenius at the House of the latter."

"Van Dinando," the "sober Merchant in that Town, a serious Seeker after God," was that "Da: [David] van den Enden Merchant in Cullen upon the Rhine" to whom Robert Barclay wrote a letter dated Aberdeen Prison 17th of the month March 1677.[183] Addressing him as Well Beloved Da:

---

[183] "Reliquiae Barclaianae," pp. 24–27.

van Enden, Barclay says that he had "diverse times understood the christian salutation of thy love (transmitted by
my dear Brother Benjamin Furly),". and had been "informed that thou has so much understanding in the English
language as to read it." He then expresses his deep concern
for "the great seed in Germany which longed to be re-
deemed," and said that he would be rejoiced to hear of any
of those in whom the seed is awakened. Then follows a long
discourse on Quakerism; and after the signature "Thy
reall Friend in the Lord, Barclay", comes the postscript:
"Salute in my name thy partner Milt: as also J.D. resident
for the King of Denmark there as I understand."

This letter was doubtless written by Barclay at Penn's request in preparation for the latter's journey in the Rhineland, and is one of many examples of the close coöperation
of the early Quaker missionaries with one another and with
Furly and other Quakers in Holland.

DOCENIUS

The "Resident of several Princes", as Penn calls him
in the above place in his Journal, or "the King of Denmark's Resident, at Colen", as he calls him in another,
signed his name as Dozen, or Docenius. George Fox[184] refers to him as "ye King of Denmarks Resident whom William Penn had visited in Germany", and adds: "so hee
hearing yt W P was at Rotterdam, came to see him, being
Convinced." Fox also says that Docenius came with Penn to
visit him at Benjamin Furly's house in Rotterdam, on the
18th. of the 8th. Month [October], 1677.

It was probably in his ambassadorial capacity, in part,
that Docenius came from Cologne to The Hague, in 1677,
while Penn, Fox and their party were still in Holland; although Penn says that the resident of the King of Denmark
had come from Keulen to have another interview with him,
and that he met with him at The Hague. He accompanied
Penn to Rotterdam and attended the meetings there; and,
when the English Quakers left that city to return home, he
went with them as far as Brielle.

A half-dozen years later, when Penn was founding his

---

[184] The Haistwell Diary, p. 254.

colony beyond the Atlantic, Docenius desired to become one of his colonists, but was prevented from doing so for the reason stated by Francis Daniel Pastorius as follows[185]: "Anno 1683. the 2nd. of April J set out from Francfort, came the 5th. of ditto to Collein, where J was kindly received of David van Enden, Daniel Mitz and ———— Dozen, the then Resident of the King of Denmark in the sd City, (This Dozen had strong Jnclinations for Pennsilvania, & desired me to prevail with his wife, but her Reply was that there they were carried in a Coach from one door to the other, but if they should happen to come hither, she was afraid that she must look after the Cattle, and milk her cows, &c.)"

DUISBURG

Penn's next stopping-place was Duisburg, about forty miles north of Cologne, and in the immediate vicinity of Krefeld and Mülheim-on-the Ruhr. At his inn at Herford, Penn had met with "a Young Merchant of a sweet and ingenious Temper, belonging to the City of Bremen";[186] and he also refers to another "Young Man of Bremen, being a Student at the College at Duysburgh." Penn had been informed by the latter "of a sober and seeking Man of great Note in the City of Duysburgh"; and now was his opportunity to follow up this clue. But meanwhile, at Cologne, Penn had heard through a letter from Elisabeth of an even brighter prospect, and he gives the following account of his pursuit of it. "We set out towards the City of *Duysburgh*, of the Calvinist Way, belonging to the Elector of *Brandenburgh*; in and near to which we had been informed there were a retired and seeking People.

"We arrived there next Day about Noon, being the first Day of the Week. The first thing we did after we came to our Inn, was to inquire out one Dr. *Mastricht* a Civilian, for whom we had a Letter to introduce us, from a Merchant of *Cullen*: Whom quickly finding, we informed him what we came about, desiring his Assistance; which he readily promised us".

---

[185] Pastorius, "The Beehive", p. 223. Quoted in M. D. Learned's "The Life of F. D. Pastorius," 1908, p. 111.

[186] *Infra*, p. 175.

The Countess of Falkenstein and her Father

"The first thing we offered", Penn continues, "was an Access to the *Countess* of *Falchensteyn* and *Bruch*:[187] He [Dr. Mastricht] told us she was an extraordinary Woman, one in whom we should find things worthy of our Love; that he would write to her to give us an Opportunity with her; that the fittest time was the present time, in that we might find her at the Minister's of *Mulheim,* on the other side of the River from her Father's Castle; for that she used to come out the first Day Morning, and not return till Night: That we must be very shy of making our selves publick, not only for our own sakes, but for hers, who was severely treated by her Father for the Sake of those Religious Inclinations that appeared in her, although her Father pretended to be of the *Protestant Religion.*

"We therefore dispatched towards *Mulheim,* having received his Letter, and being also accompanied by him about one third of the way: But being six English Miles, and on foot, we could not compass the Place before the Meeting was over; for it was Past Three before we could get out of *Duysburgh*; and following that way which led to the backside of the *Graef's* Castle and Orchard which was also a common way to the Town, (tho' if we had known the Country we might have avoided it) we met with one *Henry Smith* [Heinrich Schmidt], Schoolmaster and Catechiser of *Speldorp,*[188] to whom we imparted our Business, and gave the Letter of Dr. *Mastricht* of *Duysburgh* to introduce us to the Countess.

"He told us, he had just left her, being come over the Water from Worship, but he would carry the Letter to her, and bring an Answer suddenly; but notwithstanding staid near an Hour. When he came he gave us this Answer, *viz.* that she would be glad to meet us, but she did not know where; but rather inclined that we should go over the Water

---

[187] This was the Countess Charlotte Auguste of Dhaun-Falkenstein, of the House of Broich. She was still a young woman, but her precocious piety had long caused her to be derided as a "Quakeress".

[188] "Speldorp" is probably the Château of Heltorf, about five miles from Duisburg and just outside of Mülheim.

to the Minister's House, whither, if she could, she would come to us; but that a strict hand was held over her by her Father. After some more serious Discourse with him, concerning the Witness of God in the Conscience, and the Discovery, Testimony, and Judgment of that *true Light,* unto which all must bow that would be Heirs of the Kingdom of God (recommending him to the same) we parted; he returning homewards, and we advancing to the Town. But being necessitated to pass by her Father's Castle, who is Seignour or Lord of that Country, it so fell out, that at that very instant he came forth to walk: And seeing us in the Habit of Strangers, sent one of his Attendants to demand who, and from whence we were? And whither we went? Calling us afterwards to him, and asking us the same Questions. We answered, That we were Englishmen come from *Holland,* going no further in these Parts than his own Town of *Mulheim.* But not showing him, or paying him that worldly Homage and Respect which was expected from us, some of his Gentlemen ask'd us, if we knew whom we were before? And if we did not use to deport our selves after another manner before Noble-men, and in the presence of Princes? We answered, We were not conscious to our selves of any Disrespect or Unseemly Behaviour. One of them sharply replied, Why don't you putt off your Hats then? Is it respect to stand covered in the presence of the Soveraign of the Country? We told them it was our practice in the presence of our Prince, who is a great King, and that we uncovered not our Heads to any but in our Duty to Almighty God. Upon which the *Graef* called us *Quakers,* saying unto us, We have no need of *Quakers* here; get you out of my Dominions, you shall not go to my Town.

"We told him that we were an innocent People that feared God, and had good-will towards all Men; that we had true Respect in our Hearts towards him, and would be glad to do him any real Good or Service; and that the Lord had made it Matter of Conscience to us, not to conform our selves to the vain and fruitless Customs of this World, or words to this purpose. However he commanded some of his Souldiers to see us out of his Territories; to whom we also declared somewhat of the Reason and Intention of our coming to that Place, in the Fear and Love of God; and they were civil to us.

"We parted with much Peace and Comfort in our Hearts; and as we passed through the Village where the School-master[189] dwelt, (yet in the Dominions of the *Graef*) we called upon him, and in the sense of God's Power and Kingdom open'd to him the Message and Testimony of Truth, which the Man received with a weighty and serious Spirit. For under the Dominion of the *Graef* there is a large Congregation of Protestants called *Calvinists,* of a more religious, inward and zealous frame of Spirit, than any Body of People we met with or heard of in *Germany.*

"After we had ended our Testimony to him, we took our leave, desiring him not to fear, but to be of good Courage, for the Day of the Lord was hastning upon all the Workers of Iniquity: And to them that feared his Name, wherever scattered throughout the Earth, he would cause the *Sun of Righteousness to arise* and visit them, with *Healing under his Wings*: And to remember us with true Love and Kindness to the *Countess,* Daughter to this *Graef,* and to desire her not to be offended in us, nor to be dismayed at the Displeasure of her Father, but eye the Lord that hath visited her Soul with his holy Light, by which she seeth the Vanity of this World, and in some measure the emptiness and deadness of the Religions that are in it, and he would preserve her from the Fear of the Wrath of'Men, that worketh not the Righteousness of God. So we left the Peace of Jesus with him, and walked on towards *Duysburgh,* being about six English Miles from thence, and near the eight Hour at Night. The Lord was with us, and comforted our Hearts as we walked, without any outward Guide, through a tedious and solitary Wood, about three Miles long, with the Joy of his Salvation: Giving us to remember, and to speak one unto another of his blessed Witness in the Days past, who wandred up and down like poor Pilgrims and Strangers on the Earth, their Eye being to a *City in the Heavens, that had foundations, whose Builder and Maker is God.*

---

[189] This was "Henry Smith of Speldorp".

"Betwixt nine and ten, we reached the Walls of *Duysburgh,* but the Gates were shut, and there being no Houses without the Walls, we laid us down together in a Field, receiving both natural and spiritual Refreshment, blessed be the Lord. About three in the Morning we rose, sanctifying God in our Hearts that had kept us that Night; and walked till five, often speaking one to another of the great and Notable Day of the Lord dawning on upon *Germany,* and of several Places of that Land that were almost ripe unto Harvest. Soon after the Clock had struck five, they opened the Gates of the City, and we had not long got to our Inn, but it came upon me, with a sweet, yet fervent Power, to visit this *Persecuted Countess* with a Salutation from the Love and Life of Jesus, and to open unto her more plainly the Way of the Lord: which I did in the following Epistle."

The "Minister of Mulheim", at whose house the countess was accustomed to spend Sunday was probably Arnold Sibel, an Evangelical preacher, or Reiner Copper, the husband of Mlle. de Reneval, one of the Princess Elisabeth's companions at Herford. The Princess, in a letter to Penn which he received at Cologne, had written:[190] "If this find you at Cleve, I wish you might take an occasion to see the two Pastors of Mülheim, which do really seek the Lord, but have some prejudice against your Doctrine, as also the Countess there. It would be of much use for my Family to have them disabused; yet God's Will in that, and all things else, concerning Your Loving Friend in the Lord Jesus, Elisabeth." Penn's attempt to see the Countess was a failure; and his conversations with one of the two ministers was, as will be seen, of but little avail.

The letter which Penn wrote in his inn at Duisburg to the "Countess of Falckensteyn and Bruch at Mulheim", after his encounter with her father, was a very long one, but contained only the following brief reference to the encounter: "I had seen thee, had not thy Father's strange sort of severity hindred. I confess I do not use to be so treated in my own Country, where the Lord hath raised up MANY

---

[190] This letter (A. L. S., dated 4/14 of Sept. '77) is in the Granville Penn Collection of the Pa. Hist. Soc.

THOUSANDS of Witnesses, that he hath gathered, out of
All Sects and Professions, to worship him, not in their
Spirits or Wills, but in his Will, Spirit and Truth: And we
are generally, after much Affliction and Suffering, in good
Esteem, even with the great Ones of this World. And this let
me add for thy particular Comfort, that though I have
been a Man of great Anguish and Sorrow, because of the
Scorn and Reproach that hath attended my separation from
the World, (having been taught of Jesus to turn my back
upon all for the sake of that Glory that shall be revealed)
yet to God's Honour I can say it, I have an hundred Friends
for one, yea, God hath turned the Hearts of my Enemies
towards me; he hath fulfilled his Promise, to turn the
Hearts of the PARENTS UNTO THE CHILDREN. For
my Parents, that once disowned me for this blessed Testimony's sake, (of the Jew, Christian, Circumcision, and Baptism inward, against the fleshly Christian) have come to love
me above all, and have left me all; thinking they could never
do and leave enough for me."

A very fervent religious note was the one chiefly struck in
his letter; but he illustrated his precepts by the following intimate references to his own experiences: "Tho' unknown,
yet art thou much beloved for the sake of thy Desires, and
Breathings of Soul after the Living God: The Report
whereof, from some in the same State, hath made deep impression of true Kindness upon my Spirit, and raised in me
a very singular and fervent inclination to visit thee; and
the rather, because of that SUFFERING and TRIBULA-
TION thou hast begun to endure for the sake of thy Zeal
towards God, my self having from my Childhood been both
a Seeker after the Lord, and a great Sufferer for that Cause,
from Parents, Relations, Companions, and the Magistrates
of this World. The Remembrance whereof hath so much the
more endeared thy Condition unto me . . . . .

"Let This that hath visited thee lead thee: this Seed of
Light and Life, which is the Seed of the Kingdom; yea, 'tis
Christ, the true and only Seed of God, that visited my Soul,
even in my young Years; that spread my Sins in order before me, reproved me, and brought Godly Sorrow upon me;
making me often to weep in solitary Places, and say within

my Soul, O that I knew the Lord as I ought to know him! O that I served him as I ought to serve him! Yea, often was there a great Concern upon my Spirit about my Eternal State, mournfully desiring that the Lord would give my Soul rest in the great Day of Trouble. Now was all the Glory of the World as a Bubble; yea, nothing was dear to me that I might win Christ: For the Love, Friendship and Pleasure of this World were a Burden unto my Soul. And in this seeking-state I was directed to the Testimony of Jesus in my own Conscience, as the true shining Light, giving me to discern the Thoughts and Intents of my own Heart. And no sooner was I turned unto it, but I found it to be that which from my Childhood had visited me, though I distinctly knew it not: And when I received it in the Love of it, it shewed me all that ever I had done, and reproved all the unfruitful Works of Darkness; judging me as a Man in the Flesh, and laying Judgment to the Line, and Righteousness to the Plummet in me. . . .

"In this state of the new Man all is new: Behold new Heavens and a new Earth! Old things come to be done away; the old Man with his Deeds put off. Now, new Thoughts, new Desires, new Affections, new Love, new Friendship, new Society, new Kindred, new Faith; even that which overcometh this World, through many Tribulations; and new Hope, even that living Hope that is founded upon true Experience, which holds out all Storms, and can see to the Glory that is invisible (to carnal Eyes) in the midst of the greatest Tempest."

The letter which he wrote at the same time and place to "the Graef or Earl of Bruck and Falckensteyn" was doubtless designed to be irenic, but it contained the following "little expostulation": "Friend, I wish thy Salvation, and the Lord reward thee Good for the Evil that thou shewedst unto me and my Friends the last Night, if it be his Will: But since thou art but a mortal Man, one that must give an Account in common with all, to the Immortal God, let me a little expostulate with thee.

"By what Law on Earth are Men not Scandalous, under no Proscription, harmless Strangers, about lawful Occasions, and Men, not Vagabonds, but of good Quality in their own Country, stopt, menaced, sent back with Souldiers, and that at Sun-set, exposed to the Night in an unknown Country, and therefore forced to lie in the Fields: I say, by what Law are we judged, yea, thus punished before heard? Is this the Law of Nations, or Nature, or Germany, or of Christianity? Oh! Where's Nature? Where's Civility? Where's Hospitality? But where's Christianity all this while? Well, but we are Quakers: Quakers! What's that for a Name? Is there a Law of the Empire against that Name? No: Did we own it? No: But if we had, the Letters of that Name neither make up Drunkard, Whore-master, Thief, Murderer nor Traitor: Why so odious then? What harm hath it done? Why could Jews pass just before us, that have Crucified Christ, and not Quakers that never Crucified him? . . . .

"What art thou for a Christian? A Lutheran? Yes; Canst thou so lately forget the Practices of the Papists, and with what Abhorrence thy Ancestors declared against such sort of Entertainment? Were not they Despised, Mocked and Persecuted? And are their Children treading in the steps of their old Enemies? Friend, 'tis not Reformed Words, but a Reformed Life that will stand thee in stead. 'Tis not to live the life of the Unregenerate, Worldly-minded and Wicked, under the Profession of the Saint's Words, that will give an Entrance into God's rest. Be not deceived, such as thou Sowest, such must thou Reap in the day of the Lord. Thou art not come to the Berean-state that tried all things, and therefore not Noble in the Christian sense. The Bereans were noble, for they judged not before Examination.

"And for thy saying, We want no Quakers here, I say, under favour, you do: For a true Quaker is one that Trembleth at the Word of the Lord, that worketh out his Salvation with fear and trembling, and all the Days of his appointed Time waiteth in the Light and Grace of God till his great Change cometh; . . . . Yea, he is one that Loveth his Enemies, rather than feareth them; that Blesseth those that Curse him, and Prayeth for those that despitefully treat him; as God knoweth we do for thee. And O that thou wert such a Quaker! Then wouldst thou Rule for God, and act in all things as one that must give an account to God for the Deeds done in the Body, whether Good or Evil, Then would Temperance, Mercy, Justice, Meekness, and the Fear of the Lord dwell in thy Heart, and in thy Family and Country. Repent, I exhort thee, and confider thy latter End, for thy Days are not like to be many in this World, therefore mind the things that make for thy Eternal Peace, lest Distress come upon thee as an Armed Man, and there be none to deliver thee, I am

Thy Well-wishing Friend,

Duysburgh 3d 7th
M. 1677. S.V.   W. P.''

This forthright attitude towards one of the local nobility and rulers, Penn carried into his conversation with Dr. Mastricht, to whose house he went after writing the letters. "This being done," he says, "we went to Dr. Mastricht's to inform him of what had past, who tho' of a kind Disposition, and very friendly to us, yet seemed surprized with fear, (the common Disease of this Country) crying out, What will become of this poor Countess! Her Father hath called her Quaker a long time, behaving himself very severely to her, but now he will conclude she is one indeed, and he will lead her a lamentable Life: I know (said he) you care not for suffering, but she is to be pitied. We told him that we both loved her, and pitied her, and could lay down our Lives for her, as Christ hath done for us, in the Will of God, if we could thereby do her good; but that we had not mentioned her Name, neither was the Letter, that he gave us to her, so much as seen or known of her Father. But still he feared that our Carriage would incense the Graef so much the more against both his Daughter, and all those serious and inquiring People up and down his Country. We answered with an earnestness of Spirit, That they had minded the Incensings and Wrath of Men too much already, and that true Religion would never spring or grow under such fears; and that it was time for all that felt any thing of the Work of God in their Hearts to cast away the slavish fear of Man, and to come forth in the boldness of the true Christian Life; yea, that Sufferings break and make way for greater Liberty, and that God was wiser and stronger than Man.''

Dr. Mastricht responded to this challenge by giving Penn a clue to other "seekers", who also occupied high position, though less exalted than that of the count and the countess. "We askt him," Penn continues, "if there were any in that City who enquired more diligently after the way of the Lord, he recommended us (as we had already been informed in another place) to the Family of the Praetor, or chief Governour of the Town; whose Wife, and Sister more especially, were seeking after the best things: so we parted with him in love, and by the help of his Daughter, were conducted to this family.

"We had not been long there before a *School-master* of *Dusseldorp,* and also a *Minister* came in enquiring after us, having heard of us at *Mulheim,* where he preached the day before to the People, or else by the way of our attempt to Visit that place, and the Entertainment we received at the hands of the *Graef.* He sate down with us, and tho' we had already a sweet oportunity, yet feeling the Power of God to rise, the Meeting renewed: And O magnified be the Name of the Lord! He *witnessed* to our Testimony abundantly in all their Hearts and Consciences, who were broken into much tenderness; and certainly there is a blessed *Power* and *Zeal,* stirring in that young Man; yea he is very near the Kingdom. So we took our Leave of them, leaving the Lord's *Peace* and *Blessing* upon them."

The young man "very near to the Kingdom" was probably Neander, whom Penn met later at Düsseldorf; and the next young man—also "near to the Kingdom"—may have been Arnold Sibel, although his identity is not revealed in Penn's next paragraph, which reads as follows: "It was now something past the 12th Hour of the Day. In the way to our Lodging we met a Messenger from the *Countess of Falckensteyn,* a pretty young tender Man, near to the Kingdom, who saluted us in her Name with much love; telling us, That she was much grieved at the Entertainment of her Father towards us, advising us not to expose our selves to such Difficulties and Hardships, for it would grieve her Heart, that any that came in the Love of God to Visit her, should be so severely handled; for at some he sets his Dogs, upon others he puts his Soldiers to beat them: *But what shall I say, That it self, must not hinder you from doing good,* said the *Countess.*

"We answered him, that his Message was joyful to us, that she had any regard to us, and that she was not offended with us: We desired the Remembrance of our kind Love unto her, and that he would let her know that our Concern was not for our selves, but for her. We invited him to eat with us, but he told us he was an Inhabitant of *Meurs,* and was in haste to go home. So we briefly declared our *Principle* and *Message,* recommending him to Christ the true Light in his Conscience, and parted. So we went home to Dinner, having neither eaten nor drank since first-day Morning, and having lain out *all Night* in the Field.

"We had no sooner got to our Inn, but the Man was constrained to come after us, and sate down with us, and enquired concerning our Friends, their *Rise, Principles* and *Progress,* and in all things that he desired satisfaction about, he declared himself satisfied, Dinner being done, and all cleared, we departed that City, being about the fourth Hour in the Afternoon, and for want of Accomodation were forced to walk on foot Eight *English* Miles to a Town called *Holton,* where we rested that Night."

Before leaving Duisburg, Penn wrote the following post-script to his letter to the Countess: "My dear Brethren and Companions *G.K.* and *B.F.* with me salute thee in the dear Love of God. The enclosed I received from a religious young Woman at *Franckfort:* We have a blessed Opportunity in this Town with some that have a desire after the Lord, in which we are abundantly comforted. We have just now received thy Message and Salutation from *H.S.* [Heinrich Schmidt] which hath exceedingly refreshed and revived us, for our trouble was not for our selves, but for thee, and we hope our Love will not turn to thy Disadvantage, for we mentioned nothing of thy Name, nor the Name of any other Person, onely that we desired to speak with the Minister of *Mulheim,* and that was only to the Souldier. The Lord made us a good Bed in the Fields, and we were very well satisfied. We are going this Afternoon out of the Town towards *Wesel,* from thence to *Cleve,* and thence to *Herwerden* (the Lord willing) so farewell in the Lord."

The letter he had signed: "Thy great and faithful Lover for the blessed and holy Truth's sake."

A letter which Penn wrote a week later to "Joanna Eleanora Marlane [von Merlau], the Noble Young Woman at Franckfort," reveals that it was she, "the Religious young Woman at Franckfort", who had written a letter introducing him to the Countess of Dhaun-Falkenstein and Broich; for he says in his letter: "So dear J.E.M. know that the Lord hath brought us well to Amsterdam, not without good service by the way: For at Cullen we had a pretious Meeting, and were received with much gladness of Heart. We also went to Duysburg, and from thence towards Mulheim, being the first Day of the Week, hoping to get an opportunity with the Countess of Bruch, and to deliver thy Letter: But her Father (who is a cruel and severe Man) meeting us near his Castle, stopt us; and after some little time, finding what we were, said, There wanted no Quakers there, and sent us with some of his Souldiers out of his Territory. It was about Sun-set, so that we were forced to return towards Duysburg: But the Gates of the City being shut, and there being no Houses without it, we were forced to lye in the Fields all Night, where the Lord made us a good and comfortable Bed. We told the Graef at parting, we were Men that feared the Almighty God, we desired the good of all Men, and that we came not thither for any evil design; but he would not hear; the Lord, if he pleaseth, forgive him. Nevertheless we had a good Meeting at Duysburg, were we had our Heart's desire, the blessed power and life of God making its own way in the Hearts of those that heard our Testimony. I also writ a large and tender Letter to the Countess, and received a sweet and loving Message from her; and I have great hopes that all things will work for the best."

Duisburg Revisited

In pursuit of this hope, and probably encouraged to persevere by Elisabeth after his second visit to her at Herford, Penn returned at the end of September to Duisburg, where, he says, "we visited the Schult, or Chief Governour that Night whom we found at home; he received us with much

Kindness. His Wife and Sister, we fear, have been shaken in their good belief of our Testimony since we were last there; some Fowls of the Air have devoured the Seed that was sown. O that sweet and tender frame in which we left them the time before! However, the entrance we had upon the Spirit of the Schult, a little consolated us. Hence we sent Maria Martha's Friend, a Letter, desiring him to let us have his Answer the next Night at Dusseldorp, inclosed to Neander, when and where we might see him, either at Dusseldorp, Mulheim, or Duysburgh; and if it were possible, we would gladly visit the Countess of Bruch."

"Maria Martha" was Mlle. de Reneval, and her "Friend" was Reiner Copper; but the latter was too wary, or too timid, to bring about a meeting with the Countess. "Kuper," Penn says, "was so far from endeavouring our visit to the Countess, that he would not meet us himself, either at Dusseldorp, Mulheim, or Duysburgh: Nay, it did not please him to send us an Answer, much less any the least Salutation."[191]

Copper having failed him, Penn went again at the beginning of October from Düsseldorf to Duysburg, where, he says, "We first visited Dr. Mastricht, a Man of a good natural Temper, but a rigid Calvinist. I perceived by him, that they held a Consultation about seeing us at Bruch; but they all concluded, it was best to decline meeting with us because of the Graef, he being ready to fling our Name, in reproach, upon them, in his displeasure; and this would confirm him in his Jealousies of them. This might excuse the Countess, but by no means Kuper; and if I had any sense, Mastricht was there with them upon design to frustrate the hopes we had conceived of meeting with her. We from that descended to other things of weight, and in love and peace parted.

"From his House we returned to our Inn, and after Supper we visited the Schult, who with much civilty and some tenderness, received us. His Sister also came to us, and we

[191] From Mülheim, Copper went as pastor to Duisburg, and from there went in 1683 to join the Labadists at Wieuwerd. After the dispersion of the latter, he was invited by the Countess of Hoorn to settle at Bielefeld, a few miles from Herford, to which latter place the Countess retired after the death of her friend, the Princess Elisabeth.

had a good little Meeting with them, and our God was with us, and his pure and tender Life appeared for our Justification, and pleaded our innocent Cause in their Consciences: And so we parted with them, leaving our Master's Peace amongst them.''

The Dr. Mastricht to whom Penn refers so frequently in his account was one of the German Pietists who, on November 12, 1686, formed the ''Frankfort Company'' for the purpose of promoting the colonization of Pennsylvania. His name was Gerhard von Mastricht, and both his first and his last name indicate a Netherlands descent. The impression which Penn had made upon him in Duisburg is evidenced by his membership in the Frankfort Company and his purchase of 1666 2/3 acres of land in Penn's colony. Mastricht did not go to Pennsylvania, and together with the other members of the company was dispossessed of his land by fraud in 1700.

WESEL

After the first visit of Penn and his party to Duisburg at the beginning of September, they went by way of ''Holton'' (Holten) to the east of the Rhine, to the city of Wesel, at the confluence of the Rhine and the Lippe. Here, says Penn, ''the first thing we did (as had been our Custom) was to enquire who was worthy, particularly for two Persons recommended to us by the Countess of Hornes, that lives with the Princess Elizabeth. But upon enquiry, we found one of them was gone to Amsterdam with his Wife, who had been formerly a Preacher, and being conscienciously dissatisfied with his own Preaching, laid it down, and is now in a seeking State. But in lieu of him we found out three more, with the other Person that had been recommended to us. We bespoke a Meeting amongst them after Dinner, which accordingly we had at a Woman's House of good Note in the Town; who told us, That she had been long in a solitary Estate, dissatisfied with the Religions generally profest in that Country, waiting for Salvation, and she hoped that now the time was come, and that we were the Messengers of it.

''The Lord was with us in the Meeting, and their Hearts

were opened by the Word of God, to receive our Testimony as glad Tidings of Salvation, Meeting being done, we immediately returned to our Lodging, desiring we might see them together in the same place the next Morning, to take our Leave of them; to which they readily assented.

"Next morning we came, and had a precious Meeting with them, and there were some present that were not there the Night before. So we left them in much Love, and went to our Inn; where, after having refresht our selves, we went to Rees."

In his letter to Joanna Eleanora von Merlau, a fortnight later, Penn wrote: "From Duysburg we went to Wesel, where we inquired out who was worthy; and there we found four or five separated from all Congregations, waiting for the Consolation of Israel, with whom we had two precious Meetings."

At the end of September, Penn was again in Wesel, accompanied this time by Jan Claus of Amsterdam. The Kingdom of Prussia absorbed this Rhenish town, with many others, in its westward expansion two centuries ago, but many traits characteristic of the Netherlands are stamped upon it and its people, as is the case with other places in the Rhineland adjacent to Holland. Jan of Wesel, or Johannes Wesselius Gansfortius, one of the most eminent of the "Reformers before Luther", was a native of the Netherlands city of Groningen, and took his Dutch ways and traditions to the town whose name he has made illustrious in the history of Mysticism. Wessel's writings, although nearly two centuries had elapsed since he laid down his pen, had helped greatly to make the Rhineland of Germany and Holland promising soil for the seed of Quakerism.

William Penn and his companion, Jan Claus of Amsterdam, felt this congeniality of spirit occasionally when they travelled from Herwerden to Wesel in September, 1677. They had come by wagon over the two hundred English miles of the journey, riding three days and nights without lying down in a bed, and contenting themselves, perforce, with the wagon-floor. The wagon was not quite an open one, but was covered only "with an old ragged sheet"; and since the passengers were twelve in number, they were sufficiently cramped and straitened. "The passengers," says Penn, "were often, if not always Vain; yea, in their Religious Songs, which is the fashion of that Country, especially by Night, they call them *Luther's Songs,* and sometimes *Psalms.*" Penn often reproved them for their hypocrisy, for "they are full of all vain and often profane Talk one Hour, and sing Psalms to God the next."

At other times, and in some of the towns through which they passed, the company was more congenial. "Many discourses we had," Penn continues, "of Truth and the Religion and Worship that was truly Christian, and all was very well: they bore what we sayd. But one thing was remarkable, that may not be omitted: I had not been six Hours in the Waggon before an heavy weight and unusual oppression fell upon me; yea it weighed me almost to the ground,[192] that I could almost say, My Soul was sad even unto Death. I knew not at [the time] the Ground of this Exercise: It remained about twenty-four Hours upon me. Then it opened to me that it was a travail for the Seed of God, that it might arise over all in them I had left behind, and that nothing might be lost, but the Son of Perdition. O the strong crys, the deep agonys, many tears, and sincere bowings and humblings of soul before the Lord! that his holy sense which was raised in them might be preserved alive in them, and they forever in it! That they might grow and spread as heavenly plants of righteousness to the glory of the name of the Lord." This deep concern was later fully expressed in a long letter which he wrote, probably from Amsterdam, to the Princess Elisabeth.[193]

In his letter a fortnight after leaving Wesel to the Countess of Hoorn, Penn says: "We had a good time [at Wesel] with Dr. Schuler, and Rosendale, and the Woman we mentioned to thee, but the Taylor was shy and fearful of coming to us at the Doctor's."

The "Woman" referred to here was probably the Countess' sister, of whom Penn writes in telling of his fourth visit to Wesel, as follows: "We understood by Dr. Shuler

---

[192] The printed Journal has *GRAVE.*
[193] See *supra,* pp. 45–53.

that thy Sister desired we would be so kind as to see her when we returned: Upon that we went and visited her; she received us very kindly. Thy Brother in Law's two Sisters were present; we stayed with her at least two Hours. Many Questions she put to me, which I was glad to have an Opportunity to Answer, for it made way for a Meeting: She intreated us to come again if we stayed, and told us our Visit was very grateful to her: Adding, That because we past her by the last time, she concluded with her self we had no hopes of her; with more to that effect. From thence we went to Dr. Schuler's who freely offered us his House for a Meeting next day: And indeed, the Man is bold, after his manner.

"The next day about Seven I writ a Billiet in French to thy Sister, to inform her of the Meeting to begin about Eight: She came, and her two Sisters with her; there was Rosendale, Colonel Copius and his Wife, and about three or four more, and to our great Joy the Lord Almighty was with us, and his holy Power reached their Hearts, and the Doctor and Copius thereby confessed to our Testimony.

"The Meeting lasted about Four Hours: Being ended, we took our leave of them in the Spirit of Jesus, and so returned to our Inn. The Taylor was all this while affraid of coming to our Inn, or to the Doctor's to the Meeting: Great Fears have overtaken him, and the poor Man liveth but in a dry Land. After Dinner, we visited Copius and Rosendale, and at Copius's we had a blessed broken Meeting, he, his Wife, Rosendale, his Wife, and another Woman (Wife to one Dr. Willick's[194] Brother) present; they were extreamly affected and overcome by the power of the Lord, 'twas like one of our Herwerden Meetings; indeed, much Tenderness was upon all their Spirits.

"This done, and having left Books, both there, and with thy Sister, we left Wesel with hearts full of Joy and Peace; And let me say this, That more kindness, and openness, we have scarcely found in all our Travels. O that this blessed Sense may dwell with them. A Seed there is in that place that God will gather; yea, a noble People he will find out;

---

[194] This was Dr. Thomas van Wÿlick; see *infra*, p. 325.

and I doubt not but there will be a good Meeting of Friends in that City before many Years go about; my love is great to that place."

Although Penn's visits to Wesel appear not to have resulted in the establishment of a Friends' meeting, their fruitfulness was shown a half-dozen years later, when the Frankfort Company was formed for the purchase and settlement of land in Germantown, Pennsylvania, and when two of the townsmen of Wesel became charter members of the Company.

That a Friends' Meeting may have been temporarily formed in Wesel itself, or at least that it was at one time in a crystallizing condition, is indicated by the Amsterdam Epistle of the 11th. of 1st. Month, 1680, which says: "And a New Planting of the Lord has Arisen in the Country of Meurs in the small town of Krefeld . . . . ; Wesel and Kleef are places which lie not far away, and which manifest some inclinations towards the Truth (*Laaten zich eenige begeertens na de Waarheyd zien*)." These inclinations doubtless helped to carry their possessors from Wesel, as has been seen was the case in Kleef and Krefeld, to the "New plantings" beyond the seas.

When Penn came to the Rhineland again in 1686, he visited Wesel, where Jan Streypers and his son-in-law, H. J. van Aaken, met him and accompanied him to Kirchheim and Krefeld.[195] His colony in Pennsylvania was well started by this time, and he could give a very definite invitation to the persecuted to seek that haven of refuge.

DÜSSELDORF AND JOACHIM NEANDER

After Penn's second visit to Duisburg, at the end of September, he went up the Rhine to Düsseldorf to visit Neander, apparently to arrange for another attempt to visit the Countess of Falckenstein: but on their arrival, Penn says, "Neander was gone to Mulheim, in order to Preach on the Morrow [Sunday]; so that we were disappointed of our Intelligence." Penn went on up the Rhine to Cologne the next day, but took the night boat that evening for Düssel-

---

[195] *Infra*, p. 235.

dorf. "Arriving there next morning," he continues, "we presently sent for Neander: who came to us, and three more in company. We had a blessed meeting, with them, and one of the three that came with him, our Souls were exceedingly affected with. The Meeting done, they went away, but *Neander* returned. . . . .

"It grieved us now for Neander, the Young Man hath a Zeal for God, and there is a Visitation upon him, my Soul desireth that it may not be ineffectual: But I have a great fear upon me. For this I know certainly from the Lord God that liveth for ever, and I have a Cloud of Witnesses to my Brethren, that *Retirement* and *Silence* before God, is the alone way for him to feel the heavenly Gift to arise, and come forth pure and unmixt. This *only* can *aright* preach for God, pray to God, and beget People to God, and nothing else. But alas, his office in that family is quite another thing; namely, to perform *Set* Duties, at *fixt* times; Pray, Preach, and Sing, and that in the way of the World's Appointments. His very office is *Babylonish,* namely, a *Chaplain;* for 'tis a *Popish* Invention.

"In the good old Times, Godly *Abraham,* that was a Prince, and *Joshua* a great General, and *David* a King, with many more, *instructed their Families* in the knowledge and fear of God: But now People are too Idle, or too Great to pray for themselves, and so they worship God by *Proxy.* How can a Minister of the Gospel be at the beck of any Mortal living, or give his Soul and Conscience to the time and appointment of another? The thing in it self is utterly wrong, and against the very Nature and Worship of the new and everlasting Covenant. You had better meet to read the Scriptures, the Book of Martyrs, *etc.* if you cannot sit and wait in *silence* upon the Lord, *till his Angel move upon your Hearts,* than to uphold such a *formal, limited* and *ceremonious* Worship. This is not the Way out of *Babylon.* And I have a deep sense upon my Soul, that if the Young Man thrive beyond the Talent, God hath given him, to answer his Office, and fill up his Place, and wait not for the pure and living Word of God in his Heart, to open his Mouth, but either studieth for his Sermons, or speaketh his own Words, he will be utterly ruined."

This account is given by Penn in a letter from Amsterdam a week later to the Countess of Hoorn, whom he appeals to as follows: "Wherefore, *O Dear Friend* have a care thou art no Snare to him, nor he to thee! Man's Works smother and stifle the true Life of Christ; what have you now to do but to *look to Jesus,* the Author of the holy desires that are in you, who himself hath visited you. Tempt not the Lord, provoke not God. What should any Man Preach from, but Christ? And what should he Preach People to, but Christ in them, the hope of Glory? Consider, nothing feedeth that which is born of God, but that which cometh down from God; even the *Bread of God,* which is the Son of God, who giveth his Life for the World. Feel it and feed on it; let none mock God, or grieve his Eternal Spirit that is come to seal them up from the Mouth of Man, that hath deceived them, that Jesus the Annointing, may teach them and abide with them for ever.

"Be stedfast and immovable, and this will draw the Young Man nearer to the Lord, and empty him of *himself,* and purge away *mixtures,* and then you will all come to the *Divine Silence.* And when *all Flesh* is silent before the Lord, then is it the Lord's time to Speak, and if you will *hear,* your Souls shall *live.*"

In concluding the interview, Penn says, "we tenderly yet freely spoke our Hearts to him, before we parted, which done, in God's love we took our leave of him at Dusseldorf, and got that night to Duysburgh."

This young man in whom Penn took so deep an interest was Joachim Neander, who is famous chiefly for his Reformed or Calvinistic hymns. Martin Luther's great hymns were his inspiration, and his best efforts at rivalling them are considered to be "Lobe den Herren, den mächtigen König der Ehren" and „Der Tag ist hin, mein Jesu bei mir bleibe".

He was born in Bremen in 1650; found "a spiritual father" in Theodor Undereyck; studied in Heidelberg; came under the influence of Spener and the early Pietists in Frankfurt-am-Main; and was called to Düsseldorf in 1674 to become the rector of the Latin School of the Reformed Church. Falling still more deeply under Pietist and Labadist influences, he was suspended from his position in the spring of 1677 and spent the following summer (just before Penn's arrival) in great poverty, but in the composition of his hymns. These probably procured for him the office of chaplain to the noble family, which Penn so severely criticized. Two years after Penn's visit to Düsseldorf, Neander was called to a pastorate in Bremen, where he died soon afterwards at the age of thirty. His collection of fifty-six hymns were set to music and were published in numerous editions as well as very widely sung.

At the time of Neander's death in Bremen, Theodor Undereyck (1635–1693) was still pastor in that city, where Neander had first come under his influence at the age of twenty. Undereyck had been born in Duisburg; had come under the influence of Coccejus in Leiden and Labadie in Geneva; had been pastor of the Reformed church in Mülheim-on-the-Ruhr, where he made a deep impression of piety,—in contrast with the frivolities of the court of the Lutheran Count of Dhaun-Falkenstein, during his residence of eight years (1660–1668); for two years, he was preacher at the court of the Countess Hedwig Sophie, at Cassel; and then went to Bremen, where he preached for twenty-two years until his death in 1693. Although he published a condemnation of the Quakers and other fanatics as dangerous cranks (*gefährliche Grillen*),[196] his preaching differed so markedly from that of the strict Calvinists that he continued himself to be called a Quaker; and his Pietist and Labadist teachings had helped to make easier the advent of Quakerism in the Rhineland, especially at the courts of the Countesses and Princes.

EMMERICK

Leaving Wesel after his first visit, Penn and his companions went to Rees, Emmerick and Kleef, towns which have since become Germanized, but which were then largely Dutch. They lie close to the border of the Netherlands province of Gelderland; and at Rees, Penn says that they met with a "Counsellor of Gelderlandt", with whom they

---

[196] „Christi Braut unter den Töchtern zu Laodicaea", 3 Thle., Hanau, 1670.

"had a good opportunity to declare the Testimony of Jesus, who received it, and parted with us in much kindness."

At "Emrick," Penn says, "we called upon an eminent Baptist-teacher, recommended to us by one of Wesel: We spent some time with him, opening to him the Way of Life, as in the Light it is manifested to all that love and obey the Light; and of that more spiritual and pure Ministry that from the Living Word of God is received by many true Ministers in this Day. The Man was somewhat full of Words, but we felt the living Visitation of the Love of God reacht to him, and so we left him, making all the haste we could to get to Cleve that Night, which accordingly we did, though late, being forced to walk one third-part of the way on foot."

In his letter to Fräulein von Merlau, Penn refers to his talk with "the chief Baptist-teacher" at Emmerick, "who confessed to our Testimony, and received us lovingly. We directed him to that Gift of God in himself, that pure and eternal Word in the Heart, that he might know the pure Ministry of that, from the Ministry of Man's Spirit, which cannot profit or give life to the Soul."

In this letter, Penn also said that he hoped to go to Emrick again; but, although he returned to Wesel and Kleef a few weeks later, he does not speak of stopping again at either Rees or Emmerick.

KLEEF

The English *Cleves* or *Cleve*, the German *Kleve*, lies in Prussian territory, but only four miles from the Netherlands' border, and may still be called by its old Dutch name of *Kleef*. It is famous in operatic history as the scene of *Lohengrin*, and in England's history as the home of that Princess Anne who became for a short time the fourth wife of Henry VIII., whose aesthetic taste she did not suit,—except in Holbein's portrait,—and whose decapitatory humors she escaped by a judicious retirement from her position of perilous eminence.

The English Quakers were attracted to it, naturally, by neither its music nor its history. William Ames, the first of

Quaker preachers who visited it, went there to sow the seeds of Quakerism among its Mennonite inhabitants. In a letter which he wrote to George Fox, dated, Amsterdam, the 3rd. of 7th. Month, 1661[197], he says: ''After J passed from amsterdam J took my journy towards the palt[e] [Palatinate]: but by the way between holland and Coln [Cologne] J had som seruice, for the sound of truth hath ben much amongst [them], to wit in gelderland and Cleueland, where many baptists [Mennonites] dwells, amongst whome J haue laboured pretty much, yet though a loue is raised in seuerall and that seuerall haue ben Conuinced yet little is brought forth though in time J hope there may.''

The ''Cleueland'' referred to by Ames is the old Kleefland, or Duchy of Cleves, of which Kleef was the capital. Eight years after William Ames first preached Quakerism in the land and city, Steven Crisp and Jan Claus made a preaching tour through them, going to the city and lodging at ''the house of Mary Ann Boome.''

It was eight years after this that Penn and his companions arrived in the town. Although it was late and they were tired after their walk from Emrick, Penn says ''that Night, notwithstanding, one of us went to a certain Lady,[198] to whom we had Recommendations from the Princess, and that was particularly known to one of us, informing her that we were come to that City, desiring to know what time next day we might give her a Visit; she appointed Eight in the Morning.

''About that time we went to see her; she received us (considering her Quality and Courtship) far from any appearance of Offense at our Deportment. We told her our Message and Visit was to those of that City, that had any Inclinations or Desires, Hunger or Thirst after the true and living Knowledge of God; for that end we had left our own Country, and had wandred up and down in several parts of Germany. She told us, That some there were that searched after God, but she feared the Name of Quaker would make them shy, because they were called Quakers themselves, by

---

[197] A. R. Barclay MSS. 7. The year should probably be 1657: cf. *infra*, p. 191.
[198] Lady Hubner? See *infra*, p. 171.

People of the same Profession, only for being more serious and retired in their Conversation.

"We replied, That it was an Honour to the Name, that all Sobriety throughout Germany was called by it; this ought to make the Name less odious, yea it will make the way easier for those that are truly called so, or that are Quakers indeed: It will take off much of the wonder, and, if may be, of the Severity of the Places where we come, that the Name is gone before us, and hath received a Dwelling-place in their Towns and Cities. In fine, to all such God had committed to us the Word of Life to preach, and such we seek out in all places where the Lord bringeth us: And hitherto we can say it to the praise of our God, he hath vindicated our Service and Testimony, by his own blessed Power, shed abroad in their Hearts to whom we have been sent.

"So she told us she would send for an Attorney at Law, one that was more than ordinarily Eminent; having deserted the Church, and being therefore reproached with the Name of Quaker. In this Interval we had close discourse with her, a Woman certainly of great Wit, high Notions, and very ready Utterance: So that it was hard for us to obtain a true silence; a state in which we could reach to her. But through some travel of Spirit more than ordinary, we had a sweet time of refreshment, and the Witness was raised in her; and we really and plainly beheld a true Nobility, yea, that which was sensible of our Testimony, and did receive it.

"By this time the Person she sent for came, and a blessed sweet time we had: For the power and presence of the Lord our staff and strength, unto which our Eye hath been throughout all our travels, that we might only be acceptable in that, plenteously appeared amongst us (the Lord have the glory of his own work) both confessing to the truth of what had been said, and the Attorney to the living sense in which the truth had been declared.

"We would have returned to our Inn, to eat, according as we had appointed in the Morning, but she laid a kind of violent Hands upon us, and necessitated us to stay and eat with her; which we did. And we had no sooner sate down, but her Brother-in-law, a Man of Quality and Employment

in the Court of the Elector of Brandenburg, came in, who
Dined with us.

"As we sate at Meat, we had a good Meeting, for the
time was much taken up about the Things of God, either in
answering their Questions, or minstring to them about the
true Christen Nature and Life; in all which her Brother
behaved himself with great sweetness and respect.

"After Dinner we took our Christian leave of them in the
fear of God, recommending unto them the Light of Christ
Jesus, that brings all that receive it into the one Spirit, to
live in holy Peace and Concord together; particularly and
alone speaking to the Lady, and the Attorney what was
upon us as to their States."

In his letter to Fräulein von Merlau, Penn makes a
further reference to this visit: "We went to Cleve, where at
a Lady's House, belonging to the Court, we had a precious
Meeting: And we found some that had deserted the publick Ministry, as not being anointed of God to preach,
neither knowing by a true experience the way and travail
of the new Birth, but are made and maintained by Men: We
sounded the joyful Gospel amongst them."

A month later, Penn and Jan Claus came again to Kleef
where, Penn says, "we had a very pretious Meeting at an
honest Procurator's House, who received us with much
love: Four or Five more were present, all Grave and
Tender: Our Hearts were greatly affected with their love
and simplicity. We also visited the Lady Hubner, who was
kind to us."

William Ames, as we have seen, had travelled in Kleefland in 1661 and "sounded the truth" there; but it is not
certain whether he referred, in speaking of the "many
baptists", to the Dutch Mennonites, or to the German
Seekers or Pietists of whom the "lady of quality" spoke
to Penn. It is particularly interesting, therefore, to learn
that Penn heard in 1677 of those German-Dutch Pietists
who were afterwards to play so important a part in his
Quaker colony. Quakerism, however, did not flourish among
the Pietists in Germany, as they themselves flourished
among the Quakers in America; and we have record of only
one other visit of Quaker missionaries to Kleef. This was

made in 1710 by Mary Ellerton, of England, and her companion, and Pieter Leenderts, of Haarlem.[199]

With "Cleveland", Penn ended his efforts in the Rhineland until his next and last visit to the Continent in 1686. He did not keep, or publish, a Journal of this visit, and very little is known about it. He spent some time, about a month, in the Rhineland on this journey and definitely visited Krefeld, Kaldekerk, Krisheim and Wesel. He probably revisited the communities of "seekers" in various other places in pursuit of toleration for the sectarians in Europe and of colonists for his own "land of liberty", since his journey through the Netherlands in this year was devoted to this two-fold object.[200]

EMDEN

The Rhineland and the parts of Germany immediately bordering on the Netherlands made their appeal to Penn for the reasons stated; but he felt no call to extend his travels much further among the German people. Emden, which was so largely Dutch, so close to the Netherlands, and the center in Penn's time of a stern persecution of the Quakers, made a special appeal to him, and he was led on eastward as far as Bremen. His religious mission, here as elsewhere, was to defend and sustain the Quakers who were under persecution, and to seek out the "seekers" who had separated themselves from the Lutheran and Reformed churches. It is rather amusing to find him, therefore, in the very midst of this mission, writing a letter "To Friends everywhere concerning the present Separatists [that is, those from the Society of Friends], and their Spirit of Separation." This was a letter of condemnation and appeal relating to the "Wilkinson-Story" controversy and separation which had been condemned by the London Yearly Meeting of Ministers in June of that year.

Penn's letter was written, he says in his Journal, "in the Ship, between Delfzyl and Embden, upon the 16th. of the 7th Month [September], 1677", after the separation in

---

[199] Amsterdam Epistle, the 10th. of 5th. Month, 1711. See Monograph Number Six ("Dutch Quaker Leaders, 1665–1800").

[200] Cf. especially The Hague, *supra*, p. 118.

England "hath several times been opened unto me, and had remained some days upon my Spirit." His postscript contains the encouraging news that "God's blessed Work encreaseth and prospereth in these Lands, magnified be his Everlasting Name"; but it was precisely because of separation from the established churches in Holland and Germany that, as Penn said in his letter, "the Fields are even white unto the Harvest, up and down the Nations." It was this separation, too, quite as much as it was the "pernicious doctrines" of the Quakers that caused them to be persecuted.

Quakerism appears to have made its advent in Emden during the Sixteen Sixties, and its persecution there began in 1674.[201] Three years before this latter date, Penn had made a flying visit to Emden, after or before a visit to the Labadists at Herford; and he stopped there again in 1677, after another visit to the Labadists at Wieuwert. He tells of his activities in Emden, in both 1671 and 1677, in the Journal of his travels in the latter year, at which time he devoted himself chiefly to persuading the city authorities to cease their persecution of the Quakers. This persecution continued, however, until 1686, by which time Penn's colony had profited greatly by the flight of fugitives from it.

BREMEN

Penn's call to Bremen appears to have come from two of its citizens whom he met on his journey of 1677 in Herford and the Rhineland,[202] and to the example and probable request of George Fox.

Fox's "Haistwell Diary", of 1677–78[203] makes brief reference to his own stay in Bremen on his way both to and from Hamburg and Fredrikstad. On his first visit, he says that he and Jan Claus "hyred a Wagan [at Delmenhorst] and passed to Bremen (wch is a Statly Citty) and after ye Souldiers and officers had Examined us, wee went to an Inn at ye Signe of ye Swann, where wee hyred

---

[201] See Monograph Number Seven ("The Persecution of the Quakers in the Netherlands and Western Germany").

[202] *Supra*, p. 147.

[203] Cambridge and Philadelphia edition, 1925, pp. 242 and 246.

a Wagan and passed" . . . on towards Hamburg. The date of this stop is given in the Diary as the 18th. of 6th. Month [August], 1677; and the date of his return to Bremen, the Diary gives as the 1st. of 7th. Month [September], 1677. It was less than three weeks later, then, that Penn arrived in the city. On Fox's second visit, the Diary states that he and Claus "hyred A Wagā: and went In it to the Citty of Breman, where yᵉ Souldiers & officers did Examin us, and then wee went to an Inn, and Stayed a while (and yᵉ Lords power was over yᵉ Citty, and his Seed Reigned and Reigneth, though my Spirit suffered much in that place for yᵉ peoples sake)."

Jan Claus returned with Fox as far as Harlingen and then accompanied Penn from that place by way of ship along the coast of the North Sea and up the River Ems to "Lier" (Leer), and thence by wagon to Bremen. Here, Penn says, "we met our Friends and Companions G.K. [George Keith] and B.F. [Benjamin Furly] who were come hither some Hours before us from Amsterdam. In this City [Bremen] there is a work of the Lord begun, though yet obscurely: We had a travail upon our Spirits, that the blessed and precious Truth of our dear Lord and Master might find a place to rest its foot upon.

"To that purpose we wrote to two *Ministers,* under some Suffering from their Brethren, because of their great Zeal against the *formality* and *deadness* of the so called Reformed Churches. This we sent by a Merchant, whom we formerly met at *Herwerden.* With some difficulty we got to them, but the Person chiefly struck at was shy to speak with us:[204] His reason was this: 'It was known that we were in Town, and it was one of the Accusations against him that he was a Fosterer of all the *Strange* Religions that came through the Town. Also he was then actually under Process, and that the People that had heard of the innocency of his cause conceived a prejudice against our *Name,* though it might be without cause: Therefore he could not at present confer with us; and said he was sorry for it with all his heart, but what we should say to his Brother should be the same as if it had been said to him; to whom he referred us'.

---

[204] This may have been Theodor Undereyck; see *supra,* p. 167.

"However I took hold of his Arm and said, I have this Message to deliver to thee, that I may disburden my self before the Lord, which was this: *Mind that which hath touched thy heart; let that guide thee, and do not thou order that: Consult not with* Flesh *and* Blood, how to maintain *that cause, which Flesh and Blood in thy enemies persecuteth thee for.* He answered, 'Rather than I will betray that cause, or desert Christ, by God's strength, *they shall pull my flesh off my bones'.* So he left us in his House, and truly we had a good time with his Companion, the other Minister, about three Hours testifying unto him, that the day was come and coming, in which the Lord would gather out of all Sects (that stand in the oldness of the Letter) *into his own Holy Spirit, Life and Power;* and that in *This* the Unity of Faith and Bond of Peace should stand. And therefore that he and all of them should have an Eye to the *Principle* of God in themselves, that being turned to it, they might speak from it; and that therein they would Glorifie God and be edified. So we parted, leaving the Man in a sensible and savoury frame. We visited the Merchant twice, and had a very good time with him; the Man is of a loving and sensible Spirit, and the Love of God opened our Hearts to him."

"The merchant" referred to in this paragraph, was evidently the "Young Merchant of a sweet and ingenious Temper" whom Penn had met the first night at supper at his inn in Herford. He "took occasion," Penn writes in his Journal, "from that Night's Discourse, the sixth day at Dinner and Supper, and the Seventh day also, to seek all opportunities of conference with us, and (as we have reason to believe) he stayed Twenty Four Hours in that City on our Account. We opened to him the Testimony of Truth; I know not that in any one thing he contradicted us. At last he plainly discovered himself unto us to be a Follower of a certain Minister in *Bremen,* that is even by his Fellow-ministers and Protestants reproached with the Name of *Quaker,* because of his singular sharpness against the formal lifeless Ministers and Christians in the World. We laid fast hold upon this, and askt him, in case any of us should Visit that City, if he would give us the opportunity of a Meeting at his House? which he readily granted us: So we gave him some Books, recommending him to the true and blessed Testimony of Christ Jesus the Light and Judge of the World, and Life of them that receive him and believe in him, and so we parted.

"We also visited Doctor *Johan Sophrony Cozack,* an odd Compositum of a Man. He has had great and strange Openings; he hath writ several scores of Tracts: He is a great Enemy to the Priests, and in Society with none: Of a merry, yet of a rough disposition, without any method or decency in his Cloaths, Food, Furniture and Entertainment. He wants but three of four-score, yet of a wonderful Vigour and Pregnancy.

"We were twice with him, and we have reason to think he was as loving to us as to any Body. And truly he did show at parting some serious and hearty kindness: But we could fasten little upon him as to God's Power, or any inward sense of us or our testimony: Yet we had little to object against what he said too; nay, some things were very extraordinary.[205]

"From him we went to Doctor *Belingham,* an *English* Physician, a Man of a lowly and tender Spirit, who received us in much love, lamenting when we left him, that he had no more time with us.

"At the Inn we had frequent opportunity to declare the way of Truth, and we must needs say, we were heard with patience and sobriety; particularly of a *Doctor of Law,* who lodged at the House, and an ancient Man of *Kiel* in *Holstein.* We left *Books* amongst them all, and in the Love and Fear of God we took our leave of them on the fifth day after Dinner, and begun our Journey towards *Herwerden,* the Court of the *Princess.*"

Penn's visit to Bremen and its vicinity in 1677 appears from his Journal to have been solely a religious one; but it is significant that several Quaker preachers from Pennsylvania and active in the promotion of colonization there

---

[205] It would appear from his name that this "odd Compositum of a Man" came from the Hungarian city of Soprony (German Oedenburg), and to have descended from or been connected with the Russian Cossacks; but outside of Penn's pages, he is unknown to fame.

came to the city during the years when that colonization was being supported largely by emigrants from Germany. These included Roger Longworth, in the 1680's and 1690's; Thomas Chalkley, in 1709; and Thomas Story, in 1715. Roger Haydock of England went there in the 1680's also; and Mary Farmer and Mary Wyatt, of England, journeyed to Bremen in 1725, when the German emigration to Pennsylvania was still running strong. In "bramon", Mary Farmer wrote, "we found a few frindly pepell with whom we had a Leetell meeting." By 1814, when Stephen Grellet, a Quaker preacher from Philadelphia, arrived in Bremen, the "greene country towne" of Penn's founding had become a populous city, and his colony a great commonwealth, both of them owing much of their growth and prosperity to many thousands of immigrants from German lands.

CHAPTER IV

THE DUTCH QUAKER FOUNDERS OF GERMANTOWN

The name "Germantown" implies that this first settlement in Pennsylvania next to Philadelphia was founded by Germans; and Pennsylvania's local historians[206] have assumed that the inspiration for its settlement came from German Mennonite sources, and that its actual founders were German Mennonites themselves. But a study of European sources in Krefeld and Krisheim reveals the fact that the founders of Germantown were not really Germans, but Netherlanders, and not Mennonites, but Quakers. Pastorius, in his preface to Germantown's „Grund- und Lagerbuch", states: "We named the place Germantown, which means the Brother City of the Germans (*der Teutschen item Brüder Statt*)." Evidently the Dutch and Germans were not going to permit the English settlers in Philadelphia to monopolize the beautiful title of "the City of Brotherly Love", or the cohesive power of a communal name!

Geographically, the pioneers from Krefeld and Krisheim were "Germans", insofar as that term had a definite meaning in the Seventeenth Century; but politically, the Krefelders were subjects of the Prince of Orange (William III), while the Krisheimers were ruled by the Elector Palatine, and both were constituent parts of the Holy Roman Empire. Nearly two centuries were yet to elapse before the Rhineland, annexed by the Kingdom of Prussia, was to be grafted into the German Empire.

---

[206] John F. Watson (1828, 1830, 1857), Oswald Seidensticker (1870), Willis P. Hazard (1879), Samuel W. Pennypacker (1880, 1899), Marion D. Learned (1908). Julius F. Sachse (1895, 1903) lists the Germantown settlers as follows: Mennonites, 1683; (Labadists, 1684); Kelpian Pietists, 1694; Dunkers, 1719; New-Born, 1725; Schwenkfelders, 1734; Moravians, 1734–42. How even a contemporary colonist, James Claypoole, confused the German "Frankfurters" with the Dutch "Krefelders" is shown *infra*, p. 254.

Krefeld, about 1700 A. D.

In nationality, that is, in origin, language and customs, the Krefelders were Netherlanders, while the Krisheimers were Netherlanders and German-speaking Swiss.[207] From the point of view of religious affiliations, they were not German Lutherans, but had been Dutch Reformed or Zwinglians, then Mennonites; and having been converted from the Mennonite to the Quaker faith and organization, they were Quakers in full standing before, during, and for some time after their settlement of Germantown.

Numerically, the pioneers from Krefeld and Krisheim during the years of Germantown's founding (from 1683 to about 1690) largely outnumbered those from other German places who may properly be regarded as Germans. About 175 persons settled in the town during those years, and of these all but eight or ten came from Krefeld and Krisheim and their neighboring villages, or from various places in Holland.[208] By 1701, there were sixty families, (about 300 persons) in Germantown, and the Dutch were still largely in the ascendant; and as late as 1709, when the great tide of German immigration set in, the Dutch settlers continued largely to outnumber the Germans.[209]

The Krefelders and Krisheimers purchased their land as individuals and went out as colonists, while the Germans formed a corporation and did not themselves emigrate. Pastorius attached himself to the German corporation and, although he went on the great adventure, he was rather encouraged by, than the promoter of, the proposed emigration of the Dutch Quakers of Krefeld and Krisheim.

---

[207] Krefeld was a part of the Principality of Orange-Nassau and was ruled by William III of Orange, later William III of England, during the emigration of its Dutch Quakers to Pennsylvania, and was not annexed to Prussia until 1702. Krisheim was in the Lower (Rhenish) Palatinate, an electoral principality of the Holy Roman Empire; and when this principality was divided among various powers after Napoleon's conquests, the village was included in Rheinhessen (Kr. Worms, A. G. Pfeddersheim), which was incorporated in the German Empire in 1871. Its Calvinist princes died out in 1685, and were succeeded by Catholics, under whom occurred the emigration of the "Palatines."

[208] Infra, Appendix B (p. 395).
[209] Infra, Appendix C (p. 399).

The "German Society", or "Frankfort Company", which had been formed in the autumn of 1682, in Frankfurt, to promote colonization in Pennsylvania, purchased 15,000 (later 25,000) acres of Pennsylvania land through Pastorius. This purchase was made in London, in May and June, 1683,[210] and Penn reserved 18,000 acres in a single tract to which he gave the name of "New Franconia", with the expectation that the Frankfurt purchasers would form a rival settlement to that of the Krefelders. But Pastorius was the only one of them to go to Pennsylvania; hence, as the learned biographer of Pastorius admits, "it appears that without the Crefeld Purchasers the founding of Germantown could scarcely have been effected, as Pastorius had with him neither the purchasers of his German Company or Society, nor settlers to take up the land which the Society had purchased."[211] Indeed, Pastorius himself did not settle in Germantown until nearly two years after the Krefeld pioneers.

After 1709, the tide of German immigration rose so high through all of Eastern Pennsylvania as to submerge the Dutch settlers from Krefeld and Krisheim and their descendants; and intermarriage, as well as superior numbers and the adoption of the German language, speedily obliterated the Dutch origins of the town.

Thus, the fate of the Dutch founders of Germantown was similar to that of the one hundred Pilgrim founders of Plymouth, who were swallowed up in the later deluge of Puritans in Massachusetts Bay; or even more like the Dutch of Nieuw Nederland who were overwhelmed by the English of New York and New Jersey. But, thanks to the splendid history of the Pilgrims by their fellow-pioneer, William Bradford, their place in Massachusetts history is assured. De Vries and Van der Donck have given us contemporary accounts of New Netherland; John Romeyn Brodhead wrote a notable history of it; and Washington Irving by his amusing caricature and persiflage has enbalmed it in popular

[210] The Krefelders bought their land in March and June, 1683.
[211] M. D. Learned, "Francis Daniel Pastorius", Philadelphia, 1908, p. 133.

literature and made it live, even though fantastically, in the nation's memory.

But the Dutch founders of Germantown had no literary chronicler of their own to sound their praises and preserve their story, their character, and their fame to posterity. A gifted German writer, Pastorius, who was the only university-trained and legal and literary man among them, wrote of them naturally from the German point of view; and following him, a New England poet of a century and a half later (the Quaker Whittier), permitted the German to eclipse the Dutch, and even the Mennonite and Pietist to obscure the Quaker, in his "Pennsylvania Pilgrim."

Francis Daniel Pastorius and Quakerism

Francis Daniel Pastorius, the young German scholar and historian, who had been of much service to the Dutch pioneers in the location of the lands which they had bought from William Penn, became their mouth-piece and historian, and so magnified his own and the German influence that he claimed to have founded the town and called it Germantown. But, although he arrived in Philadelphia August 20, 1683, and the vanguard of the Krefeld pioneers did not arrive there until nearly seven weeks later (October 6, 1683), he did not settle in Germantown until some time after May 30, 1685, while the Krefelders began to settle there on October 25, 1683.[212]

Pastorius had drawn a lot of six acres in Germantown on the same day as the Krefelders; and when he finally settled there, his household consisted of himself and eight other persons. But these included only one, or perhaps two Germans (one of them from Mainz,[213] the other, Thomas Casper, or Gasper, of unknown origin, perhaps from England); a Swiss (Georg Wertmüller, of Berne); four persons from

---

[212] S. W. Pennypacker, one of Germantown's foremost historians, says of Pastorius: "He was the most conspicuous, if not the most important figure in the settlement of Germantown. . . . The typical man of letters of his period in America." (*Pa. Magazine*, 33:125).

[213] His name was Jacob Schumacher, and he may have been a relative of the Dutch or Swiss Quaker Schumachers of Krisheim and Germantown.

Holland;[214] and a youth from some unstated place, but with a Dutch or Low German name.[215]

So non-German was his own family, that Pastorius wrote to his parents:[216] "In regard to my household, I should like to arrange it in good German style in which Jacob Schumacher and the old Swiss are very serviceable, but the Hollanders who are with me are not of much use in it, especially the maid.... I very much desire as soon as possible to bring here a German maid, whom I can trust better than I can do [the Dutch maid] now, alas! If you wish that your hope [of successful settlement] should not be disappointed, send only Germans, for the Hollanders (as sad experience has taught me) are not so easily satisfied, which in this new land is a very necessary quality."

The "German Society" of Frankfurt had appointed Pastorius their agent for the purchase and administration of Pennsylvania land on the 2nd. of April, 1683, the day on which he set out from Frankfurt for America. In London, between the 8th. of May and the 6th. of June, 1683, Pastorius bought from Penn's agents for this Company, 15,000 acres of Pennsylvania land. On the latter date, he left London for America, and arrived in Philadelphia August 20, 1683. From that time until November 14, 1685, he patiently awaited the arrival of his Frankfurt friends, the members of the "German Society", to settle on the land designed for them in "New Franconia", as Penn called it, or in "our own town of Frankford", as Pastorius called it, "about half an hour from Philadelphia." But when he became convinced that his Frankfurt friends would not make the great adventure, while the Krefelders and Krisheimers were making noteworthy progress at Germantown, he wrote to the "German Society", November 14, 1685, and asked to be released as their agent.

---

[214] These were Isack Dilbeeck, Marieke Blomers, his wife, and their two sons, Abraham and Isack.

[215] Koenradt Rutters (alias Conrad Bacher), who may have gotten his name from Thomas Rutter, a bailiff and blacksmith in Germantown, to whom he was appenticed. "Cunnard Rutter of Germantown" became a Quaker and a member of Abington Monthly Meeting, which loaned him in 1708 the sum of £ 4 with which to buy a cow.

[216] A letter dated, Philadelphia, March 7, 1684.

After considerable correspondence, the "German Society", which by this time had "jointly purchased five and
twenty thousand acres of unseparated land, English measure, in the American province of Pensulvania", was re-
organized on the 12th. of November, 1686, under the name
of the "Frankfort Company." But this company also failed
to do as the Krefelders and Krisheimers had done, namely,
to emigrate in a body and settle together as a separate
community. Pastorius very reluctantly consented to act as
the agent of the new company until 1700; but it too had very
little success in colonization, and was soon afterwards dispossessed (fradulently, he thought) of all its land. Meanwhile, he had himself thrown in his lot definitely with
the Germantown settlers,—economically, socially and re-
ligiously.

His former Pietist leader in Frankfurt, J. J. Spener, appears to refer to the conversion of Pastorius to Quakerism
in one of his letters, dated August 1, 1689, as follows: "Such
as take their refuge thither, I leave to their own opinions."
Three years before this, Pastorius had written: "We have
built here in Germantown anno 1686 a little church (*Kirchlein*) for the community (*Gemeinde*)." This was the
Quakers' first "meeting-house", a word which had no German equivalent: hence *Kirchlein*. It was built of wood, and
Pastorius refers to its builders as "not looking towards an
externally large stone building, but that a temple of God
(which we believers—*wir Glaubige*—ourselves are) should
be built, and that we may be altogether pure and un-
spotted."[217]

Pastorius's library contained a large number of Quaker
books, and he claimed to have read everything that William Penn and James Nayler had written! Of Robert Barclay and his "Apology", he wrote: "Barclay has a vein of
pure gold and his *Apology* I would compare to pure pearls,
to rubies and diamonds; against the gates of hell it stands a
witness for the mystery of godliness and piety." He was
the school-master of the Quaker school in both Philadelphia
(1698–1700) and Germantown (1702–1718). In the Keithian
secession, he sided against the reactionaries, and in favor of

[217] „Beschriebung", p. 34.

the orthodox Quakers. His acceptance of Quakerism appears to have dated from the eight weeks' voyage to Pennsylvania, on which he became an intimate friend of the eminent Quaker, Thomas Lloyd. Twenty years afterwards, Pastorius wrote of this friendship as an unspeakable blessing, a favor sent to him from heaven.[218]

Pastorius died towards the end of 1719; his will was dated the 16th. of 12th. Month, 1719, and witnessed by three Friends; and he was buried in the old Friends' graveyard in Germantown. A worthy Quaker "Pilgrim" and pioneer he was indeed, and may well be called "the Pioneer of German immigration into Pennsylvania"; but not "the Founder of Germantown."

THE QUAKERS AND THE MENNONITES

When the religious affiliations of the Germantown settlers are considered, it is found that the pioneers from Krefeld and Krisheim were Quakers almost without exception. In their fatherland, during a dozen or fifteen years before their emigration, they and their parents had accepted the Quaker faith, become members of the Quaker society, and suffered varied persecutions in consequence. In Germantown, they had their own local meetings for worship, and were constituent members of Dublin or Abington Monthly, of Philadelphia Quarterly, and of Philadelphia or Burlington Yearly Meetings for organization and "discipline." The records of these meetings show that many of the Dutch Quakers at Germantown were appointed to varied services. Thus, not only Philadelphia, but Germantown too had its origin in the Quaker faith and Quaker settlers.

Jan Lensen appears to have been the only one of the

---

[218] Not only did Pastorius himself remain an active member of the Friends' meeting during the rest of his life, but he endeavored to hold his children loyal to the Quaker faith. In a postscript to one of his last letters, dated Germantown, November 27, 1714, and addressed to his son Henry, he says: "Caspar Hood was the day before yesterday at our house and told us that a fortnight ago he was at friends Meeting on Duck-Crick, and there did see our abovesd Cousin [Marieke ———], but not thee, Pray! do not neglect to meet with God's people, and there to wait upon the Lord, of whose hands all our Blessings, both Temporal and Spiritual, must come."

pioneers of 1683 who remained a Mennonite; and the small number of Mennonites in Germantown as late as 1708 is indicated by the following contemporary, and later Mennonite, authorities. The Rev. Rudolphus Varick, a Dutch Reformed minister of Long Island, writing to Classis of Amsterdam, April 9, 1693, of a journey he had made to Pennsylvania in the summer of 1690, says:[219] "I then came to a Dutch village, near Philadelphia where, among others, I heard Jacob Telner, a Dutch Quaker, preach, . . . This village consists of forty-four families, twenty-eight of whom were Quakers; the other sixteen are of the Reformed Church. I addressed those who had been received as members by Mr. Oyer [?]. The Lutherans, Mennonites and Papists, all of whom are much opposed to the Quakers, meet lovingly every Sunday, when a Mennonite, Dirck Keyser from Amsterdam, reads a sermon from a book by Joost Harmensen."

Jacob Gottschalk, formerly of Goch, was chosen the second Mennonite preacher in Germantown,[220] in 1702, and ten years later he wrote the following account of the beginning of the first Mennonite Church in America:[221] "The beginning of the Church of Jesus Christ which is called Mennonite took place on this wise at Germantown. A number of friends out of Holland and other places in Germany here came together. Now the most of these were Quakers, so they could not agree with them, and they began to have a meeting, although as sheep without a shepherd. Since they had no preacher, they endeavored to admonish one another. Later, in the year 1698 others of our brethren in the faith came in from Crefeld and other places in that country. They met with us for meeting in the house of Isaac Jacobs van Bebber." In 1702, they chose Gottschalk and Hans Neuss of Crefeld as preachers; and in 1707, more Mennonites from the Palatinate arrived, who united the next

---

[219] "Ecclesiastical Records of the State of New York", Albany, 1901, Vol. II, p. 1053.

[220] Willem Rittinghuysen was chosen the first preacher, apparently in 1698.

[221] Gottschalk's very brief account, written originally in Dutch is given in English translation from a German version (the Dutch original having been lost) by Dean Harold F. Bender, of Goshen College, Indiana, in *The Mennonite Quarterly Review*, Vol. VII, No. 4 (October, 1933), pp. 203–4.

year with those already in Germantown.[222] They then formed a church, Gottschalk says, "consisting of a total of thirty-four brothers and sisters including preachers and deacons." Eleven more were baptised in 1708; and in 1712 (after the arrival of "the Palatines") the number of Mennonite members is given as ninety-nine.

A modern authority on the Mennonites, Professor C. Henry Smith, of Bluffton College, Ohio, states in his recent book[223] that down to 1702, nearly all of the Mennonite colonists in Germantown were of Dutch descent, from Holland or from Dutch congregations in Lower Germany; that in 1707, the steady Mennonite immigration from the Palatinate began; that in 1708, the list of Mennonites in Germantown (exclusive of the Skippack congregation) numbered forty-four men and the wives of seven of these; that in 1712, the Mennonites in Germantown reached their zenith, at which time there were ninety-nine (including Skippack) in a population of about 250; that all but three or four of the "original thirteen" founders appear in the Quaker meeting records of the first half of the Eighteenth Century; and that perhaps one of these (Jan Lensen) died too soon to become a Quaker.

Another authority on the Mennonites in America, Dean Harold S. Bender, writing in 1933, of "The Founding of the Mennonite Church in America at Germantown",[224] states that the documentary history of the Mennonites shows that there were thirteen male Mennonite members in Germantown before 1708; that the name Mennonite does not occur in any public American document earlier than two deeds of a church-yard plot in 1703 and 1714; that there had been no baptism and probably no observance of the Lord's Supper, in the Mennonite church in Germantown, before 1708, and

---

[222] Gottschalk says that these newcomers "kept to themselves for the space of an entire year." This delay in forming a united congregation was probably due to the fact that the Dutch language and perhaps other Dutch customs were still being used in the services by the Dutch pioneers.

[223] "The Mennonite Immigration to Pennsylvania in the Eighteenth Century, Part XXXIII of a Narrative and Critical History, Prepared at the Request of the Pennsylvania-German Society", published in the Proceedings of the Pennsylvania-German Society, Norristown, 1929, Part II, pp. 1–412.

[224] *The Mennonite Quarterly Review*, Vol. VII (1933), pp. 249–250.

that the probable explanation of this omission is "to be found in the influence and example of the Quakers, who were strictly opposed in principle to the outward observance of all ordinances, in particular baptism and the Lord's Supper". This influence would have been exerted directly because there were so few Mennonites left outside of the Quaker fold.

The division among Pennsylvania Quakers which was led by George Keith in the early 1690's caused the Dutch Quakers of Germantown to take different sides in the controversy. The "Keithians" were denounced by the "orthodox" Friends, who were in the large majority, and the former followed George Keith into "secession." This separation began in the year 1692; and thereafter, the displeasure of the majority party was visited upon the minority leaders, who ceased to be elected to public office. This religious segregation and political boycott were doubtless accompanied by social ostracism, until most of the minority decided to unite or re-unite with the Mennonite Church. With the arrival of the German Pietists under the leadership of Johannes Kelpius in 1694, the Keithians met with them in the home of Jacob Isaacs van Bebber, where H. B. Köster preached to them in German and English, until some of them transferred their meetings to Philadelphia.

Another result of the Keithian schism was the opportunity it afforded, in 1694, to Heinrich Bernhard Köster to persuade a number of the Quaker seceders to join his own peculiar sect, which was called by him "The Contented of the God-loving Soul", and popularly known as "The Society of the Woman in the Wilderness." Köster returned to Europe about 1700 and continued his attempt to recruit the Quakers of Amsterdam and elsewhere on the Continent to his Society. A number of the former Germantown Quakers, also, removed from Germantown in 1702 to the "patroonship" of one of their Mennonite comrades, which was called after him for a half-century "Bebber's Township".

It would appear, then, that at this time (a quarter-century after the first settlement) the adult members of the Mennonite church together with their children, forming a total of perhaps eighty-five persons, constituted only about one-tenth of Germantown's population. The bulk of the towns-people, before the great immigration of the Germans in 1709 and subsequent years, were Dutch Quakers, with a sprinkling of English and Welsh Quakers, German Lutherans and Pietists.

As an illustration of the persistence of Quakerism among the founders of Germantown, a score of years after its settlement, the following record is significant. It is an "Account" (written on Rittenhouse Mill paper, in the handwriting of Francis Daniel Pastorius) of the contributors to the building of the stone meeting-house of the Friends at Germantown in 1705.[225] "Anno 1705 the 20th. of 4th month", the record reads, "Friends of Germantown bo't of Heivert Papen a Lott or fifty acres of land for the sum of Sixty Pounds Curr't silver money of Pensulvania. Subscription of Friends belonging to Germantown Meeting and paid as followeth, by Aret Klincken, John Luken, William Strepers, Denis Kunders, Lenert Arets, Peter Shoemaker, Paul Wolff, Thomas Potts, Sen'r, James Delaplaine, Isaac Shoemaker, Jacob Shoemaker, Matthew Milan, William Wilkinsen, Abraham Tunes, Francis Daniel Pastorius, Peter Clever, Johannes Kuder, Dirk Jansen, Wolter Simens, Simon Andrew, John Griffith, Paul Kästner, Andrew Kramer, Elias Burley, Mary Doeden, Anthony Loof, Cunrad Cunders (in all £48, 15s. in cash and £70.5s.2d. in work and materials)." In addition to these members of the Germantown Meeting, the following contributors are listed in the "Account" as members of the Abington Meeting: William Clinkins (Klincken), Stephen Clinkins, Reiner Tyson, George Gottschick, Geo. Shoemaker, Lenart Arets ("for lime sold"); and the following as members of the Philadelphia Meeting: Caspar Hood, Levin Harberdinck, Solomon Cresson, John Hendricks, Arnold Cassel.

1. THE KREFELD PIONEERS

The Lutheran revolt from the Catholic church opened the door to an aggressive freedom of thought which resulted not only in the establishment of such "orthodox" Protes-

---

[225] From the records of the Germantown Preparative Meeting.

tant churches as the Lutheran, the Reformed and the Anglican, but also in the rise of a large number and variety of Protestant "sectarians". The theory of a national church, as united and uniform as a national state, clashed violently with these sectarians, and the religious persecution of Protestants by Protestants became the order of the day in both the Europe and the America of the Seventeenth Century.

Persecution in the homeland led to flight from the homeland, frequently to other lands quite as hostile, but in which obscurity of life might lead to temporary although precarious toleration. Among these religious exiles, were companies of Dutch Mennonites who left their homes in Holland, for both religious and economic reasons, and took up their abode in the German Rhineland, in parts of which their hereditary rulers of the house of Orange-Nassau held sway.[226] They settled on the great river as far south as Frankfurt (350 miles from Rotterdam) where we find such good Dutch families as Van de Walle, Hasevoet, Laurens and others whose names end in the characteristic *sz, tz* and *sen*.

KREFELD

About one-third of the way up the Rhine Valley from Rotterdam to Frankfurt, and on its left bank three miles from the great river, stands the modern city of Crefeld, with a population at present of 130,000. During four centuries after its first mention in history, it lived the humble life of a small peasant and market-town; but about 1600, it passed from the rule of the Counts of Mörs (Meurs) to that of the Princes of Nassau and Orange. In accord with the policy of this princely house, toleration was granted (at least sporadically) to the Protestant sects, whose members came sifting into it in the 17th. Century from Holland and from the neighboring German duchies of Jülich and Berg, and the Archbishopric of Cologne. They brought with them the art of making linen-cloth and, in the next century, the making of silk. Annexed to Prussia in 1702, the town grew rapidly in population; silk and velvet manufactures made

---

[226] *Supra*, p. 178.

it wealthy and famous; railroads found an important center in it; our own Bret Harte, who was of Dutch descent, mingled his literary labors in the city with those of a United States consul; and the modern Crefelders marked their patriotic love of Germany by erecting a statue to Karl Wilhelm, the author of the music of *Die Wacht am Rhein*. Wilhelm lived in Krefeld for a time and was so influenced by his Dutch neighbors that he borrowed two measures for his famous song from the national anthem of Holland.

Krefeld was a very small town of handicraftsmen, however, that witnessed the first rise of the Quakers in it and their departure from the Old World to the New. Views of the town and its environment, contemporary with its Dutch Quaker inhabitants, reveal not only its quaint and picturesque aspects, but also the simplicity and intimacy of the life led by its citizens within and outside its walls. The Dutch and German names of its land-holders appear on the map, together with the names of dikes, fords, woodlands, the by-ways and the high-ways (to Kempen and Fischeln), the "old mill" and the "new mill", the ponds and cisterns (some privately owned, others belonging to the *Volk*), the stocks, the small jail and the large jail, the private and public bleacheries.

The Dutch and German names of the villagers are familiar in Mennonite history; for even before 1600, a Mennonite community took refuge in the city.[227] Among these was Herman (Isacks) op den Graeff, who was born in the neighboring village of Aldekerk, in 1585, and twenty years later married Grietjen Pletjes, a Mennonite girl of Kempen, another village close to Krefeld. Eighteen sons and daughters were born to them, and some of their descendants became Quakers and pioneers in the settlement of Germantown, Pennsylvania, while others remained among the Mennonites. In 1670, the clergy induced the town authorities to refuse permission to the Mennonites to build a meeting-

---

[227] The flight of Mennonites from Switzerland into the Palatinate appears to have taken place chiefly after 1673, when 1500 of them are said to have arrived. Many of these went on down the Rhine to Krefeld; but in both places, they found the Mennonites of Holland, who had preceded them by nearly a century.

Das alte CREFELD und seine Umgebung vor d. J. 1692.

A Map of Krefeld, before 1692 A. D.

house; but soon afterwards, twenty-nine of their families accepted the offer of citizenship, and finally, in 1695, they were permitted to build their first house of worship, but on a back street, without a tower or bell, and to hold their services one hour later than those of the established Reformed Church. The Labadists, too, found a place of refuge in Krefeld, and aided the Mennonites both to stir up the local clergy against "the heretics" and to attract the Quaker missionaries to these fields supposedly ripe for the harvest.

THE QUAKER MISSIONARIES

Quakerism was first introduced to the residents of Krefeld by William Ames, that most energetic of Quaker missionaries on the Continent, who began his labors in the Rhineland as early as 1657. Accompanied by George Rofe, he travelled up the Rhine as far as Heidelberg, and wrote to Margaret Fell:[228]"After I passed from amsterdam I took my journy towards the Palt^e: but by the way [between] holland and coln [Cologne] I had some service, for the sound of truth hath been much among [them ?] to wit in gelderland and Cleveland, where many baptists [Mennonites] dwells amongst whome I had . . [torn] pretty much, yet though a love is raised in severall and that severall have been convinced, yet little is brought forth, though in time I hope there may." It is significant that Ames who had been a Baptist preacher before his conversion to Quakerism, directed his message on the Continent largely to the Mennonites, out of whose fold the Baptists of England, and many of the Quakers of Holland and the Rhineland came.

Four years later, in 1661, Ames again went through the Rhineland, accompanied this time by his youthful companion and successor, William Caton. In the summer of that year, Caton had been engaged in Rotterdam upon literary and proselyting labors in behalf of Quakerism; and among these was an apparently successful appeal to a "German Earle" whom he met there to grant religious toleration to

---

[228] From Utrecht, 17th. of 2nd. Month [April], 1657 (Swarthmore MSS., I, 71–74). Cf. *supra.* p. 169.

his heretical subjects.[229] Writing to George Fox from Rotterdam one month later,[230] Caton speaks of his intention to go soon to the Rhineland with William Ames, "especially to the Prince of Palatine and to that other Prince or Earle that hath proffered so much Lyberty." In preparation for this visit he had had some Quaker literature translated into German; but as the translator had since left Holland, he hoped to find another translator in Germany. Finally, in September, 1661, Ames and Caton left Holland for the German Rhineland, and Caton gives in his Journal the following account of the first part of their journey:

"About that time it was upon me to go into Germany, partly to visit Friends, and partly to speak with the Prince Palatine, and some one else in that country: in order thereunto I took my leave of Friends in Holland with much tenderness of heart, committing them to the custody and protection of the Almighty. And about the tenth of the Seventh month [September] 1661, I with my dear brother William Ames set forwards on our journey towards Germany, and in due time we got well to Cologne; from thence we travelled towards the Grave de Whitt's country, who had promised large liberty to all sorts of people, that would come and inhabit in his dominion. When we came there, we went to his house, and had an opportunity to speak with him; and he reasoned very moderately with us a pretty while, and we endeavoured to inform ourselves, as much as we could from his own mouth, of the certainty of what was published in his name concerning liberty. But in the end, we perceived clearly from him, that his invitation, though promising liberty or toleration, was not so much out of love to tender consciences, as out of covetousness for what was theirs, as since hath more evidently appeared.

"After we had had a very good time with him, and had informed ourselves sufficiently, and tried the ground from whence such things had proceeded, we parted from him, and went up into the country, and had some good opportunity to speak with some of the priests and people; and after we had satisfied and cleared ourselves, we left those

---

[229] Swarthmore MSS., I, 450.
[230] *Ibid.*, I, 454.

parts, and travelled on our journey towards the Palz or Palatinate.''

By the ''Grave *de Whitt's* country'', Caton or his editor meant the County of Meurs (or Mörs), which had been ceded to the ducal house of *de Wied* in the year 1493. Krefeld had been one of the towns in this county, but it had been ceded about 1600, as has been stated above, to Prince Maurice of Orange-Nassau, son of William I, or the Silent, with whose princely house the counts of Wied were closely allied.

Krefeld, Duisburg, Mülheim-on-the Ruhr (Mülheim-Eppinghofen), and the town of Meurs (or Mörs) were near neighbors, and the two Quaker missionaries doubtless visited all of them before going on to the Palatinate. Their stay in the Rhineland on this visit lasted about six months, and many details of it are extant for other places; but no more are forthcoming for their visit in the County of Meurs. They paved the way in it for later visits by Steven Crisp and William Penn; they saw the beginnings of its Quaker Meetings; and they gave the initial impulse to the later emigration from it to Pennsylvania.

Caton's (or his editor's) remark that ''the Grave de Whitt's'' promise of toleration ''was not so much out of love to tender consciences as out of covetousness for what was theirs, *as since hath more evidently appeared*'', was justified by the count's conduct in subsequent years. For example, in May, 1670, Graf Wilhelm Wirich von Dhaun-Falckenstein entered upon a severe prosecution of ''quaeckerey''.[231]

This persecution was probably stirred up by the characteristically aggressive or enterprising activities of Steven Crisp of England, another fervent ''Quaker apostle'' to the Netherlands and the Rhine-land. In the year before it began (1669),[232] Crisp and Jan Claus, a leading Quaker of Amsterdam, made a journey through the Rhineland, coming from the Netherlands through Kleef and ''Regensburg'' (Ravestein ?) to ''Mors'' (Mörs, or Meurs) and ''Ord-

---

[231] Wilhelm Hubben, „Die Quäker in der deutschen Vergangenheit", Leipzig, 1929, p. 32.

[232] Crisp gives this year in his Journal; Claus (in the Amsterdam "testimonial" to Crisp, in 1693) ascribes it to 1667.

ingen" (Uerdingen), "where Ludovic, the Wachtmeister, received them kindly." Crisp's reference to this journey in his Journal is as usual very brief. "While travelling in those provinces [of the Netherlands]", he says, "I was moved to pass into Germany to which I gave up in the fourth Month [June] that same year; and, by the way, met with many perils and dangers, by reason of the horrible darkness, popery, cruelty, and superstitions of those lands and dominions through which I travelled, so that sometimes it was as if my life were in my hands, to offer up for my testimony; but the Lord preserved me and brought me, upon the fourteenth day of that Month, to Griesham [Krisheim]."

He does not refer in this passage to any stop in Krefeld; but Mörs and Uerdingen, both of which the two travellers did visit, lie within ten and four miles respectively from Krefeld. On the direct route to Krefeld, about thirty miles to the north, lies the town of Goch, whose Dutch Mennonite minister, Abraham Jansen, evidently denounced Crisp; for among the latter's posthumous papers, Benjamin Furly found in 1693 a paper entitled "My Answer to Ab. Jansen, of Goch, Germany, a Baptist", which Furly endorsed "Judged not needful to be printed."

Crisp did not visit the Friends of Krefeld and its vicinity again until 1678; but in 1677, William Penn, George Keith and Benjamin Furly, returning from their journey through the Rhineland, stopped at Duisburg, which lies within twenty miles of Krefeld. Penn tells in his "Travails" of the party's visit to its vicinity, but does not mention Krefeld. Their primary object was to find the Countess of Falckenstein and Bruch; and, failing in this on his first attempt, Penn returned with Jan Claus to Duisburg four weeks later, but was again disappointed.[233]

It seems strange that Penn does not even mention in his account of the journey the Quakers of Krefeld, who were to play so large a part, a half-dozen years later, in the settlement of his colony in Pennsylvania. He could not, of course, have forseen this event; but the efforts of Ames, Caton and Crisp at Krefeld must have been known to him, and he states that the primary object of his own journey through

---

[233] Cf. *supra*, pp. 147–160.

the Rhineland was to find and visit "a tender people." It might be supposed, therefore, that he would have seized the opportunity of travelling a few miles to visit the small congregation of Quakers at that place. It was a time of much persecution, however, and the dread name of "Quaker" was being hurled at everyone, from princess to peasant, who showed the least tendency to diverge from the strait path of Calvinism. Perhaps, then, it was to avoid adding fuel to the fire of persecution against the Krefeld Friends,[234] that Penn refrained from visiting them; but it may simply be that in his eagerness to "convince" the princess, he neglected to visit the peasants who were already "convinced." In view of later events, it would have been of great interest if he had revealed his impression of the Krefeld founders of Germantown on their native heath.

Crisp did not accompany Penn and his party on the Rhineland journey of 1677; but the next year (in September) he again left Holland to visit "divers cities upon the Rhine, where several had received a notion of truth in a talkative mind."[235] He appears to have gone through Kleefland and as far as Krefeld, during the summer; but severe illness compelled his speedy return to Amsterdam. The Memorial to him, drawn up by the Amsterdam Friends in 1693,[236] refers to his visits in the Rhineland and specifically mentions Krefeld as follows: "Another time [besides 1667] he made a Journey into the County of Meurs, to the Town of Crevel, where a meeting was set up."

The next Quaker missionary to appear in Krefeld was Roger Longworth, who arrived there in 1679. He was a man after Crisp's own heart, and was to play, as will be seen in the next chapter, a noteworthy part in the exodus of

---

[234] The sensitiveness of the clerical and popular mind to "heresy", in Krefeld in 1677, is illustrated by the presbytery's punishment of a "heretic" in that year, for writing some words profaning the name of God on the paper coverings of pepper-cookies (*Pfefferkuchen*) which were designed to be eaten by children and cattle (Goebel, II, 55). This faith or superstition in regard to talismans (*Anhängsel*) was carried over to Pennsylvania and practised in Germantown, notably by "the Hermits of the Wissahickon." They even practised the *Schatzkästlein* (Treasure-chest) idea, in accordance with which persons guilty of immoral conduct were given written moral verses *to eat.*

[235] Journal, 1694, p. 46.

[236] Probably written by Jan Claus, his companion.

Dutch and German Quakers to Penn's colony beyond the
Atlantic. On his release from an imprisonment of six or
eight weeks in the castle of Chester, England, because of his
Quaker activities, he spent four months preaching in the
Netherlands and north-western Germany, where he and his
companion, Jacob Claus of Amsterdam, were imprisoned
for a time because of his denunciation of the persecution of
the Quakers in Emden. Released from this imprisonment
and expelled from the city, the two missionaries proceeded
through Gelderland and thence to "the pelletinia in the
south of germania."[237] On their way to visit the Friends
in the Palatinate as far south as Krisheim, they stopped
for a time among the Friends of Krefeld; and here they
organized a regular Friends' meeting for worship, to be
held twice a week on Sundays and Wednesdays.

PERSECUTION OF THE KREFELD QUAKERS

This organized activity of the Quakers excited the anger
and complaints of the local clergy. To the Synod of Mörs
(Meurs) held in Krefeld in 1679, was brought the complaint
that Quakers from England had held services (*Dienst
getan*) "here in Krefeld"; and the next year, the same
synod heard complaints from various members that "numerous Quaker meetings had been held, to which had come
many from England and Holland, who held their meetings
also and propagated their faith (*ihre Lehre treiben*), many
of our people betaking themselves to them."[238] The complaints of the clergymen to their synod that they were being
slandered (*gelästerd*) by the Quakers and Labadists, and
the protest of the synod to the state, led speedily to the imprisonment and exile of the recalcitrant Quakers of Krefeld.

The story of this persecution is recorded in a pamphlet
written in Dutch and published in Rotterdam and Amsterdam in 1680. Its title, in English, reads: "Remonstrance to
Baron von Kinski, Sheriff of Meurs, also to the Magistrates
and Inhabitants of the City of Krefeld, as well as to the

---

[237] Longworth's letter of 8th. Month (October), 1679: Pemberton MSS., I, 119.
[238] M. Goebel „Geschichte des christlichen Lebens in der rheinwestfalische
Kirche," Coblenz, 1852 (Vol. II, p. 294.).

Clergy of the same City, who often call themselves Servants of the Community.''[239] The authors of the pamphlet were two of the six Quaker sufferers who had been driven into exile, namely, Herman Isaaksz op den Graeff and Hendrik Jansz.

The eight pages of the pamphlet begin with the following statement: ''Friends, It is three weeks to-day since we and two others of our Friends, together with a woman and her infant child, were led by armed men out of the City and Jurisdiction of Kreveld, without our knowing any just reason or cause therefor. Having wandered for some days in the vicinity we felt some freedom to go, for our refreshment, to make a short journey to Holland, to visit our Friends there. Then, just as we felt a freedom to do that, so we now feel impelled to return to Kreveld, to resume our occupations for the sustenance of our temporal lives, and to continue as hitherto in our dealings and intercourse with you, in modesty and in the fear of the Lord. On the other hand, it has occurred to us that perhaps some might erroneously imagine that we should not return to that place whence, as stated above, we were expelled by force; hence we have deemed it necessary, not only for the anticipation of all kinds of erroneous suppositions, but also for the instruction of all who may be concerned therwith, to give in a few words some reasons for our conduct.

''We believe that it is known to every resident of Kreveld that I, Herman Isaaksz, have been born and bred there, and that I, Henrik Jansz, have resided there for about six years past; that we have earned our livelihood by our own hands, without having been a charge or burden upon anyone: and much less have we been conscious of causing anyone loss or injury through trickery, fraud, or violence, or of having given anyone the slightest reason for resentment by leading an evil life. We touch briefly upon these facts in passing, so as to induce everyone to reflect upon what reasons could possibly justify our being expelled in such manner from our

---

[239] „Vertoog aan den Baron de Kinski, Drossaart van Meurs, Als ook aan die van de Regeeringe, En aan De Ingesetenen van de Stad Krevel, Mitsgaders aan de Predikers van de zelve Stad, die haar zelven veeltijds noemen Dienaars van de Gemeente", Rotterdam and Amsterdam, 12 mo, 8 pp., 1680.

birth-place and home. As far as we are concerned, we must say that we have requested, indeed, a copy of the charges against us, but that none has yet been given us.

"When a thief, robber, violator of the peace (*geweldenaar*), or some such person is expelled from a city or country, ought he not to be convicted previously of his misdeeds, either by his own confession, or by impartial witnesses? Should not his sentence be read to him publicly? Should not a statement of his crimes be made in his sentence? And if he requests a copy thereof, should it not be given him? We, on the contrary, have not been convicted of any crime, and no copy of our sentence has been granted us, although we have requested the same, orally and in writing. Now, would we like to have any citizen or resident so treated,—even though they may have been hitherto unknown to us?

"It is true that we have learned indirectly that the three following pretexts have been urged against us as reasons for our treatment: First, that we do not yield due respect to the authorities; second, that we renounce the outward sacraments; third, that we hold separate conventicles. Our Friends have often been subjected to similar wicked accusations, especially in the year 1675 by the magistrates of Embden. These have been so clearly disproven by letters and short replies written to them by one and another of our Friends,[240] that no further contradiction of them is needful (*dat 'er geen tegen zeggen opvalt*)."

The authors of the pamphlet nevertheless proceed to make a brief reply to the accusations, in the. course of which they cite the fact that Charles II. did not resent the wearing of hats in his presence by the Friends. "As to baptism and the Lord's Supper, we answer again, as we did in a letter to the Sheriff, dated the 29th. of the last month, that we observe the true baptism and Lord's Supper, but not the outward ones." As to the third charge: "It was made against the Reformed a century ago. We only wait in silence upon the Lord, to feel his powerful working upon our

---

[240] At the end of the pamphlet, five of these replies (printed in the Dutch from 1675 to 1679) are referred to, with title and authors: W. Pen, T. Green and I Kroock [John Crook], Steven Crisp, Pieter Hendriksz.

spirits. And who is injured or offended thereby? If anyone come to us, we do not prevent them; if no one come, we do not fetch (*halen*) and much less compel them."

Then follows a fervent appeal for justice to the Sheriff, the magistrates, and the inhabitants of Kreveld: "Remember the invasion of the French a few years ago,[241] when they lay so close to Kreveld: would you have been permitted to dwell side by side with their mass-saying? May they not come again?[242] Should you not do justice to receive justice? Remember how our ancestors strove against the Catholics for religious liberty."

Such is the burden of the appeal to magistrates and people. Then comes an appeal to the ministers of religion: "The blood of the martyrs is the seed of the church,—as old Prince William of Orange stated in 1566. Even the Spanish Inquisition-masters know well now that their hidden tricks and traps (*listen en streken*), by means of which they made the magistrates the executors of their sentences, are thoroughly understood by other people,—as is proven in the widely-known History of the Netherlands by the famous P. C. Hooft, published in the year 1656."[243]

This appeal to history, to reason, and to conscience, which the exiled Quakers made to their fellow-townsmen of Kreveld was signed by Herman Isaaksz and Henrik Jansz, and dated "Holland, the 22nd. of the 2nd. Month, 1680, Holland style."

An account of some aspects of this persecution of the Krefeld Friends is given by Pieter Hendricks, in a letter to Roger Longworth dated, "Amsterdam 4 yᵉ 6/m 1680 H: Acct."[244] In this, Pieter speaks of his own illness which had prevented him from attending London Yearly Meeting that year and also, probably, from accompanying the Amsterdam Friends on the visit which they had recently made to the Krefeld sufferers. Hendricks's account of the persecution and the visit referred to is as follows:

---

[241] This was probably the first ravaging of the Palatinate by Turenne in 1674.

[242] The second and more terrible ravaging of the Palatinate by the French occurred in 1688.

[243] The two volumes of this famous History were published between the years 1642 and 1654.

[244] Etting MSS. (Misc.), Vol. 4, p. 9.

"Concerning the Crevelt friends, they have beene banished and sent away twice with a threatening from yᵉ deputie of Crevelt the last time if they come in againe, they should be whipt and burnt on theire backs, sweareing by his soules salvation he should doe it; but they have beene theire againe peacably a prettie while, about 6 or 7 weekes; only yᵉ husbandman Johannes,²⁴⁵ was beaten grievously of late, by 2 of his neighbours, when he was passing by them, and they saying to him good Even, and he not answering them, they kicked him and strook him downe and tread upon him & dragged him by yᵉ haire soe yᵗ he was necessitated to keepe his bed in greate paine, but begins to Come up a little sometimes; it is a man yᵗis spoken well of, allmost by all for his honestie and Jnnocencie, it seems yᵉ magistr: there will take yᵉ thing in hand, and they say they will suffer such things in noewise—My wife [Elizabeth], geerti: [Geertrud Dericks] & Sitie Adams of Haerlem²⁴⁶ have beene there lately & are satisfyed verie well in theire Journey, and weare verie much refreshed with friends theare in yᵉ lord; they Continued there 3 dayes, and had 4 meetings and another on yᵉ first day in yᵉ forenoone, many strangers came in, friends things [think] a great part of halfe yᵉ towne, but all was prettie quiet & peaceable . . . .,²⁴⁷ it is thought, they will let friends live peaceably at Crevelt, but time will make yᵗ appeare—about yᵉ same time when they persecuted friends there, J had one of theire burgermasters here at our house, but knew it not then; but J laid friends sufferings prettie hard upon him; he was inquisitive about our principles & seemed prettie well satisfyed, except in our practice concerning yᵉ hat—B :F: [Benjamin Furly] & A :S: [Arent Sonnemans] had an opportunitie to speake with yᵉ drost of Meurs, beeing then in yᵉ hague, who had 2 priests with him and severall others, but the priest was [?] away twice from them; but whether yᵉ Prince of orange received W Penˢ letter we know not, not knowing by whom it was sente, but its possible it is come to his hande—because

---

²⁴⁵ Johannes Bleikers: cf. *infra*, p. 230.

²⁴⁶ For these Dutch Quakeresses cf. Monograph No. 6 ("Dutch Quaker Leaders").

²⁴⁷ Hendricks refers here to their visit in Kaldekerk; cf. *infra*, p. 234.

friends have had soe much libertie at Crevelt soe long. Friends in yᵉ Pallatinate weare well, and have desired theire loves to be remembered to friends in England, & soe have they at Crevelt . . . Petter Hendricks. [P.S.] J have written something concerning womens speakeing, Containeing about one sheet, wᶜʰ J have sente to yᵉ priest at Kriesheim some weekes agoe, its printed in high-dutch, and spreading bot there and at Crevelt where the people was much wondering at it when our women weare there, the baptists [Mennonites] in yᵉ paltz are quiet now since they had our last answer—if thou has an opportunitie thou may read this letter to G: f: [George Fox].''

Appeals for Toleration

Besides the appeals for toleration of the Krefeld Quakers which Hendricks, Furly and Sonnemans made in Holland to the local rulers of Krefeld, Crisp, Longworth and Penn made their appeals also, Penn writing a letter to the Prince of Orange, which was referred to by Hendricks in the letter just quoted. Crisp, who had become well acquainted with the Krefeld Friends during his visits of 1667, 1669 and 1678, hurried over from England in 1680 as soon as he heard of the renewed outbreak of persecution against them. ''In this time [August, 1680],'' he says,[248] ''it came upon me in the great love of God, to visit a little innocent remnant that had believed in the Lord Jesus Christ, and professed his name, in Crevelt, in the land of Meurs, who, for their testimony, had suffered many things and grievous, and been several times banished from house and home, and made to wander with wife and children to seek harbour or shelter in strange cities and places. These I found now returned to their dwellings, and was joyfully received by them, and much refreshed by them; beholding their faith and courage, and their steadfastness in the testimony they had to bear for the Lord. I tarried with them about three days, and had several precious public meetings in the city, and sounded the day of the Lord's tender visitation in the ears of many of the inhabitants, who generally behaved themselves in great

---

[248] Journal, 1694, pp. 50–51; 1824, pp. 93–94.

sobriety and moderation, neither mocking nor scoffing, nor evilly intreating us.

"It is rare to find a people so moderate in those parts, which are in the borders of the dark Romish religion, and as it were intermixed with it. But I speak it to their praise, no man evilly intreated me, and the Lord's power was over all; for which we blessed and praised his Name. And having comforted and strengthened them that had believed, I did commit them to the grace of God, and left them, and returned again to Holland another way, through the Spanish Netherlands; where I saw great abominations and idolatry, and worshipping and praying to images, &c. which grieved my soul; and I could not but declare against it in several places, as the Lord made way."

Not only did Crisp labor among the persecuted, striving to console and strengthen them in their determination to stand steadfast, but he also made vigorous appeals to the magistrates and townsmen to put a stop to the persecution; and he probably inspired and aided two of the exiles to write their "Remonstrance", which he then took to Rotterdam and Amsterdam for publication.[249]

Roger Longworth, also, hearing at London Yearly Meeting of the Krefeld persecution, went once more up the Rhineland to Krefeld, where he and his companion, Roger Haydock, brought consolation and courage, albeit renewed peril, to the little company of "isolated" and persecuted Friends.[250]

William Penn's appeal in behalf of the Krefeld Friends was made in a letter to the Prince of Orange, dated from London, the 26th. of 12th. Month, 1679 [March, 1680]. In this, he reminded the Prince of the policy of toleration which had been "the steady practice of thy famous ancestors", and then continued as follows:

"There are several inhabitants of Crevelt, (a town upon

---

[249] The vigor of its style and its reference to the Emden persecution are reminiscent of Crisp's own protests (Cf. Monograph No. 6: "Dutch Quaker Leaders").

[250] Their appeals to the magistracy for toleration, on this journey, appear to have been made on behalf of the Friends of Krisheim, as well as those of Krefeld; cf. *infra*, pp. 287f.

the Rhine, near Cologne, a member of thy ancient patrimony,) that have been banished, without regard to age or sex, not for any offence by them committed against the civil government or ministers of justice, and consequently free from the charge of disloyalty or immorality; but which is worse, I cannot hear there was any reason rendered for the punishment, so that the judgment preceded the trial, and the sentence was executed before the cause was heard.

"Though I presume that which is to be alleged by the Drost or Chief Governor under thy command, is their dissent from the reformed religion: but with submission, we must never reproach the Papists with persecuting Protestants, if Protestants themselves will persecute Protestants, because of some different apprehensions about religion. . . .

"To be short, great Prince, God and Caesar divide the man; faith and worship belong to God, civil obedience and tribute to Caesar. In the first, with Prince William of Orange, (thy great ancestor,) indulge these poor inoffensive people, it is Christian, it is Protestant, it is human, for religion improves and not ruins nature; . . . Nor does variety of opinion hinder arts or ruin traffic, of which the countries under thy government are a demonstration against the clamors of superstition. Thus Caesar giving God his due, if the people shall refuse to Caesar that which belongs to Caesar, to wit, tribute and civil obedience, let the law be executed with so much the more severity, by how much their pretences to goodness exceed those of other men.

"I shall conclude, great Prince, with this humble request, that it would please thee to command the Drost of those parts to suffer these dissenting inhabitants of Crevelt now exiled, to return quietly to their habitations, and that if nothing appear against them but what relates to faith and worship, so liberally allowed in the seven provinces under thy command, they may enjoy the liberty of that their native country and the protection of its civil government, that the great God who is King of kings and Lord of lords, may bless and prosper thy affairs as he did those of thy predecessors, who took the same course I have here recommended to thee."

This appeal to "the man highest up", backed by those of the Krefeld sufferers and the Friends in Holland to "the men lower down", was successful; for the Prince of Orange issued a proclamation authorizing the holding of public meetings for worship in his realms by the Quakers and other Protestant sects, provided that admission to them was accorded also to ministers of the (Reformed) established church.

Krefeld's Quaker Meetings

The Friends in Krefeld as elsewhere were not satisfied, however, with meetings for worship only on Sunday mornings; they desired also a mid-week meeting for worship, and a monthly meeting for "discipline", for the regulation of affairs among their own fellow-members. It was precisely in this year of persecution, 1679, that they ventured to organize such meetings. The Epistle of Amsterdam Yearly Meeting, dated the 11th. of 1st. Month, 1680, notified London Yearly Meeting that "a new planting of the Lord has sprung up in the County (*Graafschap*) of Meurs in the small city of Crevelt, a hereditary place of the Prince of Orange, but not within these seven Provinces [of the Dutch Republic], and lying on the road towards our Friends and Brothers in the Palatinate." Roger Longworth also, writing of his visit to Krefeld in 1681, says:[251] "I shall give thee a short account of our traivell in the south of jeremeney. We went first to Crevelt, that is a place where there is a new gaithering of friends, and wee had verie good services. it is but about two years since they had a meeting, and now there are about twenty on a first day." Finally, about a century later (in 1770), a committee of London Yearly Meeting reported that "at Crevelt, the Meeting was first settled in 1679, and held on the first and fourth days of the week. Their Monthly Meeting was first held in 1682."

The Krefeld Quaker Wedding, 1681

The meetings having been successfully organized, the exiles safely returned, and a pledge given for toleration in the future, a very interesting event occurred in the small

---

[251] Pemberton MSS., I, 117.

Krefeld, about 1700 A. D.

Quaker community. This was a marriage of two of the members in the 3rd. Month, 1681. The groom was Derick Isacks op den Graeff, the brother of Herman, who had been one of the exiles of 1679 and one of the two authors of the "Remonstrance". Hendrik Jansz (or Janssen) another of the exiles and co-author of the "Remonstrance", also attended the wedding, as did probably the other four exiles, including "two others of our Friends, a woman and a child," and indeed most of the twenty members of the meeting referred to by Roger Longworth.

The marriage was conducted "according to the good order observed among Friends", which George Fox had begun to develop for Friends in England as early as 1653.[252] Seventeen years later, he wrote "a letter concerning certificates in matrimonial affairs", which was translated into Dutch and copied in the minute-book of the Friesland Monthly Meeting.[253] This letter was doubtless circulated in its Dutch version among the Friends of Krefeld and elsewhere in the Rhineland, and it helps to explain why the "good order observed among Friends in relation to marriage" was so uniform in all Friends' meetings.

The letter is dated the 14th. of the first month, 1670/1, "English Style" [March, 1671], and reads as follows: "While I continued at Enfield, a sense came upon me of an hurt, that sometimes happened by persons coming under the profession of truth out of one country into another, to take an husband or wife amongst friends, where they were strangers, and it was not known whether they were clear and orderly or no. And it opened in me to recommend the following method to friends, for preventing such inconveniences. Whereupon I writ the following lines:

'All friends that marry, whether men or women, if they come out of another nation, island, plantation, or county, let them bring a certificate (*Attestatie*) from the men's meeting of that county, nation, island or plantation from which they come, to the men's meeting where they propose their intention of marriage (*gedincken te trouwen*).

---

[252] Cf. George Fox's "Journal", 1694 edition, p. 347; 1800 ed., II, 125–6 (Cf. *Ibid.*, pp. 87–8).

[253] Cf. Monograph Number Eight ("The Friesland Monthly Meeting of the Society of Friends").

For the men's meeting being made up of the faithful, this will stop all bad and raw spirits (*qŭade, loose en Ruijge geeste*) from roving up and down. When any come with a certificate or letter of recommendation from one men's meeting to another, one is refreshed by another, and can set their hands and hearts to the thing. This will prevent a great deal of trouble. And then, when ye have to say to them in the power of God, in admonishing and instructing them, ye are left to the power and Spirit of God to do it, and to let them know the duty of marriage, and what it is; that there may be unity and concord in the Spirit, and power, light, and wisdom of God, throughout all the men's meetings in the whole world, in one, in the life. Let copies of this be sent to every county, nation, and island, where friends are, that all things may be kept holy, pure, and righteous, in unity and peace, and God over all may be glorified among you, his lot, his people, and inheritance, his adopted sons and daughters, and heirs of his life. So no more, but my love in that which changeth not.

G.F.' "

It was apparently four years after this letter that the London Yearly Meeting of 1675 adopted the following procedure, which was closely followed at the Krefeld meeting of 1681: "At or near the conclusion of the said meeting, after it has been held the usual time, the parties are to stand up and, taking each other by the hand, declare in an audible and solemn manner to the following effect; the man first, viz. Friends, in the fear of the Lord, and before this assembly, I take this my friend A.B. to be my wife, promising, through divine assistance, to be unto her a loving and faithful husband, until it shall please the Lord by death to separate us. And then the woman in like manner: Friends, in the fear of the Lord, and before this assembly, I take this my friend C.D. to be my husband, promising, through divine assistance, to be unto him a loving and faithful wife, until it shall please the Lord by death to separate us."

This procedure is stated in a minute of the London Yearly Meeting of 1754, and it probably shortened the procedure as stated in 1675; but in both cases, latitude of expression was permitted. The 1754 minute also repeats the earlier provision for a "certificate" to be signed by the bride and groom, the relatives, "and such others present at the solemnity as think proper." This certificate is couched in almost the same language as the Krefeld certificate, but is much shorter; and in the space for the signers, following the names of the bride and groom, are the words: "We who were present, among others, at the abovesaid marriage, have also subscribed our names as witnesses thereunto, the day and year above written." It may be, therefore, that the Krefeld signatures do not include the names of *all* who were present at the wedding.

The Krefeld Marriage Certificate

The wedding was attested by a marriage certificate written in Dutch, which gives the usual details and which, translated, reads as follows:[254]

"A certificate for Derick Isacks and NölekenVijten regarding their marriage

"This serves to notify all whom it may concern that Derick Isacks, bachelor (*Jongman*), a native burger's son of Krevel, and Nöleken Vijten, spinstress (*Jonge dochter*), born in Kempen, having informed the people of God called Quakers in Krevell that they proposed to enter into the state of matrimony with each other, also that they are free of [engagements with] all other persons, this having been also noted in the Book of the meeting of the aforementioned people, and in accordance with their desire to have the same published in a public meeting of the aforementioned people: It was accordingly consented to that their proposal may be published in the public meeting [for worship] and that, if no hindrance (*Belet*) should then arise against their proposed marriage, it may be fulfilled at a suitable time and according to the good order which is observed among the aforementioned people; which public announcement having been made in two public meetings, the first one held on the 9th. day of the 2nd. Month, and the second on the 9th. day

---

[254] See Frontispiece and Appendix D (pp. 422–423).

of the 3rd. Month, 1681, and thus having been circulated and made known (*rŭgbaar en kennelick*) both to the burgers and to [all] the inhabitants of this city; and no hindrance [to the marriage] having appeared, we the undersigned hereof do testify that they, namely, derick Isacks and Nöleken Vijten, appeared in a public meeting of the aforementioned people appointed for that purpose, and then and there in the presence of the Lord and of us all confirmed (*bevestigt*) their marriage on the 20th. day of the 3rd. Month, 1681, in krevell, he, Derick Isack declaring in the following words, saying, Friends and People, it having been announced twice within six weeks in this place, in our public meeting, that I, D.I., and N.V. were resolved to enter into the marriage state with each other, and nothing having arisen as a hindrance thereto, we propose to proceed therein to affirm and confirm (*betŭigen en bevestigen*) the same in a godly and christian manner before god and Men, as we now do in the presence of the great God, the god of abraham, Isack and Jacob, the God who created the heaven, the earth, the sea and all that is thereon and therein, and who still daily sustains the same through the power of his word (*door het wordt seiner kragt*): I say, Friends, in your presence, and in the presence of all who are here assembled, I, Derick Isack, take you (*ŭ*) Nöleken Vijten to be my wife (*Echte vroŭ*) and promise, in sincerity, fidelity and the fear of God, to dwell with you and not to forsake you until God almighty shall command us through death to separate from each other—And she, Nöleken Vijten, declared, saying, Friends, by this promise (*Beloften*) and in the presence of the living God, the God of heaven and of earth, and in the presence of this assembly, I Nöleken Vijten, take Derick Isacks for my husband (*Echte Man*) and promise in the fear of God to be faithful to him and not to forsake him until the Lord shall command us through death to separate from each other.''

Thus ends the certificate, and the signatures of the bride and groom and witnesses immediately follow as given below, the men's names in a column on the left and the women's on the right.

Derick Isacks   nölken Vijtten
Herman Isacks   Greitijen peters
Abraham Isacks   Liesbet Isacks
Tunnes Keŭnen   margrit Isacks
Herman Daŭrss   Jenneken (?) Jansen
henderijck Janssen   lijntijen teissen
Veit Scherkes   Judit preijers
Jan Siemes   mercken willems
Wolter Siemes
Lenart Arents
Johannes blijkers

This quaint marriage-certificate is of unique historical interest. In the first place it is, so far as known, the only extant marriage-certificate issued by a meeting of Friends on the continent of Europe. It was the first and probably the last marriage-certificate issued by the Krefeld Monthly Meeting of Friends; and it reveals the fact that this meeting, like its sister-meetings everywhere, had the supervision of marriages within its care as early as the 2nd. Month, 1681, and recorded this supervision in its [Monthly ?] Meeting Minute-Book. The further facts that the certificate was written in the Dutch Language, was awarded to such a good Dutch-named couple as Derick Isacks and Nöleken Vijten, and was signed by nineteen persons (nearly the entire membership of the meeting, according to Roger Longworth in 1681), all of whom bore good Dutch names, are evidence of the close proximity of the Dutch ancestry and perhaps Dutch nativity of the members of the Krefeld meeting. Finally, nearly all of the signers of the certificate emigrated from Krefeld to Pennsylvania as a single religious community and became the pioneers who settled the so-called colony of ''Germantown.''[255]

THE ISAACS OP DEN GRAEFF FAMILY

The bride-groom, Derick Isacks, was one of three sons, members of a family well-known in Pennsylvania colonial

---

[255] Familiarity of usage makes this name appear less uncouth than "Dutchtown", or "Hollandtown", or "Netherlandstown", or "New Krefeld", any one of which would have been historically more appropriate.

history under the name of Op den Graeff.[256] Their grand-father, Herman, was born in 1585 of Mennonite parents in the village of Aldekerk, a village with a Dutch name and Dutch inhabitants about twelve miles from Krefeld. Re-moving to the latter place, Herman married there in 1615, a Mennonite girl, named Greitijen Pletjes, a daughter of Pletjes Driessen of Kempen, another small town halfway between Aldekerk and Krefeld.[257] Herman died in 1642, his widow following him the next year, and leaving behind them eighteen children.[258]

One of these children, Isack Hermans, was born in Kre-feld in 1616; married Greitijen Peters, and died in 1679, having become converted along with his family to Quaker-ism. The family comprised after his death the widow, three sons (Derick, Herman and Abraham), and one daughter (Margrit).

The family's ancestral ties to the Mennonites must have been strong ones, their ancestors having been prominent members of that sect. The grandfather, Herman, for ex-ample, was the delegate from Krefeld to the council held in Dordrecht, in 1632, which adopted the Mennonite Confes-sion of Faith. But, under the persuasive preaching of Ames and Caton, or Crisp and Longworth, the family was con-verted to Quakerism and endured the fines and distraints which harassed the Quakers in the Rhineland for a score of years.

It is possible that Derick was óne of the Krefeld exiles of 1679; but if so, he was readmitted to the town and per-mitted, in 1681, to have a public wedding in accordance with the Quaker ceremony. His name stands first on the mar-riage-certificate; and opposite it is that of his bride, signed, nölken Vijtten. It is possible that the latter was a daughter

---

[256] *Graaf,* so spelled in modern Dutch, means count; and *Graafschaf,* county or country. Perhaps Herman Isaacs was so-called in Krefeld partly because he had come into the town from the county, and partly in order to distinguish him and his family from the Krefeld family of Isaacs van Bebber. Op den Graeff, or Graaf, is a common suffix to names in Holland; in the forms also of van Graef, van de Graeff and van der Graeff, it is found among many families of Huguenot descent in Dordrecht, The Hague, etc.

[257] Kempen is supposed to have been the birth-place of Thomas à Kempis, in 1471.

[258] The Schenten MSS.

of Veit Scherkes, who also signed the certificate. Next below the bride's name, comes that of the bridegroom's mother, *Greitijen peters;* and below hers are those of her son Herman's wife, *Liesbet Isacks* (van Bebber), and of her daughter, *Margrit Isacks;* while in the opposite column, below the groom's, are those of his two brothers, Herman and Abraham.

Greitijen, the mother, accompanied her children on the ship "Concord" to Philadelphia in October, 1683, but died in that city on the 19th. of November following and was buried there before the settlement was completed in Germantown. This news is given in a letter of her son Herman to a correspondent in Holland, and dated in Germantown the 12th. of February, 1684;[259] while Francis Daniel Pastorius, in a letter dated March 7, 1684, says: "Of the people from Crefeld, no one has died except the aged mother of Herman op de Graeff, who having had enough of these earthly vanities, soon after her arrival here went to enjoy the heavenly bliss."

Greitijen's daughter, Margrit, was married in Germantown, after her mother's death, to Pieter Schumacher the Younger, her marriage-certificate being witnessed among others, by "Frances Daniell prestoreys [Pastorius]."[260] Margrit's father-in-law, Pieter Schumacher the Elder of Krisheim, arrived in Germantown in 1685, being assisted to do so by Dirck Sipman of Krefeld, and becoming a tenant of Herman Isacks op den Graeff.

DERICK ISAACS OP DEN GRAEFF

Derick, the eldest of the three Isacks brothers, was the leader of the thirteen heads of families and thirty-three colonists who settled Germantown in 1683. On their way through Rotterdam in June of that year, the three brothers purchased jointly, through Penn's agents, Jacob Telner, then of Krefeld, and Benjamin Furly, of Rotterdam, 2,000

---

[259] The Könneken MSS., No. 7. This letter is attributed also to Abraham op den Graeff, coupled with the legend that an Indian squaw, who appeared when it was being written and was curious as to writing, was permitted to hold the pen while her hand was guided in tracing the words which told of the white sister's death.

[260] Records of Abington Monthly Meeting of Friends.

acres of land in the virgin colony. When they arrived in Germantown, Derick and his brothers settled on adjoining lots, set up their Krefeld trade of linen-weaving, and proceeded to participate actively and prominently in public and religious affairs.

In 1688, when the first petition against human slavery was presented to the Dublin Monthly Meeting by the Friends' Meeting in Germantown, "derick op de graeff" is the second signature upon it.[261] When it was referred by the Dublin Monthly Meeting to the Philadelphia Quarterly Meeting, as being "so weighty that we think it not Expedient for us to meddle with it here", the Quarterly Meeting adopted the following minute: "This above mentioned was Read in our Quarterly Meeting at Philadelphia the 4 of ye 4 mo. '88, and was from thence recommended to the Yearly Meeting, and the abovesaid Derick and the other two [there were three others] mentioned therein, to present the same to ye above-said meeting, it being a thing of too great a weight for this meeting to determine." Derick and his colleagues duly presented the petition to the Yearly Meeting, held at Burlington, three months later; but that meeting "adjudged it not to be so proper for this Meeting to give a Positive Judgment in the case, It having so General a Relation to many other Parts [of the Province and the World], and therefore, at present, they forbear it."

This appeal against human slavery on which Derick's name stood second was of even more historic interest than the list of signers of the marriage-certificate on which his name stood first. Although "way did not open" for its adoption at once, it sowed the seed which was to ripen in the next century, in the time of John Woolman, the Quaker apostle of freedom, into complete emancipation of the slaves among the Quakers; and the century after that into the nation-wide abolition of slavery by the proclamation of Abraham Lincoln, another scion of a Pennsylvania Quaker family.[262]

---

[261] Cf. *infra*, p. 294.

[262] It is noteworthy, too, that it was a Pennsylvania society which presented to the Congress of the United States, in 1790, its first anti-slavery petition, and that this petition received the support of Pennsylvania's Dutch and German members of congress.

The disappointment of the petitioners of 1688 is voiced by the Quaker poet, John G. Whittier, who puts the following words into the mouth of "The Pennsylvania Pilgrim":

"Dear heart, he said, our folk
"Are even as others. Yea, our goodliest Friends
"Are frail; our elders have their selfish ends,
"And few dare trust the Lord to make amends
"For duty's loss. So even our feeble word
"For the dumb slaves the startled meeting heard
"As if a stone its quiet waters stirred;
"And as the clerk ceased reading, there began
"A ripple of dissent which downward ran
"In widening circles, as from man to man.
"Somewhat was said of running before sent,
"Of tender fear that some their guide outwent,
"Troublers of Israel. I was scarce intent
"On hearing, for behind the reverend row
"Of gallery Friends, in dumb and piteous show,
"I saw, methought, dark faces full of woe.
"And in the spirit, I was taken where
"They toiled and suffered; I was made aware
"Of shame and wrath and anguish and despair!
"And while the meeting smothered our poor plea
"With cautious phrase, a Voice there seemed to be,
" 'As ye have done to these ye do to me!'
"So it all passed; and the old tithe went on
"Of anise, mint and cumin, till the sun
"Set, leaving still the weightier work undone."

The poet ascribes the reply to this depondency to the wife of Pastorius, who is made to speak as follows:

"So may the seed which hath been sown today
"Grow with the years, and, after long delay,
"Break into bloom, and God's eternal Yea
"Answer at last the patient prayers of them
"Who now, by faith alone, behold its stem
"Crowned with the flowers of Freedom's diadem."

But it might well have been the wife of Derick himself who painted the bow of promise. Derick was evidently not too bitterly or too permanently disappointed by the rejection of his anti-slavery petition; for he remained a member of the Friends' meeting in Germantown, and when the Keithian controversy arose, he sided with the conservative Friends, although his brothers, Herman and Abraham, sided with George Keith. Keith was so incensed with Derick's activity against him that he called him, in a moment of anger during a public meeting (although Derick was a high official at the time), an "impudent rascal." When Keith was "disowned" by the Yearly Meeting in Burlington, in 1692, Derick was one of the signers of the "certificate of disownment"; and the next year, he signed Philadelphia Quarterly Meeting's certified statement of the case to London Yearly Meeting.

Meanwhile, Derick took a prominent part in the affairs of the colony. In 1689, Penn granted a charter for the "German Towne" to "Dirk Jsaacs Opte Graeff Linnenmaker" and his ten associates, and appointed him and three others to be the first burgesses. In 1692, he was one of the town's six "committeemen"; the next year, he served as bailiff, the town's chief executive; and the year after that, he was appointed to conserve the town's right of exemption, under its charter, from taxation.

The eldest of the brothers, Derick was the first to die, in May, 1697; and he left to mourn his loss, his Krefeld bride of 1681, whose name of Nöleken had suffered a sea-change like his own and become *Nilcken* or *Nieltje*. The date of Nöleken's death is not known; and she and Derick apparently had no children.[263]

The pioneer Quaker bride and groom of Krefeld in 1681, who had become pioneers also in the settlement of a colony in the Promised Land of Pennsylvania, doubtless continued to believe, as the successive wars of Louis XIV rolled over Europe, that they had acted wisely in exiling themselves from their native Rhineland and in building their home anew in a land of peace and plenty. But it may well be supposed that in their forest-home, they had many a home-sick thought for the scenes of their nativity, their courtship and marriage. As Whittier in his "Pennsylvania Pilgrim" suggests:

---

[263] Their marriage-certificate is now in possession of one branch of the Teissen, or Tyson, family (cf. *supra*, pp. IX, XIII).

"Or, talking of old home scenes, Op den Graff
"Teased the low back-log with his shodden staff
"Till the red embers broke into a laugh
"And dance of flame, as if they fain would cheer
"The rugged face, half tender half austere,
"Touched with the pathos of a home-sick tear."

HERMAN ISAACS OP DEN GRAEFF

Herman Isacks, the second of the brothers, was one of the Krefeld exiles of 1679 and one of the authors of the "Remonstrance". Readmitted to Krefeld, we find his name second on the marriage-certificate of his brother Derick, and in the opposite column the name of his wife, Liesbet Isacks (van Bebber). Liesbet was a daughter of Jacob Isacks van Bebber, of Krefeld, who was one of the first purchasers of land in Pennsylvania, and a sister of Matthias Isacks van Bebber who bought four or five thousand acres of land in the vicinity of Germantown and founded Bebber Township.

Herman and his wife were among the pioneer settlers of Germantown in 1683; and there is extant a letter, in a German version of the Dutch original, which was written by one of the three brothers, probably Herman, and which gives a brief account of the voyage and settlement. This is dated from Germantown, the 12th. of February, 1684, and is in part as follows:[264] "We sailed from England to America in six weeks. The blessings of the Lord did attend us so that we had a wonderfully prosperous voyage. Upon our whole voyage we did not experience as much inconvenience as between Holland and England. . . . Our number did not decrease upon the ocean, but was increased by two, a son and a daughter. The mothers were easy in labor and were soon well again."

There follows some account of the infant Philadelphia, its religions, buildings, laborers ("with Blacks or Moors also as slaves to labor"). The land is described, with its allotments, trees and timber, grape-vines, pasturage, cattle and pigs; also "our city of Germantown", with its rivers and valleys. "The Indians", the writer says, "show them-

---

[264] Könneken MSS., No. 7; see *infra*, p. 315.

selves very kind and friendly, and we live together with them very quiet and peaceable. We travel day and night through the forest without the least fear of them. Most of us have already our own habitations, and every day more good houses are being built, all of which pleases us greatly. ... We have begun to spin flax.''

In addition to his part in the family's linen industry in Germantown and in farming his own land, Herman became the agent for the large land-holdings of Jacob Telner and Dirck Sipman, others of the Krefeld purchasers. He was one of the eleven men to whom Penn granted the charter of Germantown in 1689, being named in it ''Hermann Isaacs opte Graef, towne President''; and he was chosen one of the town's first four burgesses.

When the Keithian controversy broke out in 1692, Herman and Abraham, unlike their brother Derick, sided with Keith, and signed a ''testimony'' in his favor. Even after the Yearly Meeting at Burlington had ''disowned'' Keith, Herman was one of sixty-nine adherents of Keith who signed a paper defending him.

In consequence of this, Herman as well as Abraham appears to have lost favor among his neighbors during the few remaining years of his life, and we catch but fleeting glimpses of him. His fences were condemned, in 1696, as insufficient, and he is not recorded as having held any more elective offices. He was called to serve on a jury in a homicide case, in 1701; and he died in that year or the next, leaving his land to Abraham, his only surviving brother.[265] The date of the death of his widow, Liesbet, is not known; and she and Herman, like Nöleken and Derick, appear to have left no descendants.

ABRAHAM ISAACS OP DEN GRAEFF

Abraham, the youngest of the three brothers, signed Derick's marriage-certificate, in 1681, but it is not known when he himself was married. His wife's name does not appear upon the certificate, nor is her family name known; but her first name was *Catharina,* according to a deed of land

---

[265] There appears to be some discrepancy in the records in regard to the date of his death; cf. *Pa. Magazine,* V (1881), p. 252.

made in 1685, or *Trijntje* (a diminutive of Catharina) as it is given in a deed in 1704.

Abraham was one of the thirteen "heads of families" who founded Germantown in 1683; and the first decade of his residence in the new home beyond the seas was evidently filled with useful activities. He and his brothers transferred their weaving industry to Germantown, and were largely responsible for making it famous, as a contemporary puts it,[266] for "very fine German Linen, such as no person of Quality need be ashamed to wear." Indeed, it is claimed for Abraham that he was the most skilled of all Germantown's "High German People and Low Dutch, Whose Trade in weaving Linnen Cloth is much." We find him in 1686 among the competitors "for ye Govr's promise to him [who] should make the first and finest pece of linnen Cloath."

Two years later (1688) he was one of the four signers of the anti-slavery petition of that year. The next year, he was one of the eleven men to whom Penn granted a charter for Germantown,[267] and in that charter he was one of the six men appointed to serve as the first "committee-men." He served the town as burgess in 1692; and he was a member of the colonial assembly in 1689, 1690 and 1692.

But in this last year, the controversy kindled among the Quakers by George Keith began, and the brothers took opposite sides in it. Abraham and Herman supported Keith, while Derick sided with the conservative Quakers. When the latter repudiated Keith, in 1693, Abraham was one of five who joined with Keith in issuing a printed "Appeal" against the Quaker meeting and the Quaker Government.

Although it does not appear that the Friends "disowned" Abraham, it would seem that he fell back into his ancestral Mennonite society, and when he died was buried in the Mennonite graveyard near Evansburg, Pennsylvania. Part of his Germantown land (fifty acres), however, was conveyed in 1690 to Jacob Shoemaker, who conveyed it (in 1693) to the Germantown Friends for their first meeting-house.[268]

---

[266] Gabriel Thomas "Province . . . . of Pennsylvania", 1698.

[267] In this charter, he is called "Abraham Isaacs opte Graef."

[268] This was probably built of wood in 1693, and was succeeded in 1705 by a stone one which stood until 1812; the third one lasted from 1812 until 1871, when the existing (fourth) one was built.

His last years were marked, also, by difficulties with the civil government. The fence-overseers condemned his fences, in 1696, as insufficient. His son, Jacob, "borrowed" a neighbor's horse without permission, in 1701, and was fined a half-crown therefor, while Abraham was condemned to pay the costs of the legal action involved. He quarreled with the sheriff about these costs; and two years later, "did mightily abuse the Bailiff in open court", and was fined £2 : 10 s. for so doing. The next year (1704), he was sued by a neighbor for money due on purchased goods, and after a court-action had the debt arbitrated. That same year, an old Krefeld neighbor and fellow-pilgrim, Veit, or David Scherkes, declared that "no honest man would be in Abraham's company"; and when Abraham sued him for slander, David was acquitted.

These successive troubles apparently caused him and his wife to sell their brick house and 828 acres in Germantown, and remove to the neighboring Perkiomen. His brothers, Derick and Hermann, had died, in 1697 and 1701, respectively, and all of the 2,000 acres purchased by the three brothers reverted to Abraham, the survivor. Having sold the land in Germantown, Abraham laid out the remaining 1,200 acres on the Perkiomen Creek, and here spent the rest of his days.

Abraham and Tryntje's children were four in number, namely, Isaac, Jacob, Margaret and Anne. The descendants of the sons bear the names of Updegraf, Updegrave and Updegrove. Anne became the wife of a neighbor's son, Herman in de Hoffen; while Margaret married Thomas Howe, a tailor in Germantown. The last glimpse we have of Abraham comes from 1709, when he conveyed 300 acres of land on the Perkiomen to Margaret and her husband, on condition that they should take good care of him until his death.

Thones Kunders

Besides the seven members of the Isacks op den Graeff family who signed the marriage-certificate of 1681, there are twelve other Dutch Quakers of Krefeld and Pennsylvania whose signatures are on it. One of these was *Tunnes (?) Keŭnen,* as he signed his name on the certificate; or Tünis Künders, as it is said to appear in other Krefeld sources;[269] or Thones Kunders, as he was better known in his transatlantic home. Nearly opposite his on the certificate, is the name of *lijntijen teissen,* who was Thones' wife. *Lijntijen* is a diminutive of Helena and of Magdalena; and an American descendant of Thones and his wife[270] says of them: ''Among the number on the ship 'Concord' was Thones Kunders, a man at that time presumably of twenty-five or thirty years of age, and his wife, *Elin,* supposed to have been a sister of William Streypers, the latter being also one of the emigrants.'' Other Pennsylvania writers have referred to Kunders's wife as one of Streyper's sisters;[271] but *Elin* [Ellen], like *Lijntijen* is a form of Helen or Helena, and of Magdalena (the Hebrew Magdala). The latter form was probably the name given her by her Bible-minded, Dutch Quaker parents.[272]

Thones and Lijntijen Kunders were among the Krefeld pioneers who founded Germantown in 1683. In the house which he built there, which was doubtless at first a very crude structure, the Krefeld Quaker settlers held their first meetings for worship in the strange new world;[273] and in it the first slavery protest was signed in 1688. The land which he purchased appears to have fronted on the beautiful creek known by its Indian name of the Wissahickon; and some eighty acres of this land he and his wife sold in 1719–20 to

---

[269] Friedrich Kapp, "Franz Daniel Pastorius' Beschreibung von Pennsylvanien", Crefeld, 1884. Pastorius calls him Thones, also, Denis, Kunders.

[270] Henry C. Conrad (of Wilmington, Delaware), "Thones Kunders and his Children", Wilmington, 1891, p. 6.

[271] The Kunders' youngest son, Henry, was married in 1710 to Katherine, a daughter of Willem Streypers; and their daughter, Ann, was married in 1715 to Leonard Streypers, presumably a son of Willem.

[272] A granddaughter of the Kunders (the daughter of their second son, Madtis, or Mathias) was named Magdalen.

[273] Part of the walls of this house were still standing in 1891, at No. 4537 (in 1923, No. 5109) Germantown Avenue. In his will, dated June 19, 1722, "Dennis Kunders" made as his last bequest: "The bed and furniture Standing in the New Room To be for the use of friends."

Johannes Gumre and "the Congregation of the Brethren", popularly known as the Dunkards, or Tunkers.

In 1689, he was one of the eleven citizens to whom Penn granted a charter for the town, and was appointed in that document to serve as one of the burgesses, his name being spelled in the charter, Tenis Coenderts and Tünes Cunders. Two years later, "Touniss Kunders" was elected one of the *Fens-besichtger,* or fence-viewers. In 1696, he served the town as recorder; and in 1704 we find him serving on a Germantown jury. He died, according to a contemporary Quaker journalist,[274] in 1729.

Three of the Kunders' six children, namely, Cunraed, Madtis (Mathias) and Jan, were born in Krefeld between May, 1678, and June, 1681, and were brought with their parents to Pennsylvania; the other three, Ann, Agnes and Henry, were born in Germantown between May, 1684, and December, 1688. Several of them and their children attended the school set up by Pastorius about 1700. The descendants, who are numerous, adopted the English custom of taking their father's last name as their own; but they "made names for themselves" in several ways, and adopted various forms of his, such as Conard, Conrad, Cunard, etc. One of these descendants was Samuel Cunard, the founder in 1838 of the first regular steamship service across the Atlantic. Beginning with the *Britannia,* the famous Cunard Liners have culminated, for the present at least, in the mighty *Berengaria.* Thones Kunders, a passenger on the *Concord* in 1683, would have contrasted in amazement its 500 tons and capacity of 180 passengers and 40 crew with the *Berengaria's* 52,226 tons and capacity of 2911 passengers and 949 crew; he could not have believed either that the *Berengaria,* running $22\frac{1}{2}$ knots per hour, crosses the Atlantic in less than as many days as the *Concord* took weeks.

REINERT TEISSEN

Lijntijen Teissen's brother Reinert was also a Krefeld Quaker and one of the pioneer settlers of Germantown in 1683. His name does not appear upon the marriage-certifi-

---

[274] Thomas Chalkley's "Journal". Chalkley calls him *Dennis Conrad.*

cate of 1681, for the reason, perhaps, that although he became a man of large wealth and much influence he is said never to have learned to write his name; hence he too may have attended the famous wedding, but if so he left no memorial of the fact.[275]

He does not appear to have been married at the time of his emigration to Pennsylvania, but was married later, probably in Philadelphia, to an English colonist's daughter, Maria ————. It was perhaps due to her influence that he was one of the sixty-four citizens of Germantown to whom Penn's Deputy Governor, Thomas Lloyd, granted naturalization papers on the 7th. of 5th. Month, 1684. He also promptly built a house, which evidently became a kind of public center, since we find it used as a place of public auction in 1692.[276] He had already been elected, the year before, the first of four burgesses, and he filled that office in 1692, 1693, 1694, and 1696. His fencing was found insufficient, in 1696; and he performed jury service in 1701. By 1702, his children were old enough to be sent to Francis Pastorius' school. Such are the meagre notices concerning him on the public records.

Reyner's religious activities led him to participate in the opposition of the Friends to the Keithian Schism, and his is one of the four names of Germantown Friends which appear on the Quarterly Meeting's statement of the case which was sent to London Yearly Meeting, in 1693; and it appears also on the testimony issued against Keith by the Philadelphia Yearly Meeting in 1692. Other small evidences of his Quakerly activities are the extant records that in 1715 he was appointed by the Germantown Monthly Meeting one of its three representatives to the Quarterly Meeting; in 1725, he was made an elder by Abington Monthly Meeting; and in 1735, "Ryner Tyson, senior", was appointed with two

---

[275] Charles F. Jenkins, in a note in the *Pennsylvania Magazine*, Vol. 14 (1890), pp. 326–7, attributes to his illiteracy the varied forms of his name, which he has found spelled in Pennsylvania documents as follows: Reynear, Rynear, Reyner, Rhiner, Rheinert, Reinert, Reinier, Reynier, and Reiner, and Tyson, Thysen, Tisen, Tysen and Tissen. Perhaps it was because of such an embarrassment of choice that he refrained from writing it at all!

[276] Perhaps he was himself for a time the auctioneer.

other Friends by his Monthly Meeting "to visit families of Friends for the promotion of the religious concerns of the Society."[277]

An obituary notice of him says:[278] "He continued faithful to the manifestations of Truth received, and grew in the esteem of his friends to be a father in the church. In the year 1725, he was appointed an elder, and continued faithful in fufilling the duties of the station until prevented by age and indisposition. His friends say: 'He was innocent and inoffensive in life and conversation and diligent in attending his religious meetings.' He lived beloved and honoured to a good old age, dying the 27th. of 7th. Month, 1745, aged about eighty-six years."

Although he does not appear to have been prominent in connection with the Anti-Slavery Petition drawn up by the Germantown Friends in 1688, we may well suppose that "freedom for the slave" was a familiar and ardent topic in his family for several generations. His great-grandson, Elisha Tyson, who was born in a house standing on the site of Ryner's original homestead five years after Ryner's death, removed when a young man to Baltimore, Maryland, and there, in the midst of a strong pro-slavery and slave-owning community, devoted his wealth and influence for nearly a half-century to an indefatigable and highly successful defense of the Negro slave and freedman.

CORNELIS TEISSEN

Another of the Teissen family, Cornelis, who was probably a younger brother or nephew of Ryner, removed from Krefeld to Germantown in 1703. He died there thirteen years later, and over his grave in Axe's graveyard, Germantown, Francis Daniel Pastorius erected what is said to be the oldest existing tombstone in memory of a Dutch or German emigrant to Pennsylvania. It bears an inscription, probably composed by Pastorius, (with echoes of Latin, German, Dutch, and English) as follows:

---

[277] *Friends' Miscellany*, Vol. 8: 285 and Vol. 9: 30.
[278] *The Friend*, Philadelphia, Vol. 30 (1857), p. 229.

"Obijt Meiy 9, 1716	Died May 9, 1716
"Cornelis Tiesen	Cornelis Tiesen
"Out 63. Jaer	Aged 63 years
"Salig sin de doon [dood]	Blessed are the dead
"Die in den Here sterve	Who die in the Lord
"Theilric is haer Kroon	Hallowed is their Crown
"Tgloriric haer erve."[279]	Glorious their inheritance.

JAN LUYKENS

Ryner Teissen's sister Maria married Jan Luykens, another of the Krefeld Quakers, who did not sign the marriage-certificate of 1681, but who was one of the pioneer settlers of Germantown in 1683. Jan served as constable of the town in 1691–95, as sheriff in 1694–95, and lived until 1744. The Dutch Bible which he brought with him from Krefeld is in the possession of one of his descendants, and the original of his will (dated 9th. of 8th. Month, 1741) is preserved in Philadelphia's Registry of Wills. The inventory of his estate is preserved with his will and it gives a vivid picture of some aspects of the daily lives of the well-to-do colonists. It is as follows :[280]

An Inventory of all & Singular the Goods Chattels and Creditts of John Lucken, late of Germantown Deceased, appraised the 24th of the 11th mo. 1744 by Mathias Adams and John Johnson.

	Pounds	Shillings	Pence
To his Wearing apparrel	11	10	
Bed Bedstead & Bedding	5		
Another Bed Bedstead &c	3	15	
Some more Beding	1	10	
Two old spinning wheels		7	
Four old bags		4	
Three old Barrels old Iron & things in the Garret		10	
A Bedcase		7	
70 yds Whitned linen at 2/3 P yd	7	17	6
36 yds Brown linen at 2/ P yd	3	12	
9½ lb. of fine yarn at 3/3 p yd	1	10	10
10 lb. of white yarn at 3/ P yd	1	10	

---

[279] S. W. Pennypacker's "Settlement of Germantown," Philadelphia, 1899, p. 140 (note) ; a photograph of the tombstone on the facing page shows some discrepancy in Judge Pennypacker's transcription.

[280] Contributed by Annie Lukens Daniels, a graduate of Swarthmore College and a lineal descendant of Jan Luykens.

A little bundle of Tow yarn		3	
3½ yards of worsted & linen at 3/ P yd		10	6
Two old sheets & a pillow case		9	
A Cupboard		15	
Two Blankets old		12	
An Oak Table		8	
6 chairs and three wooden stools	1		
Half a Dᵒ Knives & forks		3	
a pair of scales & weights		3	
A maul 2 wedges & an ax		6	
14 yds of Linen at 2/3 P yd	1	11	6
8 sheets	2		
4 yds striped linen at 3/ P yd		12	
4 old Table cloaths		8	
To 8 old pillow cases		12	
4 Towels		2	
2 lb. or better of thread		10	
Three Remnants of new linen		6	
a Cupboard		15	
26 lb. of Linen yarn at 2/ P lb.	2	12	
Some potts and pans		15	
And-Irons Shovel & Tongs and old Grid Iron		7	6
Mortar, Pestil, Choping knive flesh fork & ladle		9	
A Box with several Iron tools		11	
Some Books		10	
A Reel [for spinning?] a Cagg & an earthen Jug		3	
a parcel of pewter	2		
Some earthenware & Trenchers & a parcel of Bottles		10	
A Barrel 2 Cags & a peal [a baker's shovel?]		4	
an old Dresser		5	
a wheel-barrow Hoes, fork & some Tools &c		10	
Some half priced Bord		5	
A Cow & some Hay for fodder	2	10	
Money Scales & weights to ᵗʰ two Boxes		7	
Some Remnants of linen & some yearn		8	
a Chest		7	
Cash	9	4	
Bond, Bills, Notes &c	846	15	2
The House & Lott in Germantown	170		
Two Hundred acres of Land Joyning Spipenk	200		

Sum £ 1287   12

Appraised by us { Mathias Adams
{ Jⁿ Johnson

The progress which was made in the accumulation of material goods by the colonists, as evidenced by the above inventory, may be measured also by the list of the personal possessions of Enneke Klostermann in 1688 when she married Francis Daniel Pastorius. This list was made by the latter, and is as follows:[281] 50 acres of land and a house-lot in Germantown (for which she paid a yearly rent to the Frankfort Company); "in silver coins: 36 Reichsthaler or 10 £ 16 s. of this land (*disslandisch*)"; "in house-furnishings": 1 new chest; 1 spinning-wheel and reel; "in books": 3 "edifying writings" (*erbauliche Schriften*); [282] in clothing: 1 black silk cape (*Kaper*) 12 s.; 3 bodices (*reichleiber*); 1 pair of cloth sleeves (*zeugerne Ermel*); 1 cloth smock (*tüchern hembdrock*); 2 black serge pinafores (*gronrasch Leibergen*); 1 black serge apron; 1 blue linen apron; 6 apron bands (*Schürtzeltücher*); 2 blue gowns; 3 pairs of striped stockings; 2 pairs of shoes, and 1 pair of slippers; "in linen goods": 1 yard of muslin (*Nesseltuch*); 11 Hollands ells of fine linen; 8 chemises; 8 towels (? *Nastücher*); 3 bed-sheets; 4 napkins; 5 neckerchiefs; 4 suits of underclothes; 6 wimples (*Kroplappen*); 5 sun-shades; 5 caps; 18 dust-caps (*Dreckmützen*).

Jan Luykens's wife, Maria, lived until 1742, and twenty-six years before her death witnessed the marriage of her daughter Hannah to John Samuel, the elder son of Francis Daniel Pastorius. Jan and Maria Luykens had five daughters and six sons, and the American family of Luykens, or Lukens, is very numerous.

HERMAN DAÜRSS

Herman Daürss, whose name follows that of Thones Kunders (Tunnes Keünen) on the marriage-certificate of 1681, was not one of the pioneer emigrants to Germantown in 1683, but he arrived there the next year. Twenty years later, he acted as witness (under the name of Herman Dors)

---

[281] „Res Propriae", p. 33. Quoted by Seidensticker and Learned.

[282] These were *Jeremiah Dyckens* „Würdiger Tischgenoss (A Worthy Table-companion)"; *Saldenius* „Christliche Kinder-schuel (Christian Kindergarten)"; and „Christliches Gedenckbüchlein (Christian Remembrancer)."

in a suit for slander which Abraham Isacks op den Graef brought against Veit Scherkes; and as late as 1739, there occurs the following notice of his death: "One Herman Dorst near Germantown, A Batchelor past 80 years of Age, who for a long time lived in a House by himself, on the 14th Instant there dyed by himself."[283]

The name of Jenneken Jansen appears on the marriage-certificate of 1681, just opposite that of Herman Daürss, and it is possible that she was his wife. No trace is found of her in Pennsylvania's archives, and if she died before Herman's removal to Germantown, her illness in 1683 may have accounted for his not sailing in that year; while her death the next year would have enabled him to follow his Krefeld comrades to Germantown, but left him to live there the lonely life of a widower. It is true that the notice of his death refers to him as a "Batchelor"; but this term was loosely used for a "single" person, and he had lived unmarried in Pennsylvania for fifty-five years. Jenneken Jansen may have been a sister of Henderijck Jansen.

HENDERIJCK JANSSEN

Henderijck Janssen (or Henrik Jansz), who signed the marriage-certificate of 1681, was one of the Krefeld exiles of 1679, and co-author of the "Remonstrance". In this, he stated that he had resided in Krefeld for about six preceding years. When the rest of the wedding company emigrated to Germantown in 1683, Hendrik and his family remained in Krefeld, and were the last Quakers in that city. The Epistle of the Amsterdam Yearly Meeting in 1690 reports that there were two Friends still remaining in Krefeld; and the postscript of a letter from Pieter Hendricks to Steven Crisp, dated Amsterdam, the 23rd. of 6th. Month, 1692,[284] refers to these Krefeld Friends as "Hendrik Jansen, his wife and four children." It is possible that Hendrick Janssen was the son of Jan Hendriks of Worms and Krisheim, who had

---

[283] The *American Weekly Mercury*, October 18, 1739, and *The Pennsylvania Gazette*, quoted by I. Daniel Rupp, "Thirty Thousand Names", Philadelphia. 1875.

[284] Colchester MSS. 18, and Devonshire House "Copy-book", 16.

been converted to Quakerism by William Ames in 1657 and went with Ames four years later on a missionary tour to Danzig, where they were examined by the magistrates and banished from the city.

Judit Preijers, whose name appears on the certificate just opposite Hendrik Jansen's, may have been his wife, and therefore remained with him in Krefeld; no mention of her appears in the Pennsylvania records.

The Jansen clan was a numerous one, even among the Dutch Quakers; and it is difficult to trace their relationship with even approximate certainty. The four children of Hendrik Jansen doubtless followed the Dutch custom of taking their father's first name for their last one. There were several Quaker emigrants named Hendricks from the Rhineland to Germantown, and it may be that these were Hendrik's children, who left Krefeld after their parents' decease. The Germantown records state that Cornelis, Willem and Barnt Hendriks were landholders in the town; Willem received his citizenship in 1698, and was town constable in 1704; Cornelis served on a jury in 1704, and was constable in 1706; both sent children to the school kept by Pastorius, and both settled in 1708 in the township laid out by Matthias Isaacs van Bebber. Barnt settled in Germantown in 1703.

VEIT SCHERKES

Veit Scherkes is the next name after Henderijck Janssen's on the marriage-certificate of 1681; and indeed it would appear from the name of the bride, Nöleken Vijten, that she was Veit's own daughter. One of the first Friends in Krefeld, Veit was also a pioneer settler in Germantown, although he did not go with his fellow-Quakers of Krefeld in 1683, but followed them the next year. In Germantown's records, he is known as Vijt Sgerkis, David Scherkes, and David Scherges.[285] In 1691, he was *Schrief*, or sheriff; he sided with George Keith in the controversy which arose the next year; in 1704, Abraham Isacks op den Graeff sued him

---

[285] One of these forms may have been the origin of the wide-spread Pennsylvania name of Yerkes.

for slander, accusing him of having said that no honest man would be found in his (Abraham's) company. The jury acquitted Veit of this charge; but we hear no more of him in the town's history.

JAN AND WOLTER SIEMES

Jan Siemes signed the marriage-certificate of 1681, and was one of the thirteen pioneer heads of families who founded Germantown in 1683. He was the first of the (men) pioneers to die, probably in the winter of 1683–84. His wife, Mercken Willems, also signed the certificate of 1681 (just opposite the name of her husband), and accompanied him to Pennsylvania. Here, as his widow, she was married again in October 1685, to a member of Jan Luyken's family, and was afterwards referred to as Mercken Williamsen Lucken. She appears to have been the sister of Jan Willems Boekenoogen, a Quaker of Haarlem, who went to Pennsylvania in 1684.

Wolter Siemes [or Seimens ?], as he signed his name on the marriage-certificate of 1681, was doubtless a brother of Jan. He was not one of the original thirteen pioneers of 1683, but arrived in Germantown before November, 1684. Under the names of Walter Simens and Wolter Sijmens, we find him elected in 1691 to the office of public messenger and town-crier (*Bott v. Schreier*); in 1703, to that of constable; and serving in 1704 on a jury called to try a suit of Mattheus Smith against Abraham op den Graeff. He was one of the Dutch and German settlers naturalized by an act of the Assembly in 1708–09.

LENART ARENTS

Lenart Arents, the next signer of the marriage-certificate of 1681, was one of the Mennonite linen-weavers of Krefeld who were converted to Quakerism and emigrated to Pennsylvania in 1683. On June 10 and 11 of that year, he received from Penn a grant of 1,000 acres of land in the new colony. When the land was surveyed and formally allotted to the settlers, in May, 1684, Lenart received as his share 501 acres in Germantown. The preamble of Penn's deed for this reads as follows: "Whereas by my Indentures of Lease & Release bearing date the tenth & eleventh days of June in the year one thousand six hundred eighty three for the Considerations therein Mentioned I granted to Leonart Arretts then of Crevelt in the County of Meurs in the borders of Germany Linen Weaver (but now of Germantown in the sd Province) the quantity of one thousand acres of land to be laid out in the sd Province ...."[286]

"Lenert Arets" was one of Germantown's four burgesses in 1691 and again in 1706; and in 1704, he served on the jury in the suit for slander of Abraham op den Graeff against David Scherkes. His wife was a sister of Jan and Willem Streijpers,[287] of Kaldekerk (Kaldekirchen), a village near Krefeld, and probably members of the Friends' meeting in that place. Lenart's wife and brothers were cousins of the Isacks op den Graefs, but they did not sign the marriage-certificate of 1681; but his wife and her brother Willem went with the first Krefeld pilgrims to Germantown in June, 1683.

JAN AND WILLEM STREYPERS

Penn had granted to Jan Streypers 5,000 acres of land in March, 1682; and from this, Jan granted his younger brother Willem one hundred acres, and commissioned him to act as agent for his share of the linen industry which was to be set up in Germantown. In February, 1684, Willem wrote to Jan that the land had been allotted in Germantown, and he had settled on it, ready to clear and sow it and build a house, but that he had no resources as yet, and must have a year's equipment. Jan accordingly sent him the following articles: "Box with 3 combs, and 3 ——— [for spinning and weaving ?], and 5 shirts and a small parcel with iron ware for a weaving stool." He told him also to "let Jan Lensen weave a piece of cloth to sell, and apply it to your use." Eight months later, Willem wrote to his brother the cheerful news: "I have been busy and made a brave dwelling house, and under it a cellar fit to live in, and have so much grain, such as Indian Corn and Buckwheat that this winter

---

[286] Exempl. Rec. I, p. 708.
[287] This name is variously spelled in Pennsylvania records: Streijpers, Streypers, Streipers, Striepers, Streepers and Strepers.

I shall be better off than I was last year.''[288] By 1685, it is recorded, Willem Streypers was the owner of two pairs of leather breeches, two leather doublets, some handkerchiefs, stockings and a new hat. His prosperity increased so rapidly in the New World that his brother Jan wrote in 1687: ''I intend to come over myself.'' Jan did so, at some time before 1706, and signed a petition to the Assembly in that year to become a naturalized citizen of Pennsylvania. But evidently the call of his native land was too strong to be resisted, and he returned to Kaldekerk, where he entered upon the sole ownership of the family estate. As compensation to Willem for his share in this, Jan conveyed to him all his lands in Pennsylvania, amounting at the time to about one hundred acres more than the 5,000 of his original purchase. Willem, though now a considerable landowner, drops out of the records about this time,[289] and he may have died soon afterwards.

JOHANNES BLIJKERS

The last name on the marriage-certificate of 1681 is that of Johannes Blijkers. He was one of the Krefeld exiles of 1679; and on his return, he suffered the severe beating which Pieter Hendricks graphically describes in his letter of June, 1680.[290] By the following March, he had recovered sufficiently to attend the wedding-ceremony, and two years later, he accompanied the pioneers on the ''Concord'' to Germantown. His wife's name does not appear upon the marriage-certificate, and perhaps he was not married at that time. But he was married before the departure for Pennsylvania; and on the voyage across the Atlantic, his wife bore him a son, who was given the name of Pieter.[291] While en route in Rotterdam, Johannes bought through Benjamin Furly 200 acres of Penn's land; and a half dozen years later, he acquired fifty more acres in Germantown. Two years afterwards, he was chosen one of the town's four *Fens Besichtgers* (fence-viewers, boundary overseers). In

---

[288] Streper MSS.; quoted by Pennypacker, *op. cit.*, p. 26.
[289] He served as bailiff of Germantown in 1707.
[290] *Supra*, p. 200.
[291] Abington Meeting Records.

1702, he was one of the subscribers to the school opened by Pastorius; and in 1708–09, he was naturalized by an act of the Assembly.

WEDDING GUESTS AND COLONISTS

Having reviewed the signers of the Krefeld marriage-certificate of 1681, it is seen that seven of the eleven men who signed it, namely, the three Isacks op den Graeff brothers, Thones Kunders, Jan Siemes, Lenart Arents, and Johannes Blijkers, were among the thirteen men who were the pioneer settlers of Germantown in 1683. Three of the other men who signed the certificate, namely, Herman Daurss, Veit Scherkes and Wolter Siemes, settled in Germantown in 1684; and they may have been left behind partly for the purpose of completing necessary details of the emigration from the old home to the new.[292] Only one of the eleven men signers of the certificate, namely Henderijck Janssen, did not join the pioneers; but three of his children probably went to Germantown before or about 1700.

Six of the thirteen pioneers of 1683, namely, Reinert Teissen, Jan Luykens, Willem Streypers, Pieter Keurlis, Abraham Tunes, and Jan Lensen, did not sign the certificate of 1681; but they were all members of the Krefeld Quaker Community and were nearly all connected by blood or marriage with one or another of the wedding guests. Reinert Teissen (if indeed he was not present in person) was represented by one sister. Jan Luykens was the husband of another sister; Willem Streypers was a cousin of the Op den Graeffs, and his sister was the wife of Lenart Arents; Abraham Tunes was a relative of Thones Kunders.

Of the eight women who signed the certificate, six went as pioneers to Germantown in 1683; one (Jenneken Jansen) apparently died before the voyage was made; and only one (Judit Preijers) remained in Krefeld. The bride; the mother, sister and sister-in-law of the groom; the wives of Thones Kunders and Jan Siemes, all went with their menfolks on the great adventure. Thus the thirteen men and the twenty women and children who founded Germantown

---

[292] Cf. *infra*, p. 257.

were a single community, united by the ties of consan-
guinity, of a common ancestry and language (that of Holland), and of a common religion (that of the English
Quakers).

This flight of an entire religious congregation, the Pilgrim Fathers and the Pilgrim Mothers of Dutch descent,
from a land of persecution to a land of liberty was paral-
leled in the Seventeenth Century in both England and
America; but it was new, at least during that century, in
the annals of Continental Europe. Perhaps not in the history of colonization can be duplicated the story of the Krefeld Quaker wedding-party of 1681, from which were transplanted the bride and groom and nearly all the guests from
the banks of the Rhine to the valley of the Schuylkill![293]

The End of Quakerism in Krefeld

Meanwhile, the few Friends left in Krefeld continued to
suffer persecution. Pieter Hendricks in a letter to Roger
Longworth, dated Amsterdam, the 1st. of 12th. month, 1683,
says:[294] "At Crevel is also alles still, also in the paltz
[Palatinate] friends in the paltz as also som at Creveld
have som tauchts [thoughts] for pensilvania, butt wee
hoope that friends at the paltz will remaijn in thar place."
But farther on in this letter (the last item in it), Hendricks
adds: "After this was written resave wee letters from Crevelt that thij have robt friends of thaer goeds, moor than
iver bevoor."

Despite an Epistle of love and encouragement "to
Friends in Holland, . . . Crevelt, etc.," which Gertrud Deriks, one of the Amsterdam Friends who had visited Krefeld during the persecution of 1679–80, wrote and distributed among them in the form of a Dutch pamphlet,[295]
the Krefeld Friends were by no means re-assured that the

---

[293] The Pilgrims of Scrooby and Plymouth, the Puritan settlers of several
towns in Massachusetts and Connecticut, illustrate the migration of religious
congregations for colonization.

[294] Pemberton MSS., II, 43.

[295] Dated, Rotterdam, the 15th. of the 7th. Month, 1682, and printed without
place or date.

renewed persecution would soon come to an end. To strengthen them in standing firm, also, the Krefeld Quaker meeting was separated in 1683 from the Amsterdam Yearly Meeting (established in 1677) and made a constituent part of a Yearly Meeting for Friends in Germany. But this measure, too, was unsuccessful in checking the persecution.

It was partly because of it, no doubt, that Herman Daurss, Veit Scherkes and Wolter Siemes, in 1684, followed the pioneers of 1683 to Pennsylvania, leaving only Henderijck Janssen, his wife and children to "remaijn in thar place", as Pieter Hendricks expressed what might be called (rather inappropriately for pacifists) "holding the fort for Quakerism." It was of this emigration that the author of the Könneken Letter Number 8 wrote as follows:[296] "From Crefeldt, many more persons (as I learn) will come hither [to Philadelphia] in the near future. It seems as if God has great things in store for this place."

Two years later (the 16th. of 5th. Month, 1686, the Amsterdam Epistle reports: "The meeting of friends in the Palatinate [at Krisheim] is in effect dissolved, by reason that most of the friends of that place have removed themselves from thence to Pennsylvania .... The meeting that was at Crevelt is brought into the same condition; for they are likewise all, that were convinced of Truth, gone thither, except one man and his wife."

Two months after this was written, William Penn made a brief journey through the Rhineland, pleading for religious liberty, or at least toleration, for the persecuted, but at the same time making a strong bid for more recruits for his colony beyond the sea. He got many hundreds of these in subsequent years; but there were no more Dutch Quaker colonists to be procured in Krefeld. The Amsterdam Epistle of 1687 reports: "At Creveld there remains yet one man and his wife that bear a testimony for the Truth; and one single ancient Friend in the Palatinate [at Krisheim]; all the rest of Friends of both these places being gone to Pennsylvania." The Amsterdam Epistle of 1690 reports that there were two Friends still remaining at Crevelt; and the

---

[296] See *infra*, p. 331.

letter of Pieter Hendricks to Steven Crisp in 1692, quoted above,[297] refers to these Friends as "Hendrik Jansen, his wife and four children." Within a few years after this, some or all of the Jansen children also departed for Pennsylvania leaving Hendrik and his wife the last of the Quakers of Krefeld. Like "the last of the Mohicans", they had lived to speed all the rest of their Quaker comrades on the long journey towards the setting sun; and if any of their children and grandchildren remained in Krefeld and continued with the old folks within the Quaker fold until their elders' death, it is probable that they became merged with the Mennonites' congregation, out of which their ancestors came.

QUAKERISM IN KALDEKERK

Krefeld's village neighbor, Kaldekerk, or Kaldenkirchen ("in the county of Iuliers in the borders of Germany", as Penn's deed of land to Jan Streypers defined it), had experienced, as has been seen,[298] the impact of Quakerism and had vigorously resented it. Complaint had been made of this *Qüakerei,* in the Synod of Jülich in 1680 and 1681, and Pastor Eylert of Kaldenkirchen reported that he had exerted himself with his best endeavors, but in vain, to restore to their senses (*zurecht zu bringen*) the women who had been bewitched or contaminated (*berüchtigten*) by Quakerism in that place.[299]

The endeavors which were used to cure the Kaldenkirchen Quakers were not solely clerical and kindly, as is evident from the experience which Elizabeth Hendricks and her two Quaker companions had there in 1680. Elizabeth's husband, Pieter, writes of their visit:[300] "They weare also at Kaldekerk, but there was little openings for a meeting, onely they visited them that weare convinct [of "the Truth", that is had accepted Quakerism], but yᵉ people was verie Tumultuous, giving them many Evill names, & when they was to pass away, they threw much dirt at them—ye Calvinist priest

---

[297] *Supra,* p. 226.
[298] *Supra,* p. 200.
[299] Wilhelm Hubben, *op. cit.,* p. 31.
[300] To Roger Longworth, Amsterdam 4 yᵉ 6/m 1680 H: Acct. (Etting MSS., Misc., Vol. 4, p. 9).

stood by and countenanced it, there are both papists and Calvinists in that place; and yᵉ papist have proclaimed it from theire pulpits that none was to Entertaine or take into their houses any quaker; but yᵉ papists Custos or keeper of theire steeple house little regarded it but being an Innkeeper entertained friends when they came there, and was friendly.''

The Streypers family, as has been seen,[301] were among the Quaker residents of Kaldenkirchen and among the Quaker settlers of Germantown. The two brothers, Jan and Willem, bore the name of Streypers, but their two sisters bore the name of Isaacs; hence their father many have borne the first name of Isaac. They were cousins of the Isaacs op den Graeff of Krefeld, and two of the sisters signed the marriage-certificate of 1681. One of the sisters married Lenart Arents; and another, Geertruid, married Paulus Kuster of Krefeld and went with him and their three sons to Pennsylvania some time before 1693.

Jan Streypers and his son-in-law, H. J. van Aaken, met William Penn in Wesel, on his journey through the Rhineland in 1686 and went with him to Krefeld; and four years later, Jan yielded to Penn's and others' persuasions and followed his old friends and relatives to Germantown. The Van Aaken family clung to their old home in Kaldenkirchen, however, in spite of continued or sporadic persecution. We find H. J. van Aaken writing a letter on September 30, 1699, to William Penn, requesting him to use his influence with the magistrates of the County of Meurs to grant toleration for the holding of Quaker meetings. His letter reads in part as follows:[302] ''I understand that Derrick Sypman uses for his Servis to you, our Magistrates at Meurs, which Magistrates offers their Service to you again. So it would be well that you Did Kyndly Desire them that they would Leave out of the High Dutch proclomation which is yearly published throughout ye County of Meurs & at ye Court House at

---

[301] *Supra*, p. 229.

[302] Samuel W. Pennypacker, "The Settlement of Germantown", Philadelphia, 1899, p. 129, note, gives this letter with the statement: "An English translation of this letter in the handwriting of Matthias Van Bebber is in my collection."

Crevel, that ye Quakers should have no meeting upon penalty, & in Case you ffinde freedom to Desire ye sd Magistrates at Meurs that they may petition our King William (as under whose name the sd proclomation is given forth) to leave out ye word Quackers & to grant Leberty of Conscience, & if they should not obtaine ye same from the said King, that then you would be Constrained for the truth's Sake to Request our King William for the annulling of ye sd proclomation Concerning the quackers, yor answer to this p. next shall greatly oblige me, Especially if you would write to me in the Dutch or German tongue, god almayghty preserve you and yor wife in soule and body. I myself have some thoughts to Come to you but by heavy burden of 8 Children, &c., I can hardly move, as also that I want bodyly Capacity to Clear Lands and ffall trees, as also money to undertake something Ells.''

Penn's influence, if it was exerted in response to this appeal, did not avail. Religious persecution continued in the Rhineland and many thousands of its residents emigrated within the next quarter-century to Penn's colony of Quaker toleration. But Jan Streypers returned to Kaldenkirchen in 1706, to reside there permanently, and the Van Aaken family appear also to have continued their residence there. With the first and second generation, Quakerism evidently died out in the village; for we hear no more of it in Quaker annals.

Motives of the Krefeld Pioneers

The motives for the emigration of the Krefeld Quakers to Pennsylvania are not far to seek. The persuasive words and personality of William Penn must have counted largely with them. They doubtless read with avidity the story of the founding of Pennsylvania, and especially Penn's own ''Account of the Province of Pennsylvania, in America'', the Dutch translation of which (probably by Benjamin Furly) was published in Rotterdam, and its German version (probably by Jan Claus) in Amsterdam in 1681, the year in which its English original was published in London.[303] The German ''Pennsylvania Pilgrim'', too, Francis Daniel Pas-

---

[303] *Infra*, p. 311.

torius, who came to Krefeld in April, 1683, travelling on foot from Frankfurt, and visited the Isacks op den Graeffs, the Kunders and other members of the Quaker meeting, exerted the strong influence of his enthusiasm in re-enforcing their own.

Both religious and economic motives animated the prospective emigrants; for both of these were appealed to in Penn's pamphlet; and Pastorius when setting sail on the "America" wrote: "I have entered upon this journey and passage across the great ocean under God's guidance the more cheerfully in order to escape temporal and eternal ruin. A number of persons in High and Low Germany among others were led to purchase . . . land in the above mentioned Province of Pennsylvania, with the confident expectation that by fleeing hither from Europe, as it were into a second Pellam, we might escape the disturbances and oppressions of that time, and likewise transport other honest and industrious people in order that we might lead a quiet, peaceful Godly life under the rule of the oft-mentioned William Penn, which it is hoped will be just and benign."[304] Religious persecution at home, religious liberty in Pennsylvania, and the devastation of the Rhineland by Louis XIV's armies which threatened their very existence, proved too much even for the Krefeld Quakers' endurance.

A political motive, also, was strong in the minds of the Krefeld pioneers; for not only did the defense of the Rhineland against the French invasions threaten to sweep them into the German armies, but emulating the example of the Pilgrims and Puritans of New England and of Penn himself, they aspired to found "a little Province" of their own within the larger Province of Pennsylvania. There, as in the Provinces of their beloved Netherlands, they hoped to enjoy complete self-government, and to defend their consciences against militarism in all its forms and the fruits of their toil against excessive taxation from outside. Complete exemption from militarism they did find in the Quaker colony. But when the inevitable taxes for the building of roads were imposed upon them by Philadelphia County, they appealed to the Provincial Council of Pennsylvania

[304] "The Beehive".

against this "taxation without representation", and demanded that taxes should be laid upon them only by their own General Court of Germantown. But their appeal was denied; and, worse than that, Queen Anne acting during the eclipse of William Penn, adopted the report of one of her attorneys that the Court itself was illegal, and abolished it (in January 1707). With it, fell Germantown's dream of complete self-government in an autonomous "Province"; but self-government within the increasingly democratic Commonwealth of Pennsylvania was assured to their descendants.

Swayed by the realization and recollection of religious, economic and political hardships at home, and by the anticipation of religious, economic and political benefits to be enjoyed in the Land of Promise beyond the Atlantic, they set forth upon their journey. This journey was aided by at least three other Dutch merchants, all of them prominent Quakers. These were Arent Klincken, Jacob Telner, and Benjamin Furly.

ARENT KLINCKEN

A Pennsylvania annalist, John F. Watson, who began the publication of his materials relating to Germantown in 1828, relates that "Arents Klincken came from Holland with William Penn in his first voyage in 1682. He had seen and known Penn in Holland. He built the first *two* story house ever raised in Germantown; and Penn was present and partook of the raising dinner: the same old stone house on Justis Johnson's premises. He died at the age of eighty."[305] As usual, Watson cites no contemporary record of these statements; and in his own list of passengers on board Penn's ship, "The Welcome", he does not include the name of Arent Klincken. There was an "Aret Klincken" who served as a "committee man" in Germantown in 1691, a justice in its court of record in 1695 and 1697, an overseer and one of the first patrons of its school in 1701–2, and a collector of its rents in 1705.

Later historians have repeated Watson's legend about

---

[305] "Annals of Philadelphia and Pennsylvania in the Olden Time", Philadelphia, 1857, Vol. II, p. 20.

Klincken's voyage with Penn in 1682, and have called him "a Krefeld merchant" who prepared the way for the coming of his Quaker comrades from that city the next year. That he was a Quaker, appears from a minute of Philadelphia Monthly Meeting, dated the 30th. of 1st. Month, 1705, which records his ("Arnett Clinken of Germantown's") request on behalf of the Germantown Friends for aid in building their new meeting-house. But there is no evidence that he was a resident of Krefeld, and his name is not on the marriage-certificate of 1681, or on the list of the Krefeld pioneers on board "The Concord" in 1683.[306] On the other hand, his daughter Ann, who married a son of Thones Kunders in 1704, is stated in the Quaker marriage-records of Pennsylvania to have been born "at Toppenburk, Germany". If "Toppenburk" was Trompenberg, a village about twenty miles from Amsterdam in the province of Utrecht, and close to Hilversum, and if Arent was a merchant of that place,[307] it is quite possible that he transacted business with the Rhineland Quakers and that he "had seen and known Penn in Holland". The fact, too, that his daughter Ann was born "on 6th. Month 4th, 1683", may account for the absence of his name and that of his family on the list of the Krefeld pioneers on their journey which began that month. Just when he settled in Germantown is not known; but it was at some time before 1691, and it may have been in 1684, when Herman Daurss, Veit Scherkes and Wolter Siemes of Krefeld crossed over.

JACOB TELNER

Another Dutch Quaker merchant who was of much assistance to the Krefeld founders of Germantown was Jacob Telner. At first a Mennonite of Krefeld and Amsterdam, Telner became later a Quaker of Krefeld and Pennsylvania. He was baptized, as an adult, in the Mennonite Church in

---

[306] A Friend of Haarlem, Tanneken Willems Boekenoogen, daughter of Willem Boekenoogen and Tanneken Tymons, was married at Haarlem in 1666 to Matheus Matheusz Klinkert, and had five children; "Aret Klincken" *may* have been one of these.

[307] One Pennsylvania record ascribes him to Dalem; Dalen is far to the northeast, in the province of Drenthe.

Amsterdam on the 29th. of March, 1665; but some time before 1676, he became a Quaker and a prominent member of
the Friends' meeting in Amsterdam. In the latter year, he
signed with twenty-six other Dutch Friends the Amsterdam Epistle; and in 1678, with five other Friends he signed
the "Testimony" issued by the Amsterdam Quarterly Meeting against the ill conduct of Cornelis Roelofs.[308]

Telner was a well-to-do merchant, and perhaps it was his
opulence or his lack of Quaker "plainness," or his criticism of George Fox, which caused Pieter Hendricks, in a
letter to Roger Longworth, dated Amsterdam, the 17th. of
5th. Month, 1678, to say: "And (to speake it is familiarity
to thee) we have alsoe some feare concerning Jacob Tellner,
he is prettie high and it does not diminish but rather increase, but my heart's desire is y^t he may be preserved."
An echo of this unsatisfactory attitude of Telner is found
in the pamphlet of J. R. Markon, printed in 1684,[309] in which
its author, criticizing the Amsterdam Quakers, says: "I
could mention by name several examples of such people
who are thus proscribed in your Inquisition-book, and of
some others who will become thus proscribed unless they
accept and confess the infallibility of your Friend George
Fox; if they do not so confess, then some of them are told,
'You have in you the spirit of Jacob Telner.'"

There is extant, also, a letter from Steven Crisp to Telner,
which is without date, but doubtless assignable to Telner's
(and Crisp's) troubles at this time. It is a very frank letter,
and runs as follows:[310]

"Deare freind Jacob Telner it hath beene some time in my
heart to visit thee with a few lines to expresse that true loue
that I haue had to thee ever since I knew thee which loue
hath beene the cause of my dealing for truely & playnly with
thee from time to time for I have always had an eye And desire to thy preservation in that truth which thou wert Convinced & I have always taken notice that thy progresse

---

[308] See Monograph Number 6 ("Dutch Quaker Leaders").

[309] „Een Vriendelijcke Samenspraack, tusschen een Huysman en een heden-
dagsche Quaaker . . .", Amsterdam, 1684.

[310] Colchester MSS., 20; cf. Samuel Tuke's "Memoirs of Stephen Crisp",
York, 1824, pp. 13–17.

in the truth hath beene made harder & more difficult to thee
then it is to many by reason of thy naturall temper which
is forward & vnstable & hath beene mixt with a zeale to
get forward & to attaine to high things whereby sometimes
the enemy hath taken his advantage vpon thee to thy hurt
& then the tender loue of god hath againe visited thee &
showed thee thy hurt and thou hast beene sensible that the
lords hand hath been ouer thee for good & this hath broken
& melted thee for a season but the enemy who is always
upon his watch; hath sought euen out of that tenderness
to lift vp thy mind into the conceipt of some great attainments againe & then the former tenderness hath beene as it
were shutt vp & closed for that neither the true workeing of
y^t power nor the loue & tender counsell of thy freinds &
brethren could be discerned for a time which hath beene a
great greife & exercise to vs the lord knows: yet notwithstanding the loue we have borne to thee hath not ceased, but
for my part I can truly say that from time to time I haue
had an Inward travaile upon my spirit how to doe thee
good & I thanke god that my labour of loue hath not beene
in vayne to thee ward: deare Jacob I was exceedingly refreshed in ye Account I received from deare G d n [Gertrud
Deriks] that thou wert open hearted to freinds & that a
tender loue was in thy heart working thee into more vnity
then formerly well deare freind nothing saves vs but loue
for god is loue & nothing redeemes vs but righteous Judgment administered in that loue & where this loue is retained
in the heart & this pure Judgment dwelt in such must needs
haue fellowship one with another for there all are kept
meeke & humble and they have nothing nor noe body to
exalt, but onely the name in which they find their saluation.

"Now deare Jacob let mee tell thee I doe not believe that
all thy temptations are overpassed or that thy enemy hath
given ouer his seeking to winnow thee & therefore there is
a great necessity for thee to keepe vpon thy watch & when
thou feeles most of ye Inflowings of Joy then to be most low
& carefull to keep thy heart open to the lord & to his people
& soe shalt thou retaine that which is giuen thee whereas if
thou giues way to that which leads into exaltation & much
talking thou may talke it away and then be dry & empty in

thy selfe, the nature of the true seed is first to take a deep root down ward & then to bring forth its fruit vpward therfore let thy soule affect the Inward Invisible rooting & growth of truth more then the outward appearance for where there is an Inward grouth to godward it is seene & discerned by a spirituall eye that god hath opened in his children by which we doe Appeare louely Amiable & Comfortable to each other & in this it is that the lasting fellowship stands for if I speake with the tongue of men and Angells & want this the life of the seed will be burdened & oppressed in them where it is risen though otheres whose life stands in the affection may be greatly Joyed & lifted vp thereby, but this will neuer bring to god nor add any to the body of Christ nor edify his church. Therefore I haue always found it safe to keep something in the storehouse for my owne food, & to breake onely that bread to others that was given me for that purpose & the same that I haue learned by experience declare I vnto thee because I loue thee & I hope thou will be sensible of my love & receive these lines as a token of it..... Noe more but my true & vnfeigned loue to you all I rest thy freind

In truth S. C."

From the tone and terms of this letter, we may conjecture that Telner was one of Crisp's own converts to Quakerism, perhaps as early as his visit of 1667. We learn of no later communications between them, and one wonders if the letter proved too frank for Telner's "naturall temper" and put an end to their intimacy, if not to their friendship.

Whether because of this unpleasantness between him and the other Amsterdam Friends, or in the course of his business affairs, he removed soon after 1678 (perhaps after his return from America in 1681) to Krefeld. He had doubtless become acquainted with William Penn during Penn's visit to Amsterdam in 1677; and when the news came of the purchase of West New Jersey and the grant of Pennsylvania, Telner threw himself actively into the promotion of emigration thither from the Rhineland. During the years 1678 to 1681, at the time of the great exodus from England to West New Jersey, Telner travelled through the Middle Colonies on the Hudson and the Delaware, and thus prepared himself to become Penn's chief agent in the promotion of Quaker and Mennonite emigration from Krefeld and its neighborhood to the New World. That this American visit was also a religious one is shown by the records of the Friends in New Jersey, which record that among "the Friends who came from Europe on Truth's account to visit their brethren in North America between the years 1678 and 1681", were five from England and "Jacob Tillnor from Holland, who all passed thro' these provinces [West and East New Jersey] and their services were well accepted."[311]

Telner was (with Dirk Sipman and Jan Streypers) one of the three original purchasers of Pennsylvania land, buying from Penn 5,000 acres on the 10th. of 3rd. Month, 1682. William Penn's deed or "indenture" for this land refers to "Jacob Telner of Amsterdam in the Province of Holland March^t." This would imply that Telner, even though he had removed his home to Krefeld, still considered himself a merchant in Amsterdam.

Having interested his Krefeld neighbors by precept and example in the purchase of land in Pennsylvania, he accompanied the original thirteen families of pioneers as far as Rotterdam on their way to Pennsylvania in the summer of 1683; and here he sold 1,000 acres each to Govert Remke, Lenart Arents and Isaac Jacobs van Bebber, and 2,000 acres to the three brothers, Abraham, Dirck and Hermann Isaacs op den Graeff. All of these purchasers had been residents of Krefeld, and all became settlers in Germantown. Francis Daniel Pastorius records that he consulted with Telner and other Dutch Quakers in Rotterdam on the eve of their voyage. Telner's personal acquaintance with the Quakers in London, with friends in New York, and with conditions in America and on the voyage thither, must have enabled him to give wise counsel to Pastorius and to be of much assistance to the departing pioneers.

He evidently coöperated with Benjamin Furly, also, another of Penn's agents for Pennsylvania; for we find his name signed as witness to a deed dated in Rotterdam, the

---

[311] Hazard's "Register", Vol. VI. (1830–31), p. 183.

8th. of June, 1683, transferring land from Furly and
Johannes Bleijckers to Jacobus van de Walle.[312] And he
himself evidently bought more land in Pennsylvania; for he
owned a large tract on the Skippack Creek, not far from
Germantown, which was known for many years as "Telner's Township".

It was not long before he himself, accompanied by his wife
and daughter, set sail for the land of promise. The voyage
was a long one, of twelve weeks' duration, from Rotterdam
to New York, and ended, apparently, in the autumn of 1684.
During that autumn, and on December 12, 1684, he wrote
from New York to Jan Laurens of Rotterdam, who summarizes his two letters as follows:[313]

"Jacob writes to me that he supposes there are many who
are desirous of knowing how he and his family are and how
it had fared with them, and requesting me to inform such
persons briefly out of his letters. He says that they have had
a long and hard voyage (that is to say, to New York,
hitherto New Amsterdam); that they were twelve weeks
under way, others having made the trip in five, six or seven
weeks; that they had very contrary winds and calms; that
they therein found and experienced remarkably the presence
and protection of the Lord; that on their arrival they were
received by all their acquaintances with much love and affection; that his wife has now forgotten the hardships of the
sea; that he found it a very pleasant country, overflowing
with everything (that is to say, in New York, where he was),
where people can live much better and with less expense
than in Holland; that if men are industrious in what they
undertake, and live in a Christian manner, they need not
work many days in the week; that he had heard a good re-

---

[312] Pennsylvania Historical Society MSS. 7.

[313] This summary, together with a letter of December 12, 1684, from Cornelis
Bom, of Haarlem, who was then in Philadelphia, was published in their Dutch
original in Rotterdam, in 1685: „Missive van Cornelis Bom . . . . verhalende
de groote Voortgank van de selve Provintie. Waer by komt De Getuygenis
van Jacob Telner van Amsterdam." The Moravian Archives in Bethlehem,
Penna., is said to possess "the only known" copy of the printed version. S. W.
Pennypacker, "The Settlement of Germantown," 1899, pp. 107–8, gives the
above English translation of the summary of Telner's letters, and on pp. 102–7,
an English translation of Bom's letter.

port of Pennsylvania; and that there was a very wonderful increase in the production of everything in proportion to the time, although it was impossible in a short time to have things as abundant as in New York; that when he went to Pennsylvania he hoped to give a true report of everything there.''

Telner succeeded in making a visit to Pennsylvania, and Laurens gives the following summary of his account of it:

''He writes, December 12, 1684, that he found a beautiful land with a healthy atmosphere, excellent fountains and springs running through it, beautiful trees from which can be obtained better firewood than the turf of Holland, and that in all things it might be considered an exceptionally excellent land, and that those who belittle it are unworthy of attention; that Philadelphia grows rapidly, having already several hundred houses of stone and wood and cottages; that he, with his family, intends to move there in the spring, and further, that he is very well, and that his wife and especially his daughter are in good health and fat.''

This intention of the Telner family to remove to Pennsylvania in the spring of 1685 was duly carried out, and they probably settled on the 989 acres in Germantown which Pastorius had drawn for Telner by lot on May 2, 1684. Here he lived for thirteen years, a pillar of support in many ways to the infant colony. The largest landowner in the settlement at Germantown, he was in close touch and coöperation with the leading men in Philadelphia, where also he maintained a residence. He appears to have kept in touch with people and affairs in New York, also, and this for religious as well as mercantile reasons. On September 20, 1685, O.S., Rev. Henricus Selyns, a Dutch Reformed clergyman in New York City, wrote to the Classis of Amsterdam in part as follows:[314]

''Concerning the Labadists—their blustering has mostly been quenched; but now, upon the arrival of some more from the house at Wiewarden [Wieuwerd], they again protrude their heads above the water. They have been reinforced also by Dutch Quakers, who have come to Long

---

[314] "Ecclesiastical Records of the State of New York", Albany, 1901, II, 906–7.

Island. Their impudent head and teacher, Tellenaer, intended to go and live in Pennsylvania, but he remained here and has not yet left, because of Domine van Zuuren's departure. He has dared, may God help us, to disturb public divine service at Breuckelen and Midwout, on one Sunday at the former place, and on the next Sunday at the latter. He comes assisted by his confrater,[315] singing into the church. He pushes himself forward and sits down near the pulpit. After public prayer he rises and calls out loudly, that it has been revealed to him by God to say something to this congregation which is now without a pastor: that they had been deceived by a false divine service, he is sent to them to preach the true and living God. One of the Elders ordered Tellenaer to be silent and pushed him, amid great commotion and disturbance, away from the baptismal fount. The constable then led him out of the church. After the service they went to the school house. There, with great audacity, he boasted of being without sin, and spoke against original sin, psalm singing, baptism, communion, and the righteousness ascribed to Christ. He shook his head, brushed the dust from his feet, and delivered up all, who were not willing to listen to his word, to the evil one.''

A year later, September 9, 1686, the Rev. Rudolph (or Domine Rudolphus) Varick, a Dutch Reformed Clergyman of Long Island, New York, wrote to the Amsterdam Classis, as follows:[316] ''A certain German Quaker, Jacob Tellenaer, who travels through city and country here with other Pharisees, has somewhat meddled with a few simple-minded members of my congregation. But I think they will quickly be led back to the right path.'' The official summary of this letter stated:[317] ''A certain Quaker, Jacob Telner, had taken in some people on Long Island, but he seemed to be almost through; and there were, singularly enough, no other sectaries, only there were several preachers with whom he hoped to associate.''

Again, on September 30, 1688, the Rev. Varick wrote to

[315] Perhaps John Delavall; see *infra*, p. 248.
[316] ''Ecclesiastical Records, II, 922–3.
[317] *Ibid.*, II, 944.

the Classis:[318] ''The German Quaker, Jacob Tellenaer, has not preached in our district for more than a year and a half, and he does not any longer endeavor to convert any of our people. We have only two English Quaker families among us. One of these will apparently soon move away.''

On the 10th. of October, 1688, Mr. Selyns wrote to the Classis:[319] ''The tempest which arose in connection with the arrival of the Separated Labadistic . . . [mutilated] Bruta and Brutalia lightning flashes of fantastic Quakers, has mostly disappeared in smoke without any further violence. . . . Tellenaer has packed up his whole Quaker establishment in order to become a Justice of the Peace in some village in Pennsylvania. It was impossible for him to accomplish what was beyond his powers, without God. . . . Would that sin could be diminished and piety increased throughout our whole country! We have to lament that dykes and dams will break—the longer they are, the quicker —and this country is deluged with awful iniquity higher than the clouds. . . . May God shield us from further iniquities that we may be preserved from corresponding punishment.''

A year and a half later, in June 1690, Domine Varick was forced to flee from English persecution on Long Island and become temporarily a preacher for the Dutch Reformed congregation in New Amstel (Newcastle), Delaware. Writing to the Amsterdam Classis of this visit, he says: ''I came to a Dutch village near Philadelphia, where, among others, I heard Jacob Telner, a Dutch Quaker, who preached there. Subsequently, I lodged at his house in Philadelphia.''[320] From this it would appear that either the sermon or the proffered hospitality of Telner, or perhaps Varick's own taste of persecution, had overcome his former aversion to his Quaker host.

Meanwhile, Telner had been rendering civil as well as religious service in his new home. In 1689, he was allotted

---

[318] *Ibid.*, II, 956.

[319] *Ibid.*, II, 958. A summary of this letter (*Ibid.*, II, 970) states: ''The Quaker, Jacob Tellenaer, has not preached for a long time now, and no longer tries to seduce any one.''

[320] *Ibid.*, II, 1053.

25 more acres of "the first next portion to Germantown"; and in that year he was one of the citizens to whom Penn granted the first charter for the "German Towne". He was the first burgess of the town named in the charter, and took office when the charter was recorded in 1691. In 1692, he and Pastorius were appointed by the General Court of Germantown to "request the Governor for the confirmation of the Charter of Germantown, as friends in Philadelphia deem that advisable." Three years later, he presented the town with a half-acre of land, and his friend Jacob De la Plaine (James Delaplain)[321] presented another half-acre, on which to erect a market-house, "in the road or highway where the cross street of Germantown goes down to the Schuylkill," for the holding of a weekly market.

During these years of secular life and civic activities, he was not neglectful of religious demands. In 1687 (the 3rd. of 3rd. Month), for example, we find him and Cornelis Bom in Germantown presiding over the marriage, by Friends' ceremony, of Jan Duplouvys, a Dutch baker, but apparently not a Quaker, to Weyntie van Sanen. Two years later, he and his daughter Susanna attended the wedding of Francis Rawle and Martha Turner, and signed the marriage certificate. In 1692, he and his friend John Delavall (a member of Pennsylvania's Provincial Council at the time) went as travelling ministers on a tour through New York and New England. The names of these two men had been associated together for several years; for example, a letter from Alexander Beardsley of Pennsylvania to Jacob Tyzack [of England ?], in or before 1690, included the item: "Several have come to Inhabit with us from New York, as John Delavall and Jacob Tellener." The "List of Publick Men and Women Friends that have visited New England since the Year 1656"[322] refers to them as follows: "1682 [sic; an error for 1692] Jacob Tilner from Germany (a Dutchman) and John Lilovale from Philadelphia (Interpreter)."

---

[321] "James Delaplain" was assessed in Philadelphia County, in 1693, £72, and taxed 6s. His house was at the corner of Germantown Avenue and School House Lane; and in it, as in Thones Kunders's house, the Friends held their meetings.

[322] Manuscript Collection, Friends' Historical Library, Swarthmore College.

Another reference to Delavall comes to us from the list of "Eighty-seven Publick ffriends y^t have dyed in Pensilvania since ye first Settlement of Friends there", which is as follows: "John Delavall The Sonne of Thom^s Delaule Mc^{e}h^t in N. York where he was conserned and recd a Publick Testimony [that is, recommending him as a minister] he removed to Philad^a and was buried y^e ... 10th : 6 m^o : 1693." The tax-list of Philadelphia County for 1693 assesses the property of "Widdow Delaval" at £250, and taxes it at £1 0 s. 6 d.

The religious and ecclesiastical schism among the Germantown and Philadelphia Quakers developed by George Keith from 1690 to 1692, was participated in by Jacob Telner, but on the orthodox side; and it was probably to counteract the Keithian doctrines that he wrote the "Treatise" referred to by Francis Daniel Pastorius, but apparently never published. This treatise he may have taken to London with him in 1692 or 1693 for the purpose of helping to block Keith's appeal to the English Friends made at that time. He appears to have spent considerable time among Friends in Colchester, on this visit, as well as in London. Among the Colchester Manuscripts[323] is one entitled "Jacob Telner's Answer to George Keith's doctrine in his Catechism", and this may be the "quarto treatise" to which Pastorius refers.[324] A letter, also, from Jan Claus of Amsterdam to John Furly of Colchester, dated the 1st. of 12th. Month, 1693, says that Jacob Telner was then in Amsterdam, and desired to have his love sent to the Furly family and his salutation to all the Colchester Friends.

On this visit to Europe, Telner doubtless went up the Rhine from Holland to his old home in Krefeld; and he may have pursued his merchandizing journeys, mingled with missionary and colonizing efforts, back and forth between the Continent and England. Indeed, it seems probable that he made up his mind to give up his Pennsylvania home and

---

[323] No. 11.

[324] If the Answer was in reply to Keith's "Christian Catechisme", which was not published until 1698 (instead of to his "Plain Short Catechism", published in 1690), it could scarcely have been taken over by Telner in 1692, unless he had seen Keith's manuscript, or part of it, before its publication.

settle permanently in Europe. Returning to Germantown
and Philadelphia to systematize his business affairs and to
place them in the hands of his attorneys, Robert Turner
and Samuel Carpenter, he again sailed for Europe in 1696.
On his departure, his friend Pastorius dedicated to him
two poems, the first of which is inscribed, in Latin, "This is
to Jacob Telner returning to Europe (aeuropaeantem)",
and its single verse translated from the German reads:

"One should struggle for such merchandize
    As, when the ship by storm is wrecked,
Can be rescued by the stripped refugee alone.
    And that is neither gold nor silver;
Paper too, though lighter, is then too heavy.
    Nothing else than Intelligence and Skill (?*Fremigkeit*),
When times are precarious on sea and land
    Are safe from spoil and robbery."

This allusion to the desirability of leaving paper behind
when starting on a voyage may be accounted for by one of
Pastorius' other notes, which reads: "J endeavoured at
Spare times to make this present Hive[325] on a Quire of fine
Paper which a friend of mine departing for Europe did give
me."[326]

The second poem addressed to Telner (or perhaps a con-
tinuation of the first, has three stanzas in German and a
concluding one in Latin. The last one, translated, reads as
follows:

After rumbling, after roaring,
After thunder and downpouring
Comes again the clear sunshine.

We must press through storm and cleave it;
If today will not achieve it,
Jacob, tomorrow shall be thine!

---

[325] This is the famous "Beehive" of Pastorius, which is regarded by German-
Americans as "the Magna Charta of German culture in colonial America."
It is the first American Encyclopaedia, and antedates the French Encyclopaed-
ists by two generations.

[326] Telner may have been the donor of the paper.

Therefore cease not now from hoping:
Rescue comes from all thy moping;
There comes again the opposite mood:
What God wills is fair and good.

Dei Voluntas mea felicitas.	The will of God is my felicity.
Haec ego properè, Tu prosperè.	These I send with speed to wish thee good speed.
Vale ac Salva; iterum iterumque.	Fare well and keep well,—again and always.

These verses may hold a clue to the reason for Telner's return to Europe, namely, an attack of melancholy or disappointment due to religious or mercantile difficulties. Perhaps the hope referred to has to do with the renewal of his activities in promoting emigration from the Rhineland to Pennsylvania. That he continued to be closely associated with Penn in relation to Pennsylvania affairs is evident from a letter to James Logan, in 1703, in which Penn says: "I have been much pressed by Jacob Telner concerning Rebecca Shippen's business in the town [i.e. Philadelphia]."

In England, he acted as agent both for the Mennonite fugitives from the Rhineland en route to Pennsylvania, and for the Mennonites of Amsterdam, Haarlem and Rotterdam who added their charity to that of the English Friends in aiding them.[327] A letter which he wrote on their behalf, dated in London, the 6th. of August, 1709, states that eight of the families had gone to Pennsylvania, but that there were many other Rhineland fugitives who desired to reach a haven of refuge in Pennsylvania. "The truth is," he writes,[328] "that many thousands of persons, old and young, and men and women, have arrived here in the hope and expectation of going to Pennsylvania, but the poor men are misled in their venture. If they could transport themselves by their own means, they might go where they pleased, but because of inability they cannot do it, and must go where they are ordered. Now, as there are among all this multi-

---

[327] Cf. *infra*, pp. 386ff.
[328] Pennsylvania Historical Society MSS., 8.

tude six families of our brethren and fellow-believers, I
mean German Mennonites, who ought to go to Pennsylvania,
the brethren in Holland should extend to them the hand of
love and charity, for they are both poor and needy. I trust
and believe, however, that they are honest and God fearing.
It would be a great comfort and consolation to the poor
sheep if the rich brothers and sisters from their super-
fluities would satisfy their wants and let some crumbs fall
from their tables to these poor Lazaruses. Dear brethren,
I feel a tender compassion for the poor sheep, for they are
of our flesh, as says the Prophet Isaiah, lxviii. 7 and 8.''

Telner's mercantile, charitable and colonizing efforts did
not put an end to his religious activities on the Continent,
but were evidently associated with and inspired by them. It
appears from his letter last quoted that he had returned to
the Mennonite fold; but there are evidences that he remained
in close personal relationship with the Quakers and continued
to participate in their religious meetings. For example, the
Amsterdam Epistle of 1711 refers to the frequent religious
visits of ''our dear ffriend and Brother John Claus and of
our ffriend Jacob Telner to Haarlem.'' This is the last
recorded reference to one of the most useful Quakers of his
time, laboring as he did and with such success in various
capacities, on the Continent, in England, and in America. As
one of the pioneer promoters of settlement in Germantown
and Philadelphia, his memory deserves to endure; and it is a
satisfaction to learn that the founder of Pennsylvania was
so appreciative of his services that in partial compensation
for them, he granted him a hundred acres of ''Liberty
lands'' in Philadelphia's suburbs.[329]

The death of his wife is not recorded, nor is it known
where she spent her last years, though it was probably in
her daughter's home in Philadelphia. This daughter, Susanna, was her parents' only child. We catch our first
glimpse of her in the long letter quoted above from Crisp to
Telner. The last paragraph of this letter reads: ''& remember my very deare love to thy wife & to thy daughter J am
glad tell her to heare good news of her & if thou writes to

---

[329] Pennsylvania Archives, 2nd Series, 19:256.

me let me heare how it goes with her she is now come to yeares of vnderstanding & knows the leadings of the light in her owne conscience what she may doe & speak & what not & as she is obedient therunto she will find pease in her owne bosome be a comfort to you & will appeare lovely to all her friends.''

There is every reason to suppose that Susanna fulfilled this cheerful prophecy. She accompanied her parents to New York in 1684, and to their Germantown home the following spring. Here, she attended the wedding and signed the marriage-certificate of Francis Rawle and Martha Turner, in 1689, and was herself married to Albertus Brandt, who was recorder of Germantown in 1694. The next year, Brandt, who did business as a merchant in both Germantown and Philadelphia, was fined for failure to serve on a jury in Germantown, ''having no other excuse but that in court in Philadelphia he was wronged upon the account of a jury.'' After his death in 1701, Susanna was married again to David Williams of Philadelphia, who may have been a son of one of the Dutch Willems or German Wilhelms who helped to found Germantown, although his name has a decidedly Welsh flavor.

BENJAMIN FURLY

Benjamin Furly, a Hollandized Quaker of Rotterdam, aided largely the escape of both the Quaker and Mennonite colonists from the Rhineland and their colonization in Pennsylvania.[330] He became Penn's chief land-agent on the Continent, and sold for him nearly 50,000 acres in the colony before the year 1700. Telner appears to have received his grant from Penn in person. But Jan Streypers and Dirck Sipman bought 5,000 acres each from Furly under date of March 10, 1682 [? 1683 ?]; and on the 11th. of June, 1683, Furly sold 1,000 acres each to three more Krefeld residents, namely, Lenart Arents, Govert Remke and Jacob Isaacs van Bebber.

Govert Remke was a Mennonite, and did not go to Penn-

---

[330] Cf. Monograph No. 5 (''Benjamin Furly and the Rise of Quakerism in Rotterdam'').

sylvania, but sold his land on January 14, 1686, to Dirk Sipman. Sipman did not go to Pennsylvania, but appointed Herman Isaacks op den Graeff his agent and sold his Germantown land in 1685 to Gerhard Hendricks and Pieter Schumacher of Krisheim, and Hans Peter Umstat of Krefeld; and the balance of his 6,000 acres in 1698 to Matthias Isaacs van Bebber. The last named was a brother of Isaac Jacobs van Bebber, who arrived in Germantown in 1684, and a son of Jacob Isaacs van Bebber whom he brought with him to Germantown in 1687. The Van Bebber estate finally included more than 6,000 acres, in the vicinity of Germantown, and it was rapidly settled by German and Dutch Mennonites during the next quarter-century. It was long known as Bebbers Township; but in 1704, the two Van Bebber brothers removed to "Bohemia Manor" (or "New Bohemia"), in Cecil County, Maryland. Sipman, Remke and the Van Bebbers appear to have remained Mennonites; or, if they were at any time Quakers, to have returned to the Mennonite fold.

The Voyage to Pennsylvania

When the Quaker pioneers left Krefeld in June, 1683, they were accompanied by Telner, Streypers and Sipman as far as Rotterdam, where they were welcomed by Furly, and aided by him in their varied preparations for their great adventure. He and Telner procured passage for them through James Claypoole, a Quaker merchant of London, the brother of John, Lord Claypoole, the husband of Oliver Cromwell's daughter Elizabeth. Claypoole was himself going with his family to Pennsylvania on the ship "Concord", which was scheduled to leave Gravesend on the 6th. of July. Furly sent to him a list of the thirty-three Krefelders and their passage-money, and he procured accommodations for them on "The Concord;" but preparations for the voyage detained them in Rotterdam, and Claypoole wrote several letters to Furly urging him to speed them on their way. He was able to delay the ship's departure until July 24, by which time the Krefeld pilgrims were safely on board.

In these letters he told of shipping arrangements for "ye Ffrankfurtrs," that is, for the thirty-three emigrants from Krefeld whose names Furly had sent him, and whom Claypoole calls in another letter "the 33 Dutchmen." In the last of these letters, (London, July 10, 1683), Claypoole says: "It troubles me much that the friends of Crevillt are not yet come and the wind being still contrary, I doubt we shall goe away wthout them, the ship ["The Concord"] went to Gravesend the 7th and intends for the Downs the 17th and then to be gone wth the first fair wind, we have loytered severall days on their account, and shall doe still, wch may be 50 ℔ domidge to the ship, but we cannot blame them, but if it were the will of the Lord I should be heartily glad they might come before we goe, for it troubles me to think w^t a great disappointment it will be to the poor friends besides the loss of their money wch I have pd to the M^r long since."

Furly had sold the Pennsylvania land and made out the deeds for it to the individual Krefeld purchasers, but had promised that this land should be in a solid block so that the Dutch and German settlers would not be scattered among the English. It was finally agreed that thirty families should be settled within one year upon the land in three townships with ten families each.

The voyage, although it was long, lasting seventy-four days (from July 24 to October 6), was a comfortable one and, unlike those of Penn's ship, "The Welcome", the year before, and Pastorius's ship, "The America", from June 10 to August 20 of the same year, there was but little illness among the passengers, no deaths, and two births;[331] but, as Claypoole wrote,[332] "The blessing of the Lord did attend us so that we had a very comfortable passage, and had our health all the way."

As Furly and Telner had waved the voyagers off from ancient Rotterdam, so Penn and Pastorius welcomed them on their arrival in the infant Philadelphia; and it was not long before they travelled up the Schuylkill and the Wissahickon to view the Promised Land of their vision. Penn's gratification at the arrival of these, the first fruits of his labors on the Continent of Europe, was expressed in a letter

---

[331] See *supra*, p. 215.
[332] James Claypoole's "Letter-book", June 5, 1683.

which he wrote one month after their arrival (November 10, 1683),[333] in which he spoke of "the continued good fortune of this Province", and stated that within a single month there had "arrived five vessels, among others one which brought many people from Crevelt and neighboring places in the land of Meurs."

It is interesting to reflect upon the joyous impressions which the banks of the Delaware, the Schuylkill and the Wissahickon, clad in the golden October days of 1683 even more beautifully than now in their wondrous autumn leaves, must have made upon the minds of the Krefeld pilgrims. For they had not only been tossed for ten weeks in their sail-boat out of sight of land upon the Atlantic's waves, but they had come from a part of the Rhineland which was not at all famous for its beauty. A German guide-book of one century ago[334] admits that a "journey down the Rhine from Düsseldorf to Holland offers little to please either eye or spirit; on all sides stretches a dreary heath (*traurige Haide*)." A century and a half before that, Krefeld's environments must have been even more dreary and unattractive.

Old Krefeld and New Germantown

The town of Krefeld itself had always been an "open place", undefended by fortress walls; hence its early, inner section was not circular, but had the form of a large checkerboard or rectangle such as Penn planned for his "green country-town" of Philadelphia. The town's architecture, the guide-book quoted above describes as being "neat (*nette Bauart*) and as already reminding one of Holland's." Old Germantown's architecture rejoiced in many reminiscences of the Dutch fatherland; but the town's shape was determined by an Indian trail which developed into the Main Street, on which every settler desired his home to face. Hence the visitor's impression of the early settlement was that of "a long, long trail a-winding."

A characteristic touch of the Old World which was re-

---

[333] Quoted by Benjamin Furly in a letter dated Rotterdam, March 6, 1684, in „Recüeil de Diverses pièces Concernant la Pensylvanie"; cf. *infra*, p. 313.

[334] „Handbuch für Reisende am Rhein von seinen Quellen bis Holland," Heidelberg, 1831.

peated in Germantown was the planting of gardens and vineyards, in which the linen-makers and other craftsmen enjoyed their leisure, and added to their incomes. How interesting to find, in the ''New Deal'' of this Twentieth Century by which the National Recovery Administration is attempting a partial solution of America's industrial problem, the persuasion of factory laborers to live in the suburbs of our large cities on ''subsistence homesteads'' which would seem quite home-like to Germantown's first settlers. Whittier's picture of Pastorius and his wife discussing the Anti-Slavery Protest in their ''garden, forest-walled'', is true to history as to poetry. Outside of the town and its gardens, ''alles ist nur Wald'' (all is forest), one settler wrote; but the Dutch Quaker did not take so kindly to the woodman's axe as did another of Pennsylvania's families, that of Abraham Lincoln; hence he rejected logs for his dwelling and, lacking the clay sufficient for the beloved brick cottages of Holland, built roughly of stone.

The characteristic Dutch discontent with things as they are and his love of progress and reform in the art of daily living which had made Holland the school-mistress of Elizabethan England and of Dutch New York, caused itself to be felt in other ways than in this rejection of logs for stone; and his ''divine discontent'', his determination not ''to stay put'', caused the more German-minded Pastorius to write home as early as 1684: ''Send only Germans, for Hollanders are not so easily satisfied, which in this new land is a very necessary quality.''

Accordingly, in that same year we find some Germans coming to Germantown from Mülheim, Mörs, Neuwied, and Cologne; but the stream of Dutch settlers from those places and others in the Rhineland flowed steadily on, and brought with it settlers bearing such *echt Hollandsche* names as Herman op de Trap, Jan Lindeman (the silversmith of Mülheim, patronized by Penn), Evert in den Hoffe, Reinier Hermans, Klas Jansen, Kornelis Siverts, Jan Neusz, Hendrik and Maria Buchholtz, and Arnold van Vossen. While from Krefeld itself came Wolter Siemes and Herman Darss (both of whom signed the 1681 marriage-certificate), Jacob and Mathias Isaacs van Bebber, Willem Hosters and Cornelis Teissen. Most of these were Quakers as well as Krefelders;

for the Rev. Rudolphus Varick wrote in 1693, of a visit he had made to Pennsylvania in 1690, that of the forty-four families then in Germantown, twenty-eight were Quakers. Indeed, Jan Lensen is believed to have been the only one of "the original thirteen" settlers who did not leave the Mennonites to become a Quaker—perhaps because he died quite soon after the settlement; and Pastorius, the leading German colonist, threw in his religious, as well as economic, political and social lot with his Quaker neighbors. Most of the settlers before 1690 were related by blood or connected by marriage with one another; and until that year, when a Mennonite congregation was formed, they participated in Quaker meeting affairs in Germantown, and in the Monthly Meetings at Philadelphia and Abington.

The reference in the Krefeld marriage-certificate of 1681 to "the book of the meeting", and the granting of the certificate itself, are evidence of the fact that a meeting for "discipline" or business had been begun, if not thoroughly established by the Germantown pilgrims in their old home. They continued to meet, as has been seen, at the home of Thones Kunders as soon as they settled in Germantown until a meeting-house was built in 1686; and their meeting was recognized as a "preparative meeting", a constituent first, of Abington, then of Philadelphia Monthly Meeting. Later it came to share this status with Frankford, the preparative meeting alternating between the two towns.

Since the settlers desired to be farmers as well as handicraftsmen, the 5,700 acres of woodland which they purchased spread far and wide throughout the township of Germantown, but farmers' villages were laid out in 1687, for convenience' sake and in accordance with the precedent in their old home. These villages were four in number, namely, Germantown (nearest to Philadelphia and extending to Washington Lane, with 2,750 acres); next, Crisheim, or Cresheim (extending to Mermaid Lane, with 884 acres); Sommerhausen (extending to Chestnut Hill, with 900 acres); and Crefeld (extending to Whitemarsh, with 1,160 acres). Thus were commemorated, by the third name, the Franconian birthplace of Francis Daniel Pastorius, and, by the second and fourth, the old homes of the settlers from **Krisheim and Krefeld in the Rhineland.**

Germantown's Monument to the Krefeld Pioneers, 1920

GERMAN MONUMENTS TO THE DUTCH PIONEERS

Hence it was that the noble stream of Dutch Quaker emigration to Pennsylvania, having its rise in Krefeld and Krisheim beside the Rhine, found a home in Krefeld and Krisheim beside the Schuylkill. But the stream of German emigration, which rolled over Philadelphia and eastern Pennsylvania within the next generation and made of Germantown "the cradle of the German race in America", entirely engulfed the Dutch settlers, and founders. It was not until nearly two centuries and a half had elapsed (November 10, 1920) that Philadelphia (which had incorporated "Krefeld", "Krisheim" and "Germantown" alike within its bounds) erected a monument to the Krefeld pioneers. By that time, the Dutch origins and the memory of them having become completely Germanized in the public mind, the monument gave first place to the German late-comer, Pastorius; and although it names the thirteen Dutch founders, in the inscription on its base, it permits the past, present and future to be dominated (unhistorically and most inartistically) by a grandiose statue of "Germania".[335]

Krefeld in the Rhineland was absorbed in Prussia in 1702, and it too entirely neglected or forgot its Dutch citizens who had founded Germantown; hence, in 1931 (May 27), when a bronze memorial was presented to the city by the German-American National Society, the Carl Schurz Memorial Foundation and the Wyomissing Foundation, the German element in the emigration was alone portrayed. The memorial was made by a German-American sculptor, Otto J. Schweizer, and it commemorates the landing of the thirteen Krefeld weavers and their families "under the leadership of *Franz Daniel Pastorius*", and celebrates the contributions of *Germany* to American achievement![336] These contributions were very real and excellent; but they did not come primarily through Dutch Quaker Germantown.

---

[335] See photograph of the monument facing p. 258.

[336] The original of this monument was presented by its author to the Germantown Society of Philadelphia, and is preserved in the library of that society. It received only "second prize" in the competition for the "Pastorius" monument in Germantown, where its rival was set up in Vernon Park. Its replica stands in Krefeld, Germany. Cf. photographs facing p. 260, and Appendix E (p. 424).

2. THE KRISHEIM AND PALATINATE PIONEERS

The same motives which carried the Dutch Mennonite emigrants up the Rhine from Holland to Krefeld, and the Dutch Quakers from Krefeld across the sea to Pennsylvania, caused the tide of Mennonite migration to flow up the Rhine from Holland and down the Rhine from Switzerland to Krisheim, and to send a Quaker offshoot thence across the Atlantic to a New World Krisheim in Germantown.

The founder of Pennsylvania made to the European Krisheim a visit which was of much brevity, but of lasting importance. Leaving Frankfurt in the afternoon of September 1, 1677, Penn and his companions drove to a village which Penn calls "Crisheim in the *Paltzgrave's* Country."[337]

GRIESHEIM, KIRCHHEIM, KRIEGSHEIM, KRISHEIM

A Prussian village, *Griesheim*,[338] is on the River Main, six miles west of Frankfurt; but since Penn left Frankfurt on Wednesday afternoon and did not arrive in Crisheim until the next day, this Griesheim was evidently not Crisheim. Another village called *Griesheim* is in Hesse about six miles south of Darmstadt and about twenty miles north of Worms; but since Penn says that he arrived at Crisheim "by way of Worms", it is not probable that *this* Griesheim is Crisheim, for he would not have gone twenty miles too far south to Worms and then retraced his steps, especially since he was going on to Worms within a few days, and especially since he says later that "Crisheim is about six English Miles from Worms." If he went south through Worms on his way to Crisheim, the latter must have been either south, east or west of Worms. But there appears to be no place named Crisheim within this district.

---

[337] They probably drove through Darmstadt, the capital of the Grand Duchy of Hessen, about seventeen miles south of Frankfurt; but Penn's only mention of the city is in connection with "the German of, or near Darmstad", whom he met with at Leiden (see *supra*, p. 95).

[338] W. C. Braithwaite, "Beginnings of Quakerism", p. 414, follows some early Quaker authors in calling the village *Griesheim;* Sewel calls it *Kriesheim*, in both his Dutch and English editions; and Croese calls it *Kirchem* (in his Latin edition), while his English translator makes it *Kirchheim*. There is a *Kirchheim* in Alsace and a *Kirchheim* in the Palatinate.

Krefeld's Monument to the Krefeld Pioneers, 1931

There is still another village about six miles north of Worms whose modern name is *Kriegsheim,* and whose former name (used as late as 1856) is said to have been *Krisheim*; hence it seems certain that this village was the one Penn visited, and the home of a small Quaker community. There, Penn says, ''we found to our great Joy a Meeting of tender and faithful People.'' The tenderness of this people had been developed and their faithfulness to Quakerism had been proved during a score of years before Penn's arrival.

The Background of Quakerism in the Palatinate

The background of Quakerism in the Palatinate and in sundry other parts of the Rhineland is a period of eight centuries of warfare between the French and the Germans for the possession of the valley, culminating in the terrible Thirty Years' War which had ended only nine years before the arrival of the Quaker missionaries. Especially during this last war, wholesale depopulation had occurred, followed by a slow and furtive re-settlement of the land, not so much by the former peasants as by new-comers from the Netherlands and from Switzerland. Many of these new-comers were religious sectarians, chiefly Mennonites, who had renounced the established churches, and whose religiosity had been greatly emphasized by the horrors of the century of so-called religious warfare. To attract them to the depleted lands, the rulers of the Palatinate conceded to the Mennonites, in the midst of the Thirty Years War (1626), equality with members of the Reformed Church in religious and civil rights. Prince Charles Louis invited the Huguenots of France and the Huterites of Hungary; but the Mennonites from up and down the Rhine were made especially welcome, and (in 1664) they were promised toleration to the extent of being permitted to worship in private houses, *provided* not more than twenty families should meet at one time, that no outsiders should be re-baptized and received as members, that no political disaffection or religious heresy should be preached, and that the Mennonites should pay an annual tax or tribute of three gulden per family for the first year, and six gulden afterwards. The penalty of exile was affixed to these terms; but restricted though they were, they were confirmed from time to time by Charles Louis' successors, and attracted numerous Mennonites from Zurich and Bern, who were just then undergoing another siege of bitter persecution. In the early 1670's especially, the Mennonite stream poured into the Palatinate, some coming by way of Alsace, and stopping there for a time before going on to the Rhine and across the Atlantic.

Thus during the generation following the close of the Thirty Years' War, colonies of anxious peasants and artisans strove to cling to their new homes and to make good their right to life, liberty and the pursuit of happiness in the face of a reluctant and capricious government and of successive rumors of invasion and waves of actual warfare. It was to such a perplexed and harried community that Ames, Caton, Crisp and other publishers of Quakerism came; and not only did they find its members unsettled as to religion, but their successors, like Penn, Furly and Longworth, found a good opportunity for persuading the peasants, harassed by new attacks of war and persecution, to remove their homes to a more peaceful and promiseful land.

AMES AND CATON IN KRISHEIM

William Ames was the pioneer Quaker missionary in Krisheim. Accompanied by George Rofe, he made his first visit there as early as 1657. Of this visit, Besse says:[339] "By Means of their *Preaching*, some Persons there became convinced. . . . This alarmed the Priests, who excited the Rabble, disposed to do Evil, to abuse those Persons by scoffing, cursing, reviling, throwing Stones and Dirt at them, and breaking their Windows. The Priests also applied to the Magistrates to suppress and banish them, and prevailed so far, that *Philip D'Auber*, the Land-Shriver, gave Command that *none should entertain the said William Ames and George Rolfe, on pain of forfeiting forty Rix-Dollars;* and they not being willing that any of their Friends should suffer for harbouring them, and being not free to leave the Country, endured much Hardship by lodging in Barns and

---

[339] *Op. cit.*, Vol. II, p. 450.

Stables on Straw, &c, until at length *W. Ames* found an Opportunity of speaking to the Prince Elector, who heard him favourably, and finding nothing against them worthy of Punishment, disannulled the Land-Shriver's Order, and gave Liberty to those of their Persuasion to travel in his Country, or to reside there." Sewel[340] adds the touch that the Prince Elector did not even take offense at William's keeping on his hat at the table, even though the other prominent noblemen present kept theirs off (*altoos ongedekt waaren*).

There is extant an open letter from William Ames, dated Crisheim, 1657, and printed in the Dutch language, evidently for the sake of the Friends both in the Palatinate and in the Netherlands. It is only one printed page in length, begins "Dear Hearts" (*Waarde harten*), and is an ardent, heartfelt appeal to them to be "faithful to that which delivers from pollution."

John Stubbs and Samuel Fisher, on their perilous visit to Italy in 1658 went down through the Palatinate; and in the same year, Ames was again besought by the Friends in the Palatinate to return to them. But he evidently did not comply immediately with this request; for, in a letter to William Caton, dated, "Neer Amsterdam 22th of y[e] 5th mo 1658",[341] Ames says: "And in germany friends desires is greatly but thou knowest this [Amsterdam] is a place w[ch] cannot well be left."

Again, in 1661, Ames visited Krisheim, accompanied this time by William Caton, who writes of their visit in his Journal as follows: "About that time it was upon me to go into Germany, partly to visit Friends, and partly to speak with the Prince Palatine, and some one else in that country; in order thereunto I took my leave of Friends in Holland with much tenderness of heart, committing them to the custody and protection of the Almighty. And about the tenth of the Seventh month [September] 1661, I with my dear brother William Ames set forwards on our journey towards Germany . . . . . ." Coming by way of Cologne and the country of "the Grave de Whitt" (on whom they urged religious

---

[340] "History", Amsterdam, 1717, p. 249.
[341] A. R. Barclay MSS., 5.

toleration),[342] the two travellers arrived at "a place called Kriesheim", where they found "a small remnant of Friends, that bore their testimony to the truth." With them, Caton says, "we were refreshed, after our long and pretty tedious journey. There we continued some time, helping them to gather their grapes, it being the time of their vintage; and when we had had a time of refreshment among them, we travelled towards Heidelberg, the place of the prince's residence." Henry Fell coöperated with Ames and Caton on this visit, at least in Krisheim and Heidelberg.

After their visit in Heidelberg, Ames and Caton returned "again to Friends at Kriesheim" and "staid some time with them." Ames then departed by way of Amsterdam on a long journey to Bohemia and Poland, taking with him "a Friend of the Pfalz" ("for", he wrote to George Fox, "they were not at all free that I should goe alone").[343] Caton accompanied him "to a place called Alstone; where the governor of those parts lived." *Alstone* was probably the town of Alzey, the District City (*Kreisstadt*) of Rhein-hessen, on the west side of the Rhine, half-way between Worms and Bingen. Here, Caton's Journal continues, "it was upon us to go to him the [governor] to lay some abuses before him that were sustained by Friends. He was moderate towards us, and a good service we had with him; and after that he gave me an order for the officer of the place where Friends lived, for him to take care that the rude multitude did not abuse Friends. After we had been with him, we took leave of each other in the endearedness of our Father's love, and he [W.A.] went for Holland, and I returned to Kriesheim again; there I staid with Friends some certain time, and afterwards went to Heidelberg again, for I was not clear of that city."

---

[342] *Supra*, pp. 191ff.
[343] Barclay MSS., 7. His companion was Jan Hendricks, a "convinced Friend" of Worms and Krisheim. When Ames arrived in Frankfort-on-the-Oder, he wrote a brief account of this journey, in a letter to Margaret Fell, dated the 18th. of 2nd. Month, 1661/2, in which he said: "I was som time with oure dear friends there [in the Palatinate], and was with the prince who shewed more friendship than ever. . . . I have an honest man with me, a friend of palatine, who could not be Cleare to let me pass alone"; (Devonshire House, "Early MSS.").

It was during his stay in the Palatinate, in 1661, that the sad news came to Caton of the death of ''Niesie Dirrix, of Amsterdam, who'', he says, ''had been a dear extraordinary, and special friend of mine, and a true and faithful servant to the flock of God in the Low Countries.''[344] On the same date that he wrote the above letter to the Friends in London, he wrote another, more personal one to them, which was chiefly an expression of sorrow for the death of Niesie Dirricks and the sickness and death of other Friends in Amsterdam; but it gives us no further particulars of Friends in Krisheim and the Palatinate.[345]

Sewel devotes a brief paragraph to one of Ames's visits to the Crisheim Friends as follows:[346] ''Now whilst William Ames was in the Palatinate, he got acquaintance with the Baptists (*Doopsgezinden*) at Kriesheim, a town not far from Worms; and among those people he found so many listeners that some families became his fellow-believers, and under much opposition (*veele tegenheden*) stood fast in their new faith until the settlement of Pennsylvania in America, when they departed thence all together (*gezamentlyk*); and they soon recognized that their longing towards that land was to be attributed to Divine Providence; for not long after their departure, war began in Germany, and the Palatinate was most pitifully laid waste by the French, while thousands of people were bereft of all their possessions and reduced to poverty.''

Croese is more interested in Ames's visits to the Electoral Prince in Heidelberg, but has the following brief reference to Crisheim: ''When *Ames* had left the Court and City, he wanders over the Countrey, and there makes several Essays to promote his Design, but it came to nothing; and therefore he returns to *Holland*. But having afterwards taken Two of his Companions along with him, to wit, Bat and Higginson [these are *Catano* and *Higginsio* in the

---

[344] See Monograph Number Four (''The Rise of Quakerism in Amsterdam'').
[345] Swarthmore MSS., I, 466–8.
[346] Sewel says in his English edition, under the year 1659: ''I think that it was in this year that William Ames went into Germany, where being come into the Palatinate . . .''. (N. Y., 1844, I, 253). In his Dutch edition (1717, p. 249), he says: ''Eenigen tyd daarna'' (that is, some time after his imprisonment in Rotterdam in 1659).

Latin; i.e. Caton and Higgins] he goes again for *the Palatinate,* and addrest himself to the Prince. . . . So they went their ways elsewhere but yet kept, in this part of the Countrey, and followed their design, and after many windings and turnings, found some Countrymen at *Kircheim,* near *Wormes,* whom, after they had for some time heard them, they brought over to their way [*disciplinam*] and this was all they could, after all their indefatigable Labour and Toil, effect and bring about."

QUAKER PERSECUTION IN KRISHEIM

Persecution of the Krisheim Friends began early. Besse records that in the years 1658 to 1660, the Friends of "Cresheim" were arrested, imprisoned and fined for such offenses as refusing to bear arms or contributing towards the cost of the militia, refusing to pay tithes, working in the fields on a holiday, reproving "a priest" for neglecting his flock. The chief persecutors of the Friends were "John Shoffer, an Officer", "Egidie Janson and Casper Hendricksz, Priests", and "the *Romish* Priest at *Worms*"; while the victims mentioned were "John Hendricksz (Jan Hendriks), Jacob Janson (Jansen), John (Jan) Philip Laubeck and Christopher Moret (Stoffel Murrett)". The imprisonment was in "a nasty Prison", at one time a whole day without food; while Jan Laubeck was imprisoned in 1659 three days for "reproving one Egidie Janson, a Priest, for the Neglect of his Flock." The fines exacted were excessive, such as, "fourteen Rix-Dollars for a Demand of four Guilders (to support the militia); one-half of a Friend's Increase out of his Barns (for not paying tithes to "the Priest"); the tithe of Christopher Moret's Cabbage out of a young Vineyard [sic], "which was contrary to the Law and Custom of the Country"; twenty-six Sheaves of Corn out of fifty; a Seizure of Wine out of two Friends' Cellars, and Tithes of a vineyard."

This persecution and the "openings" it afforded brought a speedy response from Friends in England. To the first business meeting of the Society of Friends for all England, which was held at Skipton in 1660, there came "from some Friends of London certain information of the great work and service of the Lord beyond the seas, in several parts and regions, as Germany, . . . Palatine . . . , through all which Friends have passed in the service of the Lord." Backed by such enthusiasm at home over "the spread of the Truth" abroad, the call to Germany could not be denied. Accordingly, we find in a letter from William Caton to George Fox, dated, Amsterdam, the 28th. of 10th. Month, 1660, that William Ames "is pressed in spirit to hasten toward p . . . [the Palatinate] in Jermany"; [347] and in William Caton's Journal, occurs the statement: "I was much alone [in Holland], especially about that time [1660–1661], for William Ames who had had very good services in those parts [the Netherlands], was sometimes in Germany [that is, up the Rhine in the Palatinate], and sometimes at Hamburgh; and once he travelled through Bohemia, and to Dantzic, and from thence to Poland." On this occasion, John Higgins accompanied Ames to the Palatinate, where they visited the Krisheim Friends before going on to Heidelberg to appeal to the Elector in behalf of toleration.

AMES APPEALS FOR TOLERATION

Ames gave an account of his visit to the Elector in 1661, in a letter to George Fox, dated, "aneserdam the 3th of the 7th/mo. 1677 [1661], as follows:[348] "After I passed from amsterdam I took my journey towards the Palte; hauing littel seruice by the way and being for [torn] sometime amongst friends (whom I found well) I passed to heidelburgh to visit the prince was the seruice that Chiefly lay vpon me, and to giue him seuerall volums as well latin as english and dutch which I judged might be best for him, which in holland I had caused to be bound vp for him and coming into the citty the captaine of his life guard saw me in the street and although there were others in his company, not of the meanest yet he really came [torn] to manifest his great affection towards me, taking me by the hand in the street and desire [torn] to his house which accordingly I did.

---

[347] Swarthmore MSS., I, 425.
[348] A. R. Barclay MSS., 7.

"and that same day in the euening the prince vnderstanding of my being thear, as he was wont to doe (to witt to send
for me) sent a seruant with a torch to light me vp to his
palace and when I came theer he tolde me I was wellcom,
and began to aske me what I thought of that report consern-
ing friends riseinge against the king. I tolde him I knew it
was a false report and many moderate words past between
vs to that purpose; he shewing me the diurnall printed in
english for it was just about that time, but I Could not see
that he was very ready to beleeue any such thinge of vs,
and alsoe the captaine of his guard said that he had written (to witt the capt) to a good friend for the certainty of
the matter, and had receiued answere, that we were innocent
in it.

"soe after supper (after I had giuen him the bookes which
he gladly receiued, he caused [me] to follow him into an
other roome where in the presence of them all, it may be
about [torn] persons, I had freedom to declare that which
was in my heart to him, shewing him the truth on the one
side, and on the other side the wickednes of the priests the
falsnes of [their] doctrine, the vnjustnes of tithes and the
sufferings of my friends in that Country, which he heard
without seeming to be offended at all, but asked me whether
I did not know that priests were needful as to the vpholding
of theire politique gouerment, then I shewed him that they
were the men who were destructive to good gouerment &
I also manifested the loue of friends towards him and tolde
him his name was mentioned in one of those bookes for his
deuotion &c. which seemed to please him very much and he
saide he would read them, soe I having ben long with him I
desired to pass to my lodging being without the Citty and
fearing the gates should be shutt; whearvpon at his Command one was apointed to accompany me with a torch, to
my lodgeing, and to cause the gates to be opened for me,
and the next day (I desireing to know whether he had anything more to say to me) he sent me word that if I did Com
to visit him I should be welcom but as for that which he
had to say to me I need not stay.

"in that Country alsoe I had good seruice with a Countis
(soe called in english) [the Princess Elisabeth] which is

[torn] moderate woman and I beleeve doth loue us; for the goods sake which shee doth Judged [torn] vs, though shee is not soe Conuinced as in all things to Joine with vs, but doe hang to the priests, not for theire goodness but because of their Cerimonyes truth in that country hath a great dominion though few com into the obedience of it as yet."

The book cited to the prince as mentioning his name was probably the contemporary account of the visits of Ames, John Higgins, Samuel Fisher, and John Stubbs to the Elector between the years 1657 and 1661, which comes to us from George Bishop's "New England Judged", London 1661. This account is as follows:[349] "Shall I pass the Sound, ... and so to *Heidelberge,* the chief City of the *Palatinate,* and there stay a little; there I shall understand of a quiet Passage in and through them all, and of the *Prince Elector Palatine* of the *Rhine,* his sending to *William Ames* (who first ministered and gathered a People in those Parts) and of his own Accord taking off the Fine of Twelve Pound, laid upon whosoever should Entertain *William,* by his Chief Magistrate, and giving him free Liberty to Declare against Evil in his Dominions. I shall there also Understand of the said *Prince Elector's* forbidding him to go to the *High Council of the Church* (as it is called, they having summon'd him to appear) saying, *That he would take him off*: And when the said Council notwithstanding summon'd him again, the Prince hearing that he was in the City (*viz.* at *Heidelberge,* where his Palace was, and the Convocation of the Priests) I shall find that he sent two of his Servants, one after the other, for him to come and Dine with him; and when he came, that he told him, *That he knew not of his being in the City before*; that the Priests had no such Power as to send for him, nor should have such Power; that he had reproved the Priests for what they had done; and bad him, if ever they sent for him again, not to obey them; that he rebuked one of the chiefest of the Priests of that Council for saying, *That they* (viz. the Priests) *would give our Queries in Writing to him to Answer*—and that he charged the said Priests, in the presence of *W. Ames,* that they should give forth none, (tho' *William* was as ready

to answer as the Priests to give forth) that the Prince used
much Moderation, as did also his Sister [Elisabeth]; that
she received very friendly what was spoken by him in the
way of exhortation to her; that neither of them were offended at what was spoken by him to them, nor at the Hat,
nor with plain Language, *Thou* and *Thee*. I shall there also
understand, that when about the space of a Year after, he
and another Friend (*viz. John Higgins*) came to visit him,
that he very lovingly received them; that the Captain of
his Life-guard told the said *William, That his Prince was
very glad that he was come into the Country again*; that *he
had given him Order to supply them* (tho' they neither
wanted, nor asked, nor received) *with what-ever they
wanted, either Money or Clothes;* in which his Love was
seen and accepted; that he very friendly received divers
Books from them, both then, and at times before: And, that
when at another time *Samuel Fisher* and *John Stubbs* were
there, from *England,* and had given Notice to his Secretary,
that they had something in Writing to present the Prince;
that he sent for them into his Presence Chamber (where
was also his Sister) and received it gladly from them, and
a Book enclosed (their Hats being on) expressing much Desire after Friends Books; and receiving at another time a
great Book of *George Fox's,* and a Letter from *William
Ames,* by the Hands of *John Higgins,* and charging him to
thank William for that his Book. Moreover, I shall find that
he had much Discourse with them; that he told them, that
he took their coming in Love; that *he believed they spake
in Love to their Souls;* that he gave them thanks for their
Love; That after a while, being called to Supper, he took
them with him; that he shewed them his House; that he
stayed them by him whilst he did Eat; that they had Discourse with his Chaplains, and divers of his great Men
whilst they did Eat; that neither HE, nor any of them, during all that time (tho' it was a Season of greater Pomp
and State than ordinary, the Prince and his Nobility being
met about the choice of a New Emperor) manifesting any
Offence at their Discourse, or at their being Covered, tho'
(according to their Custom) the Prince and his Nobles sate
with their Hats off; but on the contrary, the Prince mani-

festing much Satisfaction with what they said; and enquiring after *William Ames,* and how he did, saying, *he was not well when he was last with him;* that in Friendship and Love they departed; that they had free Liberty to Meet in any part of his Dominions, in the very Heart of which there is a Meeting of Friends, gathered into the Truth by the said *William* aforesaid, who Meet together with the said Prince's Knowledge; whose Meetings are Peaceable.

"*Lastly,* I shall there find, that when *John Stubbs* and *Samuel Fisher* were afterwards in *Germany,* that the *Land-Scriver* (the next Officer in Power under the Prince, and Divers of their Ministers sent to them, to give him and the said Ministers a Meeting, that *Samuel Fisher* met them alone (*John Stubbs* not being well) that he had much moderate Discourse with them, and Liberty a pretty time, and that he quietly passed away, after that the *Land-Scriver* and the Ministers had expressed much Thankfulness to him, for his Love, who were not offended at his Hat, nor Plainness of Speech. All which makes ye [New England persecutors] manifest.''

CATON APPEALS FOR TOLERATION

William Caton tells in his Journal of his own visits to Mannheim and Heidelberg, where he too had interviews with the "countess (so called)'' and the Electoral Prince. "I was several times,'' he writes, "at a city called Manheim, where there were a sort of Baptists, who lived together as one family, and had their goods common; with whom I was several times; and did bear my testimony among them to the truth of God, though few of them received it. I was several times with the governor of that city at his own house; and he was very courteous to me (at least seemingly,) and desired me as often as I came to the city, to come to his house. I was also in the country with a countess (so called,) who was very loving to me, and pretty open to hear the truth; and at her house I found a great lord (so called,) who formerly had been general of the emperor's army, (as I was informed;) and a great conference I had with him in the countess' presence, who was rather one with me in her judgment than with the great man before mentioned; and after I had had some very good service with them, I left them.''

Of his visits to Heidelberg, Caton says: ''When I came there I hired a lodging in a goldsmith's house, and sometimes I went up to the prince's palace, and had good service there; and sometimes I was with some of the great ones of the city, with whom I had also very good service, and some of them were very courteous and *respective* to me; and more love did appear in some of them towards me than others could well bear. Then began the enmity in the clergy to get up against me; and through the means of some that were envious against me, I with another young man (who were all the Friends that were in the city,) were ordered to appear before the council, as also the man that entertained us; which accordingly we did, and a very good service we had, for never had their been any Friend there before; so that they had many things to query of me; and the Lord was pleased at that very time to give me enough wherewith to answer them, as also utterance, boldness, and dominion, even to the admiration of some. They were moderate towards us, and suffered me to speak pretty freely and largely among them; but in the end (that they might appear to do something,) they would have me to depart out of their city, though they had nothing to lay to my charge, except for declaring the truth, and dispersing some books which testified of the truth; nevertheless, they suffered us then to depart from their judgment-seat in peace.

''Afterwards the prince came to hear of it, at which (as we were informed,) he was very highly displeased with the council for troubling us, when we had given them no just occasion. After that I went to the president's house, who had examined me before the council; and after a little discourse with him, he became pretty moderate, and did reason very familiarly with me, and asked me many things concerning our Friends in England; as also concerning the magistrates' proceeding towards them; and I was very free to give him a full account thereof for his information. Before we parted he seemed to be very loving to me, and thanked me for the present I had given him, which was some Friends' books; and yet before the council, my giving of such books to people was the greatest crime they had to lay to my charge, though both the prince and he did receive them from me and accept of them."

Of another visit to the Prince, he writes: "Upon a certain time when I was at Heidleberg, there came two of my dear brethren to the city, viz, John Stubbs and Henry Fell, who had been at Alexandria in Egypt, and in Italy, &c. The postmaster of the place seeing them, did bring them to my lodging, (for he knew me well,) for they had not knowledge of my being in the city; presently after, came the captain of the prince's life-guard, having seen them in the street; and he being a very courteous man to us, discoursed very friendly and familiarly with us, and afterwards told the prince of the aforesaid Friends being in the city. Soon after, the prince sent his secretary to my lodging to desire us to come up to the castle to speak with him, which accordingly we did; and when we came there, he began to speak friendly and familiarly to us, as his manner was, and did ask them much concerning their travels, and how it had been with them, &c. And a very gallant opportunity we had with him in the presence of the nobles, (so called,) that were conversant with him. After he had discoursed long with us, he parted very lovingly from us, and soon after we went out of the city."

Caton spent six months of "very good service for the Lord" in the Palatinate, making Crisheim his headquarters, preaching "the Truth"; distributing Quaker literature; interviewing the Prince and "other great ones"; being prosecuted by the clergy; examined by the council; trying to induce printers to print Quaker pamphlets in German; going into churches and synagogues with his hat on and trying to address the congregation; getting "sorely beaten and left bleeding in the temple"; arguing with teachers and students in a Jesuit college; and performing the many other ingenious and arduous tasks which "the first publishers of Truth" enthusiastically entered upon.

A long letter which he wrote "to Friends at London" was dated "Cresheim near Worms in Germany, the 30th.

of the Eleventh Month, 1661.''[350] It is devoted chiefly to
an appeal to the English Friends to stand steadfast under
persecution; but it doubtless expressed the spirit of his
messages to the Friends in Krisheim and is reflective of the
persecutions and dangers which they also endured. "It is
like," he writes, "that some of you have heard in Part of
the good Service which I have had in this Country, and of
my being several Times with the Prince, who hath indeed
been very courteous and moderate towards me and Friends,
yet I believe in some Things he is subject to that which
befalls most Princes, that is, to be overswayed in too many
Things by the Clergy, as Princes almost universally are,
yea, and as some have been to their Ruin. This Week I was
with him, and with the Governour of *Manheim,* and when I
had been about an Hour with the Prince, there came some
Jesuits to speak with him, and I was very willing to have
discourse with them before the Prince, that he and all his
Nobles, that were then present, might sufficiently have seen
that we were none of their Emissaries; But the Prince was
called forth upon some Occasion, and the *Jesuits* went out
of the Room, so that I had little Opportunity to speak to
them.''

That Caton was not unduly hopeful of toleration from the
Elector is evidenced by the following passage in his letter,
which was probably intended as much for the persecuted
Quakers in the Palatinate as for those in England. "And let
not your Minds," he writes,[351] "be drawn out with Reports
that are abroad of Liberty here or there, or else where, or
that which you hear, that *such a Prince hath said so, and he
hath promised thus and thus:* and *such an Earl or a Duke, he
hath writ and promised such and such Things, and it might
be we might there enjoy Peace and Liberty.* Let not these
Things, I say, enter into your Minds, to unsettle them, lest

---

[350] Besse, II, 451–454; Caton's Journal, 1839 edition, pp. 107–8. It is dated
from "Kreisheim, near Worms, in Germany, 30th. of 11th mo., 1661 [February,
1662]." Its opening paragraphs were probably suggested by the persecutions
suffered by the Krisheim Friends and the refuge they had found in "the
Truth." The original of this letter, under date of "Cressinge neare Wormes in
Germany, y⁰ 30ᵗʰ of yᵉ 12ᵗʰ [sic] month 1661", is now [1930] in Friends
House, London.
[351] Besse, II, 453.

that thereby you become the more incapable to endure your Sufferings in the particular Places where the Lord hath set you, and where it is required of you to bear your faithful Testimony, and this is expedient for every one of you to know, that the present Sufferings and Trials, which you are exercised in, come not without the Permission of the Almighty: And if it be his Determination to exercise you in such Things for your future Benefit, though it may seem to some to be for your present Disadvantage, you may be assured, that they could not be long escaped, nor avoided elsewhere.

"For I may tell you how that I have observed in my Travels, in the sundry Dominions where I have been: Sundry Things, I say, I have seen and observed, which undoubtedly would bring great Sufferings upon us, if we should come as Pilgrims and Strangers to inhabit in them, notwithstanding the Large Promises and fair Pretences of some of their chief Rulers, who in the Pomp and Vanity wherein they are found, are subject to change, and easy oftentimes to be moved by their Councils and Consistories; and very hard it is to find one among the Potentates of the Earth, that is not so much leavened by the Spirit of the Clergy of that Sect of which he is, as that he is not imbondaged by it, and is and may be at Times brought through their Persuasions and Importunities to do what is contrary to the just Principle of Equity in himself: And where the Spirit of Enmity rules in a Dominion (though a pretty moderate Man may have the Name) in such a Dominion there is not much Liberty to be expected by us to be enjoyed in Matters of Religion, for it is well known to you, how that through that Spirit we have suffered from the Beginning, which hath wrought mightily aginst us in our native Country, especially in them that were called the Clergy or Ecclesiastical Men, and the very same untoward malicious Spirit doth evidently shew itself in such Sort of Men, when the Truth of the Lord is held forth to them."

In this letter, he inveighs vigorously against the three tolerated sects, namely, the Papists, the Lutherans, and the Calvinists, who "seem to be bent against us of all others, as the offensivest, the irregularest, and the perturbatiousest

people that are of any sect; and notwithstanding the great
variance that is and hath been among themselves, yet they
can, as it were, join hand in hand against the Truth and
us." The Calvinists, or members of the German and Dutch
Reformed Church, in the Palatinate, who had had so long
and terrible a struggle with the Roman Catholics for survival, were evidently determined not to permit Quakerism
or anything that savored of it to undermine their present
dominant position. Calling to their aid the arm of the government, they began in 1663, to persecute with especial
vigor the Quakers and Mennonites alike.

Renewed Persecution

Besse gives a brief record of the Quaker persecution in
Krisheim during the years 1663 to 1666, citing the fines
amounting to 250 Guilders (£37.10 s.), besides the annual
tithes of about one-fifth of their yearly produce, which were
forcibly collected from the Krisheim Friends. The fines
were imposed for refusing to bear arms, and for meeting
together for religious purposes; they included one shilling
sterling (imposed upon every Friend for attendance at each
religious meeting), numerous cows, hogs ("a fat sow"),
an ass, bedding, pewter, and from one-seventh to one-fifth
(instead of one-tenth) of their garden produce. Even the
cattle were subjected to imprisonment: "The distrained Cattle were kept under the Town-hall three Days, and fed there
with Fodder taken from their Owners, and then sold by the
Burggraff at Altzij [Alzey], and when some of the People
expressed their compassion to the Sufferers, the fore-named
Officer, John Shoffer, forbad their speaking much about it."
The victims mentioned in these years were "John Hendricksz, Hendricsz Gerrits, Velter Eberten, Agnes, widow of
John Johnson, Christopher Morett, John Philip Laubeck,
George and Peter Shoemaker"; while the prosecutors this
time were "John Shoffer and the Earl George Wilhelm of
Hëydelsheim [Heidesheim]."

On his first visit, in 1661–62, Caton had said farewell to
the adventurous Quaker missionaries, John Philly and William Moore, who had stopped at Krisheim on their way to
Austria and Hungary. William Moore returned to Krisheim

in October, 1663, after the barbarous cruelties to which he
had been subjected in Hungary, and wrote to Caton from
Amsterdam as follows: "I arrived at Christein among
Friends, and being there kindly entertained and abundantly
refreshed, I tarried there some Weekes, waiting to have
heard of John [Philly]."

Philly had been released from his Hungarian dungeon in
September, 1663, and he also found his way back to Krisheim, but did not reach there until the winter of 1663–64,
or the spring of 1664. So grieved was he that religious persecution existed not only in eastern Europe but also in the
more cultured Rhineland, that he wrote a letter to the
Electoral Prince in behalf of the persecuted Krisheim
Quakers. This appeal was dated "Am—Tag des vierten
Monats [June] 1664", was signed J. W. Philley, and addressed *Freund!*[352] It begins:

"Since I was with thee [at Heidelberg], I have been in
Kriegsheim, where I found that little despised flock who
fear the Lord in thy dominions, serve Him and walk in the
fear of God, but who have informed me that much violence
and extortion have been committed upon them by one
Johann Arend, who pretended to act on thy commission,
but who presented no written order from thee. Because they
refused to pay him one shilling per person whenever they
assembled to worship God, he has taken from them eight
cows, bedding, and other things valued at one hundred
Reichs-dollars, an exact account of which is enclosed herewith: This, in spite of the fact that they are people who
labor daily to eat their own bread in peace and honesty, and
who have never transgressed a just and righteous law,
which is what their religion demands, without having any
such compulsion imposed upon them.

"Now, what he did, was done without thy knowledge and
command; and thus he has not only thereby oppressed the
poor and innocent, but has greatly dishonored and abused
thy name and credit, and it is only right and reasonable that
their cows, bedding and other things which were unjustly

---

[352] The letter is quoted in full, in German, by Wilhelm Hubben („Die Qüaker
in der deutschen Vergangenheit", Leipzig, 1929, pp. 65–66) from the *Men-
nonitische Blätter*, Hamburg-Altona, 1911/12, p. 18.

taken from them be either restored or paid for. This is not
the time to exercise oppression and violence upon the poor
and innocent, when the just and righteous judgment of
God hangs over the nation for such deeds.''

Then follows an appeal to Christ's teachings and the
tragic experience of Ahab and ''other oppressors in ancient
times'', and the warning that dethronement here and punishment hereafter may follow the prince's neglect to do
justice upon the guilty officer and to the innocent Quakers.

Prince Charles Louis did not make compensation to the
Quakers; but a few months after Philly's letter to him
(August 4, 1664), he granted some judicial safeguards and
religious toleration to them and to the Mennonites, with
whom they were usually identified.[353] The Quakers continued, however, to refuse to pay a poll-tax levied especially
upon them, and continued to suffer in consequence.

This refusal was made more exasperating to the officials
by the Quakers' neglect of treating Sunday in the strict regard demanded by the Calvinists. The Inspector of Osthofen
(a town a mile or so from Krisheim), Johann Jakob Löf-
fler by name, wrote a complaint in regard to this offense to
the electoral administration, as follows:[354] ''The Kriegsheim Anabaptists (*Wiedertäufer*: i.e. Mennonites) and
their Quaker brood (*Quäkergebrütsel*), on the holy Sabbath
and holy days of every kind, pursue their housework and
run around in the village and fields, thereby not only griev-
ing our people and others confessing the evangelical faith,
but also causing the Palatinate churches to be ridiculed by
our neighbors of adjoining Leiningen and elsewhere.''

When the bailiff from the neighboring town of Alzey sum-
moned the so-called ''Mennonites'' of Kriegsheim to defend
themselves, the Quakers declared baptism and the laws regarding the Sabbath to be mere human institutions; and
there followed, on the 5th. day of March, 1669, an electoral
threat of banishment. This threat was repeated when the
Quakers continued to refuse payment of the special tax;
and it was decreed that ''the Quakers should either pay a
tax for their freedom of worship, as the Anabaptists did, or

---

[353] Hubben, *op. cit.*, p. 67.
[354] *Ibid.*

else be driven (*geschafft*: herded ?) from the land.'' This
threat was evidently not carried out, but was held *in terrorem* over the Krisheim Quakers' heads.

STEVEN CRISP IN KRISHEIM

Steven Crisp, ever alert against persecution, began his
series of visits to "Germanie" soon after this. The "Testimony of the Yearly Meeting of Friends Held at Amsterdam,
The Fifth Month, An. 1693, concerning . . . Stephen Crisp''
relates that "In the Year 1667 [sic; it should be 1669] he
visited the small Company of Friends, then living at a Place
call'd Kreysheim, in the Palatinate; Also he went to Heydelberg, the Residence of the Prince Elector Charles Louis, to
acquaint him with the Unrighteous Dealings of the Magistrates of Kreysheim, in taking from Friends, Three or Four
Times the Value of Goods for an imposition which Friends
for Conscience sake could not pay; and was Friendly received and Discoursed by the Prince; whereby Friends were
somewhat eased in their Sufferings.'' That is, the Count
Palatine, recognizing the justice of Crisp's appeal, annulled the tax of four Rix-dollars per family, which had been
imposed upon the Quakers for meeting together for the purpose of religious worship.

Of his journey to Germany in 1669, Crisp writes: "I was
moved to pass into *Germany,* to which I gave up in the
Fourth Month [June] that same Year, and by the way met
with many Perils and Dangers, by reason of the horrible
Darkness, Popery, Cruelty and Superstitions of those
Lands and Dominions through which I Travelled, so that
sometimes it was as if my Life were in my hands, to offer up
for my Testimony; but the Lord preserved me, and brought
me upon the 14th. Day of that Month to *Griesham* nere
Worms, where I found divers who had received the Everlasting Truth, and had stood in a Testimony for God about
Ten Years, in great Sufferings and Tribulations, who received me as a Servant of God; and my Testimony was as a
Dew upon the tender Grass unto them. I had Five good
Meetings among them, and several were reached and convinced, and Friends established in the Faith. It was also
just in an hour of Temptation and time of Tryal among

them, that the Lord had cast me there, for the Prince of that Land, called the Palsgrave, had imposed a Fine upon them for their Meetings, to wit, Four Rix-dollars the Year for each Family, which they (for Conscience sake) not paying, he sent an Order to take the Value in Goods; whereupon his unreasonable Executioners came and took away the trible Value, but they suffered the spoiling of their Goods with great Joy and Gladness, and counted it a Happiness that they were counted worthy to suffer for his Names sake, who had called them to the knowledge of his blessed Truth, and to bear a Testimony in that dark Desert, to the Light of the Lord Jesus. So I went to Heydelburgh to the Prince of that Land, and had a good opportunity with him, and laid before him the danger of his proceeding on in Persecution; he heard me with a great deal of Friendliness, and discoursed things at large with me, and in several things promised it should be better, as it did also after come to pass: So having finish'd that service in *Germany,* I returned . . .'' to the Netherlands.[355]

It is to be hoped that the Pfalzgraf kept his oft-repeated promise to Caton and Crisp, and that the persecution of the Krisheim Friends was at last somewhat abated. We are left in the dark concerning their welfare, however, during the eight years which followed Crisp's visit, before the arrival of William Penn.

PENN IN KRISHEIM AND MANNHEIM

Penn found at Krisheim a survival or revival of the persecution; for, he says, "it seems the Inspector of the Calvinists had injoined the Vooght, or chief Officer, not to suffer any preaching to be among our Friends; who (poor Man) fearing the Indignation of the Clergy, came next Day to desire Friends not to suffer any preaching to be amongst them, lest he should be turned out of his Place. To whom we desired Friends to say, that if he pleased he might appre-

---

[355] It was on this journey (and possibly at Krisheim) that Crisp wrote the "Letter from Germany to Friends", which is extant now as a "Postscript," (pp. 24–27) to the 2nd. edition (London, 1687) of George Keith's "Benefit of Silent Meetings", London, 1670.

hend us, and carry us to the Prince, before whom we should give an Account of our Testimony. But, blessed be the Lord, we enjoyed our Meeting quietly and comfortably; of which a Coach-full from *Worms* made a part, amongst whom was a Governour of that Country, and one of the chief Lutheran Priests.''

During his stay of two days at Krisheim, Penn wrote a long letter of religious exhortation to the Princess Elisabeth and Countess of Hoorn, but gave them no details concerning the Krisheim Friends. Penn's desire to meet with the Electoral Prince either at Mannheim or Heidelberg must have been strong, both because of the influence for religious toleration which he hoped to exert upon him through his sister, the Princess Elisabeth, and because of the experiences which Ames, Caton, Crisp and other Quaker missionaries had met with at his court. Elisabeth, too, expressed her desire, in her letter to Penn, dated the 4/14 of September, 1677, to know what reception he had received at Frederisbourg (or ''Manheim alias Frederisbourg'', as Penn called it).

Leaving Krisheim for Mannheim, where he hoped to find the Electoral Prince, but failed to do so as the latter had gone to Heidelberg, Penn wrote him a letter and then returned to Krisheim, where he had ''appointed'' another meeting with the Friends.

In his letter to the Prince, Penn not only advocated religious toleration in general, but appealed for it specifically in behalf of the Krisheim Friends and suggested that some Friends persecuted outside of the Palatinate might be induced by a policy of toleration to immigrate and settle in it. ''The next thing'', he writes, ''I should have taken the liberty to have discours'd, would have been this; What Encouragement a Colony of vertuous and industrious Families might hope to receive from Thee, in case they should transplant themselves into this Country, which certainly in it self is very excellent, respecting Taxes, Oaths, Arms, &c.

''Further, to have represented the condition of some of our Friends, and thy own Subjects; who though they are liable to the same Tax as Mennists, etc. (not by part the

Case of other Dissenters) yet the Vaught of the Town where they live, came yesterday to forbid all Preaching amongst them, which implies a sort of Contradiction to the Indulgence given.''

Lest another wave of persecution should sweep over the Friends after the Prince's death, Penn took the precaution to appeal to him as follows: ''One thing more give me leave to recommend to thee, and that is, to be very careful of inculcating [to inculcate] generous, free and righteous Principles into thy Son, who is like to succeed thee, that when thou art gone, the Reputation of the Country may not sink by contrary Practices, nor the People of divers Judgments (now thy Subjects) be disappointed, distressed or ruined. Which, with sincere desires for thy temporal and eternal Good, conclude this,

Thy unknown, but sincere Friend,
William Penn.
From Manheim, 25th of 6th Month, 1677.''

Leaving Mannheim and staying over night at Worms, Penn and his companions, ''the next Morning (being the first day of the Week) walked on Foot to *Crisheim,* which is about six English Miles from *Worms.* We had a good Meeting from the tenth till the third Hour, and the Lord's Power sweetly opened to many of the Inhabitants of the Town that were at the Meeting; yea, the *Vaught* or chief Officer himself stood at the Door beind the Barn, where he could hear and not be seen; who went to the Priest and told him, that it was his Work, if we were Hereticks, to discover us to be such, but for his part he heard nothing but what was good, and he would not meddle with us.

''In the Evening we had a more retired Meeting of the Friends only very weighty and tender; yea the Power rose in an high operation among them, and great was the Love of God that rose in our Hearts at the Meeting to visit them; and there is a lovely, sweet and true Sense among them: We were greatly comforted in them, and they were greatly comforted in us. Poor Hearts, a little handful surrounded with great and mighty Countries of Darkness; 'tis the Lord's great Goodness, and Mercy to them that they are so finely kept, even natural in the Seed of Life. They were most of

them gathered by dear *William Ames*. The next Morning
we had another Meeting, where we took our leave of them,
and so came accompanied by several of them to Worms.''
Perhaps it was a discreet regard for princely suscepti-
bilities in civil affairs which caused Penn to refrain from
writing in his Journal and in his letters to the Princess Elisabeth and her brother the Elector, of what must have been
his strong hope, namely, that the Princess would be able
through her influence to secure complete toleration for the
Quakers in the Palatinate, and that Krisheim might become
a place of refuge for the Quakers persecuted in other parts
of the Continent. This was not to be; but Penn's sojourn in
Krisheim and his comradeship with the Quakers there were
soon to bear fruit in the migration of most of them to Pennsylvania, where they were assured of a more permanent
toleration than they could find in the ark of refuge for which
Penn had appealed to the Electoral Prince of the Palatinate.

Gerard Croese's characteristic summary of Penn's efforts in the Palatinate and their results is as follows:[356] ''In
pursuance to these mens Practices, *William Penn, Barclay*
and *Keith,* at that time they came with *Fox* into *Holland,*
steered their Course for these Parts, but being ignorant in
the *German* Tongue, they took some of the Natives of the
Country along with them to be their Interpreters; but there
was nothing done by them that is worthy of mentioning. But
those few Quakers, who I have said, lived in these places,
did afterwards increase to Seven or Eight Families; who
after they had by little and little united Men, and Associated together, they declined to go to the publick Churches,
and refused to pay for the subsistance of the Clergy, and
therefore as well the Rectors and Pastors of the Churches
thereabouts, as also the Priests of the Territories of
Wormes looked with an evil Eye upon them, and so going
on from one thing to another began to accuse and sue them,
and when they could not be satisfied in their demands,
which the others would not comply with, alledging the unlawfulness of paying such Tythes and Products from their
Lands they did, instead of the Money due upon the account, take what they pleased from among their Sheep,

[356] The Latin edition, pp. 530-2; English edition, II, 235-6.

Swine, and other Cattle, whereas those Men did in the mean
time by their diligence, as it were, singular Providence
bear up still against their losses and poverty, so as that they
had yearly wherewithal both to subsist upon, and for fear
of trouble, or greater constraint and violence to satisfy their
Adversaries; but after they had for some years lived in this
manner, they did that very year that preceded the German
War [Louis XIV's forcible "Reunions" began in 1680, and
the first devastation of the Palatinate occurred in 1683–84],
wherein all that Fruitful and Delicious Countrey was
wasted with Fire and Sword, by those Men [the French]
who shewed themselves so much more skillful and ready to
Destroy then to Conqer especially these late years, of their
own accord and in a considerate manner, so as if they had
foreseen so great a War and been afraid of such an impend-
ing Calamity, forsake their Native Countrey, those Villages
and Cottages, which they could scarce bear up with props
and stakes, and entred into a voluntary and perpetual
Banishment, so passed over into *Pensilvania,* being that
part of *English America* that I have before described in
which part of the world, each of them having Land Distributed and Assigned unto them by the Proprietor of that
part, *William Penn,* they live now in the greatest Freedom
and plentifully enough.''

PERSECUTION AND EMIGRATION

The renewed persecutions which resulted in this emigration, Croese rightly ascribes to the clergy, who were not only
incensed by the doctrinal heresy of the Quakers, but also
alarmed by their opposition to the union of church and state
and the influence exerted by the ecclesiastical upon the
political power. Penn, for example, in his letter of 1677 to
the Elector wrote: "The clergy in most countries is not
only a co-ordinate power, a kind of duumvirateship in government, *imperium in imperio,* at least an eclipse to
monarchy; but a superior power, and rideth the Prince to
their designs, holding the helm of the government, and
steering not by the laws of civil freedom, but certain ecclesiastical maxims of their own, to the maintenance and

enlargement of their worldly empire in their church. And all this, acted under the sacred, peaceable, and alluring name of Christ, his ministry and church; though as remote from their nature as the wolf from the sheep, as the Pope from Peter.''

Among the practices of the Quakers which most incensed the clergy was the custom of their women to preach in public; and this outrage upon their feelings was added to their score against the Krisheim Friends. When Elisabeth Hendricks and Gertrud Deriks of Amsterdam came on a preaching tour up the Rhine in 1678, they stopped in Krisheim and their daring public attempts to make converts to Quakerism brought a storm of opposition there as it had done in Krefeld.[357] These two ''hussies, said to have come from Holland (*Weibsbilder aus Holland*)'' were accused in an official report of sojourning among the Quakers at Kriegsheim, one of them permitting herself to be used as a preacheress (*Prädikantin*), and distributing among both young people and adults, without let or hindrance, trashy publications (*gedruckte Scharteken*) as proved by an appended sample, entitled 'Eine Warnung'.''

The sample seized and delivered by the official reporter was James Parnel's ''A Warning for all People'', published in London, in 1660, in quarto. A Dutch translation of this, in broadside, was published, without place or date, under the title „Eene Vermaninge aen alle Volckeren"; and, it would appear, in a German translation also. To the latter was added a rhymed declaration or challenge by the Quakers of Krisheim, which was dated the 7th. of November, 1670, but reprinted and distributed on this opportune occasion in 1678. Its verses, in German, smack of the tongue of Holland, and read as follows:[358]

„Las die stoltzen veindten widen	Let our proud foes fume and rage,
las nur Doben ihre macht,	Let their power vainly storm!
Gott üst bey uns in der mitten,	God is with us in this age;
ihren hochmut er veracht,	He regards their threats with scorn.
haltt sie uns vor ihren spott	Though they hold us for their sport,
steht unsere Hoffung doch zu Gott."	Our hope still is stayed on God!

[357] See *supra*, p. 200.
[358] Hubben, *op. cit.*, p. 69.

This declaration was dated in Krisheim (*Dattum gries-heim*) and signed by Christoffel Morrell, Hans Plibus Laubach, Peter Schumacher, Jörg Schumacher, and Gerret Hendricus.

To make assurance doubly sure, were added to the signatures (by the public informer, or by the authors of the declaration) the words: "All these [are] Quakers." Hans Plibus may have come from Laubbach, near Coblenz, as his name implies; but the others resided in Krisheim, and two of them, as will be seen in the sequel, were of much importance in the Quaker history of Pennsylvania.

The claim of the women preachers in Krisheim to have been moved to speak by the Spirit stirred up the Rev. Joh. Reinh. Hermann, a pastor in the neighboring village of Niederflörsheim, to write a letter against the Quakers, whom he denounced as blasphemers against the Holy Ghost. A Mennonite preacher of Gerolsheim, or Görlisheim (one of the numerous *heims* near Alzey and Krisheim), by the name of Heinrich Kassel, also attacked the Quakers of Krisheim in a pamphlet entitled, "An Exposure of the Quakers or Shakers (*Beber*)." In this he dealt also with those Mennonites who had gone over to Quakerism, including some of his own relatives. Jacob Claus, "of Strassburg" replied to these clerical attacks in another pamphlet ("The Exposer Exposed"),[359] in which he quoted Kassel as saying that "the so-called Quakers, especially here in the Palatinate, have fallen off and gone out from the Mennonites." Hermann, the Niederflörsheim pastor, replied to Claus, denouncing him and his fellows as traducers and stealers of honor (*Verleumder und Ehrendiebe*); and Pieter Hendricks (*Heinrichs*) replied to Hermann in another pamphlet, entitled "Answer to a Writing of a so-called Reformed Preacher of Niederflörsheim in the Palatinate, Johann Reinhard Hermanni [sic], Pastor, which he conveyed to those People in

---

[359] „Der Entdecker entdeckt oder eine kurtzte Antwort auff das Schreiben eines Predigers unter den Mennonisten, Nahmens Heinrich Cassel von Görlisheim, welcher er nennet Eine Entdeckung der Quackers oder Bebers, und an etliche der also genanntten Quakers zu Kriesheim hat eingehändelt". Von Johannes Claus von Strassburg, Gedruckt Amsterdam bey C. C. 1678.

Kriesheim who are mockingly called Quakers, that is Shakers or Tremblers."[360]

The civil authorities also took a hand in the conflict, the electoral government at Heidelberg ordering the two women to be fined ten reichs-dollars and deported [back to Holland?]. It commanded the pastors to engage, neither in public nor in private, in useless speech, disputation, or quarrel (*Gespräch, Disputat, oder Gezänk*) with the Quakers on account of their sect, so that the less they were shamed and abused, but on the contrary were treated in a friendly, gentle, edifying, and irreproachable manner, they might be won over from the error of their ways. The Quakers, too, were commanded under "infallibly greater penalties" to print no more such things, nor to let them come otherwise into the hands of the people.

The Amsterdam Yearly Meeting's Epistle of 1680 informed the English Friends of this persecution in the Palatinate; and in response to it, Roger Longworth and Roger Haydock, accompanied by Jan Claus of Amsterdam, set forth to do what they could to stay the persecution and relieve the "sufferings", financial and otherwise, of the victims in the Rhineland and elsewhere. After a long summer's tour, they made their visit to the Krisheim Friends and then, accompanied by two of the latter, they crossed the Rhine and went to Alzey, the town where Ames and Caton had had their interview with the district officials in 1661, and which they called "Alstone", but which Longworth called "Alsaca" and Roger Haydock's editor called "Altry."

The editor of Haydock's "Writings" (1700) says that "an order was sent from the High Court at Altry, by which he [Haydock; Longworth and the others are not mentioned] was brought before the Chief Magistrate there, who kept him Prisoner eleven days, being twice brought to the Anthouse [*Amthaus*: court house] and there examined, & at last released."

---

[360] „Antwort auf ein Schriftlein eines sogenannten Gereformirten Predigers zu Niederflössheim in der Pfalz, Johann Reinhard Hermanni, Pfarrer, welches er an die Leute zu Kriesheim, die man spöttischer Weise Quaker d. h. Beber oder Zitterer nennet behändigt hat." Durch *Peter Heinrichs*, Amsterdam, C. C., 1680.

Roger Longworth, writing to Phineas Pemberton, probably at Amsterdam on his return from this journey, says :[361] "I shall give thee a short account of our traivell in the south of jeremeney. We went first to Crevelt, ... from thence we went up by the pelletiney [Palatinate] & there [at Krisheim] we had a fine time with friends & took our leave of them in much brokenness of heart, & 2 friends came along with us to a cittie called Alsaca [Alzey] where we weire to apeare before the magistrates & to give account of our bissiness in that countrie & when we came before them the [they] weir moderat & said wee must stay their till the had sent to the prince but we might be at our inn & we might have the liberty of the citty: & that day weeke the sent for us again to come before them, & the had a priest with them & toke our penimacion [affirmation?], and said we might yet stay till answer came from the prince but we might have the same liberty we had, & upon the ii [XI] day of our confinement we were set at liberty & came to Amsterdam & we are verie well blessed be the name of the Lord."

Longworth appears to have written another letter concerning this journey to James Harrison, who replied to it under date of "Boulton" (Bolton, England), the 4th. of 8th. Month, 1681, in which he says:[362] "I am glad to hear of your safe arrival & well-being & also prosparaty of truth in those parts where you have beene, god allmighty continue the same while the sun & moone endures, amen." The "prosparaty of truth", as Harrison's correspondents understood it, did not outlast the "sun & moone" on the Continent of Europe; but in the same year of their journey and just one month before their entering upon it, an event occurred which was to induce many of the adherents to "the Truth" in the Old World to transplant their religion and their homes to the shores of the New. This was the grant of the Province of Pennsylvania to William Penn.

In his letter to Longworth, Harrison mentions the significant fact that he and Elinor Low,—the financée of Roger Haydock,—are about to "bargain for" [i.e. for the sale of]

---

[361] Pemberton MSS., I, 117. This *may* have been the letter written, or posted, in Harwich; the date and place of writing are torn off.

[362] Pemberton MSS., I, 172.

Harrison's house, "in case I should goe with w: pen"; and in Longworth's letter from London, dated the 3rd. of 8th. Month, there occurs the statement: "Will: penn doth not goe to pensilvania, he is about Bristall, their is a shipe going from thence, with many passhenars."

The German records in regard to this visit allege that Longworth and Haydock pretended to have come to Krisheim as merchants desirous of buying wine, "if the wine were cheap"; that they had only spoken in English to their Friends;[363] and they denied the suspicion that they had seduced others to their sect. Thereupon, the Elector Charles ordered their release.[364]

But after the alien Quaker preachers had departed, the Friends of Krisheim had still to meet the church-tithes and the Turkish-war taxes which were demanded of them, both of which they steadfastly refused to pay as being contrary to their religious principles. Their refusal also to stand sentinel at the town's walls was the last straw which broke the patience of the electoral steward at Hochheim, Herr Schmal by name, who was spurred on by it to petition the government to order the banishment of "the foolish sect."[365] The influence of the Princess Elisabeth at the electoral court was evidently still too strong in behalf of the Quakers, and the edict of banishment was not issued. But Steward Schmal was rejoiced to report on the 9th. of May, 1685, that three Quaker households (*Hausgesäss*), to the great joy of the entire community, desired to sell their belongings (*das Ihrige*) and betake themselves to Holland or England. Schmal enclosed with this report the following request of the Quakers:

"We, the undersigned, herewith make known to the Hochheim administration under which we reside, in so far as it can be permitted us by the administrator (*Amtsschaffner*)

---

[363] They were interpreted by Jan Claus in Dutch or German!

[364] Hubben, *op. cit.*, p. 71.

[365] There is a brief memorandum in the Karlsruhe archives, dated Kriegsheim District, Florsheim, August 11, 1684, as follows: "The Quakers at Kriegsheim, formerly Mennonites but now Quakers: Henrich Gerhards, Peter Schumacher, Georg Schumacher's widow, Johannes Castle, Stofel Morett, Johannes Gerhard's widow." Pfals Generalia, 4337 (quoted by C. H. Smith, *op. cit.*, p. 94, footnote).

and not forbidden by God, to transport ourselves and our households to Holland; therefore it is our request that the administrator supply us with a certificate (*Attest*) permitting us to pass unhindered through the customs; for we would gladly depart in good will with our neighbors and acquaintances, and we earnestly hope (*verhoffen*) that we have conducted ourselves towards them and they towards us in such fashion that no one has any complaint to make on that account; and we hope that it may be granted to us.

Gerhardt Hendricks   Hans Peter Cassel

Peter Schuhmacher, widower, aged sixty years (*Witmann in die 60 Jahre*). Kriegsheim, 8. Mai 1685.''[366]

The Journey to Pennsylvania

The ultimate goal of the emigrants, of course, was neither Holland, the home of their Dutch ancestors, nor England, the home of their new religion, but the Quaker colony of Pennsylvania. They had been turning the adventure over in their minds during the three preceding years. Penn's visit of 1677 was still fresh in their remembrances; and his definite invitation of 1682 was cordially seconded by Roger Longworth, and made practicable by the aid of Benjamin Furly and Jacob Telner, Penn's agents in Rotterdam and Amsterdam. Francis Daniel Pastorius, too, stopped on his way from Frankfurt to Pennsylvania, in the spring of 1683, and paid a week's visit, he says, "to Friends at Krisheim, to wit, Peter Shoemaker, Gerhard Henrix, Arnold Cassel, etc.''

Pastorius went on down the Rhineland to Krefeld to encourage the Friends of that place in the Pennsylvania venture; and found that three of them had already, on the 10th. of March, 1683, bought 5,000 acres each of Penn's land. The Krisheim Friends communicated with those of Krefeld; and one of the three land-purchasers, Derick Sipman, having contracted with Penn to induce colonists to settle on his land, made an agreement with Hendricks and Schumacher to become co-tenants or associates of another Krefeld Quaker, Herman Isacks op den Graeff.

The Op den Graeffs and the other "original thirteen"

---

[366] Hubben, p. 71.

founders of Germantown sailed for Pennsylvania in July, 1683; but the Krisheim Friends did not petition for their passports, as has been seen, until May, 1685. They may have experienced some delay in procuring these;[367] for it was not until August 16 following that Hendricks and Schumacher received a deed from Sipman (apparently in London) conveying to each of them 200 acres of land in Pennsylvania. The deed was accompanied by an agreement (written in Dutch) that they were to proceed "with the first good wind" to Pennsylvania, receive their land from Hermann op den Graeff, build dwellings upon it, and pay a quit-rent of two rix dollars a year.

The "first good wind" soon blew, for George Fox in his Itinerary Journal under the date of the 18th. of the 6th. Month (August), 1685, records that he went "to John Cashamers [in London] to see some Germaine fri[ds] y[t] were going to pensilvania"; and on the 12th. of October 1685, the ship *Francis and Dorothy* arrived in Philadelphia, having on board the Schumacher and Hendricks households. The household of Hans Peter Cassel, the third signer of the passport petition, was delayed for some reason another five months, and did not arrive in Philadelphia until March 20, 1686; and with these latter colonists came another branch of the Schumacher family from Krisheim, namely, that of Georg (or Jörg), who *may* have "died on the voyage and been buried at sea," leaving his widow, Sarah, and her seven children to continue on the great adventure.[368]

THE KRISHEIM QUAKER PIONEERS

Reviewing the story of the Dutch Quaker leaders in Krisheim, the co-founders (with those in Krefeld) of Germantown, Pennsylvania, we find that Jan Hendriks, Jakob Jansen, Hans Philip Laubach, Christopher (Christoffel, or

---

[367] For example, Herr Schmal, when reporting their request for passports, inquired if he should humor them *(ihnen willfahren)* and let them go *after they had paid the ten-penny tax*. This tax, too, may have been obnoxious to their principles.

[368] Benjamin Hallowell, one of the founders of Swarthmore College, was a descendant of Georg, and a letter from him regarding the family was printed in the *Pennsylvania Magazine*, Vol. 6 (1882), p. 497. (Cf. *infra*, p. 408.)

Stoffel) Morett, Jörg Schumacher, and Peter Schumacher the elder were the pioneers who were "convinced" of Quakerism by William Ames, and suffered for their faith as early as 1658, 1659 and 1660; that Hendriks, Laubach (or Laubeck), Morett (or Morrell, or Murrett), Hendricks Gerrits, Görg (or Jörg) and Peter Schumacher, Agnes Jacobsen (the widow of Jan or Jakob Jansen), and the wife of Velter Eberten were the sufferers in 1663 and 1664; that Hendriksen, Morett, Jörg and Peter Schumacher, were the sufferers in 1666; that Morrett, Laubach, Jörg and Peter Schumacher and Gerrit (or Gerhardt) Hendricks signed the rhymed defiance of 1670, and helped to distribute copies of James Parnel's "Warning to all Men", in 1679; that Peter Schumacher, Gerhardt Hendricks, and Hans Peter Cassel petitioned for a passport to Pennsylvania in May, 1685; that Peter Schumacher (with his children, Peter, Mary, Frances and Gertrud, and his cousin Sarah), Gerhard Hendricks (with his wife Mary, his daughter Sarah, and his servant Heinrich Frey of Altheim, Alsace) and Heivert Papen, arrived in Philadelphia in October, 1685; and that Hans Peter Cassel (with his children Arnold, Peter, Elisabeth, Mary and Sarah), and Sarah, the widow of Jörg Schumacher (with her children George, Abraham, Barbara, Isaac, Susanna, Elizabeth and Benjamin) arrived in Philadelphia in March, 1686.

The End of Quakerism in Krisheim

Thus it was that the stream of emigration to Germantown on the Schuylkill rapidly and completely exhausted the reservoir of Quakerism at Krisheim on the Rhine. Jan Claus, in the Amsterdam Epistle of 1686, wrote its epitaph as follows: "The meeting of Friends in the Palatinate is in effect dissolved, by reason that most of the Friends of that place have removed themselves from thence to Pennsylvania; and the rest, save one ancient man, are ready, as we hear, to come away too this summer." Willem Sewel, commenting on this emigration, says: "Some families receiving the doctrine he preached [i.e. William Ames at Krisheim, in 1657], bore a public testimony for it there, and so continued till the settlement of Pennsylvania in America, when they unanimously went thither, not as it seemed without a singular direction of Providence; for not long after, a war ensued in Germany, where the Palatinate was altogether laid waste by the French, and thousands of people were bereft of their possessions, and reduced to poverty."[369]

Professor Seidensticker, who visited Krisheim in 1874, says that "no remembrance of Penn's visit clings to the place. The old Quaker families, mentioned by Besse, Sewel and Pastorius, are not represented by descendants of the same names; and to make oblivion complete, the church records, containing registers of births, marriages, and deaths, were destroyed by fire in 1848. The disappearance of the old Quaker families is accounted for partly by their emigration to Pennsylvania, partly by the sacking and burning of Palatine cities and villages during the French invasions."[370]

THE KRISHEIMERS IN PENNSYLVANIA

The story of these Krisheim colonists in Pennsylvania is a worthy one, and in the case of Gerrit Hendricks it is one of much historic importance, reaching even beyond the primary step of taking part in founding a colony which grew into a great commonwealth. Hans Peter Cassel and Heivert Papen were among the citizens to whom a charter of self-government for Germantown was granted in 1691. Papen accepted the office of recorder of the court in 1696, but manifested his Quakerism, five years later, in a rather excessive conscientiousness which caused him to decline the office of burgess. Arnold Cassel became "Rekorder" in 1691, but proved *his* orthodox Quakerism the next year by signing the certificate issued against George Keith. Peter Schumacher signed the certificate against Keith, and was justice of the Germantown court. In his house, which stood in "the meadow", on Shoemaker's Lane (now Penn Street), the Friends held their early meetings, and Penn is said to have

---

[369] "History of the Quakers", Amsterdam, 1717, p. 250; N. Y., 1844, I, 253.
[370] *The Pennsylvania Magazine*, Vol. II (1878), p. 265, note 2.

preached to Germantown's citizens from its door-step. Peter Schumacher the third[371] was one of the charter grantees in 1691, and a founder of the first school in Germantown in 1701.

GERRIT HENDRICKS AND ANTI-SLAVERY

Gerrit Hendricks was the son of Hendrick Gerrits, two of whose cows ("worth twenty-seven Guilders") were confiscated in 1663 because he persisted in attending Quaker meetings. Hendrick disappears from the records after this, but his son Gerrit took up his father's leadership in Krisheim's Quaker circle, and came with his family to Pennsylvania in 1685. Only three years then elapsed before he showed his desire for freedom for *all* men by signing the famous Germantown Friends' protest and petition against human slavery. His name is the first of four on the petition, two of the others being those of Derick and Abraham op den Graeff, Dutch Quakers from Krefeld, and the fourth that of Francis Daniel Pastorius, a German "Pietist" who was an active member of the Germantown Friends' meeting.[372]

The last paragraph of the petition has two corrections in it, namely, "This was", changed to "This is"; and "our monthly meeting at Germantown", changed to "our meeting at Germantown". There was no "monthly meeting" set up at this time in Germantown, but only a "preparative meeting" which was a constituent part of the monthly meeting at Dublin, a few miles distant.[373] It is probable that the protest was adopted by *all* the members of the Germantown meeting, and that "gerret hendericks" signed his name as clerk to the copy to be sent to the monthly meeting, while the other three Friends signed theirs as members of the com-

---

[371] He was Peter the second in America, grandson of Peter the Quaker of Krisheim.

[372] See photograph of the original document, *infra*, opposite p. 110. This document was known only by references to it in the meeting-records of 1688 until a Philadelphia Friend, Nathan Kite, found and published it in *The Friend* (Philadelphia), January 13, 1844. It is now preserved in the Library of the Pennsylvania Historical Society.

[373] The meeting-house probably stood in "Francfort", later Oxford Township, Philadelphia County, on the site of the present Trinity Church.

mittee who were appointed to present the petition to the monthly meeting.[374]

The petition was adopted by the Germantown meeting on ye 18 of the 2 month [April], 1688, and duly "delivered to the monthly meeting at Richard Worrels." The monthly meeting disposed of it by the following minute: "At our monthly meeting at Dublin ye 30 —2 mo—: 1688 we having inspected ye matter above mentioned & considered of it, we finde it so weighty that we think it not Expedient for vs to meddle with it here, but do Rather comit it to ye consideration of ye Quarterly meeting; ye tennor of it being nearly related to ye truth.

On behalfe of ye monthly meeting.

Signed,　　　　　　P[per]　　　　　　Jo: Hart"

It was accordingly presented to the Quarterly Meeting, which forwarded it to the Yearly Meeting, the former meeting adopting the following minute:[375]

"This above mentioned was read in our quarterly meetting at Philadelphia, the 4 of ye 4th mo 88 and was from thence recommended to the Yearly Meetting and the abovesaid Derick and the other two mentioned therein to present the same to ye Abovesaid meetting it being a thing of too great A weight for this meeting to determine.

Signed by order of ye meetting

Anthony Morris."

The minute adopted by the Yearly Meeting was as follows:

"At a Yearly Meeting held at Burlington the 5th day of the 7th month, 1688.

"A Paper being here presented by some German Friends Concerning the Lawfulness and Unlawfulness of Buying and keeping Negroes,[376] It was adjudged not to be so proper

---

[374] When the petition came to the Philadelphia Quarterly Meeting, it was forwarded to the Yearly Meeting to be presented by "the above-said Derick and the other *two* mentioned therein."

[375] The minutes of the Monthly and Quarterly meetings are written on the original document, and the Yearly Meeting's minute is recorded in its record-book.

[376] This word was substituted in the Yearly Meeting's minute for the word *Slaves*, which was used in the Protest.

for this Meeting to give a Positive Judgment in the Case, It having so General a Relation to many other Parts, and therefore at Present they forbear It.''

The protest did indeed have ''so General a Relation to many other Parts'', as was discovered throughout all of the Americas within subsequent years; and the Friends were to discover that they could ''forbear it'' only ''at present'', and that it would become their chief humanitarian task to put an end to the evil against which it was levelled. It was in fact not five years before the Quaker followers of George Keith published ''An Exhortation & Caution to Friends Concerning buying or keeping of Negroes'', New York (William Bradford), 1693, which was the first protest against slavery *printed* in America.[377] In 1696, also, the Philadelphia Yearly Meeting received anti-slavery protests from some of its Pennsylvania members (prominent among whom was Cadwallader Morgan), and it advised its members against the importation of slaves.

As to the individual personally responsible for the Protest of 1688, Francis Daniel Pastorius has been cited as its author because its handwriting resembles his. But if he wrote it, it was doubtless because he was more skilled in English than were his Dutch associates, the English of the petition, however, being very crude indeed for Pastorius, and Holland taking precedence of Germany in it. Its ''concern'' was and had been for years resting heavily upon the hearts of the leading Quakers in England and Holland. Benjamin Furly of Rotterdam, for example, who had been so active in promoting the emigration of the Krefeld and Krisheim Friends to Pennsylvania, had suggested to Penn, six years before the Germantown protest and at the very time when the Germantown pilgrims were passing through Rotterdam, that he should add the following ''Law'' to those he had drawn up for Pennsylvania: ''Let no blacks be brought in directly. And if any come out of Virginia, Maryld. in families that have formerly bought them elsewhere Let them

---

[377] On its last page is the statement: "Given forth by our Monthly Meeting in Philadelphia, the 13th day of the 8th Month, 1693, and recommended to all our Friends and Brethren who are one with us in our Testimony for the Lord Jesus Christ, and too all others professing Christianity."

be declared (as in y* west jersey constitutions) free at 8 years end.''[378] The abolition of the slave-trade and speedy emancipation, therefore, was Furly's solution of the problem of human slavery; and we may well imagine the conversations which he doubtless had on the subject when he entertained Pastorius, the Krefeld and the Krisheim pilgrims in his home in Rotterdam before speeding them across the ocean to advocate freedom for all in their own refuge from oppression.

The protest, which is full of concentrated common-sense as well as the Quaker version of Christianity, reads as follows:

"This is to y* Monthly Meeting held at Richard Worrell's.

"These are the reasons why we are against the traffick of men Body, as followeth: Js there any that would be done or handled at this manner? viz., to be sold or made a slave for all the time of his life? How fearfull & fainthearted are many on sea when they see a strange vessel, being afraid it should be a Turck, and they should be tacken and sold for slaves into Turckey. Now what is this better done as Turcks doe? yea rather is it worse for them, wch say they are Christians; for we hear that ye most part of such Negers are brought heither against their will & consent; and that many of them are stollen. Now, tho' they are black, we cannot conceive there is more liberty to have them slaves, as it is to have other white ones. There is a saying, that we shall doe to all men, licke as we will be done our selves; making no difference of what generation, descent or Colour they are. And those who steal or robb men, and those who buy or purchase them, are they not all alike? Here is liberty of Conscience, wch is right & reasonable; here ought to be lickewise liberty of y* body, except of evildoers, wch is an other case. But to bring men hither, or to robb and sell them against their will, we stand against. Jn Europe there are many oppressed for Conscience sacke; and here there are those oppressed wch are of a black Colour. And we, who know that

---

[378] The "Concessions" to West Jersey, of 1677–78, included perpetual freedom "from oppression and slavery"; but Penn rejected it on Furly's recommendation for Pennsylvania. See *infra*, p. 344.

men must not comitt adultery, some doe comitt adultery in others, separating wifes from their housbands and giving them to others; and some sell the children of those poor Creatures to other men. Oh! doe consider well this thinge, you who doe it; if you would be done at this manner? and if it is done according Christianity? You surpass Holland and Germany in this thing. This mackes an ill report in all those Countries of Europe, where they hear off, that yᵉ Quackers doe here handel men licke they handel there yᵉ Cattel. And for that reason some have no mind or inclination to come hither, and who shall maintaine this your cause or plaid for it? Truely we can not do so, except you shall inform us better hereoff, viz: that christians have liberty to practise this thinge. Pray! What thing in the world can be done worse towards us, then if men should robb or steal us away, & sell us for slaves to strange Countries, separating housband from their wifes & children. Being now this is not done at that manner, we will be done at, therefore we contradict & are against this traffick of menbody. And we who profess that it is not lawfull to steal, must lickewise avoid to purchase such things as are stollen, but rather help to stop this robbing and stealing if possible; and such men ought to be delivered out of yᵉ hands of yᵉ Robbers & and sett free as well as in Europe. Then is Pennsilvania to have a good report, instead it hath now a bad one for this sacke in other Countries. Especially whereas yᵉ Europeans are desirous to know in what manner yᵉ Quackers doe rule in their Province; & most of them doe loock upon us with an envious eye. But if this is done well, what shall we say is done evill?

"If once these slaves, (:wᶜʰ they say are so wicked and stubbern men:) should joint themselves, fight for their freedom and handel their masters & mastrisses as they did handel them before; will these Masters and mastrisses tacke the sword at hand & warr against these poor slaves, licke we are able to belive, some will not refuse to doe? Or have these Negers not as much right to fight for their freedom, as you have to keep them slaves?

"Now consider well this thing, if it is good or bad? and in case you find it to be good to handel these blacks at that manner, we desire & require you hereby lovingly, that you

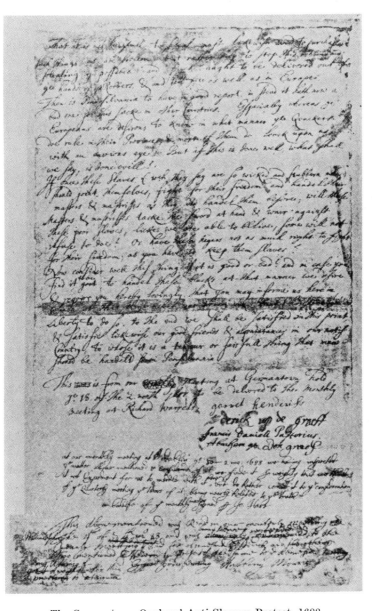

The Germantown Quakers' Anti-Slavery Protest, 1688

may informe us here in, which at this time never was done, viz., that Christians have such a liberty to do so. to the end we shall be satisfied in this point, & satisfie lickewise our good friends & acquaintances in our natif Country, to whose it is a terrour or fairfull thing that men should be handeld so in Peñsilvania.

"This is from our Meeting at Germantown held yᵉ 18. of the 2. month 1688. to be delivred to the Monthly Meeting at Richard Worrel's.

gerret hendericks
derick op de graeff
Francis Daniell Pastorius
Abraham op Den graef.''

Such is the memorable flower which blossomed in Pennsylvania from the seed of Quakerism sown among the Dutch Quakers of Krefeld and Krisheim, and which was to mature in due season into the fruit of freedom for both mind and body of the Negro slave in all America.

"Oh! if the spirits of the parted come,
"Visiting angels, to their olden home;
"If the dead fathers of the land look forth
"From their fair dwellings, to the things of earth,
"Is it a dream, that with their eyes of love,
"They gaze now on us from the bowers above?
"........ And that brother-band,
"The sorrowing exiles from their 'Fatherland',
"Leaving their homes in Kriesheim's bowers of vine,
"And the blue beauty of their glorious Rhine,
"To seek amidst our solemn depths of wood
"Freedom from man and holy peace with God:
"Who first of all their testimonial gave
"Against the oppressor, for the outcast slave,
"Is it a dream that such as these look down
"And with their blessing our rejoicing crown?''

(John G. Whittier, "Pennsylvania Hall", 1838).

This note of freedom for the slave, struck in the settlement of Germantown by the Dutch Quakers and their German associate, matches that of religious freedom struck in the settlement of Philadelphia; and it alone would make memorable the smaller and humbler settlement. Indeed, freedom of religious conviction also, and its supremacy over "the things that are Caesar's", was largely the gift to the modern world of those religious sectarians who suffered so terribly and endured so steadfastly in Holland during the Sixteenth and early Seventeenth Century. The determination that "the things that are Caesar's", but not "the things that are God's", shall be controlled by the voice of the people, they contributed to the ideal of democracy.

Along with these ideals of freedom, the Dutch settlers of Germantown brought their crafts of spinning and weaving and set going the first of those thousand mills which have made Pennsylvania famous. The neat and pleasing arts of daily living, which they inherited from their Dutch ancestors and practised in the wilderness, made sweetness and light shine in their humble dwellings. Their love of art and music and of high intellectual endeavor contributed in no small degree to the cultural life of their own and other communities enshrined within "the Woods of Penn".

Thus, both in great things and in the intimate realities of daily life they contributed noteworthy aid to the success of Penn's "Holy Experiment".

CHAPTER V

THE TREK TO PENNSYLVANIA

William Penn's journeys in 1677 and 1686 through the
Netherlands and the western German lands were perhaps
the single event of chief importance in promoting the emigration of Dutch and German Quakers and others to Pennsylvania; and for the Dutch and German colonists, as well
as for the English, he was preëminently "the Founder."
But that there were other reasons than his influence, of a
religious, economic and political kind, for that emigration,
has already been made plain.[379]
Penn led in person the settlement of his province in 1682–
84, and appears to have planned three years later to say
farewell forever to the banks of the Thames and make his
permanent home on the banks of the Delaware. A letter
from Willem Sewel, dated May 23, 1687, speaks of "a certain vague rumor" that Penn and his wife were coming to
Amsterdam "before you migrate to Pennsylvania."[380] If
such was Penn's intention, the Revolution of 1688–89 and
the cloud of suspicion which surrounded him during a half-
dozen subsequent years put an end to it. He remained in
England to face the charges of Jesuitism and treason which
were levelled against him. When these were effectually disposed of, he went with his family, in 1699, to Pennsylvania,
hoping to live for the remainder of his life amidst the colonists whom his influence and example had largely induced to
settle there. But only two years had elapsed when political
and financial difficulties in both England and Pennsylvania
caused him to decide that he could best serve his colonists'
interests by returning, for a time at least, to London.[381]
These difficulties grew heavier and more complicated after
his return and after the accession of Queen Anne, until they
broke his health and ended his life in his English home.

[379] *Supra*, pp. 236–238.
[380] See Monograph Number One ("Willem Sewel of Amsterdam"), p. 77.
[381] Cf. his speech to the Pennsylvania Assembly, on the 15th. of September,
1701.

CHARGES AGAINST PENN

The motives of Penn's preaching-tours in the Netherlands and Germany were regarded by his contemporaries as both religious and political. A young physician, Dr. John Northleigh of London, was in Rotterdam at the time of Penn's visit in 1686, and heard him preach what Northleigh calls "a good Ingenious English Sermon [through an interpreter, Benjamin Furly] to his Dutch Congregation." Northleigh does not mention Penn's name, but calls him the most eminent of the English Quakers in Rotterdam; and after commenting upon his sermon, concludes his account with the remark: "Some seriously look'd upon the Preacher to come to propagate the Gospel that was here planted among that odd sort of Christians [the Quakers]; other Waggs more witty, thought his coming was only to get some more Proselytes or Planters for his large Plantations in America."[382]

This latter motive, half-political and half-religious though it was, should have appealed even to the "Waggs" of the Seventeenth Century as entirely honorable. But Penn's advocacy of religious toleration and his praise of James II for issuing the Declaration of Indulgence were ascribed by his enemies to ulterior and sinister motives. Among these, were love of money and the desire to restore England to the Stuart monarchy and Roman Catholicism. As a Jesuit in disguise, Penn was charged with merely pretending to believe in religious toleration; and his many treatises and speeches on this topic during the years 1685 to 1689, were regarded as a means of attaining his real object.

His treatise entitled "Good Advice to the Church-of-England, Roman Catholick, and Protestant Dissenter",[383] was an eloquent appeal for the repeal of the Test Act and penal laws; and his learned book, "No Cross, no Crown",[384] stressed religious toleration among the other noblest virtues. But both of these writings were ascribed to their author's sinister motives. Willem Sewel translated both of

---

[382] Cf. *supra*, p. 117.

[383] London, 1687; Amsterdam, 1687.

[384] London, 1669 and 1682; Amsterdam, 1687.

them into Dutch and published them in Amsterdam. In a letter to Penn, dated September 24, 1687, Sewel wrote:[385] "Your book concerning the Cross is being distributed, but slowly. Indeed, I think that some of the Mennonites are doing everything within their power (*manibus pedibusq*) to instill in people a wrong opinion concerning you; for there are certain of the Collegiants, I am informed, who say that you are a Jesuit, and that a Snake lies hidden somewhere in the grass: because your admonitions to live piously and scrupulously are nothing else than bait to entice the credulous to Pennsylvania. But when such things are also said of you in your own Country (if one can believe public reports) why not also here? And indeed men of disturbance and abuse are to be found everywhere."

One of Penn's treatises on toleration, entitled "A Letter to Mr. Penn, with his Answer", was published in London, two years later; and this also was translated by Sewel, and published in Amsterdam. The author of the letter, a friendly critic named Sir William Popple, sums up the charges against Penn as follows:

"The Source of all arises from the ordinary Access you have unto the King, the Credit you are supposed to have with Him, and the deep Jealousie that some people have conceived of His Intentions in reference to Religion. Their Jealousie is, that His Aim has been to settle Popery in this Nation, not only in a fair and secure Liberty, but even in a predominating Superiority over all other Professions. And from hence the inference follows, That whosoever has any part in the Councels of this Reign, must needs be Popishly affected; But that to have so great a part in them, as you are said to have had, can happen to none but an absolute Papist. *That is the direct Charge.* But that is not enough. Your Post is too considerable for a Papist of an ordinary Form: and therefore you must be a Jesuit. Nay, to confirm that Suggestion, it must be accompanied with all the circumstances that may best give it an Air of Probability; as that you have been bred at St. *Omers*, in the Jesuits Colledge; that you have taken Orders at *Rome*, and there obtained a

---

[385] See Monograph Number One ("Willem Sewel of Amsterdam"), p. 89.

Dispensation to Marry; and that you have, since then, frequently officiated as a Priest, in the Celebration of the Mass, at *White Hall,* St. *James's,* and other Places. And this being admitted, nothing can be too black to cast upon you. Whatsoever is thought amiss either in Church or State, tho never so contrary to your Advice, is boldly attributed to it. . . .

"I have seen also your Justification from another Calumny of common fame, about your having kidnapp'd one who had been formerly a *Monk,* out of your *American* Province, to deliver him here into the Hands of his Enemies; I say, I have seen your Justification from that Story under that Persons own Hand: And his Return to *Pensylvania,* where he now resides, may be an irrefragable Confutation of it, to any that will take the pains to inquire thereinto."

Penn willingly accepted the friendly opportunity offered by this public letter to publish a specific reply to the charges against him. His reply was devoted chiefly to an advocacy of religious liberty; but in regard to himself, he said:

"The Business chiefly insisted upon, is my *Popery,* and Endeavours to promote it. I do say then, and that with all Sincerity, that I am not only no *Jesuit,* but no *Papist.* And which is more, I never had any Temptation upon me to be it, either from Doubts in my own Mind about the Way I profess, or from the Discourses or Writings of any of that Religion. And in the Presence of Almighty God I do declare, that the King did never once, directly or indirectly, attack me, or tempt me upon that Subject, the many Years that I have had the Advantage of a free Access to him; so unjust, as well as sordidly false, are all those Storys of the Town.

"The only Reason, that I can apprehend, they have to repute me a *Roman Catholick,* is my frequent going to *Whitehall;* a place no more forbid to me than to the rest of the World; who yet, it seems, find much fairer Quarter. I have almost continually had one Business or other there for our Friends, whom I ever served with a steady Solicitation, through all times since I was of their Communion.

"I had also a great many personal good Offices to do upon a Principle of Charity, for People of all Persuasions; thinking it a Duty to improve the little Interest I had, for the Good of those that needed it, especially the *Poor,* I might add something of my own Affairs too; though I must own, (if I may without Vanity) that they have ever had the least share of my Thoughts or Pains, or else they would not have still depended as they yet do.

"But because some People are so unjust as to render Instances for my *Popery*, (or *Hypocrisie* rather, for so it would be in me) 'tis fit I contradict them as particularly as they accuse me. I say then solemnly, that I am so far from having been bred at St. *Omers*, and having received Orders at *Rome*, that I never was at either Place; nor do I know any body there; nor had I ever a Correspondency with any one in those Places, which is another Story invented against me. And as for my Officiating in the *Kings Chappel*, or any other, it is so ridiculous as well as untrue, that (besides that no body can do it but a Priest, and that I have been marryed to a Woman of some Condition above sixteen Years, which no Priest can be, by any Dispensation whatever) I have not so much as *lookt* into any Chappel of the *Roman* Religion, and consequently not the Kings; though a common Curiosity warrants it daily to People of all Perswasions. And once for all, I do say that I am a Protestant Dissenter. . . .

"A likely thing indeed, that a *Prostestant Dissenter*, who from Fifteen Years old has been (at times) a Sufferer, *in his Father's Family, in the University, and by the Government,* for being so, should design the Destruction of the Protestant Religion! This is just as probable, as it is true that I *dy'd a Jesuit* Six Years ago in *America*.[386] Will men still suffer such Stuff to pass upon them? Is any thing more foolish, as well as false, than that because I am often at *White-Hall*, therefore I must be the Author of all that is done there that does not please abroad?"

Willem Sewel, in translating this pamphlet, added to it a preface of his own, in which he referred to an accusation recently published in the *Utrechtsche Courant,* and to another

---

[386] Philip Ford published in London in 1683, in two folio pages a tract entitled "A Vindication of William Penn", which denied the rumor circulated in London after Penn had sailed to Pennsylvania that he had died on his arrival in America, and had confessed on his death-bed his belief in the Roman Catholic religion. This tract also contained extracts from Penn's own letters.

appearing in a book („Engeland Beroerd") just issued in Amsterdam.[387] The first accusation was that "the Arch-Quaker (*Aarts-quaker*) Penn had fled from England and was trying to stir up the inhabitants of Pennsylvania and other places in America against the rule of the king now on the throne [William III]"! The second report was that "William Penn, a wicked instrument and an Arch-Quaker, had been arrested at White Hall (*Withal*)", and that it was commonly said he would soon be put an end to.

These charges were evidently discounted, on the Continent as in England, as the fabrications of Penn's political enemies and jealous rivals for the king's favor, and they did not detract, in the minds of the oppressed people of the Netherlands and Germany, from the attractiveness of Pennsylvania. Francis Daniel Pastorius, for example, wrote of Penn when he first met him in Philadelphia, as follows:

"Of this very worthy man and celebrated ruler, I should, in justice, write much more; but my pen, (although it is from an eagle, which a so-called savage recently brought into my house) is much too weak to express the lofty virtues of this Christian, for such he is in deed. . . . . I cannot say more than that Will. Penn is a man who honors God, and is honored by Him in return: who loves that which is good and is justly loved by all good men, &c. I doubt not, some will yet come hither themselves and experience in fact that my pen has not written enough in this matter."

James Claypoole, who bought 5,000 acres of land in Pennsylvania, and went over on the same ship as the Krefelders to settle there in 1683, wrote to a friend as follows (July, 1681): "I have begun my letter in too little a ps. [piece] of pap. to give thee my Judgmt. of Pensilvania, but in short I and many others wiser than I doe very much approve of it: and doe Judge Wm. Penn as fitt a man as any is in Europe to plant a Country". Claypoole must have exerted a reassuring influence upon the minds of his fellow-colonists as to the promise of Pennsylvania, even though his conception of the exact location of this promised land was rather vague. In another letter (March, 1682), he described it as "Pensilvania a Colony in yᵉ West Indies near Mary Land."

---

[387] Monograph Number One ("Willem Sewel of Amsterdam", p. 89).

PENNSYLVANIA'S ATTRACTIVENESS

As for the attractiveness of Pennsylvania, some idea of its successful appeal to the religious, economic and political needs of colonists is afforded by the fact that while the land along the Delaware under the jurisdiction of "New Sweden" attracted about five hundred settlers within seventeen years, fleeing from the horrors of the Thirty Years War, there came to Pennsylvania more than three thousand settlers in a single year of European peace. Comparing Pennsylvania with New York under English rule, a Swedish natural philosopher and traveller in America writes as follows:[388]

"Though the Province of New York has been inhabited by Europeans much longer than Pennsylvania, yet it is not by far so populous as that colony. This cannot be ascribed to any particular discouragement arising from the nature of the soil, for that is pretty good; but I am told of a very different reason, which I will mention here. In the reign of Queen Anne, about the year 1709, many Germans came hither, who got a tract of land from the English government, which they might settle. After they had lived there some time, and had built houses, and made corn-fields and meadows, their liberties and privileges were infringed, and, under several pretences, they were repeatedly deprived of parts of their land. This at last roused the Germans. They returned violence for violence, and beat those who thus robbed them of their possessions. But these proceedings were looked upon in a very bad light by the government. The most active people among the Germans being taken up, they were roughly treated, and punished with the utmost rigor of the law. This, however, so far exasperated the rest, that the greater part of them left their houses and fields, and went to settle in Pennsylvania. There they were exceedingly well received, got a considerable tract of land, and were indulged in great privileges, which were given them forever.

---

[388] *Peter Kalm's Travels in America, in 1747 and 1748*" (Vol. I, pp. 270, 271). Kalm, was born at Ostro, Bothnia, in 1715, traveled from 1748 to 1751 in North America, and at a later period in Russia; he became Professor of Botany at the University of Abo, and died in 1779.

"The Germans, not satisfied with being themselves removed from New York, wrote to their relations and friends,
and advised them, if ever they intended to come to America,
not to go to New York, where the government had shown
itself so unequitable. This advice had such influence that the
Germans who afterwards went in great numbers to North
America, constantly avoided New York and always went to
Pennsylvania. It sometimes happened that they were forced
to go on board of such ships, as were bound for New York,
but they were scarce got on shore, when they hastened on to
Pennsylvania, in sight of all the inhabitants of New York.''

PENN AS AN ADVERTISER

Quaker statesman and colonizer that he was, Penn did
not hide the light, either of his religion or of his colony under a bushel, but resorted to the pen, the press, and the promoter to make them seen and known of all whom he could
reach in Europe. Indeed, thanks to him and his devoted assistants who will be referred to later, Pennsylvania was
probably the best advertised of all the American colonies;
and even the "super-salesmen" of our own day cannot vie
in advertising achievements with Penn, Furly, Telner and
Longworth.

During the decade before the acquisition of his colony, and
especially after his first and second visits to the Continent,
he had at least ten of his writings translated into Dutch
(five of them into German) and published in Rotterdam and
Amsterdam.

These included: "Truth Exalted" and "A Warning to
the English Nation'';[389] "A Trumpet, Blown in the Ears
of the Inhabitants of High and Low Germany'';[390] "Missive to the Netherlands Nation'';[391] "A Letter of Love to
the Young convinced...'';[392] "Christian Liberty, or a Copy
of a Letter to the Burgomasters and Senate of the City of

---

[389] Translated into Dutch with a preface by Benjamin Furly, Amsterdam,
1675.

[390] *Ibid.*, 1672.

[391] *Ibid.*, 1672 or 1673.

[392] Translated probably by Furly, and published in Rotterdam, 1677.

Emden'';³⁹³ ''A Call to Christendom, ... Written at Amsterdam, the 20th. of the 8th. Month, 1677'';³⁹⁴ ''A Letter to the Friends of God dwelling in the Netherlands and various Districts in High Germany (*Hoogduytslandt*)'':³⁹⁵ ''A Tender Visitation in the Love of God to all People in the High and Low-Dutch Nations'';³⁹⁶ ''Tender Counsel and Advice, by way of Epistle to all who are sensible of their Day of Visitation'';³⁹⁷ ''To all who are separated from the visible Sects and Outward Congregations'';³⁹⁷ and ''Tender Counsel and Advice''.³⁹⁷

Besides these printed messages, Penn wrote a series of letters, general and personal, to correspondents on the Continent, the first of which dates from 1672. There are extant seven of these, which were written during the next seven years, addressed as follows: ''To Friends and People of yᵉ United Netherlands'';³⁹⁸ ''To the friends of God in the Netherlands and severall partes of Germany'';³⁹⁹ ''To the

---

³⁹³ Rotterdam, 1675. The Latin original of this Letter may have been written in Amsterdam, in 1671, on Penn's return from a visit to Emden, and published first (in the Latin) in Amsterdam or Rotterdam in 1672; its English version was published in London, in 1674; a Dutch reprint in Rotterdam and Amsterdam, 1681.

³⁹⁴The Dutch version of this (probably by Furly) was published in Rotterdam in 1678; but its English original was apparently not published until 1695. Its Dutch version was reprinted in Rotterdam in 1684, and a German version probably at the same place and time,—although the German version of 1750 appears to be the only German one forthcoming.

³⁹⁵ It was probably written in London, the 10th. of 12th. Month, 1674; but its first Dutch edition is not forthcoming in that year. It was reprinted in the collection of Quaker tracts entitled "Ancient Truth Revealed *(De Oude Waarheyd Ontdekt)*", Rotterdam, 1684.

³⁹⁶ It was probably written just before or just after Penn's visit to the Continent in 1677, and printed in Dutch and German at that time; it was reprinted, in Dutch, in „De Oude Waarheyd Ontdekt", Rotterdam, 1684.

³⁹⁷ These three tracts were also probably written in Amsterdam or Rotterdam in 1677, and were published together with "A Call to Christendom", in Dutch translation in Rotterdam (by Jan Pietersz Groenwout, wonende op het Speuy), 1678, under the title „Het Christenrijk ten Oordeel gedagvaart." Their Dutch versions were reprinted in Rotterdam in 1684. Their German versions may also have been published in Amsterdam at the same time; but their only German versions forthcoming now were published, together with "A Call to Christendom", in a single volume, in Amsterdam in 1750.

³⁹⁸ The Roberts MSS., 1672.

³⁹⁹ Pennsylvania Historical Society MSS., 1674.

Friends of God in Holland and Germany'';[400] ''To I. [Isaac] and G. [Gertrud] Jacobs, P. and E. Hendricks'';[401] ''To P. Hendricks;''[402] ''To P. Hendricks and Others'';[403] and ''To P. Hendricks and J. Claus''.[404] The first three of these were translated into Dutch and printed in pamphlet form for wide circulation.

After the acquisition of his province Penn wrote, between 1683 and 1687, nine letters which are extant, addressed: ''To worthy and well beloved Friends and Brethren'';[405] ''To B. Furly'';[406] ''A Missive from William Penn'';[407] ''To B. Furly'';[408] ''To S. Crisp'' (in re Pennsylvania) ;[409] ''To S. Crisp'' (in re Pennsylvania) ;[410] ''To S. Crisp'';[411] ''To the Friends of God dwelling in the Netherlands and various Districts of Germany'';[412] and ''To Jan Claus and Pieter Hendricks''.[413]

The first, second and fourth of this second series appear never to have been printed in either English or Dutch; but Dutch and German translations of the English originals were copied by hand and distributed among prospective settlers in Pennsylvania. The third was also distributed in Dutch and German manuscript form; but it was also printed in English (1683), in Dutch (1683 and 1684), and in German (1684).[414]

---

[400] The Roberts MSS., 1678. This appears to have been published in German under the title of "To all suffering Friends in Holland and Germany," 1678.

[401] Haverford College MSS., 1673.

[402] Ibid., 1677.

[403] Ibid., 1677.

[404] Ibid., 1679.

[405] The Könneken MSS., No. 11 (1683).

[406] Ibid., No. 9 (1683).

[407] Ibid., No. 4 (1683).

[408] Ibid., No. 10 (1683).

[409] Kendall's "Letters", pp. 118–9 (1684).

[410] Smith's "Crisp", No. XIII (1684)

[411] Kendall's Letters, p. 122 (without date).

[412] Pennsylvania Historical Society MSS. (1686?); this was written jointly with Thomas Green.

[413] Haverford College MSS. (1687).

[414] It was the well-known "Letter from William Penn . . . to the Committee of the Free Society of Traders". (See infra, p. 313).

The organizer of this "correspondence bureau" and of the distribution of the letters was Benjamin Furly of Rotterdam, Penn's trusted friend and agent in the promotion of the Pennsylvania venture on the Continent of Europe. The important part he played in this rôle, and the character and contents of the letters which he caused to be distributed, are described later in this book;[415] while a sketch of his life and character, and especially of the part he played in the promotion of Quakerism in Rotterdam and elsewhere on the Continent, is reserved for another monograph in this series.[416]

Penn's use of the Dutch and German press for advertising Pennsylvania directly was almost as frequent and prolific as it had been for preparing the way for the Quaker colony by promoting the Quaker faith. Five pamphlets written by him for that purpose were translated into Dutch and German and issued from the Amsterdam and Rotterdam press.

PENN'S ACCOUNTS OF PENNSYLVANIA

The first of these was an abridged Dutch translation of a pamphlet which was one of the most successful advertisements on record, namely, "Some Account of the Province of Pennsylvania, in America; ... Made publick for the Information of such as are or may be disposed to Transport themselves and Servants into those Parts."[417] Benjamin Furly was the translator of this famous "Account", and he contributed to his translation nine lines relating to the measurement of land, while in the "Account" itself, Furly states the sums of money and dimensions of the land first in English and then, in parentheses, in Dutch. In the translation, appear also an extract from the King's proclamation of March 4 and his proclamation of April 2,

[415] *Infra*, pp. 328–345.

[416] Monograph Number Five ("Benjamin Furly, 1636–1714, and Quakerism in Rotterdam").

[417] London, 1681; Rotterdam (Pieter van Wynbrugge, in the Leeuwstraat), and Amsterdam (Jacob Claus), 1681: „Een Kort Bericht van de Provintie ofte Landschap Penn-Sylvania genaemt, leggende in America. . . ."

1681;[418] Penn's letter on freedom of conscience, entitled "The King of all Kings", which was dated, London, the 14/24 of 2nd. Month, 1674, printed in 1675 in English, Latin, Dutch and German; and at the bottom of the last page (24), the announcement that "a map (*Karte*) of this Province has just been issued."

For the benefit of prospective colonists, Furly's translation includes a postscript with definite instructions from Penn's English agents, Philip Ford and others, and a statement by Furly that "further information can be obtained in Amsterdam from Jan Roelofs van der Werf, in the Heere-Straat, at the Vergulde Vijfhoek, and in Rotterdam from Benjamin Furly, English merchant, who lives at the former Brewery of the Crown, on the Schifmakers Hafen."

At the same time, from the Amsterdam press of Christoffel Cunraden, there was issued a German translation (probably by Jan Claus) of this "Account", which was supplied with the addenda published in the Dutch edition, and eleven lines "to the indulgent reader", by the translator, in regard to the difficulties of translation, together with a short glossary (*kurtze-Auflegung*) of some English words (pp. 2 and 29–31).[419]

The divisions of the "Account" itself relate, first, to the Province; second, to the Constitution, or Laws; third, to the Conditions or Stipulations (*Voorwaarden*); fourth, to the five classes of "people who, through the providence of God are best adapted (*alderbequaamst*) to become Colonists"; and fifth, to the necessaries for the voyage and what should be done on arrival. The advice included in this last division is enforced by an appeal to "the custom in England and Holland, and of the English in New England and the Hol-

---

[418] Copies of this, in the Dutch, were made for distribution in the Könneken letters (No. 5); see *infra*, p. 332. It is interesting, also to find that a non-Quaker, César de Rochefort, published a brief account of Pennsylvania, in Rotterdam, as early as 1681; this was included in his „Recit de . . . Pennsylvania, etc.", 4 to, Reinier Leers.

[419] „Eine Nachricht wegen der Landschaft Pennsilvania in America, welche jüngstens unter dem grossen Siegel in Engelland an William Penn. . . . ; nebenst beygefügtem ehemaligen in 1675. Jahr gedrucktem Schreiben ["The King of all Kings"] des oberwehnten Will. Penns". A reprint appeared at Leipzig, 1683; and another in the *Diarium Europaeum*.

landers in New Netherland, now called New York, of providing fodder (*Winter-voer*) for their animals." The "Account" is concluded by an appeal signed by William Penn to "think it over"; and Penn's "The King of all Kings" ("Letter on Freedom of Conscience") is introduced (pp. 18–24) by the words: "In order that everyone, of whatsoever outward form of religion he may happen to be, may be the better informed as to what he may expect in Pennsylvania relating to the matter of freedom of Conscience, it has been thought wise to add here a certain Letter, &c."

From these details is evident the solicitude of Penn and his translators to reassure prospective Continental colonists as to every particular of the great adventure placed before them. Nor did they overlook the value of repetition. Another enlarged English edition of the "Short [this time the Brief] Account" was published in London, in 1682; another German edition in Frankfurth [sic], in 1683;[420] a German edition in Hamburg, 1684; a French edition („Recüeil de diverses Pièces concernant la Pensylvanie") in The Hague, in 1684;[421] and another Dutch edition in Amsterdam, in 1684. The last three of these were edited and published by Furly, who supplied them with further "Explanations", by way of postscript dated Rotterdam, March 6, 1684.

Nine months after arriving in his colony, Penn wrote another famous description of it from his own personal knowledge, entitled "A Letter to the Committee of the Free Society of Traders", dated in Philadelphia the 26th. of 8th. Mo., 1683.[422] This detailed description of the new province was quickly translated into Dutch by Furly (*Missive van William Penn*) and published in The Hague (first edition)

---

[420] In a collection entitled „Diarium Europaeum."

[421] It was probably Furly's French version of his German edition (Hamburg, 1684) entitled „Beschreibung der in America neu-erfunden Provinz Pensylvanien". The colophon of this edition is an "éclaircissemens de Monsieur Furly . . .", dated Rotterdam, this 6th. of March, 1684, referring to later letters received from Pennsylvania, and especially one from William Penn dated November 10, 1683, which tells of Pennsylvania's progress and states that "in this month there arrived five ships, among others one which brought many people *(beaucoup de gens)* from Crevelt and neighboring places, and from Maryland." This is signed "Votre très-affectionné Ami, Benjamin Furly."

[422] Printed in London, in folio, 1683.

and Amsterdam, Jacob Claus, (second edition) in 1684. To it, Furly contributed a preface of three pages "to the reader, purchaser, renters, etc," and a postscript which read as follows: "Whoever is so inclined to be conveyed to the aforesaid Colony, may come to the Bourse [in Rotterdam] to speak with Captain (*Schipper*) Jacob Maurits, of the ship *Beaver,* who intends to sail towards the last of the month called April to New York (*Nieuw Jork*) and Pensylvania [sic]; or else he may apply to Adriaan Gerritsz, Bar ber (*Haersnijder*), dwelling on the Bloemgracht, in the Wapen van Vlieland, who will supply all applicants with exact information."[423]

Besides Penn's letter or "Missive" (Pages 7 to 22), Furly's pamphlet included also "A Short Account [by Thomas Holme] of the location and size of the City of Philadelphia", together with a "Sketch (*Afteykeninge*) of the City of Philadelphia in the Province of Pennsylvania in America after the London copy, engraved in Dutch (*in 't neder duyts laeten snyden*) by Jacob Claus;[424] the King's proclamation; and an extract from Thomas Paschall's letter of February 10, 1683 (*Hollandse Stijl*), addressed to "J.J. van Chippenham, in Engelland".[425] This "Missive", with the additions in its Dutch version, was also published in German, in Hamburg, 1684.[426] Its German translation was made from the Dutch by "J. W. Hamburg, 1684", and its title-page stated that it was published at the shop of Heinrich Heuss by the bank.[427]

After Penn's return to England, he wrote "A Further Account of the Province of Pennsylvania, and its improvements. For the Satisfaction of those that are Adventurers and enclined to be so," which was dated from "Worminghurst Place, 12th of the 10th Month, [16] 85," and published without place or date, but probably in London in

---

[423] This notice was circulated also in the Könneken MSS., No. 6, as a postscript to Thomas Paschall's Letter; see *infra*, p. 333.

[424] In the Könneken MSS. (No. 5); see *infra*, p. 332.

[425] This extract was not included in the first English edition, but was circulated in the Könneken MSS. No. 6); see *infra*, p. 333. The postscript was not included in the English edition. The letter is believed to have been the first one dated from Philadelphia; Cf. *The Pennsylvania Magazine*, VI, 322.

[426] „Beschreibung Der in America neu-erfundenen Provinz Pensylvanien. . . ."

[427] *In Verlegung bey Heinrich Heusz an der Banco.*

1686. It was translated into Dutch by Willem Sewel of Amsterdam, who was busily engaged at the time on a Dutch translation of Penn's "No Cross, No Crown." Various Latin letters of Sewel to Penn relating to the latter translation are extant,[428] and one relating to the "Further Account". In this letter, dated August 4, 1686, Sewel writes:[429] "I doubt not you are expecting the *Pensylvaniensis* pamphlet; it seems not improper to inform you briefly concerning it. It is not my fault that it has not been more quickly published in the Dutch translation (*Belgicum sermonem*); but the printer causes delays. He says that he is occupied with another work which he cannot put aside immediately. However, he promised, when I was very urgent, that he would do his best to have several copies ready by the third day of the coming week; if he does not break his word, I shall see to it, God willing, that these are sent to you as quickly as possible."

The pamphlet was duly published (but without date) in Amsterdam by Jacob Claus,[430] and contained on page 19 the words: "As to the Indians' laws and religious practices, I will refer the reader to my former Account, printed by Jacob Claus at Amsterdam." It included also a letter from Robert Turner to Governor Penn, dated "Philadelphia den darde 6/m Maent (Augustus) 1685." As an evidence of the faith that was in him, Penn wrote in this pamphlet: "And because some has urged my coming back [to England], as an argument against the place [Pennsylvania], and the probability of its improvement; Adding, that I would for that reason never return; I think fit to say, That *Next Summer*, God willing, I intend to go back, and carry my Family, and the best part of my Personal Estate with me. And this I do, not only of Duty, but Inclination and Choice. God will Bless and Prosper poor *America*."

At the same time, he modified his own enthusiasm by the following caution to others: "Now for you that think of going thither, I have this to say, by way of caution; if an *hair* of our heads falls not to the ground, without the providence of God, Remember, *your Removal* is of greater

---

[428] See Monograph Number One, *passim*.
[429] *Ibid.*, pp. 66–67.
[430] „Tweede Bericht ofte Relaas van William Penn," 4 to, 20 pp.

moment. Wherefore have a due reverence and regard to his good Providence, as becomes a People, that profess a belief in Providence. Go clear in yourselves, and of all others. Be moderate in Expectation, count on Labour before a Crop, and Cost before Gain, for such persons will best endure difficulties, if they come, and bear the Success, as well as find the Comfort that usually follow such considerate undertakings.''

In 1686, also, there appeared another pamphlet in Dutch, with the title, "Detailed Information and Direction to such Persons as are inclined to America, and are interested in the Province of Pennsylvania, or who are desirous of settling there.'' This is practically a second Dutch edition of the English original of a tract which was published anonymously, without place or date.[431] It was omitted from the collected Works of Penn, but was ascribed to him by the Quaker bibliographers, John Whiting and Joseph Smith. It seems probable that it was written by Robert Webb, who wrote the Preface for the second Dutch version.[432] The title-page of the Dutch translation states that the Preface contains "divers noteworthy matters (*aanmerkelyke zaken*) concerning the present condition and administration of that Province; never before this appearing in print, but now first published by Robert Webb.''

The Good News Spreads

Vague rumors of Penn's grant began to be spread abroad in Holland and Germany even before it had finally passed the privy seal. For example, on the 6th. of February, 1681,

---

[431] The English original is supposed to have been published in 1682. It is reprinted in the *Pennsylvania Magazine*, Vol. 4 (1880), pp. 329–342. Its first Dutch translation appeared under the title „Nader Informatie of Onderrechtinge voor de gene die genegen zijn om na America te gaan, etc."

[432] This version is entitled „Nader Informatie en Bericht Voor die gene die genegen zijn, om zich na America te begeeven, en in de Provincie van Pensylvania Geinteresseerd zijn, of zich daar zoeken neder te zetten," Amsterdam, Jacob Claus, 1686. The Preface *(Voorreden)* occupies eight of the eleven 4to pages. An English translation of this Dutch edition, together with notes upon it and upon Webb's preface, was printed in the *Pennsylvania Magazine*, Vol. 49 (1925), pp. 98–140.

the father of Heinrich Frey, a future settler in Germantown, wrote a letter from his home in Heilbron to his son, who was then in New York, in which he said:[433]

"Dear Son: Your letter from far away America reached us and gave us great joy; and when, a few days later, the father of your true friend came to see us, our joy knew no bounds." He speaks next of the persecution in Germany, and says that thousands would gladly leave the Fatherland if they had the means of doing so. "A merchant from Frankfurt was with us last week and informed us how along the Rhine a number of families have banded together to accept the invitation of an Englishman named William Penn, who had recently visited that community, to settle in that beautiful land and there establish new homes."

Since this month of February, 1681, was the very time that the marriage of Derick Isacks op den Graeff and Nöleken Vijten was getting under way, it is an interesting conjecture that the consummation of the marriage was a prelude to the flight of the Krefeld community of Friends to Pennsylvania. The rumor referred to in the letter was apparently connected with the Friends of Krisheim, who probably were in close touch with those of Krefeld and hoped to be ready in time to accompany them to Pennsylvania; but, as has been seen, the Krisheim Quakers were not able to reach that promised land until two years after the Krefelders.

The elder Frey's letter continues: "After I had received this information, I went at once to our minister, whose parents live at Worms on the Rhine, and begged him earnestly to learn what truth there was in these reports and to find out if possible if there would be any opportunity for us to join them and go to the New World. He then informed me that these reports were all true and that he had been informed by one who had inside knowledge that in a place called Kriegsheim near Worms many were preparing themselves to go to the New World. When I gave the good

---

[433] *The Mennonite Year Book*, Berne, Indiana, 1913; quoted by C. Henry Smith in the *Proceedings* of the Pennsylvania-German Society, Vol. 35 (1929), Part II, p. 84.

man your letter to read, he was greatly surprised and said that you were on the land to which these emigrants were going. It is the providence of God that has shown these burdened people so glorious a land. We, as also the Platenbach family, are only awaiting a good opportunity when the dear Lord will take us to you. Your brother Peter is learning shoe-making and will soon be free [from his apprenticeship]. America is the only dream of Elisabeth. Catherine, only six years old, asks us daily, 'Will we soon be going to our brother in America?' ''

It is a satisfaction to know that at least one of these youthful aspirants for America had his ambition satisfied. Peter Frey, the shoemaker's apprentice, came as an indented servant to Germantown in 1685 with the family of Peter Schumacher.

LETTERS FROM THE COLONISTS

By 1684, letters from the Pennsylvania Dutch and German settlers themselves began to be printed in Holland. Two of these, written by Cornelis Bom, of Haarlem and Philadelphia, and Joris Wertmuller (Georg Wertmüller), of Germantown, formerly of Switzerland, and dated the 16th. and 26th. of March, 1684, were printed the same year in Rotterdam.[434] Two more letters by Cornelis Bom and Jacob Telner of Krefeld, Amsterdam and Germantown, were dated October 12, 1684, and printed in Rotterdam, 1685.[435] The title-page of the latter tract took pains to point out that the Province of Pennsylvania lay "on the east [west] side of the Zuyd Revier [the Delaware] of Nieuw Nederland", and that the letters described the great progress already made by the said province.

The spirit of optimism and gratitude which pervaded

---

[434] „Twee Missiven geschreven uyt Pensilvania, d'Eene door een Hollander, woonachtig in Philadelfia, d'Ander door een Switser, woonachtig in German Town, Dat is Hoogduytse Stadt“; Tot Rotterdam, by Pieter van Alphen. Anno 1684. See *infra*, p. 332 (note 458).

[435] „Missive van Cornelis Bom Geschreven uit de Stadt Philadelphia in de Provintie van Pennsylvania . . . Waerby komt de Getuygenis van Jacob Telner van Amsterdam.“ Cf. *supra*, p. 244.

Twee Missiven

Geschreven uyt

PENSILVANIA,

d' Eene door een Hollander, woonachtig in

PHILADELFIA,

d'Ander door een Switser, woonachtig in

GERMAN TOWN

Dat is Hoogduytse Stadt.

Van den 16 en 26 Maert 1684.   Nieuwe Stijl.

Tot Rotterdam, by *Pieter van Alphen.* Anno 1684.

these letters is indicated by the following extracts. Wertmüller, the German Swiss, wrote: "The city of Philadelphia covers a great stretch of country, and is growing larger and larger. The houses in the country are better built than those within the city. The land is very productive, and raises all kinds of fruits. All kinds of corn are sown. From a bushel of wheat, it is said, you may get sixty or seventy, so good is the land. You can keep as many cattle as you wish, and there is provender enough for them and as many swine as you want, since there are multitudes of oak trees, which produce an abundance of acorns to make them fat, and other wild nuts. You find here householders who have a hundred cows and innumerable hogs, so that a man can have as much pork as he wants. There are all kinds of wild animals, such as deer, roes, etc; all kinds of birds, some tame and others wild, by the thousand, together with an exceptionally great quantity of fish. The land lies in a good climate and is very healthy. You seldom see mists or fogs. There are many great and small rivers that are navigable, beautiful springs, fountains, mountains and valleys. The farmers or husbandmen live better than lords. If a workman will only work four or five days in a week, he can live grandly. The farmers here pay no tithes nor contributions. Whatever they have is free for them alone. They eat the best and sell the worst. You can find as many wild vineyards as you wish, but no one troubles himself to look after their safety or take care of them. The vines bear so many bunches that from one vine many hundred bottles of wine should be made. Handicraftsmen earn here much money, together with their board and drink, which are very good. The natives or Indians are blackish like the heathen, who through Germany and Holland have disappeared. They are stronger and hardier than the Christians, and very mild. They go almost entirely naked, except that they cover their loins. They use no money, except beads (*kraaltjes*) and little shells like those one finds on the bridles of the train horses in Holland. If any one is inclined to come here, let him look for a good ship-master, since he cannot believe everything that they say. The freight from England to Pensilvania is five pound sterling, about fifty-six Holland guldens, but I should advise you rather to go with a Holland shipmaster to Manhates, formerly called New Amsterdam, and now New York, two or three days' journey from Pensilvania, and I should advise you to take with you what you need upon the ship, especially brandy, oranges, lemons, spices and sugar since the sea may be very trying. See that you are well supplied with clothes and linen, and it will be better than to have money, since what I bought in Holland for ten guldens, I here sold again for thirty guldens; but you must not buy too dear.

"I have written to my brother in Amsterdam that he send me a chest full of clothes. If you or any one else from The Hague, come here and are willing to bring it along and take care of the transportation, I shall compensate you well for your trouble. So if you bring or send to me here one or two of my sons who are with my brother I shall pay all the costs. If anyone can come here in this land at his own expense, and reaches here in good health, he will be rich enough, especially if he can bring his family or some man-servants, because servants are dear here. People bind themselves for three or four years' service for a great price, and for women they give more than for men because they are scarce. A good servant can place himself with a master for a hundred guldens a year and board.

"Brother-in-law B.K. [Benedict Kunts, of The Hague, formerly of Berne] if you come into these regions, bring a woman with you, and if you bring two for me, Joris Wertmuller, I shall be glad, because then we shall live like lords. My brother, who lives in Amsterdam, is named Jochem Wertmuller. He lives in Ree Street in the *Three Gray Shoes*. I have many more things to write to you, but time does not permit. Meanwhile I commend you all to God the Father Almighty, through our Lord and Savior Jesus Christ. Amen.

"I, Joris Wertmuller, Switzer by birth, at present in Pensilvania.

"N.B. if anyone comes in this land or wishes to write letters, let them be addressed to Cornelius Bom in Pensilvania, in the city of Philadelphia, cake-baker, who used to live in

Haarlem in Holland, and who came here in the same ship with me and knows where in the country I dwell.''

Bom, the former baker of Haarlem, wrote: ''The country is healthful and fruitful, and the conditions are all favorable for its becoming through the blessing of the Lord and the diligence of men a good land—better than Holland. It is not so good now but daily grows better and better. The increase here is so great that, I believe, nowhere in history can be found such an instance of growth in a new country. It is as if the doors had been opened for its progress. Many men are coming here from many parts of the world, so that it will be overflowed with the nations. Our Governor's authority is respected by all and is very mild, so that I trust the Lord will bless this land more if we continue to walk in his way. . . . During the first year or two men spent what they had saved, but now almost everything is improving. As for myself, I went through and endured great difficulties, unaccustomed hardships and troubles before I got as far as I am now, but now I am above many, in good shape, and do not consider that I have less of my own than when I left Holland, and am in all respects very well-to-do. I have here a shop of many kinds of goods and edibles; sometimes I ride out with merchandise and sometimes bring something back, mostly from the Indians, and deal with them in many things. I have no servants except one negro whom I bought. I have no rent or tax or excise to pay. I have a cow which gives plenty of milk, a horse to ride around, my pigs increase rapidly, so that in the summer I had seventeen when at first I had only two. I have many chickens and geese, and a garden and shall next year have an orchard if I remain well; so that my wife and I are in good spirits and are reaching a condition of ease and prosperity in which we have great hopes.''

Telner, the Krefeld and Amsterdam merchant, wrote the two enthusiastic letters which have already been quoted.[436]

Francis Daniel Pastorius began to write letters to his family and friends in Germany almost immediately after his arrival in Philadelphia; and these were gathered together

---

[436] *Supra*, p. 244.

and published, in their German original, in Franckfurt and Leipzig, 1700.[437] Five years before this, another German settler in Pennsylvania, who was perhaps Daniel Falckner, wrote a letter "from Germantown, in the Antipodes, Aug. 7, 1694," which was "printed (*gedruckt*) in the year 1695";[438] in 1702 there was published in Franckfurt and Leipzig another tract by Daniel Falckner relating to Pennsylvania;[439] and finally, in 1702, there was printed (without place) a "Missive" by Justus Falckner, "from Germanton in the American Province Pensilvania, otherwise *Nova Suedia* [New Sweden]".[440]

PENN'S LITERARY MASTERPIECES

Penn's own writings which were translated into Dutch or German and published on the Continent after 1686 no longer dealt with matters relating to colonization in the New World, but were designed to direct men's thoughts and conduct to matters relating to the Other World, the home of the Spirit. Among these, were two of his greatest writings, namely, "No Cross, No Crown", which was translated into Dutch by Willem Sewel, and published in Amsterdam 1687;[441] and "Fruits of Solitude", which was translated into

---

[437] „Umständige Geographische Beschreibung Der zu allerletzt erfundenen Provintz Pensylvaniae, in denen Erd-Gräntzen Americae In der West-Welt gelegen/Durch Franciscum Danielem Pastorium, J. V. Lic. und Friedens-Richtern daselbsten. Worbey angehencket sind einige notable Begebenheiten/und Bericht-Schreiben an dessen Herrn Vattern Melchiorem Adamum Pastorium, Und andere gute Freunde". Franckfurt und Leipzig/Zufinden bey Andreas Otto, 1700; later German editions were published in Memmingen, 1792, and Crefeld (Friedrich Kapp, ed.) in 1884.

[438] „Copia eines Send-Schreibens ausz der neuen Welt. . . . .“

[439] „Curieuse Nachricht von Pensylvania in Norden-America. . . . .“ This tract, with Pastorius's „Beschreibung" and Gabriel Thomas's "Historical Account" (London, 1698), was published in a German pamphlet in 1704 (in Frankfurt and Leipzig).

[440] „Abdruck eines Schreibens an Tit. Herrn D. Henr. Muhlen.“

[441] See *supra*, p. 315, and Monograph Number One, index. The first German edition appears not to have been published until 1825 (in Pyrmont), and the second German edition, in London, 1847. Sewel took pains to state on the title-page of the Dutch edition that Penn was Governor and Proprietor of Pennsylvania.

Dutch by Jan Claus, and published in Amsterdam 1715.[442]

The third of Penn's most famous writings, "An Essay towards the Present and Future Peace of Europe" (1693), was not translated into Dutch,—although it was translated by all the nations into magnificent action at the first Peace Conference, held in The Hague two centuries later.[443] Another of his books which went through many editions in English, Danish, French and Welsh, was also translated and published in Dutch and German; this was "A Key opening a way . . . . "; the Dutch version was made by Willem Sewel, and published in Amsterdam 1693.[444] The last book which came from his hand, which was published in Dutch translation, was "Gospel-Truths held and briefly Declared by the People called Quakers."[445] This was written in coöperation with three other prominent Quakers and was dated, Dublin (Ireland), the 14th. of the 3rd. Month, 1698.

After this date, Penn made another visit to Pennsylvania, but did not advertise his colony as he had done after his first visit seventeen years before. His own life lasted a score of years after 1698; but the clouds of political, financial and mental disability gathered thick around him and almost entirely incapacitated him during his last half-dozen years. By this time, however, his great work in religion and statesmanship had been done, and the seed had been sown for an amazing growth of his colony.

Through his long series of letters and treatises circulated and distributed in manuscript and in print, in Dutch and in German, Penn's personality and ideals must have been widely known and discussed among those Europeans whom

---

[442] Sewel also translated this book into Dutch, but his translation was not published; see Monograph Number One, pp. 165–166.

[443] See Monograph Number Nine ("Jean Etienne Mollet and the Aftermath of Quakerism in Holland"). Two other books by Penn which were printed in many editions in English, Danish, French, Welsh and German were probably published also in Dutch; but their Dutch editions are not forthcoming. These were "A Brief Account of the Rise and Progress of the People called Quakers", London, 1694; and "Primitive Christianity Revived", London, 1696.

[444] See Monograph Number One, index.

[445] Amsterdam, 1709.

he visited in his journey of 1677, and to whom he made his appeal in behalf of Pennsylvania during subsequent years. Pastorius, in his autobiographical "Beehive", bears witness to this direct personal influence of Penn, in the following passage: "Upon my return [from a journey to various places in Europe] to Frankfurt in 1682, I was glad to enjoy the company of my former acquaintances and Christian friends, assembled together in a house called the Saalhof, viz., Dr. Spener, Dr. Schütz, Notarius Fenda, Jacobus Van de Walle, Maxmilian Lerfner, Eleanora von Merlau, Maria Juliana Bauer, etc., who sometimes made mention of William Penn of Pennsylvania, and showed me letters from Benjamin Furly, also a printed relation concerning said province,[446] finally the whole secret could not be withholden from me, that they purchased 25,000 acres of land in this remote part of the world. Some of them entirely resolved to transport themselves, families and all. This begat such a desire in my soul to continue in their society, and with them to lead a quiet, godly, and honest life in a howling wilderness, that by several letters I requested of my father his consent . . . ."

PENN'S DUTCH AND GERMAN CO-WORKERS

But not only by means of written and printed messages, and personal contacts of his own, did Penn strive to attract colonists to his province. He made much use of his friends in Holland and Germany, and selected an admirable agent in Benjamin Furly of Rotterdam, and an indefatigable advertiser in Roger Longworth of England and America. In the score of places in the Netherlands, and the score of places in Germany, where he had visited and preached, there must have been many unnamed individuals and families who had heard him speak or spoken of, and who now talked with a personal interest about his colony when the news of it came to them; indeed, many of these became settlers in it. Among those who are known to have been his friends and to have spread the news about his colony were

---

[446] This was probably the German edition of "Some Account"; see *supra*, p. 312.

Willem Sewel, Jan and Jacob Claus, the translators and publisher of some of his writings; Gertrud Deriks, another of his correspondents and the wife of his intimate friend, Stephen Crisp; Jan and Debora Roelofs and Pieter and Elisabeth Hendricks, who corresponded with him in England, and entertained him in their homes in Holland; and, far more important than all of these, Jacob Telner, who did so much to promote emigration to Penn's colony of West New Jersey as well as to Pennsylvania, and who was especially helpful to the Krefeld founders of Germantown.[447]

These were all residents of Amsterdam; but in other places in the Netherlands also, he had good friends, such as Jacob Arentsz, of Oudesluis; Jan Jansen and Sipke Aukes, of Harlingen; and Franciscus Mercurius van Helmont, an international bird of passage, who was instrumental among other things in getting published Penn's record of his journey of 1677.

Some of the people whom he mentions by name, in his record of his journey of 1677, who lived in the various places which he visited in Germany, showed their deep interest in him and his colony by forming a "German Society" and a "Frankfort Company" for promoting its colonization. Those who participated most largely in this work were Jacob van de Walle, Dr. Johann Jacob Schütz, Daniel Behagel, Caspar Merian, Johanna Eleanora von Merlau and Johann Wilhelm Ueberfeld, of Frankfurt; Dr. Thomas van Wijlick and Johann Lebrunn, of Wesel; Dr. Gerhard von Mastricht, of Duisburg; Johan Wilhelm Petersen, Johannes Kember, and Balthasar Jawert, of Lübeck; Görg Strauss, Abraham Hasevoet, Görg Hartzfelder, of other places in Germany; and Jan Laurentz, of Rotterdam.

All of these were members of one or the other of the two Frankfurt companies; all bought land in Pennsylvania, their total purchase amounting to 25,000 acres; and, although none of them became colonists themselves, they sold their land to persons who did, and doubtless used their persuasive powers to induce these to go upon the great adventure.

[447] See *supra*, pp. 239–253.

Penn's Quaker Coadjutors

The travelling ministers of the Society of Friends from England, and later from Pennsylvania·and other parts of America, who held religious meetings in many places on the Continent, must have talked much in their social converse of the new haven of refuge and land of promise and fulfilment beyond the Atlantic. The ministers from England form a long and notable series and include, before Pennsylvania was acquired, Ames, Caton, Crisp, Fox, Barclay, Keith, Gibson, Longworth and Haydock; and after colonization began, Margaret Langdale, Mary Farmer, Mary Wyatt, Elizabeth Jacob, James Dickinson, Samuel Neale, John Kendall, John Eliot, John Fothergill, Benjamin Holme, Catharine Phillips, Robert and Sarah Grubb, George and Sarah Dillwyn, who came in the Eighteenth Century; and, on into the Nineteenth Century, Thomas Shillitoe, Mary Dudley, Maria Fox, Ann Alexander, Cornelius Hanbury, William Allen, Joseph John and Samuel Gurney, Elizabeth Fry, Martha Savory, Martha Towell, and John Yeardley.

Back from Pennsylvania itself, came Thomas Chalkley, Thomas Story, Susanna Morris, Sarah Harrison, John Churchman, John Pemberton, William Savery, Stephen Grellet and Elizabeth Walker; while from New York, came David Sands and John Griscom; and from North Carolina, William Hunt, Thomas Thornburgh and Richard Jordan.

Thus, Quakerism and the New World were kept conjointly and continuously in the minds of the Dutch and German people, by these "travelling ministers", these "publishers of Truth", some of whom exemplified in themselves the fruits of Penn's "new plantinge" beyond the seas. The international character and activities of Quakerism are well exemplified by Jean Etienne Mollet, "the last of the Quakers of Holland" (1781–1851).[448] This Friend, born in *France* and settled in *Holland,* we find actively engaged as late as 1826 in promoting the emigration of *German* separatists to an *American* colony founded by an *English*

---

[448] See Monograph Number Nine ("Jean Etienne Mollet and the Aftermath of Quakerism in Holland").

Quaker. In a letter to Stephen Grellet (another Friend of French birth and ancestry, settled in America), dated Amsterdam, the 15th. of 4th Month, 1826,[449] Mollet wrote:

"I have begun a correspondence with a German of the name of Heinrich Kiehnle, a manufacturer of Pfortzheim, who without ever having seen any Friends, but merely by reading some of their works, has become convinced of their principles and professes them openly, so that he has already undergone some persecution from the civil authorities of the great Dutchy of Baden for having had a meeting with a few Separatists (that is from the Church of Rome), when Martha Savory and her company were in his country in 11 month last. He has been enjoined by the magistrates not to distribute any of the books relating to Friends principles, and put under the surveillance of the police, so that he has almost determined to leave that neighborhood, and to settle in the kingdom of Würtemburg, where he is assured of being less exposed to these unchristian proceedings. It appears that the number of Separatists in Germany is greatly increasing, which is chiefly owing to the ignorance and loose manner of the clergy of those countries, and partly also to the revival of a religious spirit. Of this I have long had a feeling, and I have at times felt a concern to visit those countries in the love of the Gospel...

"About a year ago, some of the Separatists of the neighborhood of Pfortzheim, whom I mentioned before as having forsaken the Church of Rome, having undergone severe persecution on account of their religious principles, determined on emigrating to America, and extend their project. They had been addressed to me by Heinrich Kiehnle, but came to this country while I was at Pyrmont. The last-named Friends [of Pyrmont] had procured them some of the works of the Friends, and encouraged them when they came to America to inquire further about this Society, the principles of which I had represented to them as coming the nearest to a true pattern of Christianity. In one of his last letters, in answer to one in which I mentioned having received thine, he [Kiehnle] begged me to give thee their address, and to

---

[449] The Grellet MSS., in the Ridgway Branch of the Philadelphia Library Company.

mention that he wished thou wouldst give them a call if thou shouldst happen to come in the parts they inhabit, accordingly I annex their names, and addresses,[450] leaving it entirely to thee to do what thy feelings under a proper direction may incline thee. I forwarded to these people a letter of the same Friends [of Pyrmont] by a vessel which sailed later from Rotterdam to Baltimore, and wrote a few words of encouragement to them, engaging them, in case they should come to Philadelphia to visit John Cooke, who, I am told, speaks fluently the German language, and to whom Elliot Cresson of Philadelphia who was here last year, encouraged me to address all the Germans that should wish to become acquainted with Friends. I feel much for these poor fellows, and sincerely wish they may arrive to a settlement in their religious views which may be productive of growth in the truth. . . .''

This little rill of German emigration, which was one of countless others that swelled the great river to more than five millions of emigrants from the Fatherland to the United States during the Nineteenth Century, is an interesting illustration of the way in which even a French Friend settled in Amsterdam carried on in his small way the two-fold task that William Penn had entered upon a century and a half before, that, namely, of spreading the principles of Quakerism in the Rhineland and promoting emigration to the Promised Land beyond the Atlantic.

BENJAMIN FURLY

Penn's permanent agent on the Continent was Benjamin Furly of Rotterdam (1636–1714). This ''international Quaker'' was born and spent his youth in England, lived in Holland nearly sixty years, and was closely associated with Penn both in promoting Quakerism on the Continent and in persuading its denizens to settle in Pennsylvania. He

---

[450] These were: ''Daniel Beekman with his wife and children live at Kinsington [Kensington] two miles from Wommelsdorf near Philadelphia; Michael Kaufmann and his wife, John George Klingel his wife and three children, Sgatski with his wife, live in a country-house six miles distant from Wommelsdorf. Their correspondent in Philadelphia who knows exactly where they reside is Gottich [Gottlieb?] Klett, Brown St., No. 52.''

was a prolific writer of tracts and letters and had many Quaker treatises, including his own original writings and his Dutch translations of the works of others, issued from the press of Rotterdam and The Hague.

His acquaintance and friendship with officials in The Hague proved of great help to the Quakers of Holland in their difficult relations with the government in regard to marriage, taxes and religion. His hospitable home was the refuge of Quaker preachers travelling to and from their distant destinations, and he was able to facilitate their journeys in various ways as well as to solace their wearied spirits and assuage their physical sufferings.

To many of these preachers he became a companion and interpreter. In this capacity, he went with Penn on his journey of 1671 to Herford and Emden; he aided Robert Barclay and George Keith in their literary and missionary labors in the 1670's; and during the visit in 1677 of Fox, Penn and their companions, Furly played a leading rôle, arranging their meetings, intrepreting their sermons, organizing Quakerism in Holland and Germany, and accompanying Penn on his journeys to the Princess Elisabeth and through the Rhineland. His business connections with merchants engaged in traffic between Rotterdam and the Rhineland, as well as his varied literary and controversial activities in behalf of Quakerism, admirably paved the way for Penn's religious and colonizing activities; for these had brought him into direct contact with the sources of the stream of Dutch and German religionists that was to flow into Pennsylvania.

THE KÖNNEKEN LETTERS

Backed by his own linguistic and literary abilities, Furly developed a first-rate advertising organization, utilizing tongue, pen and press. The so-called "Könneken Letters" are a noteworthy illustration of this. They were written or sent to Furly by various persons in Pennsylvania and England, then transcribed or translated into quaint Dutch or German versions,—a mingled Dutch and German, a kind of northern *lingua franca*,—and circulated in manuscript among prospective settlers and people of influence in Holland and Germany. One of the agents used by Furly for their circulation was a commercial traveller, Johann Jawert (or Jauert), of Lübeck. This man was the son of Balthasar Jawert, sacristan of St. Mary's Church, Lübeck, and an original member of the Frankfort Company which was organized in 1683 to promote settlement in Pennsylvania. Father and son were in touch with religious circles in Germany, especially the "Pietists" and other dissenters and separatists.

One of the elder Jawert's friends was Jaspar Balthasar Könneken, a Pietist book-dealer in Lübeck, who was also one of Furly's correspondents. Könneken was prevented from going himself to Pennsylvania because of his advanced age; but he aided the cause by copying and circulating the letters and other information which he received from Furly and Jawert. One set of the copies which he made is preserved in a manuscript volume in the Ministerial-Archiv of Lübeck; and a photostatic reproduction of them, both Dutch and German, has been published by a Pennsylvania historian who makes use of the German letters in his interesting book.[451]

The first of these letters is in German, and was written by Francis Daniel Pastorius to his parents, under date of Philadelphia, the 7th. of March, 1684.[452] The second is also in German, under the same date, and is the first report of Pastorius to the Frankfort Company.[453] These two letters give a vivid and detailed account of the impression made by the new province on its first german settler under Penn.

The seventh letter in the series is also in German; but it was translated into that language from the Dutch original,

---

[451] Julius F. Sachse, "Letters relating to the Settlement of Germantown in Pennsylvania, 1683-84", Lübeck and Philadelphia, 1903. Mr. Sachse gives facsimiles of the four German and eight Dutch letters, together with an English translation of the German ones; the Dutch letters are used now for the first time in English.

[452] „Copia eines, von einem Sohn an seine Eltern aus Amerika abgelassenen Brieffes." It is translated *in toto* by Sachse (pp. 3–6).

[453] „Sicher Nachricht aus Amerika, wegen der Land-schafft Pennsylvanien, von einen dorthin gereisten Deutschen." A small quarto edition of letters number one and two were published in Germany, and an abstract of them was published later in Pastorius's „Umständige Geographische Beschreibung", 1700. An English translation is given by Sachse (pp. 7–29).

which was written by Herman Isacks op den Graeff. It was dated in "Germantown, that is, Teutschstadt, in Pennsylvania", the 12th. of February, 1684.[454] As the earliest extant report from Germantown, this letter is of much historic interest.[455]

The eighth letter is the last of the four German ones, and contains a reference to Georg Wertmüller's account of Germantown, together with a brief extract from a public letter written by Jacobus van der Walle of Frankfurt.[456] "My brother-in-law Van der Walle", the author of the eighth letter says, "has written to me that when he arrived in Holland [from Frankfurt?] a vessel sailed for Pennsylvania by way of England, and that there were more persons there than could be taken along; also that vessels are leaving almost daily. Further, that in a few days another vessel would touch there, and in a short time again a large one."

This is apparently the end of the quotation from Van der Walle, but the author of the letter continues to quote other reports from Pennsylvania as follows: "From England and Scotland, vessels leave for those parts almost daily, so that there is great increase here [in Philadelphia]. From Carolina (one of the finest places in the world) also about 700 persons have arrived here so as to live under this peaceful régime. May God maintain this, and with His blessing grant continued blessings, and rule them and us with His Holy Spirit, so that we can walk upon His paths and to our fullest capacity magnify His name with praise and honor. One of our people, Georg Wertmüller by name, has written to his acquaintance that he is well satisfied here [there?]. Many other persons have done the same, and advise and counsell their friends to come to them. From Crefeldt many more persons (as I learn) will come hither [go thither?] in the near future. It seems as if God has great things in store for this place."

Van der Walle's brother-in-law was Daniel Behagel, and together they started, in 1661, a faience industry in Frank-

---

[454] „Copia nach einander geschriebene Copia Eines Brieffes." An English translation is given by Sachse (pp. 31–34).

[455] See *supra*, p. 215.

[456] It is entitled simply „Ander Copia." Sachse gives an English translation of it on p. 35.

furt-am-Main. They both belonged to the Pietist circle, and met with Penn on his visit of 1677, and as members of the "Frankfort Company" bought more than 2,000 acres of Pennsylvania land. They were both too old to go as colonists to the new province; but when Pastorius visited them in Frankfurt, they encouraged him to make the great adventure. Pastorius, in his first report to the Frankfort Company (Könneken Letter, No. 2), refers to "what our dear friend Van der Walle mentions in his open letter"; hence the latter must have been written before March 7, 1684.[457] Who the others quoted in the letter were, is not stated.[458]

The third, fourth, fifth, sixth, ninth, tenth, eleventh and twelfth of the Könneken Letters are translations into Dutch of letters written in English. The translator of all but one of these was doubtless Benjamin Furly, by whom or to whom they were written.

The first of them[459] is by Furly himself, under date of Rotterdam, the 5th. of 3rd. Month, 1684, and was intended to be used as an introduction or preface to the next in the series, namely, the Letter of William Penn to the Free Society of Traders.[460] This well-known letter was dated in Philadelphia, the 26th. of 8th. Month, 1683, and published in London in 1683. Its first Dutch edition was published in The Hague in 1684, and its second (with Furly's preface) in Amsterdam, also in 1684.

The next two Könneken MSS. were added by Furly to his edition of Penn's Letter to the Free Society of Traders. They were "A Short Account of . . . . . Philadelphia",[461] and "An Extract from Thomas Paschall's Letter," which

---

[457] Both Behagel and Van der Walle died before 1700. The latter was probably related to the well-known Quaker family of Vandewall in Harwich, whose hospitable home entertained Penn and Fox and many other Quaker voyagers to and from Holland.

[458] It may be conjectured that the quotations were taken from the pamphlet „Twee Missiven", which contained Wertmüller's letter and, probably, the first letter written by Cornelis Bom. The only copy of this pamphlet which the author has seen is preserved in the Congressional Library at Washington, and it contains only Wertmüller's letter. See supra, p. 318.

[459] Könneken Letters, No. 3, pp. 8–10.

[460] Ibid., No. 4, pp. 11–19.

[461] Ibid., No. 5, pp. 19–21 („Een kort Verhaal wegens de situatie en groote van de Stad Philadelphia"). See supra, p. 314.

gave a glowing account of the new colony, and contained Furly's "postscript" as to directions for getting there.[462]

The next two MSS. are Dutch translations of letters from William Penn to Benjamin Furly, both dated in Philadelphia, the first in "the 6th. Month, English style, the 8th. Month [August] Hollands style, 1683,[463] the second on the 1st. of November, 1683.[464] They are both given German headings,[465] but are both translations from the English into Dutch, doubtless by Benjamin Furly.

In Letter Number 9, Penn expressed the hope that Furly might have come to Pennsylvania, but fears that he would not leave Holland to cast in his lot with the colonists. He thanks him for five letters just received by way of New York, and for the love and care which they had expressed. He speaks of the need of colonists in his great province, its large extent, the abundance and fruitfulness of its soil and other resources, and his faith that God would use it as a harborage for the Truth; but he desires, also, that no one should make the great removal unless moved to do so by the Spirit, even as Christ had appealed to the people (Mark, 8:34). He speaks of the institution of constables [justices of the peace] for the preservation of order; the necessary increase in the price of land henceforth sold to the colonists (now only 3,000 instead of 5,000 acres for £ 100 sterling, less a discount of one shilling sterling for every 100 acres), so that he might pay a fair price to the Indians for it, and in view of the fact that other Europeans sell land five German miles inland from the river [the Delaware] at the price of 100 acres for £ 10 sterling. He sends his greetings to Galenus Abrahamsz and his friends, and a long message to the effect that the Pennsylvanians were living like the ancient patriarchs whom Galenus so highly esteemed, while he and his were dwelling in Tyre and Sidon, those cities of scorn; that God's promises to the downtrodden and outcast would be fulfilled in the new world of peace and prosperity, simplicity and democracy; therefore, let him and his come over where

---

[462] *Ibid.*, No. 6, pp. 21–24 („Extract uyt . . . Paskell aan J. J.van Chippenham in Engeland"). See *supra*, p. 314.

[463] *Ibid.*, No. 9, pp. 26–28.

[464] *Ibid*, No. 10. pp. 28–29.

[465] „Ein ander copia auch auscopiert"; and „Ein ander."

they can live out their principles in reality, far from fleets
and armies, in a splendid land for pioneers, in comparison
with which Galenus's home,—he had almost said his fatherland,—is but like a prison. Penn paints a glowing picture
of Pennsylvania's marvels, and urges Furly to persuade or
constrain (*dwingt*) Galenus to remove thither. As for the
government of Galenus's company, Penn would substitute
for his own "high and low jurisdiction" such a patriarchal
family as he and Furly had seen at Wiewerd. He would sell
them a lordship (*heerlichheit*) of 20,000 acres for £ 800
sterling. The new city of Philadelphia, Penn also describes,
—with its 60 houses completed and its 300 farmsteads
roundabout, which the recent settlers had erected in addition to those of the former inhabitants. And he closes this
long letter with a renewed invitation to Furly to "come
over."

Penn's next letter speaks of the safe arrival of the High
Germans and Hollanders,—"the Krefelders",—and of his
own eagerness to provide for their present comfort and
future settlement; he renews his urgent invitation to the
Germans and Hollanders to leave the land where there is
but little comfort and where things must go from bad to
worse, and come to one where they could utilize to the full
all their talents,—their intelligence, skill, initiative and conscience: "Come, Come here, and serve God with me in a
virgin wilderness, which already begins to blossom like the
rose." He sends his greetings to the brethren and sisters
whom he thanks God for having permitted him to see, and
who, he believes, will come closer together than at present.
Jacobus van der Walle he mentions particularly in this
greeting; perhaps because Furly had already (on June 8,
1683) delivered to Jacobus a deed for land, which he had
sealed and delivered on that date, in the presence of Jacob
Telner, Weijert Jansen and Archibald Hope, his own signature being witnessed by Johannes Bleijckers.[466]

The next letter is also in Dutch with a German heading,
and is dated in Philadelphia, "the 27th. of the 1st. Month,
called March, 1683."[467] It is signed by Penn and twenty-five

---

[466] Pennsylvania Historical Society MSS.

[467] „Noch ein ander"; Könneken MSS., No. 11, pp. 29–32.

other Friends ("Your true and faithful Brothers, William Penn and twenty-five of his fellow-members as witnesses"),[468] and addressed to "Worthy and very dear Friends and Brothers,"[469] that is, the Friends in Holland and Germany. This letter is a long religious Epistle from a "solemn meeting of the eldest of the trusty [Quaker] brethren (*de outste der getrouwe broeders*) of Pennsylvania and Jersey", held in Philadelphia on that date. It is a paean of praise and thanks to God for his establishment of a realm of Truth in the Wilderness. The meetings for worship and discipline in Pennsylvania and New Jersey are mentioned and located; and a proposal is made that when Friends migrate from the Old World to the New, or vice versa, they shall be provided by their home meetings with "certificates of removal" testifying to their "clearness" in conduct (*handel en wandel*), credit, trust, debts, and unity with God's people among whom they have been living. This letter too is filled with praise of the new land, its extent, fertility, and abundance of food both wild and cultivated: "Our lot in all these things has fallen in a good place, the love of God exists and increases among us, we are a household at peace with one another, and truly our gladness (*vreugde*) is great."

The twelfth and last of the Könneken Letters in this collection is a Dutch translation of a letter from "Rodtgert Langwort" (Roger Longworth) to Pieter Hendricks and Jan Claus.[470]

FURLY AND THE COLONISTS

Reverting again to the printing-press, in 1684, Furly gathered together a number of papers relating to Pennsylvania,[471] translated them into French, and published them

---

[468] „Uwe waarde en getrouwe Broeders William Penn Nevens 25. nehmen sijner medebroeders tot een getügniss."

[469] „Waerde en seer beminde Vrienden en Broeders."

[470] „Noch een ander.—Dit is geschreeven van Rodtgert Langwort aan Peter Hendricks en Jan Claus angaande van sijn Reis in 't Land van Pensilvania"; Könneken MSS., pp. 32 (9 lines at bottom) and 33 (24 lines at top); see an English translation and a photostatic copy of the Dutch version, *infra*, p. 364.

[471] The major portion being Penn's "Some Account" and "A Letter to the Free Society of Traders."

in a single volume from the press of Abraham Troyel in The Hague. This volume is said to be now very rare and expensive, a copy having been sold in London two centuries after its publication for £ 15/15s. The British Museum's copy lacks the title-page; but there is at least one perfect copy of it in America (in the John Carter Brown Library, in Providence, Rhode Island). Furly published a German version of this collection, also, in Hamburg, 1684, which appears to be an even rarer pamphlet;[472] and to both the French and German editions he added explanatory notes of his own.

These pamphlets were evidently designed to appeal particularly to the French Huguenots who were fleeing from the persecution of Louis XIV into Holland and Germany. Furly inserts in them a note stating that "poor French Protestants" need pay for land in Pennsylvania at the rate of only a farthing per acre each year, the payments not to begin until 1685, and that those who could not pay for their voyage could indenture themselves for four years, in return for the money advanced, and would receive fifty acres of land free, at the end of their term. The pamphlets include, also, extracts from Penn's "Letter to the Free Society of Traders", from Thomas Holme's "Description of Philadelphia", and Thomas Paschall's Letter of February 10, 1683. Furly's explanatory notes are signed and dated: "Your very affectionate friend, Benjamin Furly, Rotterdam, March 6, 1684."

How many colonists were sent through Furly's influence and efforts to Pennsylvania and New Jersey, it is impossible to estimate; but there is evidence that he induced many to go, both as individuals and families and in companies. For example, the German Pietists who formed the "Frankfort Company" received private letters relating to Pennsylvania from Furly and showed them in November, 1682, to Francis Daniel Pastorius, during his visit in Frankfurt-am-Main. Pastorius accordingly went to Rotterdam, in April, 1683, talked with Furly there, procured from him cash and letters to Claypoole, Penn's agent in London, arranging

---

[472] A copy of this too is in the Brown Library.

for the voyage to Pennsylvania, and received through him the deeds for the "German" and "Frankfort" Companies' tract of 43,000 acres which Penn had conveyed to Pastorius and his associates.

These associates, as has been seen, came largely from the Dutch Quakers and Mennonites, the German Pietists, and the Dutch and German Labadists of Krefeld, Krisheim, Frankfurt and other Rhineland places where Penn and Furly had labored so valiantly together to sow the seeds of Quakerism and religious liberty. And it was Furly who negotiated the sale of lands in Pennsylvania to the Krefeld Quakers also, and dated and delivered the deeds to them; it was he who procured passage on the good ship "Concord", William Jeffries, Captain, for the thirteen pioneer families; it was he who encouraged them during their delay in Rotterdam, and waved them *bon voyage* when they finally sailed on the 24th of July, 1683; and it was his letters that they presented to Penn and Pastorius who welcomed them on their arrival in Philadelphia.

These same services were rendered by Furly to the Krisheim Quakers of the 1680's and to some of "the Palatines" who swarmed into Rotterdam en route for Pennsylvania in the early years of the next century. Farther up the Rhine, also, in Würtemberg, Furly's activities and influence set in motion another stream of emigration to Pennsylvania. This was formed by the sixteen or seventeen families of German mystics who followed their pastor, Johann Jacob Zimmerman, in his secession from the Lutheran Church, and his exodus to Pennsylvania in 1693. Gerard Croese was writing his *Historia Quakeriana* at the time of this event, and gives the following account of Furly's connection with it :[473]

"Zimmerman . . . . . writes to a certain Quaker in Holland who was a Man of no mean Learning, and very wealthy, very bountiful and liberal towards all the poor, pious and good, 'That as he and his followers and friends designed' (They are the very words of the Letter which is now in my

---

[473] Latin edition, 1695, pp. 563–5; English edition, 1696, II, 262–4. His reference to Furly, as seen in the quotation, is indirect but unmistakable.

Custody) 'to depart from these Babylonish Coasts, to those American Plantations, being led thereunto by the guidance of the Divine Spirit, and that seeing that all of them wanted wordly substance, that they would not let them want Friends, but assist them herein, that they might have a good Ship well provided for them to carry them into those places, wherein they might mind this one thing, to wit to shew with unanimous consent their Faith and Love in the Spirit in converting of People, but at the same time to sustain their bodies by their daily Labour.' So great was the desire, inclination and affection of this Man towards them, that he forthwith promised them all manner of assistance, and performed it and fitted them with a Ship for their purpose, and did out of that large Portion of Land he had in Pensilvania, assign unto them a matter of two thousand and four hundred Acres, for ever of such Land as it was, but such as might be manured,—imposing yearly to be paid a very small matter of rent [in the Latin, "unius sestertii Anglici"; one English farthing] upon every Acre, and gave freely of his own and what he got from his friends, as much as paid their Charge and Passage, amounting to an hundred and thirty pounds sterling; a very great gift, and so much the more strange, that that same Quaker should be so liberal, and yet would not have his name mentioned, or known in the matter.

"But when these Men came into *Holland* they Sailed from thence directly for *Pensilvania; Zimmerman* seasonably dies, but surely it was unseasonable for them, but yet not so, but that they all did cheerfully pursue their Voyage, and while I am writing hereof, I receive an account, that they arrived at the place they aimed at, and that they all lived in the same house, and had a publick Meeting three times every week, and that they took much pains, to teach the blind people to become like unto themselves, and to conform to their examples: This Commotion and Disturbance made among the *Lutherans,* has been not only noted here for a Commemoration of the present time, but for a perpetual memorial of that people."

It is doubtless this same incident to which "a Gentleman of Rotterdam" refers in his "Letter . . . relating to Mr.

Benjamin Furly",[474] when he says: "A distinguished Professor came from Germany to Rotterdam with about seventeen households (*Huijsgesinnen*) nearly all of whom were poor and needy and persecuted for the free exercise of their religion. Mr. Furly received all of them into his house, lodged them in his ware-house and entertained them with every comfort and necessity for a considerable time; he also, by his example, stirred up others to extend similar aid and love until this people departed, according to their intention, for Philadelphia."

FURLY'S PENNSYLVANIA LANDS

So extensive were Furly's Pennsylvania land sales to companies and individuals, in Europe, and his purchases for them in Pennsylvania, that he was obliged himself to be represented by agents. Among these are found James Claypoole, as early as 1682; Justus and Daniel Falckner, in the Nineties and later; Johan Heinrich Sprogell and Reyner Jansen, after 1700.

Reyner Jansen, of the Knijpe, had been for years a prominent member of the Friesland Monthly Meeting when, in 1690, he decided to remove with his family to the new world. Five years earlier, July 17, 1685, he had acquired from Furly a deed for land in Pennsylvania, which was duly acknowledged before a notary public in Holland;[475] and when he arrived in Philadelphia, he became, among other things, one of Furly's agents.

Furly was himself strongly tempted to emulate the Pilgrims' example and, having removed from England to Holland in his youth, to move on across the Atlantic. We find that he purchased 4,000 acres in Pennsylvania, but had some difficulty in having it surveyed and properly conveyed to him. A letter from James Claypoole to Furly dated, "London, 13 1 mo 1682-3," begins:[476] "As for thine and the Franckfordrs land to be sett out upon a Navigable River, that is only in ye power of ye Governour to doe, and not so

---

[474] „Brief van een Heer van Rotterdam . . . aangaande . . . Heer Benjamin Furly . , ." Amsterdam, 1709.

[475] Minute-Book H, Pennsylvania Archives, 2nd Series, Vol. 19, p. 598.

[476] *The Pennsylvania Magazine*, Vol. X (1886), p. 269.

far in his power as to prejudice others, or take away their lotts, if thou or any others will give mee Instructions, I shall serve you soe farr as I am capable: as for your Lotts in Philadelphia you being ye first purchasers there is no question but you will have 100 ackers for every 5000 alotted there.''

The difficulties over the land grants to the German and Frankfort Companies belong to the history of early Pennsylvania. Furly's difficulties in connection with his own land are reflected in the correspondence before and after 1700.[477]

When William Penn was leaving the colony in 1701, he ordered his deputy, James Logan, to send Furly a warranty for this land. But the next year (August 7, 1702), we find Furly writing from Rotterdam to Justus and Daniel Falckner, his agents in Philadelphia, complaining that these 4,000 acres which he had bought in 1684 and 1685 had not yet been surveyed and conveyed, although he had paid for 5,000 acres. The original agreement had been that for every 5,000 acres purchased the purchaser was to have 100 acres additional, and for every 1,000 acres purchased 10 acres additional, ''within the Libertyes of Philadelphia.'' Furly was accordingly entitled to land within the city itself, in addition to the land he had bought in the country. The Commissioners had issued a warrant on February (11th/Mo.) 3, 1684, Furly says, for ''my Lot in Philadelphia, in the High Street on the Schoolkill side. Why was it not surveyed? . . . By a map of the Town, wherein the Lots are divided by numbers my name is found painted over agt No. 38 in the High Street from the Schuylkill side which is No. 81 in the map.'' Furly had sent instructions to his agents regarding this land in a letter of April 14, 1702, in care of his friend ''Mr Hendrick Valckenbergh'';[478] and on the 5th of March 1700/1, he had sent deeds for it in care of Jacob Clasen Arentsen.[479] He therefore again instructed his agents to procure the land and dispose of it for him. His agents did not accomplish this, for we find Furly's two elder sons continuing to press his claims after their father's death.

---

[477] Much of this is found in successive volumes of *The Pennsylvania Magazine*.

[478] *The Pennsylvania Magazine*, Vol. 10 (1886), pp. 474–6.

[479] A Friend of Amsterdam, who settled in Germantown in 1701.

Furly's later agent, John Henry Sprogell, was not only unsuccessful in this task, but was accused of being highly dishonest. In a letter to him from Furly dated, Rotterdam, the 5th of April, 1709,[480] Furly expressed his sorrow for the seizure and burning of Sprogell's ship and its cargo by the French, when it was outward bound for Virginia, but upbraids him for his "unrighteous, unchristian, and ungrateful behaviour to & treatment of those two young men from whose parents & Relations you received so Signall and unparrelelled Kindness while here." Apparently these two victims of Sprogell's injustice were the sons of a Mr. Vandergraf who, Furly says, had assisted Sprogell with a loan or with credit. In view of his conduct, Furly informed him that an order had been sent to Thomas Fairman to enjoin him from acting as Furly's agent under the power of attorney that he had taken with him. The letter ends with an expression of Furly's sorrow for the grief which Sprogell's conduct would cause his "Dear Father & Mother", and with a fervent appeal to him to repent and reform.[481]

That Furly did not himself migrate with his family to Pennsylvania may be explained by his large affairs in Holland, his literary and social interests there, his advancing years, and the declining health (and probably the disinclination) of his wife, who died in 1691. His settlement in Philadelphia would doubtless have formed a chapter in the life of the city and colony as interesting in its way, though far less historically important, as that of a later "B. F.", the scholarly, ingenious and illustrious Franklin.

Like William Pitt and the map of Europe, or Abraham Lincoln and the map of the United States, so Benjamin Furly and the map of Pennsylvania kept constant company

---

[480] *Pennsylvania Magazine*, Vol. 27 (1903), pp. 376–7.

[481] A former Swarthmore College student of the author's, Harry Edward Sprogell, of Philadelphia, has made a praiseworthy attempt to clear his ancestor of the traditional charges against him; but the results of his research have not yet (1934) appeared in print. J. F. Sachse, too, in his "German Pietists of Provincial Pennsylvania" (Philadelphia, 1895), defends Falckner against Pastorius's accusations, and suggests that Pastorius forsook the German Pietists and joined the Quakers, so that it was appropriate for his place as agent of the Frankfort Company to be taken by Falckner, Sprogell and Kelpius.

in his last days. This "very accurate (*nette*) Chart of Penn-sylvania, with all its Rivers, Bays, etc., done in ink on parch-ment", as it was described in the inventory of his library, was sold at his death for four florins to Fritsch & Bohm, printers of Holland. How many times he must have poured over it and pondered upon the fate of the colony which he had done so much to aid!

FURLY AND THE GOVERNMENT OF PENNSYLVANIA

In the political work underlying the Quaker colony as well as in the sale of land and its settlement, Furly appears to have been active and influential. Penn first decided upon "The Fundemental Constitutions of Pennsylvania"[482] as the basis of the colony's government, and these received Furly's approval and perhaps his aid in drawing them up.[483] But Penn replaced these "Constitutions" by the "Frame of Government," which he signed on April 25, 1682, and the "Laws", which were agreed upon in England May 5, 1682. When Furly examined the "Frame" and the "Laws", and compared them with the "Constitutions", he was much dis-appointed and wrote a series of notes upon them expressing his strong disapproval of parts of them and his protest against their substitution for the "Constitutions."[484]

Precisely how much influence Furly's criticism had, is yet to be determined. He comments especially on the orig-inal articles Nos. 8 and 12, and the additional articles 20–24 of the "Frame"; and the 21st section of the "Frame" as adopted in the act of settlement in Philadelphia, on March 1, 1683, has been plausibly ascribed to him. This provides for the protection of the estates of aliens, and reflects Furly's interest in the welfare of the Europeans among whom he had himself become, when a young man, "a stranger in a

---

[482] The "Penn Papers", in the Library of the Historical Society of Pennsyl-vania.

[483] A number of notes commenting upon them, in Furly's handwriting, are preserved in the "Penn Papers".

[484] These notes also are in the "Penn Papers" (Vol. VI., No. 17); they are in Furly's hand-writing and are endorsed: "B. F. Abridgmt out of Holland and Germany. Laws of Govt Pense." His comments on the "Frame of Government" and on the "Fundamental Constitutions" were published for the first time in the *Pennsylvania Magazine*, Vol. XIX., (1895) Pp. 297 and 304.

strange land." The recent sufferings of the Dutch Quakers in Krefeld and Krisheim which caused their flight to Pennsylvania, were also uppermost in Furly's thoughts and his determination that they should not be renewed in their trans-atlantic homes.

The nineteenth section of Furly's notes declares: "The 26th [36] Law enjoyning all to abstain from Labour on ye first day [Sunday] may prove a vile snare to ye conscience of many in this day, who do not look upon that day as of any other then human institution, & may be pressed in spirit (whether right or wrong is not the question) sometimes to work upon that day, to testify agt that supertitious conceit that it is of divine institution, & is the Christian Sabbath."

In this, Furly reflects the Continental and Quaker reaction against the English Puritans' Sabbath; and in the following paragraph (in the same section) he expresses the Quakers' solicitude for the welfare of indentured servants. It reads: "Onely thus far there may a service be in Setting Servants at liberty from the oppressions of grinding, covetos masters, &c—that it be declared that no master shall compell his servant to labor on that day because its fit yt ye very body of man & beast should have some rest from their continuall labor—."

Other notable suggestions in Furly's notes are: that all children shall have an equal share in the estates of their parents who die intestate, but that the right of bequest be permitted, within reason, so that parents shall not be deprived of "a power of countenancing & rewarding Vertue, obedience & sweetnes, and discountenancing Vice & refractorynes in their children"; that "a certain part of every mans gain [profit] . . . be set apart, and brought into a common Treasury. . . . for erecting & maintaining of free schools and of hospitals for aged & disabled men & women, & orphans"; that the awards of arbitrators be made legal, as in Holland, for the benefit of the "many Christians in holland and Germany that look upon it as unlawful to sue any man at ye Law as to fight wᵗʰ armes"; that no "publick Tax be for longer then a year, wch will make ye Assembly always necessary, and consequently keep ministers in aw;" that "a forme of a deed be agreed upon thats short & plain that we be not bound to the tricks of ye Lawyers of England, and let possession be given & taken as in holl^d in open court, by the persons themselves or by their atturneys.''[485]

Furly's 23rd note is of much interest. It reads "Let no blacks be brought in directly. And if any come out of Virginia, Maryld. in families that have formerly bought them else where Let them be declared (as in ye west jersey constitutions) free at 8 years end.'' This note evidently means that the importation of slaves from Africa should be prohibited, and that slaves brought in to Pennsylvania from the other colonies should be emancipated within eight years. Thus, Furly at this early date would abolish both the slave-trade and slavery itself! His advanced stand on this question is especially interesting because of the fact that the first public protest against negro slavery in America was made a half-dozen years later (in 1688) by the Dutch and German Quakers who settled in Germantown, so largely with Furly's own assistance.[486]

Towards the end of his notes, Furly writes to Penn: ''That wch I have now further to add is that I far prefer thy first draught to this last, as being most equall, most faire, & most agreeing with the just, wise & prudent constitutions of our Ancestors. And most likely to keep us in a good, & fair Correspondence wth ye Nation, w^{ch} & ye Interest thereof will stand, when that of a few corrupt & guilty Courtiers will sink, &c.''

The stout old Quaker democrat, in this last sentence, seems to imply a suspicion that Charles II's ''few corrupt & guilty Courtiers'' had had an undue influence in changing Penn's plan of government for the worse; and his next sentence chides Penn for having yielded to them. ''Indeed I wonder,'' he writes, ''who should put thee upon altering them for these, And as much how thou couldst ever yield to such a thing.'' He continues his expostulation for three paragraphs, and then takes up a further contrast of the old ''Constitutions'' with the new ''Frame'', much to the advantage of the former, as expressive of sound democratic principles, especially in application to the constitution and powers of the popular Assembly. ''What I speak is with reference to future ages'', he writes; ''for to have a great na-

---

⁴⁸⁵ Furly here describes the method used in Holland.

⁴⁸⁶ Cf. *supra*, p. 297.

tion bound up to have no laws but w^t two thirds of 72 men
shall think fit to propound . . . is not consistent w^{t}h the publick safety w^{c}h is, & always will remain, the supreme Law,
& bring to certain distruction all y^t go about to make it
Void.''

How prophetic are these words of the democratic principles applied in Philadelphia a century later in the Constitution of the United States. In them, we almost hear the voice
of Thomas Jefferson; or perhaps, in very truth, an echo of
the great English democrats of the Seventeenth Century.

The ''republican martyr'', Algernon Sidney, was a friend
and correspondent of Furly, and was a frequent visitor at
Furly's hospitable home during the seventeen years after
the Restoration when Sidney was an exile on the Continent.
Having been pardoned in 1677, Sidney returned to England, but remembered with constant affection his Quaker
friend in Rotterdam, writing to him frequently during the
years 1677 to 1679. The letters for these years, at least, were
printed in 1830 for private circulation, and again in 1847;[487]
how many others passed between the two friends is not
known. Nor is it definitely known that Furly read the manuscript of Sidney's famous ''Discourses concerning Government'' which, even though unpublished, was accepted by
the fierce Judge Jeffreys as the necessary second witness (in
addition to the treacherous Lord Howard) to Sidney's
''high treason.'' How much this intimacy, and the spoken
and written exchange of views between the two friends, influenced Furly's political principles and, through him, the
enlightened government of Penn's colony is a question of
more than pleasing speculation.

ROGER LONGWORTH

Another very useful, though relatively unknown, agent
of Penn in promoting the colonization of his province, was
Roger Longworth. His Quaker contemporaries evidently
knew Longworth well and respected him highly; but the
dust of two centuries and a half has dimmed his name and

---

[487] The Letters include those that passed between Furly and Sidney (1677–
79), Locke (1686–88), and Shaftesbury (1698–99). For this correspondence
and for Furly's biography, see Monograph Number Five (''Benjamin Furly
and Quakerism in Rotterdam'').

fame, and no historian of either Quakerism in the Old World, or of Colonization in the New, devotes more than a paragraph or two to his memory. Even his contemporaries spelled his first name in such varied forms as Roger, Rogier, Röger, Rodger, Rodgert, and his last in such weird ways as Langworth, Langwordt, Langewort and Lanwory; and this is indicative of the scanty pains which they took to keep his memory green. But his ability far outran his formal education, and his deserts exceeded his reputation and his fame; hence it is a pleasure to supply here a biographical sketch of him which has been gleaned from varied and far-scattered sources.

One week after his death, in Sixth Month (August), 1687, his life-long friend, Phineas Pemberton, recorded that "Roger Longworth aforesaid was born in Longworth next house to Longworth hall in the parish of Bolton [le Moors] in County of Lancast^r in old England & dyed in the 57 yeare of his age."[488]

It is not known when or by whom he was converted to Quakerism. But it seems probable that James Harrison, first of Kendal, later of Bolton, was "the first publisher of Truth" who convinced Longworth of it. The two men were of about the same age, and we find their long correspondence with each other, during their ministerial travels, beginning as early as 1670.[489] It is said of Longworth, indeed,[490] that "near the time he came to man's estate in the Eleventh Month, 1661, he bound himself for seven years to James Harrison, of Stiall-green, in Cheshire, as an apprentice to learn the shoe-making business. . . . About the time that Roger had served out his seven years, James Harrison removed into Lancashire, and his late apprentice, now his fast friend, went with him."

Soon after settling in Lancashire, in 1669–70, he was imprisoned on at least three occasions for attending Quaker

---

[488] Streper MSS. (Phineas Pemberton's Diary, p. 5).

[489] The author has found fifty-three letters written by Longworth, most of them in the Pemberton MSS. now in possession of the Historical Society of Pennsylvania.

[490] "Biographical Sketches of Ministers and Elders . . . of the Yearly Meeting of Philadelphia," *The Friend*, Vol. 27 (1854), p. 148.

meetings. One of his fellow-prisoners was Phineas Pemberton, a young man of twenty, who married a half-dozen years later (in the 11th. Month, 1676) Phebe, the daughter of James Harrison. With Pemberton, too, Longworth established a lasting friendship and untiring correspondence.

One of Longworth's early imprisonments was in Chester Castle, from which place he wrote a letter, which is still extant, to his persecuting judge, T. Manwaring.[491] Other letters of the early Sixteen Seventies reveal imprisonments in Lancaster and Manchester, as well as Chester, jails.[492]

In 1672, he became a recorded minister in the Society of Friends; and during the last dozen years of his life, he "devoted himself wholly to the service of the Lord, travelling much in England, where he suffered imprisonment in several places; six times he passed through Holland and some others of those provinces; also part of Germany and thereabout several times as far as Dantsick."[493] Or, as another account summarizes his travels:[494] "He passed six times through Holland, also part of Germany, five times through Ireland, once through part of Scotland, twice at Barbadoes, once through New England and Virginia, twice in Maryland and the Jerseys, and twice in Pennsylvania; having travelled by land 20,000 miles and by water not much less."

Although Longworth is not mentioned in Fox's Journals until the year 1685, it is evident that much of his strenuous travel was suggested to, or urged upon him, by the founder of the Society. He is listed in 1676 as one of the ministers travelling in Ireland; and his prominence among the English Friends is shown by his signature among those of sixty ministers who signed the London Yearly Meeting Epistle of 1677.

LONGWORTH AND THE BOEHMENISTS

Longworth's connection with work on the Continent must have begun in or before 1675, in which year (ye 25 of ye 7th mo 1675) we find a religious letter from him to "the people

---

[491] Pemberton MSS., I, 28.

[492] *Ibid.*, I, 48, 49.

[493] "A Collection of Testimonies concerning Several Ministers . . . ," London, 1760.

[494] "Memorials concerning Divers deceased Ministers . . .", Philadelphia, 1787.

in and about Loupgrund neare goldburge Jn seselia Jermeney".[495] The next year, we find a letter endorsed "from Martin John from Selicia, about R. L.'s visit."[496] This is dated "Laubground", 18th. of 2nd. Mo., 1676," and is addressed to "John G. M." The Silesian "Laubgrund" is apparently the modern Lauban, or Lüben, a town in Prussian Silesia not far from the Saxon town of Zittau. "Martin John, from Selicia" would appear to have written his letter to Johannes Matern, who became a Friend and settled in England with his wife and the family of his father-in-law, Hilary Prache, in 1674. We are left in the dark as to details of this visit of Longworth to the Boehmenists and Schwenkfelders of Silesia and Saxony; but we may conjecture that he went on Matern's advice to try to convert more of the latter's former friends and neighbors to Quakerism. An English translation of part of this letter to Matern is in the Pemberton Manuscripts,[497] and reads as follows:

"Dear Friend J am glad that ye are all in good health, and that the friend Roger Longworth by Gods assistance and promotion is savely come home the Lord guide him farther into all truth. Thy Letter is read by me and many others wth great admiration seeing it doth not agree with [that which] J have told Roger. Jt appeareth out of thy letter as if the power of the Lord had been raised in them that were gathered together, but J was there too and felt nothing. Secondly as if such like silent meetings were appointed amongst us, wich never hath been. But because he desired of us we might permit him to keep a silent meeting, J was carefull that it might be done; seeing he came from a far country, and although he kept meeting more than once, yet very few came but once there, whereby he might have understood, although J did not tell it him, that they did not like it. For, among the rest thou dost write, that beeing in silence gathered together wth Roger, the Lord did not leave

---

[495] Etting MSS., IV, 6.

[496] Colchester MSS., 77.

[497] Pemberton MSS., I, 131. In the Etting MSS., IV, 5, there is a paper written by Longworth, entitled "A Few Examples, &c.", and dated the 6th. of 9th. Month, 1675, which is probably connected with his religious travels of that year.

himself without witness, but touched our hearts through his spirit in the power of Jesus, that, although we did not understand the words, yet we felt inwardly the power of the Lord, in wch he spoke, whereby we were co[n]vinced and assured, this to be the right and well pleasing worship of God: to wit in silence to wait upon God with the mind turned inwardly and the heart and spirit broken. With the latter part we agree. . . . But Rogers word hath done nothing to the purpose. . . They have known, believed, practised and felt that before they ever knew or heard of Roger. [Martin John says that he asked some if they had felt power run through them; they replied: "No."] I saw some women weeping, but J know not what was the cause of it, for they did run together confusedly . . . As the fd was wth us many came then to see strange things. . . . He being come so far, none of us wd grieve him, especially while he was so earnest upon his customs and manners of worship . . . J told him in plain words, but Roger wd not believe me. . . . He did not only desire me to pray by book, but also to groan in spirit for ye revelation of ye will of God . . . J must give myself to silence. . . J will neither be bound to any silent or vocal meeting by men without ye moving of ye Lord. . . J did take him to me [home with me] in a house which is not my own, and was very kind to him that he might live according to his will, J put away wt mt grieve him & wch he cd not bear. . . Romans 14 v. 5. . . ."

It appears from this letter also that, while the Silesians loved the works of Jacob Boehme, Longworth conceded only that "a candle had been lighted in him [Boehme] at the beginning, yet he hunted before the Lord", and that "the Behmists,—those who have Behme's books,—are puffed up in their knowledge." At Zittau, too, Longworth had tried and failed to establish meetings on the basis of the Quaker silence. There, the mystics whom he visited were under the leadership of Mark Schwaner, who had written to Martin John of Longworth's failure, but who had expressed the hope that the visit would do both of them good, revealing as it did that godly people are to be found in other countries besides one's own. At the time the letter was written,

Schwaner was in prison, for religion's sake, and "kept so close none can come or speak to him."[498]

At least one fundamental resemblance existed between the Friends and these mystics of Silesia and Saxony; for Martin John says that "everyone of them, according to his measure, seeks to find God in himself", and that "true worship is done in spirit, bound neither to place nor time." This and other basic resemblances between them, however, were not sufficient to enable Longworth to persuade the Schwenkfelders and Boehmenists of this distant land to join with the Friends of England or the Continent.

The correspondence between Longworth and Martin John was not ended here; for there is extant a letter directed "Deliver this letter to Roger Longworth in England", and signed, "Martin John a Friend of thy illumination."[499] It is dated "Loubgrund, ye 28 February 80./.", and begins: "Roger Longworth. I have received thy letter from ——— ye 22^d of ye 11/m: & seen wth no small admiration, how thou hast Confounded my Letter, wch some years agoe I sent to John George Matern, in wch I have writ no Lye ...." It then

---

[498] On Schwaner's release from prison, he followed his friends, the Praches and Materns to London, where he became an assistant secretary to the Yearly Meeting and an amanuensis of George Fox. Fox has several references to him in his Journal under the date of 1684 and 1685, in which former year he wrote, for Fox "to ye King of Denmark & the Duke of Halstine from about ye 11th hour of ye Day [Sunday!] till 9 at night." This letter to the Duke of Holstein was a reply to the duke's censure of Elisabeth Hendricks for daring to preach in public. Fox usually refers to Schwaner by his first name only, which may be a sign of their mutual affection. He wrote on at least one occasion for both George and Margaret Fox, and evidently spent many long days in this strenuous service. His work for London Yearly Meeting began as early as 3rd. Month, 1679, when the Morning Meeting and the Meeting for Sufferings agreed "that Marke Swaner the German friend bee the Correcter of friends books printed by friends order & have ye usuall and Customary allowance for ye same." For some years after Fox's death, Schwaner was employed by the meeting to prepare his writings for the press; and there are records of various negotiations with him about methods and salary between the years 1694 and 1699, when he was retired to only occasional employment (See *Journal of the Friends Historical Society*, XVIII (1921), p. 11. The second edition of Penn's "No Cross, No Crown", London, 1682, has on its title-page the statement: "Printed for Mark Swaner: and sold by...."

[499] Etting MSS. (Misc., 4:10): This is an English translation from the original German.

repeats, for more than three pages, the argument developed in his first letter.

Two letters to Martin John are extant, one from Hilary Prache, dated "London the 9th October, O. S., 1676", the other from John G. Matern, dated 30th Sept. 1676.[500] In the first of these is the following echo of the controversy as to the existence of Boehmenism among the Friends. Prache writes: "That there is a division among us on account of the writings of Jacob Boehmen, and that, therefore, some are known as Boehmists is a fearful falsehood. I do not know in the whole of London any single one among the Friends, of whom there are several thousand, who holds to the writings of Jacob Boehmen in preference to the writings of Friends, for which reason he might be named a Boehmist. The position is this. Very many friends had read the writings of Jacob Boehmen and were fond of them while they still belonged to the other sects, the papists [Baptists?] (so the Mennists are called here), the Independents; the Presbyterians; etc., and they became unsettled in their religion by their means; then they attended Quaker Meetings, or read their writings, and in that way were *convinciret* of the Truth and became united with us. All such still acknowledge the gift of the Spirit in the writings of Jacob Boehmen, and hold him to be a divinely illumined man who prophesied in particular about a people which was to come from the North, but they no longer turned to his writings, nor did they ever point them out to anyone else, for they know from daily experience that a single Quaker Meeting, of the kind that is held as it should be, makes greater demands, and is of more use, than the reading for many years of writings which talk so much of the Tree of Knowledge of Good and Evil can ever prove to be. How then can they give the occasion for anyone to call them Boehmists? Certainly he is not a Quaker who is a Boehmist. A Boehmist makes much of the outward water-baptism of infants and of the outward bread and wine

---

[500] These were published, in German, in „Unschuldige Nachrichten von Alten und Neuen Theologischen Sachen", Leipzig, Vol. for 1706, 8th section, pp. 432–446; an English translation of them by Edward Bernstein, a London Friend, is in *The Journal of the Friends Historical Society*, Vol. 16 (1919), pp. 1–8.

as very essential means of salvation, but let anyone name a single individual Quaker in the whole of London who holds such things, and is not aware of something better with regard to both these points. In this respect the Boehmists are to be sought amongst the Papists who in a like fashion lay much stress on these shadowy things. There is none such to be found among the Quakers.''

Longworth's connection with the Schwenkfelders may have given special point to his interest in the relation of state and church, which is manifested in a letter he wrote, probably in 1676 or 1677, and probably to James Harrison,[501] in regard to ''George Fox's book concerning tithes.''[502] Longworth himself quotes ''Seldons History of Tythes'' regarding their confirmation by King Ethelbert and others.

Longworth's Journeys in Holland and Germany

Having failed of his immediate object in Silesia, Longworth returned home; but probably on his journey both ways he passed through and stopped for a time in Holland. Here he began the warm friendship, which was to last throughout the next decade of his life, with Jan and Jacob Claus and Pieter Hendricks. These pillars of Quakerism on the Continent acted as guide and interpreter for him on his next five Continental journeys. With Hendricks, his friendship was particularly intimate and is manifest in the numerous letters which passed between them. One of these begins and ends characteristically as follows:[503] ''R: L: Dear friend, my love in yᵉ Lord Jes: Chr: is unto thee, and in yᵉ bonds of a heavenly fellowshipe J doe embrace thee, being oftimes mindful of thee and of those sweet opportunities yᵗ we weare soe sweetly refreshed together. . . . Soe deare Rodger noe more at present—but my love in which J imbrace thee, and J desire thee to remember my deare love to friends where thou art free—and yᵉ love of many friends is

---

[501] Pemberton MSS., I, 76.

[502] Fox wrote two tracts on tithes, in 1676: "The Beginning of Tythes in the Law, and ending of Tythes in the Gospel", and "The Law and Commandment of God concerning Tythes."

[503] The Pennypacker MSS. (Cf. Pennypacker, "The Settlement of Germantown", 1899, pp. 126–7).

to thee, and J shall long to heare from thee againe—farewell. J remaine Thy ffriend and brother in my measure Pieter Hendricks.''

In some of these letters, Hendricks writes of the various places they had visited together; while Longworth sends his love (through his ''Deare piter Henderics'') to the Friends whom they had met in ''Dansick hambourgh, fredrikstad, freesland, emden, alkemore [Alkmaar], Roterdam'', and mentions particularly his Amsterdam friends: ''deare Jo. Claus, & his wife, Jo: Rouliff & his wife, Jacob Claus & his wife Barnit [Barent] van Tongueren,'' and ''deare Mary [Maria Weyts Vettekeuken] & her brother if alive,'' of Rotterdam.

Longworth's visit to the Continent in 1677 was not associated with that of Fox's and Penn's imposing party, but appears to have been taken in company with John Hill and several Dutch Friends who had come over to attend London Yearly Meeting that year. Longworth was too strenuous a traveller to keep a journal of his travels, and we learn of his adventures almost exclusively from the scant references to them which we find in his letters. Among his fifty-three extant letters, are five or six which he wrote on this journey, two from London, two (perhaps three) from Holland, and one from Colchester. From these we learn that he planned to leave Colchester for Holland in 4th. Month (June, 1677);[504] that he returned to Amsterdam in 10th. Month (December), when he was ''verie well everie way . . . but in hast to goe to freesland and to amden and then to Returne to England;[505] that he was back again in Amsterdam in 11th. Month (January, 1678);[506] that he then hoped ''to be in England in 2 or 3 weekes time;'' and that he did arrive in Colchester at the end of February, 1678. One other of his letters (probably the one in regard to Fox's books on tithes) reached Fox, Harrison and Richard Mew, all three of whom replied to Longworth,[507] though their replies appear to have miscarried or been long delayed.

[504] Pemberton MSS., I, 65.
[505] Ibid., I, 74.
[506] Ibid., I, 75.
[507] Ibid, I, 69, 77.

James Harrison in one of his replies, states that three letters had been received from Longworth "out from holland and one from Dunkirk the first thou writt wee received not." Why he went to Dunkirk is not clear; nor have we details of his journey between June and December, 1677. He probably attended the great General Meeting in Amsterdam, in August; and then he and John Hill preceded Fox in a journey to Hamburg and Frederikstad, Hill joining Fox at Hamburg on his return, and coming back with him as far as Leeuwarden, while Longworth returned direct to Amsterdam.[508] He was in Alkmaar in September, attending the boisterous funeral of Marytie Claes;[509] and several months were spent in North Holland and perhaps the Rhineland and the Coast as far as Dunkirk. Then followed a journey through Friesland to Emden, which consumed parts of December and January; and returning again to Amsterdam, he arrived in London by way of Colchester early in March, 1678.[510]

A letter written to him by Pieter Hendricks, dated at Amsterdam the 17th of 5th Month, 1678,[511] contains among other items the following: "Thy letter to the king of poland and yͤ Councell of danzick wee understand is Come to yͤ kings hands with deare G: ffs: letter to him, after he was departed from dansick, and it is said he hath read it himselfe—but nothing further."

After travelling in England, in the spring, and attending London Yearly Meeting, Longworth set off for Ireland, whence he wrote letters to James Harrison, dated from Dublin, the 3rd. of 7th. Month and the 12th. of 9th. Month, 1678.[512] In late February, 1679, he was again in England and was arrested at "middle weith [Middlewitch, Cheshire] meeting."

The Quaker chonicler of early Quaker "sufferings"[513]

---

[508] Why Longworth was separated from "old John Hill" at this time we are not informed.

[509] See Monograph Number Six ("Dutch Quaker Leaders").

[510] Pemberton, MSS., I, 78, 80, 82.

[511] The Pennypacker MSS. (Cf. Pennypacker, "The Settlement of Germantown", 1899, p. 126).

[512] Pemberton MSS., I, 84 and 85.

[513] Joseph Besse, 1753, Vol. I, p. 322.

gives the following account of this occurrence: "Anno 1678. Roger Longworth, of Bolton, occasionally travelling into Cheshire, was by two officious Justices sent to Prison. A copy of his Mittimus[514] follows, viz.

'Com. Chester ss.

'Forasmuch as by Reason of several Expressions which we have this Day, at Holme in the County of Chester, heard from a strange Person, who calls himself Roger Longworth, of Bolton in the County of Lancaster, we do suspect that the said Roger Longworth is a Papist, and thereupon according to his Majesty's Commission, ... we have this Day tendered unto him the said Roger Longworth the Oath of Obedience, and the Oath of Supremacy, both which Oaths the said Roger Longworth, being above the Age of eighteen Years, hath this Day refused to take. These are therefore in his Majesty's Name to require and command you forthwith upon Sight hereof to receive into your Custody the Person of the said Roger Longworth, whom we have herewith sent you, and him there safely keep until the next general Quarter Sessions of the Peace, to be held in and for this County of Chester, without Bail or Mainprize. For so doing this shall be your Warrant. Given under our Hands and Seals at Holme this 28th Day of *February, Anno rni* [regni] *Caroli secundi Dei Gra. Angliae, &c, Tricesimo, Annoq; Dom.* 1678–9.

To the Keeper of   Tho. Manwaring *Bart.*
Chester Castle   Jeffery Shackerly *Knt.*'

"After he had been detained in Prison above two Months, he was set at Liberty by a private Order from the said Justice Manwaring."

It is not at all strange that this "private Order" should have been issued; but how curious that such extreme *Puritans* as Longworth, Penn and other early Friends should have been accused of being *Papists!* An illustration indeed of extremes sometimes meeting.

Longworth himself wrote an account of his arrest and four letters to Phineas Pemberton and James Harrison during the six or eight weeks of this imprisonment in Chester

---

[514] A copy of this commitment is in the Etting MSS., IV, 7.

Castle.[515] In one of these, he speaks of writing letters "to friends in Ireland & to London & Holland."

Being released and going to London, he wrote (to James Harrison, the 14th. of 4th. Month (June), 1679[516]): "I have received a letter out of Holland & friends doth expect mee there I have not sould my maier [mare] as yeat . . . I hope to write from Holland William Gibson & George Keeth intend to goe to Colchester with me." In another letter to Harrison, dated from Rotterdam the 24th. of [probably 4th. Month, June],[517] he says that he had hoped to write again before he left London, but that he "went out in haste. Did not sele my mare to pay to will: townsend. I tould him what p.p. [Phineas Pemberton] spoke to mee." This is apparently a reference to his failure to sell his riding-horse and to the money advanced for his trip abroad by William Townsend on Phineas Pemberton's guarantee; his mare, useful for short trips in England, would not be up to long ones on the Continent, and was therefore to be converted into cash.

The journey of this year, 1679, was an arduous one. Sailing on a Saturday evening from London, Longworth, William Gibson and George Keith, landed at Briel on Sunday morning, about the end of June. They held "good meetings" in Rotterdam and Haarlem; and in Amsterdam, Longworth and Gibson attended "the yeearly meeting", Longworth wrote, "where wee found friends from many parts of these eastern countries & wee had a verie glooiryeous heavenly meeting, & wee stayed 5 or 6 meetings & then deare W.G. & I [went] to Friesland. . . . ." This journey required a four months' tour.

In Friesland, Longworth and Pieter Hendricks held religious meetings "in freish places" and aided the Monthly Meeting at Harlingen in the organization and discipline of its constituent members in the Woude, the Knijpe and Lippenhuizen.[518] Leaving Harlingen in company with his interpreter, Jacob Claus, Longworth went on board ship and,

---

[515] Pemberton MSS., I, 89, 90, 92, 94 and 99.

[516] *Ibid.*, I, 102.

[517] *Ibid.*, I, 118.

[518] See Monograph Number Eight ("The Friesland Monthly Meeting of the Society of Friends").

after a twelve days' voyage, arrived in Frederikstad. Here, they held "two meetings" [on Sunday], Longworth writes,[519] "and verie good seruice and many people came in and I sounded the Lords blessed day and all was still and quiet and not a tongue lift up against the truth. I have had four meetings in this citty and the Lords power is over all. I am about to goe to Hamburg through the armies: Dannemarke's army lies about Hamburg and the French are on the South of the River [Elbe].[520] But I hope the Lord will make way." Longworth went to Hamburg to encourage the persecuted Quakers there; and he would have gone to far-distant Danzig, but heard that "friends there are all at Liberty & things are quiet."

At "amden", however, he writes that "they are very wild they have banished friends out of the citty but the Lord is pleading with them." Accordingly, Longworth, too, decided to plead with the rulers of Emden. His pleading here took the form of warnings to the magistrates and street harangues to the people, which were interpreted by Jacob Claus, and which resulted in a short imprisonment and expulsion from the city. Steven Crisp could not go to Emden and the other centers of persecution this year, and Longworth went in his stead; he contributed his report to the "Outcries" made against the persecutors by Crisp and Pieter Hendricks.[521]

Expelled from Emden, Longworth and Claus appear to have travelled up the River Ems and made a proselyting tour through Gelderland, and thence gone to "the pelletinia in the south of germania":[522] that is, to the Palatinate, probably by way of Krefeld as far south as Krisheim. It is possible that this visit helped to cause a renewed wave of persecution which drove the Krefeld Friends into exile and emigration; for it was soon after this time that Herman

---

[519] A letter to James Harrison, dated "fraderickstat in ye Dannemarke's Dominion, the 23rd. of ye 5th. mo., 1679" (Pemberton MSS., I, 106).

[520] This was during the "Skaane War" (1675–79), one of the numerous wars between Denmark and Sweden.

[521] Cf. Monograph Number Seven ("The Persecution of the Quakers in the Netherlands and Western Germany").

[522] Letter to James Harrison, 24th. of 8th. Month (October), 1679: Pemberton MSS., I, 119.

Isaaksz, Henrik Jansz and four other Friends of that town were banished, and this was followed by the departure of almost all the Krefeld meeting to Pennsylvania.[523]

Returning from the Rhineland, Longworth arrived at the end of October, 1679, in Rotterdam where he met again with William Gibson and George Keith, and where he wrote to James Harrison the letter referred to above, narrating his experiences in Emden and elsewhere. In this letter, he says: "I have had a long journey in these eastern countries and good searvices in many places where friends had never been before and noe oppossion [opposition] in my journey until this day, but only at Amden [Emden] amongst those soddommittes that would not have righteous love . . . . I have some thoughts to goe to Amsterdam and stay in these low counteries a little time & if the Lord make way, then for England."

Harrison in reply to this letter wrote from Boulton the 20th. of 9th. Month, 1679, as follows:[524] "Rodg^r Longworth: Deare And well beloved in ye Lord Jesus Christ. . . . . I received thine from Roterdam of 24: 8 mo last & we had one before & one—at London sent to William Gibson wherein J understood of thy trauell exercise & servis after W: G parted with thee. I and mine are very glad to here from thee & of thy welfare, soe are friends here and heareaways Ph: [?] Worthington desired me to remember his loue to thee when J writ, at the time when J received thy Letter, soe did Ro: [Roger] & John Haydock with others of ye meetting that knew of it; a bad bad spirit hath beene at work & yett is in Cheshire." He then proceeds to give details of the persecution of that year, especially of James Worthington.

Longworth's next letter to Harrison is dated from Amsterdam, the 2nd. of 11th. Month, 1679, (January, 1680).[525] This refers to the prevalence and large mortality of "the peste", and admits that he himself had "not been verie well of late, but now better, blessed be the Lord." His illness, the prevalent plague, and the persecutions and banish-

---

[523] *Supra*, pp. 196ff.

[524] Simon Gratz Autograph Collection, Pennsylvania Historical Society, Supreme Court Papers, Case 2, Box 12.

[525] Pemberton MSS., I, 124.

ments which he notes as occurring in Emden and Danzig, had not discouraged him, however; for he writes: "The Lords blessed work goes on & his gloarys day spreads over these darke ragiones, & peoples eyes begines to open, & a love is showing amongst sober people towards truth & friends."

Thus encouraged, he continues: "I doe intende to goe into a place called gilder Land, I have beene theire this summer, their is some convinced and [some open ?] nesse, & after my returne I hope I shall be cleare to come for England." The visit to Gelderland was presumably accomplished, although we have no details of it. And his desire to return to England soon was gratified; for we find him at William Crouch's house in London, in February, 1680, writing his Bolton friends of his safe return to England and of his own escape from Quaker travellers' perils, among them "the turks", who had captured, he wrote, "poore Deniall Baker and 3 of his sonnes with meni oether friends."[526]

The spring of 1680 Longworth spent in and around London, and the summer and autumn in Ireland.[527] Returning to Bolton, he wrote the following memorandum of a vision or message:[528] "Upon the 9 day of the 10 mo. [December] 1680 about 4 in the morning the word of the Lord cam unto me saying I will reuaille [reveal] unto thee things to com, as concerning the state of nacions . . . Write these things down & they shall come to pass. by his servant Roger Longworth at Boulton in Lancashire this was in the beginning of the siting of the perlement in the year 1680 as aboue written."[529]

The following winter and the spring of 1681 Longworth spent in England; but after attending London Yearly Meeting, he and Roger Haydock went to the Continent again, to proselyte for their faith and to defy the persecution of which the Yearly Meeting had been informed by the Amsterdam Epistle.

---

[526] *Ibid.*, I, 126, 130.

[527] *Ibid.*, I, 127–130, 138–9, 145, 149, 154–5.

[528] Etting Papers, 66.

[529] It is a somewhat singular coincidence that on this precise date, *George Fox* wrote to Longworth; but the events prophesied are not stated by either.

A letter from Longworth to Harrison, dated Amsterdam, the 3rd. of 4th. Month, 1681,[530] affords a glimpse of this visit. "Wee are verie well every way", Longworth writes; "that day that thou left us at greavesend we toke shiping about the midel of the day & we were landed at briell on the next day about 28 hours upon the sea & weire both well in health. wee had a meeting at Rotterdam on the 4th. day [Wednesday], & at harlam on the 6: day & at Amsterdam yeasterday [Sunday, the 12th.] & friends are generally well & are glad of us the yearly meeting begins the next fift day [Thursday] which is the 16 of this instant & when the meeting is over I thinke we may take our journey towards frees Land, and soe as the Lord shall order."

Not only to Friesland, does it appear that the Lord ordered them to go; but to Emden, Hamburg and Frederikstad, and thence on a long journey through a war-menaced and plague-striken country to the Rhineland. Here, at Krefeld and Krisheim, Longworth again brought consolation and encouragement, albeit renewed peril, to the little company of "isolated Friends."

From Krisheim, the two travellers, accompanied by two of the Krisheim Friends, appear to have crossed the Rhine and gone to Alzey, the town where Ames and Caton had had their interview with the district officials in 1661, and which they called "Alstone." Roger Longworth, writing of this journey to Phineas Pemberton,[531] tells of the meeting in "the pelletiney" [at Krisheim], and then of the mild confinement imposed at "Alsaca" upon the two Rogers and perhaps the two Friends who accompanied them from Krisheim.[532] From Alzey, the English travellers made their way down the Rhine to Rotterdam and thence to England, where we find them landing at Harwich in September, and Longworth going on to London.

In London, this autumn, Longworth is caught up with many other Friends into the spirit of William Penn's great adventure beyond the Atlantic. Writing to James Harrison

[530] Pemberton MSS., I, 165; see also *ibid.*, I, 160 (Longworth's letter to Harrison, dated the 7th. of 3rd. Month, 1681).

[531] Pemberton MSS., I, 117.

[532] *Supra*, p. 288.

from London, the 3rd. of 8th. Month (October), 1681, he says:[533] "Will: penn doth not goe to penselvania, he is about Bristall, their is a shipe going from thence, with many passhenars." Harrison in reply informs him that *he* is about to bargain with Elinor Low (the fiancée of Roger Haydock) for the sale of his house "in case I should goe with w: pen."[534] This news is evidently saddening, for Longworth refers in his next letter[535] to the possibility of his friend's removal "into some remote peart of the world, where wee could not com to see the feaces one of another"; but, he adds, " the Lord's will be done."

Obeying what he believed was God's will, Longworth soon left for Ireland again, in November, 1681, and spent the following winter and spring preaching Quakerism in that island, which was to send so many of its people, Quakers and others, to the New World.[536] Back again in Bristol, in April, 1682, he went on to London Yearly Meeting, and there had interviews with Penn in regard to Pennsylvania affairs, corresponding with his friend James Harrison about them.[537] With his long and intimate experience in the affairs of Quakerism in Holland and Germany, especially in connection with the persecuted Friends and others, Longworth evidently appealed to Penn as being an ideal promoter of colonization in Pennsylvania; and we can readily conceive the character of the conversations between the two men in their London interviews just before Penn started upon his Holy Experiment. In two of his letters to Harrison, written during and just after the Yearly Meeting in London,[538] Longworth speaks of these interviews and of the plans of Penn and William Gibson in connection with the expedition which was to start two months later to found Philadelphia. But before turning westward, himself, Longworth felt that he had further work to do in Europe.

---

[533] Pemberton MSS., I, 171.

[534] *Ibid.*, I, 172.

[535] *Ibid*, I, 173.

[536] Two letters to Pemberton and one to Harrison, January and February, 1682: *ibid*, I, 179, 181, 183.

[537] Harrison's letter to Longworth, Boulton, the 13th. of 4th. Month, 1682; *ibid.*, I, 189.

[538] *Ibid.*, I, 188, 190 (the 10th. and 18th. of 4th. month—June— 1682).

On the 18th. of 4th. month (June), he writes: "I am even now ready to take shipping this evening at the tower in a Duch ship with a Duch friend." A fortnight later, he wrote of his departure from Gravesend, his voyage across the North Sea to "the tagel" [Texel Island], where he "anckered" and apparently transshipped for the voyage across the Zuider Zee to Harlingen. After visiting the Harlingen Friends, "till the 1st. day over", he accompanied the representatives of the Friesland Monthly Meeting to the Yearly Meeting in Amsterdam where, he said,[539] "we have had a blessed season, the Lord has verie wonderfully apeared to the gleading [gladdening ?] of our soules."

Being informed at this meeting that the Friends in Danzig were being "percquited", he determined to "take shiping tomorrow evening towards Danckset the Lord willing. ... Soe in hast I rest & bide thee feare well in the Lord." Accompanied by an interpreter, he accordingly went to Danzig to admonish the persecutors, to hold "blessed meetings" with the persecuted, and to aid in the organization of both's men's and women's "meetings for discipline", including a yearly meeting for the Friends of Danzig, (the Amsterdam Yearly Meeting being too distant for them), and a half-yearly meeting for those of Frederikstad and Hamburg.[540]

Leaving Danzig some time in July, he records: "I trevalled with the governor of steeten [Stettin] & some oather great men to a citty called wissmoord [Wismar], with whom I had good servias, after, we had, hade some sharp dissput, we travieled foure hundred English miles in 3 dayes & 3 nights, when we came to wissmoor, he had me to the governour of that place who did treat me verie kindly, the next day I came to Lubicke, from thence of [to] freederickstat."[541]

After confirming with the Frederikstad Friends his plan for a half-yearly meeting for them and those of Hamburg, Longworth probably returned to England by way of Ham-

---

[539] *Ibid.*, I, 195.
[540] See Monograph Number Seven ("The Persecution of the Quakers in the Netherlands and Western Germany.").
[541] Pemberton MSS., I, 198.

burg and the Netherlands; but we have no record of this return journey, and it may have been direct by sea to Harwich.

LONGWORTH'S JOURNEYS IN AMERICA

Meanwhile, his Bolton friends, the family of James Harrison and that of his son-in-law, Phineas Pemberton, were on the wing for Pennsylvania. On the 3rd. and 8th. of 5th. Month (July), 1682, Phineas Pemberton had written to him (in care of "peter Hendrickes merchant in Amsterdam in Holland"), that he was making preparations for the great adventure.[542] Two months later, the 5th. of 7th. Month (September), Pemberton wrote him again, from on board "The Submission", Liverpool, en route to Pennsylvania; and this time he directed his letter "to be left with William Gibson in London."[543] Longworth, then, must have returned from the Continent sometime in the late summer; but whether or not he was in time to say farewell to his old friends we are not informed. He soon made up his mind to follow them, at least for a visit of personal observation and religious service, to the New World. This decision may have been caused or strengthened by another imprisonment which he suffered in the midst of his ministerial labors in England, during the spring of 1683.

According to Besse's account,[544] he was sent to the "Common Goal of Surry County" on the following mittimus: "I send you herewith the Body of Roger Longworth, Shoemaker, charged . . . for heading a tumultuous and riotous Assembly of disorderly Persons in the open Street, and being commanded, in his Majesty's Name, to depart, they contemptuously refused to obey: and the said R.L. took upon him by talking and other Misbehaviour to encourage the said Tumult and Riot, and for that he refused to find sufficient Sureties to answer the several Offences and Misdemeanours at the next Quarter Sessions . . . . These are therefore, in his Majesty's Name, to will and require you to receive the Body of the said R.L. into your Custody and him

---

[542] Ibid., I, 196, 197.
[543] Ibid., I, 203.
[544] Op. cit., Vol. I, p. 703.

safely keep until he shall be discharged by due Course of Law. Given under my Hand and Seal from the Bridgehouse this 11th. day of March 1682 [1683]. W. Pyers.''

During this imprisonment, Longworth's thoughts were winging their flight from his prison-cage to the land of refuge beyond the seas, and he wrote his Pennsylvania friends of his intended visit. In April, 1683, Pemberton wrote him: "I have received a letter from thee about 10 days ago, telling of thy passage towards Virginia."[545] This term "Virginia" was used in its early and wide sense, for Longworth landed in Philadelphia. His friends, the Harrisons and Pembertons, had left Liverpool on *The Submission*, the 5th. of 7th. Month (September), 1682, and "arrived at Choptank, in Maryland, the 21st 9th M°. [November], following, being brought thither through the dishonesty of the Master [Captain James Settle]." They did not reach their destination ("Apoquinemene") in Pennsylvania until the 15th. of January, 1683.

Just where and when Longworth landed in America is not stated, but in the Könneken Manuscripts, as has been seen above,[546] there is a Dutch translation of a letter which "Rodtgert Langewort" wrote to Pieter Hendricks and Jan Claus from Philadelphia, the 12th. of 5th. Month (July), 1683. The English original is not extant, and the Dutch translation is without place or date; but Hendricks wrote to Longworth on the 1st. of 12th. Month, 1683, and speaks of having received a letter from Longworth dated the 12th. of the preceding 5th. Month (July ?), to which "pritty̆ muche bisenes prevented earlier answer". It seems probable, therefore, that Longworth wrote his letter from Philadelphia some time during the summer of 1683, before he went on to New York and New England.

Translated from the Dutch back into English, the letter reads as follows:

"P.H. and Jan Claus; now then worthy and dear Friends, you may know by these few lines, that since I parted from you last I have continued in good health, down to this very day: blessed be the name of the Lord forever. We have had a

---

[545] Pemberton MSS., II, 44.
[546] P. 335.

Roger Longworth's letter from Philadelphia, 1683

good journey to this quarter of the world. I departed from Plymouth (*Plaumun*) with my companion W. Wilson, who also intended to come to these quarters, but having been taken ill he returned to London. We were about 80 voyagers who set out for Pensÿlvania. We were six weeks on the way from Plymouth to the River Delaware, and we were well all the time. We lost only 2 little children, one from small-pox and the other from consumption (*de tering*). The first place where I trod was the city of Philadelphia, where I met with the governor, W.Penn, who was very glad to see me, and in whose house I lodged while I was in the city. They have built several (*verscheide*) houses, and have 3 meetings in the Truth. I was at William Penn's for dinner with 6 Indian kings (*jndiaanse koningen*), and after dinner we went to meeting, they along with us, and the word of the Lord arose in my heart towards them, and they remained most of the time of the meeting. Thence I betook myself, to-gether with Christopher Tyler (*tÿlar*) to Burlington, where there is another meeting, and we had a great gathering. Then I went to the Waterfall,[547] where Friends dwell on both sides of the river, and where the people come to the meeting all together, and things are in good order and Friends in unity. As to the land here, or in Pennsylvania, there is good pasturage and grain, and it is much better than I had expected. In brief: here is good grain, and here is abundance: fish, fowl and fruits are overflowing: I say no more than I have seen. I am now almost ready to leave for *lang eÿlandt*, and to journey further to *Rood Eilandt*, and then towards *neuw Engelandt*. And so with my love to you dear Friends and other Friends in the Provinces (*gewes-ten*). Let the other ancient Friends be informed [share this letter], together with my love to them all. I remain your Friend and Brother in the Truth. Rodtgert Langwort.''

This homely letter not only affords some idea of Long-worth's travels in America, but it is significant of the way in which the good news about Penn's land of promise was spread among prospective colonists in the Old World.

Another glimpse of Longworth's journey to New York

---

[547] The Falls of the Delaware River, in Bucks County, Pennsylvania, where the Pembertons lived.

and beyond comes to us from a letter written by him to Pemberton, dated from "fflushen", the 24th. of 6th. Month (August), 1683,[548] in which he tells of his visit in New York and Long Island. "I went", he says, "to a place called Jerico about 20 miles & was taken with agiue and a faiver ["chills and fever"], and on the second day I came here againe, John bound [Bowne] and his wife is verie carfull off mee." He hoped to be well enough to attend the Quarterly Meeting which was to be held in Flushing on the following Saturday, and then to go on to Rhode Island and New England.

Of his farther journeyings in America this year and the next, we have but little trace. A letter addressed by Pieter Hendricks "aan mÿn waerde vriendt Roger Lanwory Toe London", and dated from Amsterdam the 1st. of December, 1683,[549] would imply that he was then, or was soon expected, in England. But he did not return when expected, and travelled far and wide in the New World; for we find him relating, in a paper of July, 1684,[550] his visit to Maryland, Virginia and the Carolinas; also, a letter from him to Pemberton dated New York, the 18th of 10th. Month (December), 1684, in regard to his mare being sent to "Rariton" [the Raritan River, probably at Middletown, New Jersey].[551] That he went on through New Jersey and New York again as far as New England on this journey is known from a manuscript "List of the Names of Publick Men & Women Friends that have visited New England since the Year 1656",[552] which includes the names of Roger Longworth and James Martin in 1683 and Roger Longworth "from Old England" in 1684.[553]

Returning from New England to Pennsylvania, he at-

---

[548] Pemberton MSS., II, 48. The Annual Catalogue of the Writings of George Fox (19, 20 G) lists a letter from Fox addressed to Longworth in Rhode Island and dated 12 mo. 25, 1683, which began: "Dear friend R. L. I receiued thy letter dated 23. 8 mo. 83." (Contributed by Professor Henry J. Cadbury).

[549] *Ibid.*, II, 43.

[550] *Ibid.*, II, 37.

[551] *Ibid.*, II, 32.

[552] Swarthmore College MSS., O 2140.

[553] The minutes of Salem, Massachusetts, Monthly Meeting contain a list of Friends "that have travelled in the worke of the ministry that have been heare at Salem," and in it also appears the name of "Rodger Longworth".

tended Philadelphia Yearly Meeting in 7th. Month (September), 1684, and was one of the signers of the Yearly Meeting's Epistle of that year. Continuing southward, he visited Friends in Maryland and Virginia, and perhaps made another visit to those in the Carolinas. A letter from some Maryland Friends to George Fox and others in England, dated "Maryland, the 13th 2d mo [April] 1685." states that their Yearly Meeting had been held "in the 8th mo Last [October, 1684]," and that "Deare Roger Longworth was at our Said meeting." They also referred the English Friends to Longworth for further information in regard to a separation which had occurred among Friends in Maryland, and in regard to a delinquent Friend in Virginia.[554] The minutes of the West River and Tredhaven (Maryland) Meeting for 1684 (p. 25) also record that "a letter of G. Fox's to our dear friends Roger Longworth and Tho: Everdon to stir up Friends to visit Virginia and Carolina and these parts was read."[555]

The winter of 1684–85 Longworth spent in the homes of his two friends, Phineas Pemberton and James Harrison, on the banks of the Delaware. Harrison was at this time steward of Penn's estate at Pennsbury, and Longworth doubtless became thoroughly versed in the advantages and disadvantages of migration to the Quaker colony. It was a season of comparative rest for him, also, and he used it to recuperate from his attacks of fever and ague, and to prepare for further journeyings. Sailing from New York early in 1685, he returned to England, making *en route* an unrecorded visit to the Friends in Barbados.

A rather obscure but commendatory reference to his work in America appears in a letter from William Ingram to Phineas Pemberton dated, London the 29th. of 6th. Month (August), 1685,[556] which reads as follows: "Friends centered in the power of Truth cause a good savor to arise in every place, as I believe was left by our Dr fd R.Longworth notwithstanding the evill indeavours of some thou gives account of who would lessen the service & testimony of that faithfull man, whom the Lord hath owned in his labours,

---

[554] *Journal of the Friends' Historical Society*, Vol. 5 (1908), p. 103.

[555] Contributed by Professor Henry J. Cadbury.

[556] Pemberton MSS., II, 97.

which I am satisfied were accepted of him & I question not but has rewarded that worthy servant with the full injoyment of eternall life & peace.'' Ingram's further statement that he and Roger Haydock approve of Longworth's "method of using the 10 £ for the service of truth'' may point to some financial accusation against him.

Another echo of Longworth's visit to America comes from a joint letter which he and George Fox wrote to John Bowne of Flushing. This letter is dated London, the 7th. of 1st. Month, 1685–6 (March, 1686), and was written soon after Longworth's return to England. It begins:[557]

"Deare John

"I have spoken with Deare G F about ye Childrens Meetings & of such as teache Children (wch it is well to instruct Children) & alsoe marchts & Tradesmen, for there is a Complaint in England, & it is good yt all yt Professeth ye Truth in words may Preach it in their Lives, Soe his Deare Love is to you all in ye Seed yt is blessed for Ever.'' These words are followed by the Letters G F; but they were probably written by Longworth, while Fox wrote or dictated the lines that follow, namely: "For a meeting of friends yt are Shopkeepers & merchants yt they may Speak one wth another, yt they make Just Returns to People yt they deale wth all, & not keep things to Long in their hands, but answere you duely yt they deale with all, & See yt long debts doe not lye in yor hands, This both among marchts—Shopkeepers & Planters must looke to, Soe yt they may owe Nothing to any man, but Love, & yt will be to the Honour of God, & their Owne Reput.''

Such was the characteristic concern of these two early Quaker travellers in America that its material prosperity should not dim the ethical and spiritual welfare of its Quaker colonists.

LONGWORTH'S LAST JOURNEY TO HOLLAND AND GERMANY

Arriving in London, probably in time for the Yearly Meeting about the end of 3rd Month (May), 1685, Longworth took up again his ministerial labors and their conse-

---

[557] Roberts MSS., Haverford College.

quent imprisonments. Within a fortnight after the Yearly Meeting, he was arrested at a meeting in Grace-church Street, and was imprisoned for nearly five months in Newgate. From a letter which he wrote to John Bowne of Flushing,[558] we learn that he "was then [i.e. the last time he wrote to him, while he was still in Newgate] a Prisoner but in a short time after was Released & then went to holland & into Germany, & some parts of the Denmark Dominions, where I had good service for the Lord, & his witness was Reached in many, in severall places, there is an Openness in those parts of the world."

From Fox's "Itinerary Journal",[559] we learn that on Sunday, the 16th. of 6th. Month (August), 1685, "Rodger Langworth declared" in a Friends' meeting held at "Rattlif" [Ratcliff, London], which, Fox states, was "Large and Peaceable within ye doors." It was probably soon after this, at a meeting which was not so peaceable, that Longworth was again arrested. After his imprisonment, which he says was short, he departed on his sixth and last journey to Holland and Germany. He had doubtless met in London with the "Germaine fri^{ds} yt were goeing to pensilvania", to whom Fox refers in the passage just quoted;[560] and when he arrived on the Continent, told the Dutch and German Friends in person of the great Quaker colony which he had recently visited.

From Amsterdam, he went to Harlingen, to visit the "pritty little meeting" there, and to hold two religious meetings appointed by himself; and thence to Emden, Hamburg and Fredrikstad. Returning to Amsterdam, he wrote a brief report of his journey to the Second-day Meeting (the Ministers' Meeting) in London.[561] This was dated the 26th. of 9th. Month (November), 1685, and reported among other things that the rulers of Emden had come to see the unwisdom of their persecuting policy towards the Friends, and were now willing or eager to change it.

He wrote of this journey to George Fox also (Amsterdam

[558] *Ibid.*
[559] Norman Penney's edition, p. 114.
[560] These were the Schumacher and Hendricks households; see *supra*, p. 291.
[561] Devonshire House MSS., Portfolio, 16, 27.

7th of 10th Month—December— 1685) referring especially to the toleration which then existed in Danzig and Emden.[562] Fox replied to this letter from London, the 29th. of 11th. Month, 1685 [January, 1686][562] acknowledging the gratifying report from Emden and Danzig, and continuing as follows: "now dr. R. it would be very well for thee and some friends, J.C. [Jan Claus] or J.Roel: [Roelofs] to visit friends at Embden while the door is open, both in the city & in the country it may be now of service, and its pity anything in that should be neglected. . . . If you find an openness in that city or country in time you may set up a monthly meeting there. And so I shall leave it to the Lords ordering by his eternal power and hand."

Longworth promptly responded to this suggestion and made the noteworthy visit to Emden, the details of which have been given elsewhere.[563] It resulted in the complete triumph of the Friends' non-violent resistance to persecution and in the establishment of full religious liberty in that persecuting city. Longworth tells the story of it in a letter which he wrote to John Bowne after his return to London, on the 7th. of the 1st. Month (March, 1786). He enclosed with this also a copy of the outspoken address which he had presented under dramatic circumstances to the rulers of the city. A reflection of this triumph is caught in Longworth's letter to Bowne, which begins as follows:

"Deare Frend:

"Thine I have before me dated ye 8th. of ye 8th. Month [October], 1685 being just come out of holland, wch I was very glad of & in the Reaadinge of it I was Refreshed in a sence & feeling of thy integrity for the Lord, who is worthy for Ever to be feared, Worshiped & Obeyed, who is our Life and Length of days, & in him wee live, move & have a being God allmighty keep ye & all frends in his Eternall power, who is our Rock and Refug to fly unto in all our Exercises, who hath bin with us unto this day, & borne us up & carryed us on, who is the same today, yesterday, & for Ever."

---

[562] "Reliquiae Barclaianae", pp. 57–58. Fox's reply is in the Etting MSS., 70.
[563] See Monograph Number Seven ("The Persecution of the Quakers in the Netherlands and Western Germany").

George Fox, when writing to Longworth of his concern for the open door in Emden and Danzig, in January, 1686,[564] speaks of "the great sufferings of friends in England," (due to the renewed persecution against which he published several tracts and broadsides, in 1684–86); and he then continues: "And therefore now the door being open as I hear, both about Poland & Danzig & some parts in Swedland, & the D of Holsteyns Country & thereaways, it is good for friends to give them a visit in the Lords eternal power & spirit that by it the minds of people may be turned to the Lord & Christ Jesus the Rock & foundation & setled upon him who is their life & salvation & in whom they have peace with God."

This was another urgent though indirect appeal to Longworth to go further afield than Emden in his proselyting endeavors; but, having gained so notable a success at Emden, he evidently felt called upon to return to England and Ireland, where the fires of persecution were still burning, and to leave the Continental fields to his friend Roger Haydock and to William Penn, who made another journey there in his two-fold religious and colonizing capacity. Roger Haydock, writing to Phineas Pemberton on the 20th of 6th. Month (August), just after his return from a five months' travel in Holland, says:[565] "R.L. came from Holland about the time I went from home westwards,[566] was at my house 2 days before I took my jorney & with my wife some time after I was gone. I think is now in Ireland, was & is I hope well."

LONGWORTH REVISITS AMERICA

Having returned to England in the spring of 1686,[567] as has been seen from this letter of Haydock and from Longworth's to Bowne, Longworth spent some time in War-

[564] Etting MSS., 63.

[565] Pemberton MSS., II, 21.

[566] He went first through western England, and then to London Yearly Meeting, before going to Holland.

[567] There is a letter extant from Pieter Hendricks to Longworth (Pemberton MSS., II, 22) which states that Hendricks had received Longworth's letter "from London the 30th. of *1st. Month*, 1686"; but this date is evidently in the English style, therefore March or April.

rington (Haydock's home) and London, and then went to
Ireland. Here he spent August and September in and
around Dublin and Cork. From the former city, four of his
extant letters were written to Hendricks, Fox, Pemberton
and Harrison; while to him, at Cork or Dublin, were addressed letters from Joan Cook (Green), John Hall, Roger
Haydock, Hendricks, Pemberton and Fox.

Fox, in his letter from London, the 15th. of 7th. Month
(September), 1686,[568] refers to his former letter in regard
to "the great service in Dantzig & that ways & Fred-
erikstadt"; and then, after speaking of William Penn's recent return from Holland and Germany and of "the great
openness" he reported in those regions, Fox continues: "I
writ to thee that if thou hadst anything to go now there is
great service in those parts. But if thy motion be to America
then I desire thee to mind Carolina for there is a great want
there of friends in the ministry as I understood by J. Arch-
dale lately come over & a great openness to hear the Truth
there." Before receiving this incentive, Longworth had
already written to Pieter Hendricks from Dublin, the 21st.
of 6th. Month (August), [569] giving an account of his work in
Ireland, which concluded with the characteristic note: "&
so friends have no cause to be dismaid or cast downe for the
Lord is with us"; stating that he "expects to go to Barbados"; and requesting him to send by Thomas Atherton
"a little amber to smock."[570]

That Roger had developed a taste for some foreign lux-
uries,—or medicaments, as he may have regarded them,—
is suggested by this request for amber, and confirmed by a
letter written to him by John Beeke and dated, "Barbadoes
ye 27-12-1685–86".[571] In this letter, Beeke thanks Roger
for an account of Friends in England, expresses gratification at hearing that "all faithfull Friends are cleer of y^e
late Rebellion [Monmouth's]", and informs him that he
has sent "one case of Sweet-meets by W^m. Jorde marked
G.F.N:s."

[568] Etting MSS., 71.
[569] Pemberton MSS., II, 20.
[570] Cf. *infra*, p. 379.
[571] Etting MSS. (Misc. 4:11).

Thomas Atherton (or Green) was then in Amsterdam; but Hendricks addressed his letters to Longworth in Atherton's care, "At ye Green Boate, in s^t Petterik Street. In Dublin" (which was Longworth's Irish headquarters), and doubtless sent him some amber to smoke away the contagion of small-pox, etc., on his voyage. To Fox, and to Harrison and Pemberton, also, Longworth wrote (on the 5th. and 10th. of September) of his intention to go to Barbados.[572] Thus it is seen that this intention was the result of a well-considered religious and colonizing concern to revisit America and complete the service which he had entered upon three years before.

How curious, then, is the following legend[573] as to the reason why he took this last journey beyond the Atlantic. This is a story "of a troublesome fellow of a Quaker, named Roger Longworth, who used to tell his neighbours of their faults, and how they, not liking him, got rid of him. A chap got secretly into Roger's shippon [cow-shed, or cattle-house] and hid himsself in a hogshead that lay there. When Roger came in the evening to fodder his cattle, the man exclaimed in a hollow voice, 'Stay not here, but go thou and all that belongeth to thee to America.' And taking it as a solemn warning, Roger soon after sold off and departed." Even though the circumstances leading up to his departure for America, which have been stated above, make it entirely explicable, this absurd story is discredited by the fact that Roger's career had been guided always by an *inner* voice, and not by external ones, especially those coming from hogsheads.

On what date in the year 1686 Longworth sailed for Barbados, is not clear. His letters to Fox, Pemberton and Harrison in September, and one from Henry Ceane "to Roger Longworth in Barbadoes", dated Plymouth the 21st. of 9th. Month (November), 1686,[574] would indicate that it was not until about November that he made the voyage. The only record that we have of his work in the island comes

---

[572] Pemberton MSS., II, 10, 8 and 9.

[573] From Brown's "History of Great and Little Bolton", 1824-5: Quoted by Norman Penney in his notes to George Fox's "Short Journal, &c.," 1925, p. 325.

[574] Pemberton MSS., II, 71.

from the following certificate or "minute of indorsement.":[575]

"From our Generall Monthly Meeting of men and women Freinds—at the Bridg Towne in Barbados the 13th of 2^d month [April], 1687.

"This is to Certifie all Freinds where this may come as there may be Accasion or A Service; concerning our Antient and True freind Roger Longworth, who Arived here from Ireland About three months since in the Publick Service of Truth; who hath Faithfully discharged himselfe therein: in this Island in wch his Service he hath Answered the wittness of God both in his ministrey and Conversation Amongst us. And Therefore for Truth Sake & his incoridgment in the same and all Faithfull Labourers in the Lords work and Service wee do: and cann doe no Less then incoridg the same; And Recommend him and Faithfull Labourers and Service for the Lord and his Truth as Afforesaid unto all— all Faithfull Freinds Bretheren & Sisters in America where the Lord may order him in his Service as Afforesaid to be helped and Assisted in the same. So wth the Salutation of our true Loves to all wee Remaine your Freinds—Bretheren and Sisters in the unity and Fellowshipp of the Gospell."

This certificate was signed by sixty-eight members of the monthly meeting,—thirty-nine of whom were men and twenty-nine women, eight of the latter being "widdows", and twenty-five of the women having their names signed for them.

Although Roger was intent on his religious mission in the New World, at least one of his friends in Ireland endeavored to enlist his services there for the secular purpose of selling American land. A brief note is extant,[576] dated "Cashale [Cashel, Ireland] ye 2th of 7 br 1686", and written by "Anth'e Sharp to R. L. (at Cork)". This authorizes Roger to sell one-half of Anthony's "30,000 acres in East Jersie at 150^l: or to sel it at 31 years or 3 lives. R.L. to have all in excess of 150^l:" A postscript to the note adds: "I doe suppose my land in East Jersie to be 30000 acres the moity is then fifteen thousand Cheap Enough."

---

[575] Etting MSS., No. 73.

[576] The Anthony Sharp MSS., Dublin (Contributed by Isabel Grubb, M.A., author of "Quakers in Ireland, 1654–1900", London, 1927).

LONGWORTH'S DEATH IN PENNSYLVANIA

The strenuous labors and long travels of this "Antient and True Freind" were now nearly over. He was only fifty-six years of age, to be sure, and was "ancient" only in the sense in which that word was used by the Friends to signify one who had been "convinced" in the early days of the Society and was therefore "old-fashioned" and distinctive. His incessant travels on sea and land from the frozen lands of Danzig to the tropic sun of the West Indies, had sapped his health, and he left Barbados for Pennsylvania to die in the home of his old friend, James Harrison. The last extant letters he had written were to Harrison and Pemberton, his revered leader, George Fox, and another old friend and co-laborer, Pieter Hendricks; while the last he is known to have received were from these four and Roger Haydock.

There was, indeed, a report of his death before he left Barbados. A letter, apparently from his brother-in-law to Phineas Pemberton, states that by a letter of the 15th. of 6th. Month its writer "doe understand that my brother is dead in barbados pray thee lett me know by thy next letter how hee dyed by sicknesse or otherwise."[577]

The catalogue of "Eighty-seven Publick ffriends yt have dyed in Pensilvania since ye first Settlement of Friends there" contains the following item: "Rogʳ Longworth of Bolton in mors [le Moors] in Lancashire he Arriued from Barbados in ye 3 mo: [May] 1687 and Was burried . . . 8.6.1687."[578] He had brought with him, probably from the Carribean, the germs of what a contemporary called "a very fatal fever", and even the blessed springtime of fair Pennsylvania could not restore him to health.

That the spring-time this year on the banks of the Delaware was not so blessed as usual, from the point of view of health, is gathered from the diary of Phineas Pemberton, who records "a great land flood" on the 16th. of 3rd. Month (May), followed by "a rupture" on the 29th. This would indicate that the river overflowed and deposited on its banks much vegetable and other refuse, which the hot sun of June and July decomposed. An epidemic of fever ensued,

[577] Without place or year; Pemberton MSS., I, 154.
[578] Devonshire House MSS., Portfolio 8.89.

and numerous Friends of the neighborhood fell victims to it within a few weeks. Among these were the father of Phineas Pemberton (Ralph, aged seventy-six), his wife's grandmother (Agnes Harrison, aged eighty-five), and James Harrison.[579] Phineas himself, his wife and children fell ill of the prevalent disease, but slowly recovered. Most of those who died of this fever were either elderly people or children; but Longworth, although in the prime of life, was weakened by his strenuous travels and perhaps by fever germs contracted in the West Indies, and was taken ill and died within a fortnight afterwards.

Phineas Pemberton, in a manuscript diary of five pages, which he kept during three or four months in 1687, says:[580] "This day above, 87 5 mo: 24 day: [That is, the 24th. day of 5th. Month (July), 1687] being first day [Sunday] Roger Longworth was not able to abide in the meeting but lay on a bed all day at the governers [William Penn's, at Pennsbury] at night came to fathers [James Harrison's] & grew ill from ague & feavor wch prevailed so over him that on the 7th. day of the 6th. Month following about 5 A clock in the afternoone it being the first day of the weeke in the yeare 1687 he dyed & was buryed in the burying place in the point over against the foot of Smectons Island in the County of Bucks in the Province of Pennsylvania, the day following being the 2nd day of the weeke & the 8 day of the said month. Recorded by me Phinehas Pemberton 16th 6/mo 1687."

Just two months later, Roger's old friend James Harrison died of the same fever, in the same home, and was buried in the same grave-yard. A contemporary,[581] linking them together in death as in life, says of them: "This Year also, died those two faithful Labourers in the Gospel of Christ, Roger Longworth and James Harrison, both of Bolton in Moors, in Lancashire; and both great Travellers at Home

---

[579] The list of "Eighty-seven Publick ffriends" mentions next after Longworth, "Jam: Harrison of Bolton in yᵉ moores in Lancashire Arriued in the Year 1681 or 1682 was Burried The 8 ᵈᵃʸ 8ᵐᵒ 1687." He was about sixty-one years old at the time of his death.

[580] The Streper MSS., p. 5.

[581] John Whiting, "Memoirs" (1696), 1715, p. 174.

and Abroad in the Service of Truth, and for the Spreading
and Propagation of it. I knew them both, but cannot say
much of them for want of Memoirs, only that they were able
Ministers of the Gospel, and labour'd much in it, for the
gathering People to it, and building up of Friends in the
most Holy Faith to the last.''

Longworth's Will and Worldly Goods

Two days before his death, Roger made or dictated a
memorandum by way of a last will and testament, as follows:[582] ''I Roger Longworth now of the County of Bucks
in the Provincie of Pensylvania being sick of Body but in
good and pfect memory—all cloathing linnen & woollen to
be divided equally between Anne [Harrison's wife] and
phebe [Pemberton's wife]; all the rest of the personalty to
the service of truth; 200 acres in Bucks County also to the
service of truth; James Harrison and Phineas Pemberton
to be executors; all books and papers to Phineas Pemberton.''[583] This will was sealed ''R L'', and to it was attached
an inventory of Longworth's possessions, which was also
probably drawn up by Pemberton's faithful but very free-
spelling hand.

The inventory reads as follows:[584] ''old shooes, old & new
boots, woosted & white stockings, saddle bag, bridle, new
felt [hat ?], camlet coate lined with furre, cloth coat, belt,
dublet, pr breechese, salinagco coat, coat with calico lining,
haire camlet coate, lether breechese, plush lined coat, wash
lether gloves, chest, cane, watch, 1 sett of shirt buttons 3 s,
seal, sea bead & bolster, pillo, rug, hameker, close stoole &
pan, 2 razors, 1 pr sizers & 1 parcell of linen, money in his
pocket = 19 s 03 d, in P Ps hand = 9£/ Total = 35.17.03.''

The ''total'' appears to refer to the entire value of
Roger's personal property; and although money went
farther in those days, it is a modest sum for such a far
traveller,—at least in comparison with the modern tourist's

---

[582] Etting MSS., I, 24.

[583] This is how they came with other Pemberton Papers to the Historical
Society of Pennsylvania.

[584] Etting MSS., 7.

outfit and letter of credit. And what pictures its various items recall of the hardships and vicissitudes of such travel as was his! His "maire" was not always available, although he carried saddle-bag and bridle with him; hence his feet must serve, even for long distances, and these had to be protected by boots and shoes and stockings of varied kinds and colors, against English mud and Irish bogs, Baltic sands and Dutch clay, Caribbean coral and American swamps.

For these varied vicissitudes, he carried goods from varied lands: white cotton cloth from the East Indian Calico; a West Indian hammock (or *hameker,* as he called it, in imitation of the Spanish *hamaca*), which Columbus defined as "a net in which the Indians sleep", but which may have been for Longworth a canvas tarpaulin, useful against the rain, or as a handy trunk; and coats of many colors. These last it is somewhat difficult to trace, because of changing fashions and of Longworth's and his friends' lordly indifference to spelling. His "salinagco coat" appears to have been a *shalloon* one, made perhaps in Chalôns-sur-marne, or named for that manufacturing origin of them, but differing in their closely woven woolen texture from the *challis* cloths of later times. His "camlet coate" must have differed greatly from that "camelott suit" of his contemporary, Samuel Pepys, who paid above £ 24 for his, and pronounced it "the best that I ever wore in my life." This was probably made of camel's hair and silk, or perhaps all of silk and velvet; but Longworth's was only an imitation of camel's hair (probably goat's), eked out with wool or silk and, with its fur lining, made as water-proof as clothes could be made before india-rubber appeared. A doublet, a plush-lined coat, ordinary and leather breeches, "wash leather" gloves, and a parcel of linen completed his wardrobe.

Roger's outward appearance, in such clothes, must have been indeed "rough and ready." But he wore a set of shirt-buttons and a watch, and carried a cane, a pair of scissors (*sizers*) in a case, and two razors; while to view his countenance, he carried "a pair (or double) spectine glass", which was doubtless the German Speckstein,—a Chinese variety of soapstone that takes on a fine polish. A sea-bed, bolster, pillow and rug, a silver spoon and case of bottles,— what a deal of luggage to carry over sea and land in his chest and tarpaulin hammock! And as defense against disease-germs, spasms and convulsions, or against perhaps the bad odors of Seventeenth Century ships, the amber which his German Friends sent him from the Baltic coast, and whose fragrance came from smoking a pipe. Did he, perchance, discover the stimulating electric rays that this precious amber emits when vigorously rubbed?

Roger Longworth's Obituary

As his epitaph, it might well be stated that he exemplified the conviction expressed in his own words, namely, "It is good y^t all y^t Professeth ye Truth in words may Preach it in their Lives."

When his travels in this world were ended, two of his life-long friends, Phineas Pemberton and William Yardley, wrote for him a personal tribute, or official "Testimony."[585] "We were well acquainted with him," they wrote, "almost from the time of his convincement, being a man of a peaceable disposition, gentle and mild, ready and willing to serve his friend to the utmost of his ability, and a very diligent labourer in the work of the Lord, willing to spend and be spent, not counting anything in this world too dear to part with, for the same. . . . And though he was often in storms and tempests at sea,[586] perils by land, and met with bad spirits and exercises of divers kinds, yet the Lord stood by him and made him a successful instrument in his hand. . . . Not being slack to labour in word and doctrine, wherever he came, to the edification of the brethren, and reconciling things where he found them amiss: Settling and establishing meetings in many parts where he came, to the great comfort and refreshment of the upright in heart, by which he got a name amongst the ancients, and is recorded among the worthies of the Lord. . . . Not long after his

---

[585] "A Collection of Memorials. . . . ," Philadelphia, 1787, pp. 4–6.

[586] They estimated that he had travelled 20,000 miles on the sea, and equally as far on land.

arrival in Pennsylvania, he was taken ill with a fever; his distemper was violent upon him, yet he bore it patiently and passed away like a lamb, leaving a good savour. And though the name of the wicked shall rot, yet·the righteous shall be had in everlasting remembrance.''

This ''Testimony'' and most of the other meagre sources of Longworth's biography give no inkling of the work which he accomplished during the half-dozen years of the founding of Pennsylvania in behalf of that great experiment. This is true even of William Penn's journal of his own travels; for it was consonant with the Seventeenth Century Quaker view that all statesmanlike activities should be entirely subordinated to and eclipsed by the religious. But that the two tasks went side by side in the hands of both Penn and Longworth is clear to all who read between the lines of what they said and wrote.

Dutch ''Certificates of Removal'' to Pennsylvania

That the eyes of contemporary Quakerism, in the Netherlands as elsewhere, were fixed eagerly and prayerfully, if sometimes critically, upon Penn's Holy Experiment, is shown by the ''certificates of removal'' which were granted by the Monthly Meetings to their members who emigrated to Pennsylvania. One of these, issued in 1684 by an ''Extraordinary Meeting'' of the Friesland Monthly Meeting to Cornelis Sioerds (or Siverts) and his wife, Sytske Wimmers, reads as follows:[587]

''William Penn, Worthy and dear friend, and all beloved friends and brothers in the Province of Pennsylvania (*het Lantschap Pinnsilvania*), in America. Our love and greeting reach out to you, and it is our joy and comfort to hear of each other's progress and growth in the precious Truth, to the honor and the glory of the name of God.

''After hearty greeting, know that Cornelis Sioerds and Sytske Wimmers, his wife, residents of Slooten in Friesland, who stand with us in the same faith and are called by the great mercy and goodness of God, and by a sense of His love, out of darkness unto the Light, are now intending to

---

[587] Minutes of the Friesland Monthly Meeting, the 8th. of 6th. Month, 1684.

depart thence [that is, from Slooten], with their two children, to the Province of Pennsylvania in America. We
therefore declare hereby that (so far as we know) the
aforesaid Friends are clear as regards their outward affairs, and that no one has anything to say against this, as far
as is known to us.

"And so with reminder of our hearty love and greeting
in the unchangeable Truth, which neither sea nor land can
separate, and through which we are often mindful of each
other's welfare.

"And so fare-well in the Lord. This is written in the name
of an extraordinary Men's Meeting of the people of God,
called Quakers, at Harlingen in Friesland. The 11th. of 5th.
Month, 1684. Jan Jansen Reijers

       willem Coenes

       gerrit Auckes

       Sipke auckes dyer (*verwer*)."

Another "certificate of removal" issued in the same year
to Jan Willems Boekenoogen, of Haarlem, by the Amsterdam Monthly Meeting reads as follows:[588]

"To the Church of God in Philadelphia. After ye salutation of our dear love in ye pure and holy Truth of God
whereof by ye grace and mercy of ye Lord we wth you are
made ptakers every one according to his measure, We doe
wish intirely and wth all our hearts y^t grace and Wisdome
may abound and be multiplied amongst you and us that
so we therby being guided in all things may be as a
fragrant odour in ye sight of all nations.

"And dear Brethren as for you ye Eyes of many nations
are turned towards you in expectation whether your government and making of lawes and also ye execution of ye same
will agree with the Testimonies of the faithfull Servants of
ye Lord in this age whose Pfession concerning those
Pticulars formerly hath bin published to the World. And
therefore tis our desire that the God of truth and wisdom
whose holy and great name we do publikly profess before
man may be pleased to guide us all in every thing to the

---

[588] From the original MS. record of certificates received by Philadelphia
Monthly Meeting from 1684 to 1758 (p. 17), preserved in the Friends' Historical Library, Swarthmore College.

honour and glory of his great name, to yᵉ praise and renown of yᵉ Truth of God and to your and our Comfort and Joy in yᵉ Lord that thus it may be is our earnest desire and supplication to yᵉ Lord in whose gratious Protection we do comitt you wᵗʰ ourselves Amen.

"The reason of this present writing is chiefly for yᵉ sake of Jan Williams Boekenooge[589] a Cooper who hauing lately liued at Haarlem, And now with his Wife and Children Intending for Pensilvania hath desired of this meeting an Attestation to shew unto you. And therefore we doe Testify that all touching his outward things is Clear as farr as we do know and he in debt to no body.

"ffrom yᵉ monthly meeting of yᵉ people of God Called Quakers in Amsterdam yᵉ third of mo/5: 1684 Stilo Loci.

"Signed on behalf of the aforesaid meeting by

B V [Barent van] Tongeren:
Peeter Hendricks."

QUAKER ANXIETY FOR PENN

An illustration of other correspondence showing mingled hope and anxiety regarding Penn's experiment in practical statesmanship comes to us from a letter of Steven Crisp and his Dutch Quaker wife, Gertrud Deriks of Amsterdam. This is dated, London, the 4th. of 3rd. Month, 1684, and is in part as follows:[590]

"Dear William, I have had a great exercise of spirit concerning thee, which none knows but the Lord; for my spirit has been much bowed into the concern, and difficulty of thy present circumstances; and I have had a sense of the various spirits, and intricate cares, and multiplicity of affairs, and these of various kinds, which daily attend thee, enough to drink up thy spirit, and tire thy soul; and which, if it be not kept to the inexhaustible Fountain, may be dried up. And this I must tell thee, which thou also knowest, that the highest capacity of natural wit and parts will not, and cannot,

---

[589] The letters *nooge* are stricken through, and *nhoven* written above them.

[590] Colchester MSS., No. 24. It was published in John Kendall's "Letters of Isaac Penington, etc.", London, 1796.

perform what thou hast to do, namely, to propagate and advance the interest and profit of the Government and Plantation, and at the same time to give the interest of Truth and testimony of the holy name of God their due preference in all things: for to make the wilderness sing forth the praise of God is a skill beyond the wisdom of this world. It is greatly in man's power to make a wilderness into fruitful fields according to the common course of God's providence, who gives wisdom and strength to the industrious; but then how he, who is the Creator, may have his due honour and service thereby, is only taught by the Spirit in them who singly wait upon him. . . . .

"I hope thou will bear this my style of writing to thee. My spirit is under great weight at the writing thereof, and much I have in my heart, because I love thee well . . . My prayer to God is for thee, and you all, that you may be kept in the Lord's pure and holy way; and above all for thee dear W.P., whose feet are upon a mountain, by which the eyes of many are upon thee; the Lord furnish thee with wisdom, courage, and a sound judgment, prefer the Lord's interest, and he will make thy way prosperous."

Penn's reply to this letter, dated London, the 28th of the 12th mo, 1684, answers various charges against him which were mentioned by Crisp, and contains a message to Gertrud in regard to his alleged reliance upon military measures in protecting that part of his infant colony which lies now in the State of Delaware. It reads in part as follows:[591] "Thy brotherly letter of the 17th instant, came yesterday to hand, with one from Gertruyd: your love therein I perceive, and your tenderness my heart turns not from . . . Now for dear G's letter: What is done since my coming away I cannot tell; but do not believe any such thing. There was an old timber house below a gaol, above the sessions-house or chamber, that had seven old iron small cannon upon the green about it, some on the ground, others on broken carriages; not one soldier, or arms borne, or militia-man seen, since I was first in Pennsylvania. So that I am as innocent of any one act of hostility as she herself; for the guns lying

---

[591] Kendall's "Letters", 1796, pp. 118–9.

so, without soldiers, powder, or bullet, or any garrison, is no more than if she bought a house with a musket in it; and the guns are to go to New York, for they belong to that place: however, I take it tenderly of her. Perhaps since Colonel Talbot's threatenings, the people of Newcastle, where they [the cannon] are, might draw them into security, and pale about their prison; but no man has a commission of war but what is natural to worldly men, self-defence; nor is there any law to that effect: so that I am clear.''

QUAKER OBJECTIONS TO EMIGRATION

Another indirect criticism of Penn's ''ark of refuge'' came from his great friend and admirer, Willem Sewel of Amsterdam. In one of his Latin letters to John Penington (July 9, 1683), Sewel wrote:[592] ''But what do you say! That you also are intent upon Pennsylvania? I can not oppose it if you are acting of your own free will; you are entirely within your rights in this matter. As far as I am concerned, although I know that there are certain men here who, beholding the troubled state of affairs and fearing a change in religious worship, are directing their thoughts thither, as though that tract of land had been bestowed by God upon the pious for an asylum; nevertheless, the thought has not come into my mind of departing thither for the sake of escaping affliction. For I do not see for what reason those men can promise themselves a happy outcome, who change their country, and run across the sea, that they may escape persecution, declining for the sake of things not ordinary (as are the profession of Truth and divine worship) to bear the cross and endure hardships and trouble.''

Again, in 1696, when Penn offered Sewel a tempting position in Bristol, England, Sewel replied:[593]

'' 'The sweet Love of one's Country' so cleaves to most Men that it is even passed into a proverb. But it is not that natural Love that chiefly affects me. There is something else —I know not what—that draws me & does not let me go free from here. The number of our people as Thou knowest is scanty, and if by my Removal I should decrease it ever so

---

[592] Monograph Number One ("Willem Sewel of Amsterdam"), p. 59.

[593] Ibid., p. 150.

Advertising Pennsylvania (See *supra*, p. X)

little, what end would await me—unless my Mind were free in every respect—may be easily conjectured. God has put me in this Country a Witness for His Name and Truth. And if I be not to be reckoned among the first, I am persuaded that the service I am accomplishing for Him in my station is not altogether in vain. And who knows what yet remains for me to do here?"[594]

It was an objection, too, felt or advanced by others besides the Quakers,—by the Frankfurt Pietists, for example, whose leader, John Jacob Spener, at first commended emigration, but later declared: "It is my opinion that we should always stay where the Lord leads us and, however long he leaves us there, to go when he summons us to go." It was partly this influence, no doubt, which caused the German Pietists of Frankfurt to yield to the Dutch Quakers of Krefeld and Krisheim the burden and the honor of becoming the founders of Germantown.[595]

This objection to emigration is reminiscent, also, of William Caton's appeal in 1661 to the Quaker victims of persecution in England and Krisheim to stand steadfast under their sufferings.[596]

Many of the Quakers in Britain shared these Continental objections to emigration and gave official utterance to them, as in the case of the Mountmellick, Ireland, men's Monthly Meeting, which stated in a certificate of removal to Pennsylvania, issued on the 25th of 12th mo. 1682: "But our friend's meeting is generally dissatisfied with his [Nicholas Newland's] removing, he being well settled with his family, and having sufficient substance for food and raiment, which all that possess godliness in Christ Jesus ought to be contented with, for we have brought nothing into this world, and we are sure to take nothing out. And he hath given us no satisfactory reason for his removing, but our godly jealousy is that his chief ground is fearfulness of sufferings here for the testimony of Jesus, or courting worldly liberty."

---

[594] Twenty-one years later, Sewel published in Amsterdam his classic "History of the Quakers," which might not have been accomplished amidst the rigors of life in an infant colony.

[595] *Supra*, p. 180.

[596] *Supra*, p. 274.

QUAKER ARGUMENTS FOR COLONIZATION

The objections to emigration to the new colony were so ominous at one time, in fact, that a pamphlet was published[597] in reply to them bearing the significant title, "Plantation Work the Work of this Generation. Written in True-Love To all such as are weightily inclined to Transplant themselves and Families to any of the English Plantations in America. The Most Material Doubts and Objections against it being removed, they may more cheerfully proceed to the Glory and Renown of the God of the whole Earth, who in all undertakings is to be looked unto, Praised, and Feared for Ever. *Aspice venturo laetetur ut India Sêclo.*"[598]

Even without such encouragement, the early Quaker impulse to sow "the seed" and to cultivate "the new plantinges of the Lord" was irresistible, and was shared by Quakers everywhere. The English Friends emulated the Puritan exodus of 1629–1640 to Massachusetts Bay, and went over by hundreds and thousands to Pennsylvania. They regarded it as a practicable means of refuge for the persecuted Quakers and non-Quakers on the Continent also, and contributed money and other assistance in aiding their emigration.

QUAKER AID TO EMIGRATION

For example, we find among other such instances, London Yearly Meeting in 1709 appropriating £ 50 to aid the Mennonites of the Palatinate in their flight from the Rhineland to Pennsylvania.

The minutes of the London Meeting for Sufferings and Yearly Meeting tell this story as follows:[599] In 3 mo., 1709,

---

[597] London, 1682, 4to, 18 pp. It bears the name of William Loddington as author, but has been attributed to George Fox, who, as early as 1672, on his visit to America, cherished the ideal of a Quaker land of refuge somewhere in the New World, and who in 1681 issued an address "To Planters and such who are transporting themselves into Foreign Plantations in America."

[598] This is an adaptation of a line from Virgil's fourth Eclogue (52): Aspice, venturo laetentur ut omnia saeclo (Behold how all things rejoice at the age which is to come). *India* was substituted for *omnia*, to fit the context. (Contributed by Professor E. H. Brewster of Swarthmore College).

[599] *Journal of the Friends' Historical Society*, Vol. 7 (1910), pp. 46–47.

Henry Gouldney made application to the Meeting for Sufferings for assistance "on behalfe of abo^t Sixty Persons y^t have been lately obliged to Leave their Native Country the Palatinate on Acco^t of General Poverty and Missery (and are now here) being by Religion them called Minists." Five Friends were appointed to make enquiries, with power "to hand to them any sume not exceeding five pounds."

The following month Henry Gouldney and Daniel Quare reported that they had "discourst them abo^t their psent Circumstances, and don't find them under any psent Necessity, having a dayly allowance from some Charitable psons." This report appears to have made Friends doubt the wisdom of their former decision, for at the next meeting, held on 4 mo. 10, we find the following minute:—

"Whereas Some Minists did lately make Application to friends for Assistance, and this meet having ordered them five pounds, its now not thought propper for this meet to allow it them. Therefore its left to pticular friends to contribute towards their Reliefe such Charity and in such manner as they shall see meet. Jt's now proposed that a Quantity of friends Books in High Dutch wch are at the Chamber be given to Simion Warner to hand to ye Minists and others lately come over from the Palatinate in Germany."

The Yearly Meeting held four days later took quite a different view of the affair, and "consents that the meet for sufferings may advance as they see meet for Relief and Assistance of some poor Palatinate People called Minists any sume not exceeding fifty pounds."

Again turning to the minutes of the Meeting for Sufferings, 4 mo. 24, we find the minute from the Yearly Meeting had been read, "And the meet being given to understand that they [the Minists] are abo^t to export themselves beyond sea—Jt's thereupon Referred to Richd Diamond, Silvanus Grove, John Whiting, Danl Phillips and Peter Bowen .. to discourse ye said People to know w^t sume will answer." On 5 mo. 1 "Dan Phillips bro^t in a Receipt of fforty-eight pounds paid on the Minists acco^t for their Passage to Pensilvania, and that ye Remainder was given to ye Surgion [on board the ship?]''. Individual Quakers also took up the cause of the fugitives. William Penn wrote to his secretary in Pennsylvania, James Logan, as follows:[600]

''Herewith comes the Palatines, whom use with tenderness and love, and fix them so [with land] that they may send over [to their home-folks] an agreeable character [of their new home]; for they are sober people, divers Mennonites, and will neither swear nor fight. See that Guy [the captain of their ship] has used them well.''

Thomas Chalkley of Philadelphia, who travelled 972 English miles through Holland and western Germany, in the spring of 1709, received a most cordial welcome as a Quaker preacher from Penn's colony, and commented upon this welcome and opportunity for Quakerism and colonization as follows:[601] ''I know not that I ever met with more tenderness and openness in people than in those parts of the world. There is a great people whom they call Menonists, who are very near to Truth, and the fields are white unto harvest among divers of them, spiritually speaking. Oh! that faithful laborers not a few might be sent of God Almighty into the great vineyard of the world, is what my spirit breathes to him for.''

The Mennonites of Amsterdam and Haarlem were appealed to in the same cause and responded liberally. Jacob Telner, who was then their agent in this affair, wrote to them from London, under date of the 6th. of August, 1709, that eight families of the fugitives had just embarked for Pennsylvania, and remarked that ''the English Friends, who are called Quakers, helped them liberally.''[602] The Mennonites of the Netherlands, thus appealed to, made representations to the States General, and the Dutch Government negotiated with the Swiss Council at Berne, with the result that the Mennonite prisoners in Switzerland were sent to Holland *en route* for Pennsylvania.

Like the English Pilgrims of a century before, some of these Pilgrims from the Alps and the Rhine lingered in the Netherlands for a number of years before sailing West-

---

[600] Penn-Logan Correspondence, Vol. II, p. 534.
[601] "Works", Philadelphia, 1749, p. 70.
[602] *Supra*, pp. 251f.

ward. In 1709–10, occurred one large exodus; in 1717, another division set out for their new homes in America; and in the years from 1726 to 1733 another large body of them poured from the Palatinate through Rotterdam and Amsterdam to Pennsylvania. The number of "Palatines" (as all the German emigrants were called) who thus sought the New World's shores is estimated[603] to have been 7,500 in 1709; about 20,000 before 1727; and about 69,000 to the port of Philadelphia between 1727 and the commencement of the American Revolution in 1775. This total of nearly 100,000 German emigrants to Pennsylvania represents about one-third of its entire population in the first half of the Eighteenth Century. The frontier lands, not only of Pennsylvania, but also of New York, Maryland, Virginia and the Carolinas, were settled largely by these hardy immigrants from the Rhineland and Switzerland.

The Friends of Amsterdam contributed a generous share to the aid of emigrants to Pennsylvania.[604] Their charity in this respect as early as 1684 was so marked that one of their opponents took pains to emphasize what he alleged to be an exception to it. J. R. Markon, in a treatise published in Amsterdam in that year,[605] has his "Houseman" taunt the "Quaaker" with the case of a Friend who had recently come from Hamburg with the intention, if he could not support his family in Amsterdam, of going to Pennsylvania.[606] "This Friend", the Houseman says, "brought a good certificate with him from Hamburg, testifying to his good conduct and standing as a Friend; but no one troubled himself in the slightest degree with his affairs or afforded him the least aid, although his need was so great that when he finally took ship, with his wife and children, for Pennsylvania, his youngest child was crying from hunger and its parents had nothing to give it. Your Friend Adriaen Ger-

---

[603] A. B. Faust, "The German Element in the United States", Boston, 1909, Vol. I, pp. 76–9, 128–9.

[604] See Monograph Number Six ("Dutch Quaker Leaders").

[605] „Een Vriendelijcke Samenspraack, tusschen een Huysman en een hedendaaghse Quaaker. . . ."

[606] The "Friend from Hamburg" was probably Paul Wolff, a weaver, from Fendern, near Hamburg, in Holstein, who settled with his family in Germantown.

ritsz demanded of one of you other Friends why he had not once invited the Hamburg Friend to dine with him, and the reply was that 'he did not know where he lived': although he had been here four or five weeks, and usually attended meeting twice a week!''[607]

To offset this alleged treatment of Paul Wolff, is the following certificate of removal granted him a score of years later by his Germantown Friends:[608]

"To the monthly meeting of friends at Philadelphia. According to ye order agreed vpon by friends that if any person belonging to any meettings Remoue himselfe to another place he shall bring a certificate from ye meetting to wch he did belong This may therefore certifie friends at Philadelphia monthly meeting that Paull Woolfe acquainting us of his remouing from us to you that ye said Paull Woollfe for many years haue walked honestly and soberly to ye best of our knowledge amongst us he haue Also liued in loue and vnity with friends and therein we part with him: still wishing and desiring his wellfare and prosperity in ye truth so with our dear loue recomended to you we Remaine Your friends in the truth from our monthly meeting at Dublin ye 24th of ye 12th month 1706/7 signed at our monthly meetting by Euerard Bolton."

GERMAN EMIGRATION TO PENNSYLVANIA

The early Quakers had been received in Germany, as has been stated, with a very hostile welcome. Religious pamphleteers had denounced them in unmeasured terms, associating them with the Anabaptists, the Socinians and others of the most radical sects, and the government had backed up the religious persecutors with political prosecution. The Quaker leaders had replied in vigorous pamphlets to the persecutors and the rank and file had endured the prosecutions.[609] But irenic Quaker tracts, explaining the new religion, had accompanied this controversial literature, Quaker missionaries had made converts, and Quaker meet-

---

[607] See Monograph Number Six.

[608] From the MS. book of Philadelphia Monthly Meeting's "Certificates Received", p. 58 (Preserved in the Friends' Historical Library of Swarthmore College).

[609] See Monographs Numbers Four, Five and Six.

ings had been established.[610] Hence, when Penn's appeal for colonists was made in Germany, by all the methods that were used in England and Holland, it met with a ready response. The same attractions to Pennsylvania were exploited, and the same repulsions from Germany operated. In particular, the universalization of military training and service, which the wars against Louis XIV and the Turks and the Great Northern War accentuated, made religious persecution doubly unendurable to Pietists, Schwenkfelders, and Mennonites. Hence as early as 1683, Pastorius started forth to Pennsylvania "with the confident expectation that by fleeing hither from Europe, as it were into a second Pellam, we might escape the disturbances and oppressions of that time, and likewise transport other honest and industrious people in order that we might lead a quiet, peaceful, Godly life under the rule of the oft-mentioned William Penn, which it is hoped, will be just and benign."[611] He regarded himself as "a forerunner presumably of many honest contrymen who are to follow"; and he was in historic truth the herald of an immense host of German emigrants who followed in his train.[612]

The Fruits of Penn's Mission to Holland and Germany

But it was the Dutch Quakers of the Rhineland who founded, close to America's chief portal, that other "town of brotherly love"—the "German Town"—which became

---

[610] See Monograph Number Seven.

[611] Pastorius, "Beehive".

[612] This emigration was greatly stimulated by a wave of persecution which swept against the Quakers and other sectarians in Germany, in the 1690's, during which decade at least eight edicts were issued against them. These edicts were gathered up, together with long dissertations in answer to some of the best known Quaker pamphlets and very bitter attacks upon the alleged practices (with many pictorial illustrations), in a huge book entitled „Quäcker-Greuel . . . ," originally published in Hamburg in 1657, with another edition in 1663, and greatly enlarged in 1702. Illustrative of the early contempt for the Quakers in Germany is a verse appended to a caricature of one of them, which reads as follows:

> „Der Quäker liegt allhie von seinem Geist gestrecket,
> „Er zittert, schaümt und bebt, die Glieder sind gerecket.
> „Der Ranter machet sich zum Narren und zum Gott,
> „Gott sey in jedem Baum, ruft seine tolle Rott."

during a century and a half, not only the cradle of a far-reaching Dutch colonization in America, but also the mecca and half-way house of a vast German Völkerwanderung.

The historic importance of the Dutch and German trek to Pennsylvania is not far to seek, although it has been largely neglected by the historians of colonial America. During colonial days, Pennsylvania was for a time the most populous and prosperous of "the original thirteen". In post-colonial years, it became and has remained one of the greatest of the forty-eight American commonwealths: the second in population and industrial wealth; "the key-stone of the Union"; the home of ten million people; the seat of two of the world's largest cities, and of three others with more than 100,000 population; the home of a score of excellent colleges, three universities, and a host of other cultural and religious institutions.

Its founder was, in moral character, religious devotion, and statesmanlike vision and ability, the greatest of colonial founders in America or in any other part of the earth, and a seer whose ideals of rational government and individual happiness the world is still struggling to realize. The Dutch Quaker settlers of Germantown share with the English Quaker settlers of Philadelphia and the eastern counties, and with the German settlers of Pennsylvania's inland districts, the fame and the praise of having given, under the God in whom they so devoutly believed and under the fruitful leadership of William Penn, the initial impulse to this great achievement.

APPENDIX A

William Penn's Itineraries in Holland and Germany

1671

Rotterdam (?)   Amsterdam   Herford

1677

[Penn's dates (of the months, but not of the days) are given below according to the New Style.]

July
- 26 Harwich (A party of nine and two servants)
- 28 Briel
- 28 Rotterdam
- 31 Leyden

August
- 1 Haarlem
- 1–6 Amsterdam
- 6 Naarden (Penn, Keith, Barclay, B. Furly)
- 8 Osnabrück
- 9–13 Herford (Barclay to Amsterdam)
- 13 Paderborn
- 15 Cassel
- 20 Frankfurt
- 23 Worms
- 23 Krisheim
- 24 Frankenthal
- 25 Mannheim
- 26 Worms
- 26 Krisheim
- 27 Worms
- 28 Mainz
- 28 Frankfurt-am-Main
- 30 Mainz
- 30 Hambach
- 30 Bacharach
- 30 Coblentz
- 30 Treis
- 31 Cologne

September
- 2 Duisburg
- 2 Mülheim
- 3 Duisburg
- 3 Holten
- 4 Wesel
- 5 Rees
- 5 Emmerich
- 5 Kleve
- 6 Nimwegen
- 7 Utrecht (Keith and Furly to Rotterdam)
- 7 Amsterdam
- 10 Hoorn (Penn and Pieter Hendricks)
- 10 Enkhuizen
- 10 Workum
- 10 Harlingen
- 12 Leeuwarden (Penn and Jan Claus)
- 12 Wieuwerd
- 13 Lippenhuizen
- 14 Groningen
- 15 Delfzijl
- 16 Emden
- 17 Leer
- 18 Bremen
- 22–26 Herford
- 27 Wesel
- 28 Duisburg
- 29 Düsseldorf
- 30 Cologne

October
- 2 Düsseldorf
- 2 Duisburg
- 3 Wesel
- 5 Kleve
- 6 Nimwegen

393

October
6 Utrecht
7–11 Amsterdam
11 Leiden
12 The Hague
12 Delft
12–16 Rotterdam
16 The Hague

16 Leiden
16 Noordwijk
17 The Hague
17 Delft
17–20 Rotterdam
20–22 Briel
24 Harwich

1686

[Calais]
[Dunkirk]
[Flanders]
Rotterdam
The Hague
Amsterdam

Alkmaar (?)
Oudesluis
Sneek (and elsewhere in
  Friesland)
The Rhineland
Rotterdam

APPENDIX B

The Dutch Pioneers of Germantown

The thirty-four first settlers of Germantown in 1683,[613] came from Krefeld, and were divided approximately as follows:

13 men;[614]

9 wives;[615]

1 unmarried woman (Margrit op den Graeff);

1 youth (Lenart Streypers);

2 infants born at sea;

8 other children.[616]

They arrived in Philadelphia on the 6th. of October; on the 12th. of that month, Penn issued to them and Pastorius a warrant for 6,000 acres, one half of which was to go to them and one-half to be reserved for the Frankfort Company; on the 24th., Penn's surveyor, Thomas Fairman, measured off for them fourteen plots of land in Germantown; and on October 25, 1683, the thirteen pioneer men, together with Francis Daniel Pastorius, met in a "dug-out cabin", the home of Pastorius on the banks of the Delaware in Philadelphia (on the present site of No. 502 South Front Street), and drew lots for the sites of their future homes. There is a "certificate", bearing the date of 1709 and

[613] The number usually given is thirty-three. This was the number of those who sailed from London on the "Concord"; but two infants were born at sea, and the mother of the Op den Graeffs died in Philadelphia *en route* to the Germantown settlement.

[614] These were: Derick Isacks op den Graeff, Herman Isacks op den Graeff, Abraham Isacks op den Graeff, Lenart Arents, Thones Kunders, Reiner Tijsen, Willem Strepers, Jan Lensen, Pieter Keurlis, Jan Siemes, Johannes Blijkers, Abraham Tunes and Jan Luykens.

[615] The women included the wives of Lenart Arents, Johannes Blijkers, Derick and Abraham op den Graeff, Pieter Keurlis, Thones Kunders, Jan Lukens, Jan Siemes and Abraham Tunes.

[616] It is not known whose these were; but it is of record that children of Abraham op den Graeff and Pieter Keurlis were complained of, in the Germantown court, in 1701; and that children of Arents, Kunders, Lensen and Lukens (as well as those of Tunes and Teissen, who were born after 1683) attended school in Germantown between 1702 and 1708. Thones Kunders brought with him three sons born in Krefeld.

signed presumably by the seven survivors of "the original thirteen", which reads as follows:[617] "We whose names are to these presents subscribed, do hereby certify unto all whom it may concern, that soon after our arrival in this province of Pennsylvania, in October, 1683, to our certain knowledge Herman op den Graff, Dirk op den Graff and Abraham op den Graff, as well as we ourselves, in the cave of Francis Daniel Pastorius, at Philadelphia, did cast lots for the respective lots which they and we then began to settle in Germantown; and the said Graffs (three brothers) have sold their several lots, each by himself, no less than if a Division in writing had been made by them. Witness our hands this 29th. Nov., A.D. 1709.

Lenart Arets

Jan Lensen

Thomas Hunder [Thones Kunders]

William Streygert [Willem Streypers]

Reiner Tysen

Abraham Tunes

Jan Lucken.''

Pastorius continued to live in Philadelphia at least as late as the summer of 1685;[618] but the thirteen pioneers immediately began to build their houses in the new settlement, and spent the following winter in them. It was the advice of Penn that they should not settle on large isolated farms, but that they should follow their ancestral custom of living together in a peasant and artisan village or town. This would greatly facilitate their social activities, especially the education of their children, in a new land without roads; and their own strong preference coincided with his advice.

There were three German families in Philadelphia in October, 1683, who desired to settle in Germantown;[619] and

---

[617] Watson's "Annals", 1909 (1857), II, 18.

[618] Pastorius's letter to Dr. J. J. Schütz of Frankfurt, dated Philadelphia, the 30th. of May, 1685. He states in this letter that he was himself still living in Philadelphia, although his thoughts flew between that city and Germantown; see *supra*, p. 181.

[619] Pastorius's letter of March 7, 1684. Two of these families would appear to have been those of Jurian (or Görg) Hartzfelder, a deputy-sheriff in Pennsylvania under Governor Andros in 1676, and Jacob Schumacher, formerly of Mainz; the third was perhaps that of the German-Swiss, Jörg Wertmuller.

they as well as Pastorius and the Krefelders drew lots for home-sites in Germantown, on October 25 of that year.

In a letter to his parents dated from Philadelphia, the 7th. of March, 1684, Pastorius states that "two hours from here, lies our Germantown,[620] where already forty-two people live in twelve homes." This would imply that the thirty-four Krefelders, living in nine or ten homes, had been joined by two or three of the German families with their eight members.

Later in 1684, five more Krefelders arrived with their families, namely, Veit Scherkes, Wolter Siemes (Seimens), Jacob Telner, Isaac Jacobs van Bebber, and Herman Daürss. How many persons came with them is not known. But we know that Telner brought with him his daughter Susanna; and we find in the Germantown records about 1700 the names of Anton and Johannes Scherkes (or Jerghjes, Gerckes) and Jacob Seimens (or Simons), who may have been sons of David Scherkes and Wolter or Jan Siemes (Seimens); while as early as 1690, Isaac Jacobs van Bebber held a meeting of Mennonites in his house. Hence it is probable that the Krefeld settlers of 1684 represented a company of at least fifteen and perhaps twenty persons.

One year later (October 12, 1685), Hendrick Boekwolt (or Heinrich Buchholtz) and his wife, and Hans Peter Umstat, his wife Barbara, his son Johannes, and his daughters Anna Margaretha and Eva, joined the other Krefelders in Germantown. Between 1685 and 1690, Krefeld sent to Germantown Jacob Isacks and Matthias Isacks van Bebber; Willem Hosters; Arent (or Arnold), Hermannus, Johannes and Paulus Koester (or Küster); Jan van Lovenigh; Jan and Mattheis Neusz; Dirck, Hendrick and Martin Sellen (or Seelen); Jacob Seimens; and Jan Streypers. The records refer to wives and children of most of these fifteen later settlers; so that they probably numbered about sixty, making a total of about 120 from Krefeld and Kaldekerk.

The second stream of pioneer settlers in Germantown

---

[620] In the same letter, he calls Frankford ("about half an hour from here", *i.e.*, from Philadelphia) "our own town", that is, the "German", or "Frankford" Company's town.

came from Krisheim. The vanguard of these settlers arrived in October, 1685, and numbered twelve persons. These included three men (Gerhard Hendricks, Peter Schumacher and Heivert Papen) ;[621] two women (Maria and Sarah, the wives of Hendricks and Schumacher); and seven children.[622]

The next year (in March, 1686), two more families, including fifteen persons, came from Krisheim. The heads of these families were Johannes Kassel and his wife, and Sarah Schumacher, a widow; and their children were two sons and three daughters,[623] and four sons and three daughters,[624] respectively.

The migration of twenty-seven pioneers from Krisheim nearly exhausted the spring; but during the next few years, we find in the Germantown records the names of four more men from Krisheim[625] and one from Flomborn, a neighboring village.[626] These sent children to the Germantown school, and presumably brought their wives with them, thus adding to the population perhaps a score of persons, and making a total of about fifty-two from Krisheim and Flomborn.

Adding together the pioneer settlers in Germantown from 1683 to 1690, we find the population in the latter year to have been about 175, of whom all but eight or ten were Dutch.

---

[621] Heivert (Heifert, Huffert) Papen was a bachelor at the time, but married later in Germantown Elisabeth, the daughter of Willem Rittinghuysen.

[622] These were Sarah, the daughter, and Lambert and Willem, the sons, of Gerhard Hendricks; and Peter, the son, and Mary, Frances and Gertrud, the daughters, of Peter Schumacher.

[623] These were Arnold, Peter, Elisabeth, Mary and Sarah Kassel.

[624] These were Georg, Abraham, Isaac, Benjamin, Barbara, Susanna and Elisabeth Schumacher.

[625] These were Willem, Cornelis and Johannes Dewees, and Hendrick Kassel.

[626] Hendrik Pannebecker.

APPENDIX C

DUTCH AND GERMAN SETTLERS IN GERMANTOWN, 1683–1709[627]

The following list, derived from both Pennsylvania and European sources,[628] is approximately complete for the first quarter-century of Germantown's history. It begins with the first settlement in 1683 and ends in 1709, when the great influx of immigrants from Germany began.

The list has been compiled with care, but with considerable difficulty, and it doubtless contains errors which discerning critics and proud descendants will take pleasure in pointing out. All such corrections will be gratefully received.

When both Dutch and German forms of a name are given in the list, it is probable that the Dutch form is the original one; for, as small bodies tend to be drawn towards and absorbed in larger ones, the tendency was to Germanize (and Anglicize) the Dutch names, and not to Hollandize the German ones. Indeed, the German names were in their turn largely Anglicized. These changes occurred in remarkably small space of time, often within a single generation, as is evidenced by inscriptions on the tomb-stones in Germantown grave-yards.

It is true, of course, that in the low lands of northwest Germany the line of demarcation between the Low German (*Plattdeutsch*) and the Dutch peoples and languages (*Hol-*

---

[627] The immigration of the Dutch and German settlers into Philadelphia and elsewhere in Pennsylvania outside of Germantown is beyond the scope of this study.

[628] The most important source of all, namely, the lists of arrivals at the port of Philadelphia, are in very fragmentary condition before the year 1726; while the Archivist of Rotterdam has informed the author that the shipping lists of that port—covering the years desired—are also not extant.

Illustrative of the paucity of the knowledge of Germantown's history until quite recent times is the fact that Pennsylvania's first excellent historian (Robert Proud, 1797) devoted to it only one-half page of his two volumes, and, after referring to the work of William Ames and the persecution of the Quakers in the Rhineland (quoting from Willem Sewel), merely says that Germantown was founded by German Friends from Krisheim or Cresheim, a town not far from Worms, in the Palatinate. He gives a footnote on "Dennis Conrad", the Friends' meeting at his house in 1683, and the date of 1729 for Conrad's death; but he does not so much as mention Krefeld!

landsch) had been for centuries far from being sharply defined. But by the end of the Seventeenth Century, a hundred
and fifty years after Martin Luther's Bible and hymns had
given enormous impulse to the fusion of all the German
dialects into Modern High German, the distinction between
the Low German and the Dutch was well established. Hence,
the appearance of Dutch names in these Low German lands,
as in the Rhineland, was not due to the survival of pri-
mordial types, but to the spread of the Dutch people and
language eastward along the German margin of the Baltic
Sea. The fishing industry, trade and handicrafts, as well as
agriculture (or, rather, the familiar Dutch style of horticulture), lured them on even as far as Danzig, to which city
Dutch and English Quaker missionaries followed them.

In the Rhineland, too, the Dutch people followed the great
river in pursuit of trade, handicrafts and horticulture
among the larger though less dense population and the more
naturally fertile soil than could be found in their own low
lands and polders which their forefathers had been obliged
to rescue from the sea and the inland rivers.

Thus, long before the migration to Pennsylvania, the
Dutch of Holland had been migrating to neighboring lands;
and their descendants in the Seventeenth Century when
migrating to Pennsylvania, were following the example set
by earlier generations.

† Signifies that the person listed was naturalized (under the name following
in the parenthesis) in 1709, in accordance with an Act which is given *infra*,
pp.

* Signifies that his children attended the Germantown Friends' school.

I. FROM HOLLAND (STATED PLACES)

Amsterdam

Arentsz (Arentsen), Jacob Claessen: in Germantown, 1701.

Keyser, Dirck: to Germantown, 1688; fence-viewer; subscriber to the
school; witness in court; † (Dirk Keyser); Mennonite
reader, 1690.

Keyser, Dirck, Jr.: witness in court.

Keyser, Peter: son of Dirck;† (Peter Keyser);*; wife = Margaret
Souplis; attended evening school.

Rittinghuysen, Willem: born 1644, in "Mongowerland" (Monnicken-
dam?), or Broich; took the citizen's oath in Amsterdam,
June 23, 1679; to Germantown, 1689 or 1690; first
paper mill in British America; first Mennonite minister,
1698–1708.

Rittinghuysen, ———: Willem's wife.
Rittinghuysen, Gerrit (Gerhard) : Willem's son.
Rittinghuysen, Klaas (Klaus) : Willem's son;† (Claus Ruttinghey-
      sen) ; Dutch Reformed; married Wilhelmina de Wees
      in New York, 1689; to Germantown, 1689 or 1690.
Rittinghuysen, Elisabeth: Willem's daughter; married Heivert Papen.
Vanderwerf, Anna: Richard's daughter.
Vanderwerf, Annetje Jans Boekenoogen: Richard's wife.
Vanderwerf, Barent: Richard's son.
Vanderwerf, Jan Roelofs: Richard's son;† (John Roelofs Vander-
      werf).
Vanderwerf, Richard: recorder;† (Richd. Vanderwerf) ; witnessed
      Heyvert Papen's will, 1708.

Arnhem (?) [The ancestral home of the Rittinghuysens]
Holtzhooven, Jacob Gerritsz: from "Guelderland"; in Germantown
      before 1702.
Petersen, Isaac: from "Guelderland"; in Germantown before 1702.

Bergen
Jansen, Dirck ("der Knecht") : a nephew of Arent Klincken; bachelor
      servant of Johannes Kuster; subscribed to school.

Dordrecht
Karsdorp (Kasdorp), Isaac: Penn's correspondent, 1677.

Haarlem
Boekenoogen, Jan Willems: with wife and *children* to Germantown,
      1684; wife = Sijtgen Gerrits of Alkmaar; sister =
      Mercken Willems, who married, first, Jan Siemes and,
      second, ——— Luykens.
Boekenoogen (Bockenhoven), Sophia: daughter of Jan; a Quaker
      preacher; married Richard Armitt, 1701; died, 1740.
Bom (Bon, Bonn, Van Bon), Hermann: charter member, 1689; com-
      mitteeman; subscriber to school; built prison and stocks,
      1704.
Bom, Koenradt (Cönrad) Herman: Aug. 10, 1687, bought from the
      Frankfort Company 50 acres of Germantown land.
Bom (Bon, Bun), Peter: subscriber to school; wife was Gerritje
      ———; to the Skippack, 1696.

Leeuwarden
Dewees (De Wees), Cornelis: son of Gerrett; married Margaret Kös-
      ter;*; constable, 1706; to Bebber's Township, 1708.
Dewees (De Wees), Gerritt Hendricks: Germantown land, 1690; wife
      was Zijtijen ———.
Dewees (De Wees), Willem: son of Gerrett; Germantown land, 1703;
      in Bebber's Township, 1708, and in Crisheim Town-
      ship; built second paper-mill on Wissahickon, 1710, in
      Crefeld Township; constable, 1704; sheriff, 1706;*.

Dewees (De Wees), Wilhelmina: daughter of Gerrett; married Nicholas (Claus) Rittinghuysen.

Willems, Jan: granted "certificate of removal" by Friesland Monthly Meeting; †(Jan Williams).

Slooten

Siverts (Sioerdts), Cornelis: his wife, Sytske Wimmers, and two children, also mentioned in his certificate of removal from the Friesland Monthly Meeting, 1684;*; burgess; †(Cornelius Siorts).

Siverts, Hanna: attended evening school.

Siverts, Sophia: received a certificate of removal from Abington to Philadelphia Monthly Meeting, dated 29th. of 2nd. Month, 1717, when she removed from Germantown to Philadelphia.[629]

Sneek

Jansen, Alice: Reynier's daughter; married John Piggot (or Pickott), whose "certificate of clearance" was received by Philadelphia Monthly Meeting from West River Monthly Meeting, Maryland (dated 11th. Month 29, 1702/3, and marriage authorized by the former 8th. Month 27, 1704).

Jansen, Imity (Jinity): Reynier's daughter; married Matthias Millan ("Matthew Mc Lean").

Jansen, Joseph Reyniers: Reynier's son; he carried on for a few years his father's printing business.

Jansen, Reynier: Benjamin Furly's agent in Pennsylvania; the first official Quaker printer.

Jansen, Tiberius: Reynier's son and associate as printer (an Almanac of 1703 bears his imprint).

Trompenberg (? See supra, p. 239).

Klincken, Ann (Anneke): Arent's daughter; married Kunrad, son of Thones Kunders.

Klincken, Anthony: Arent's son; "the great hunter";*.

Klincken, Arent (Aret): wife was Niske ———; committee-man, burgess, justice, bailiff, treasurer (?); collected for the school;*; active in Friends' meetings; subscribed £ 10 4 s. to the Friends' meeting-house, 1686.

Klincken, Elin: Arent's daughter; married ——— Williams.

Zierikzee

Plockhoy, Pieter Cornelisz: leader of Dutch colonists to New Netherland (Hoorn Kill, on the Delaware), 1662; his "Quaking society" was destroyed "to a very naile" by an English attack in 1665, and nearly thirty years afterwards (in 1694) he found a last refuge in Germantown.

---

[629] MS. book of Certificates Received, p. 102 (Swarthmore College).

II. FROM HOLLAND (UNSTATED PLACES)

Blomerse, Marieke: married Isaac Dilbeeck.

Dilbeeck, Abraham: Isaac's son.

Dilbeeck, Isaac: with Pastorius as servant, 1683; committeeman, 1691; †(Isaac Dilbeck).

Dilbeeck, Jacob: Isaac's son; †(Jacobus Dilbeck).

Duplouvys, Jan: a baker; married in Germantown, 1687, Weyntie van Sanen; "John Deplove" assessed in Philadelphia County, 1693, £ 200, taxed 16 s. 6 d.

Jansen, Coenrad: he and *wife* were Mennonite members, 1708; he a deacon and overseer; †(Cunrad Jansen);*.

Jansen, Dirck: Reynier's son (?); married Margaret Millan (Cf. R's daughter, Imity); subscriber to school;*.

Jansen, Dirck, Jr.: juryman, 1704; †(Dirk Jansen, Junr.).

Jansen, Jan: son of Klaas; †(John Jansen).

Jansen, Klaas: Mennonite teacher; to Bebber's Township, 1702; †(Claus Jansen).

Jansen, Peter: †(Peter Jansen).

Jansen, Willem: son of Klaas; †(Wm. Jansen).

Sluys, Adrian van der: son of Reiner; †(Vander Sluys).

Sluys, Hannes van der (Vanderslice): naturalized, 1709 (?).

Sluys, Reiner van der: †(Vander Sluys).

Sprogell, Johan Heinrich: versus Pastorius; naturalized, 1705.

Sprogell, Ludwig Christian: Jan Hendrick's bachelor brother; naturalized, 1705.

Vandewoestyne, Katharine: from Zeeland; Quaker preacher; died in Germantown, 1704.

III. FROM KREFELD AND KALDEKERK

Arents, Lenart:[630] a weaver; one of "the original thirteen"; subscribed £ 6 1 s. to the Friends' Meeting-house, 1686; burgess, auditor; †(Lenhart Arrets);*; *wife* was Agnes, a sister of Willem Streypers and of Thones Kunders's wife.

Bebber, Isaac Jacobs van: son of Jacob; recorder; Mennonite, 1698; to Bohemia Manor, 1704.

Bebber, Jacob Isaacs van: a baker; charter member; committeeman, burgess, recorder; pro Keith, reverted to Mennonites and moved to Philadelphia before 1698.

Bebber, Liesbet Isaacs van: daughter of Jacob; wife of Herman op den Graeff.

---

[630] "Leonard Aratts & Agnistan [Agniscan] his wife late of Crevelt near Rotterdam in Holland came in the ――― of Lond. Wm. Jefferies com^der arrived here the 6th. of mo,/8 1683." (A Partial List of Arrivals in Philadelphia, 1682–1687: *Pa. Magazine*, 8 (1884): p. 329).

Bebber, Matthias van: son of Jacob; founded Bebber's Township about
    1700, but never lived in it; removed to Bohemia Manor,
    1704: a Dutch "Patroon"; †(Matthis Van Bebbez).
Blijkers (Bleikers), Johannes: one of "the original thirteen"; *wife*
    had son born at sea on "The Concord"; original sub-
    scriber to the school; †("Johannes Bleikers of the
    County of Bucks").
Bleikers, Peter: Johannes' son, born at sea, 1683.
Daŭrss (Dors), Herman: a court witness.
Graef, Hans: *; to Lancaster County, 1716; descendants now
    "Grove".
Graeff, Abraham op den: a weaver; one of "the original thirteen";
    charter member, burgess, assemblyman; "Protest"
    versus Slavery; pro Keith; removed to Perkiomen; *wife*
    was Catharina (Trijntje) ——;*.
Graeff, Anne op den: daughter of Abraham; married Herman in de
    Hoffen.
Graeff, Derick op den: a weaver; one of "the original thirteen"; char-
    ter member, burgess, bailiff; opposed Keith; defended
    charter; "Protest" versus slavery.
Graeff, Herman op den: a weaver; one of "the original thirteen";
    charter member, burgess; Telner's and Furly's agent;
    pro Keith; wife was Liesbet Isacks van Bebber.
Graeff, Isaac op den: son of Abraham; attended the school.
Graeff, Jacob op den: son of Abraham: attended the school; in trouble
    with the sheriff.
Graeff, Margaret op den: daughter of Abraham; married Thomas Howe.
Graeff, Margrit op den: sister of the three pioneers; married Peter
    Schumacher III.
Graeff, Nöleken (Neeltje) Vijten op den: wife of Derick.
Hosters, Willem: a weaver;*.
Keurlis (Kerlin, Courlin), Martha: daughter of Pieter; married
    Thomas Potts.
Keurlis, Matthias: Pieter's son (?); attended the evening school;
    a shoemaker; had as apprentice Henry Pastorius.
Keurlis, Pieter: one of "the original thirteen"; inn-keeper, probably
    the first beer-brewer in America; constable; attended
    evening school;*; children in trouble; wife was Elisa-
    beth ——; tax collector and assessor, 1693.
Kunders, Agnes: daughter of Thones; born in Germantown.
Kunders, Anna: daughter of Thones; born in Germantown the 4th.
    of 7th. Month, 1684; perhaps the first child of Dutch
    or German parentage born in Pennsylvania.
Kunders, Ann Klincken: daughter of Arent Klinken; married a son
    of Thones Kunders.
Kunders, Coenraed (Conrad Conrads): son of Thones; born in Kre-
    feld; †(Cunrad Cunrads).
Kunders, Elisabeth: daughter of Thones; born in Germantown.

Kunders, Hendrik: son of Thones; born in Germantown; married
  Catharina Streypers (Willem's daughter).
Kunders, Jan: son of Thones; born in Krefeld; attended evening
  school; †(John Cunrads).
Kunders, Johannes: †(John Cunrads, Senr.).
Kunders, Margaret: married Rynier Teissen (?).
Kunders, Matthis (Madtis): son of Thones; born in Krefeld; attended
  evening school; †(Matthis Cunrads).
Kunders, Thones: one of "the original thirteen"; wife was Lijntijen
  (Elin) Teissen, sister of Reinert; charter member, bur-
  gess, recorder, fence-viewer; first Quaker meeting at his
  house; subscribed £ 10 11 s. to the Friends' Meeting-
  house, 1686;*; †(Dennis Kunders).
Kuster (Küster), Arent (Arnold): son of Paulus;*.
Kuster, Elisabeth: daughter of Paulus (?); Mennonite in 1708.
Kuster, Hermannus: son of Paulus; to Bebber's Township, 1708;
  trustee of Mennonite Church in Bebber's Township,
  1725.
Kuster, Johannes: son of Paulus; constable, burgess; led petition for
  naturalization, 1706.
Kuster, Paulus: a mason; on 1693 tax-list; wife was Gertrud Streypers, sister of Jan;*.
Lensen, Jan: a weaver; one of "the original thirteen"; subscribed to
  the school;*; †(Jno. Lenson).
Loevenigh, Jan van: Kelpius's messenger to Long Island, 1699.
Luykens (Lückens), Jan: one of "the original thirteen"; wife was
  Maria Teissen (who died, 1742); subscribed £ 10 5 s.
  to the Friends' Meeting-house, 1686; constable, burgess,
  sheriff;*; †(John Lurhen); died 1744; Jan and Maria
  had eleven children born between 1684 and 1705: Elisa-
  beth, Elsje ("Alitze Conrad", wife of Jan Kunders, son
  of Thones Kunders), Willem, Sarah, John, Mary, Peter,
  Hannah (married John Samuel Pastorius, 1716),
  Mathias, Abraham and Joseph.
Neus, Cornelis: †(Cornelius Neus); son of Jan (?).
Neuss, Jan: a silversmith (sold Penn a half-dozen silver spoons);
  naturalized, 1698;*; †(John Neus).
Neuss (Neues), Hans: brother of Jan; Mennonite teacher, 1698–
  1702;*; †(Hans Nous).
Neuss (Nice), Mattheis: son of Jan; †(Matthis Neus).
Scherkes (Sgerkis, Scherges, Jerghjes), Anthonij: Vijt's son (?);
  burgess.
Scherkes, Johannes: Vijt's son (?); attended evening school.
Scherkes, Vijt (Veit, David): sheriff; pro Keith.
Sellen, Dirck: brother of Hendrick.
Sellen, Hendrick: agent for Dirck Sipman and Jan Streypers;*;
  †(Henry Sellen); gave site for Mennonite Church;
  built an oil mill, 1714.

Sellen, (? Seelen, Sell), Martin: in Germantown by 1694.

Sellen, Maria: a Mennonite member, 1708.

Siemes (Seimens), Jacob: son of Jan or Wolter (?); subscribed to the school.

Siemes, Jan: one of "the original thirteen"; died early; *widow* re-married in 1685.

Siemes, Wolter: in Germantown, 1684; constable, messenger, town-crier;*; †(Walter Simons).

Teissen (Tyson), Altien: a Mennonite, 1708.

Teissen, Cornelis: *.

Teissen, Derick: Reynier's younger brother; died unmarried.

Teison, Leonard: he is stated to have been the brother of Lenart Arents.[631]

Teissen, Lijntijen: married Thones Kunders.

Teissen, Margaret: a Mennonite, 1708.

Teissen, Maria: married Jan Luykens.

Teissen, Mattheis: †(Matthis Tysen).

Teissen, Pieter: son of Reynier; married Mary Roberts.

Teissen, Reynier: one of "the original thirteen"; burgess, bailiff; nat-uralized, 1691; †(Reiner Tysen);*; married Margaret Kunders (?) or Margaret Streypers (?); very active in Friends' meetings.

Telner, Jacob: see Index.

Telner, Susanna: daughter of Jacob; married first, Albertus Brandt, second, David Williams.

Tunes (Tünes), Abraham: a weaver; one of "the original thirteen"; subscribed £ 5 to the Friends' Meeting-house, 1686; bur-gess;*; †(Abraham Tunnis).

Tunes, Herman: *.

Tunes, Maria:

Umstat, Anna Margaretha: daughter of Hans Peter.

Umstat, Eva: daughter of Hans Peter; married Hendrick Panne-becker.

Umstat, Hans Peter: in Germantown, 1685; weighmaster; *wife* was Barbara ———.

Umstat, Johannes: son of Hans Peter; subscribed to the school; re-moved to Bebber's Township, 1702.

(FROM KALDEKERK: KREFELD)

Streypers (Strepers), Catharina: married Hendrick Kunders.

Streypers, Gertrud: sister of Jan and Willem; wife of Paulus Kuster.

Streypers, Jan: in Germantown between 1687 and 1706; gave 1/2 acre for the Lower Burying-Ground.

Strepers, Johannes, Sr.: †(John Strepers, Senr.).

Streypers, Lenart: son of Jan; apprenticed to Jan Lensen.

Streypers, Willem: one of "the original thirteen"; subscribed £ 9 4 s. to the Friends' Meeting-house, 1686; fence-viewer; †(Wm. Strepers).

---

[631] Cf. *supra*, p. 403 (Note 630).

IV. FROM KRISHEIM, WOLFSHEIM AND FLOMBORN

Hendricks, Barnt (Arent) : in Germantown by 1703; will, 1708; children = Hendrik, Agnes, Anneta.

Hendricks, Gerhard (Gerrit) : first *wife* was Sijtie Boekenoogen, second was Maria ———; in Germantown, 1685; on taxlist, 1693; "Protest" against Slavery, 1688.

Hendricks, Hendrick: son of Willem; †(Hendrick Hendricks).

Hendricks (Gerrits), Lambert: son of Gerhard; attended evening school.

Hendricks, Lorentz: son of Willem (?); †(Laurence Hendricks).

Hendricks, Sarah: daughter of Gerhard; born in Krisheim, 2nd. of 10th. Month, 1678; married Isaac Schumacher; died June 15, 1742.

Hendricks (Gerrits), Willem: son of Gerhard; attended evening school; citizen of Germantown, 1698; †(Wm. Hendricks).

Kassel, Arnold: Hans Peter's son; court witness; recorder; versus Keith.

Kassel, Elisabeth: Hans Peter's daughter.

Kassel (Cassels), Hans Peter: a weaver; signed passport petition, 1695; to Germantown, March 1686.

Kassel, Heinrich:*; he and his *wife* Mennonites, 1708, he a deacon and overseer, 1708.

Kassel, Johannes: Bought land from Frankfort Co.; charter member, committee-man.

Kassel, Mary: Hans Peter's daughter.

Kassel, Peter: Hans Peter's son.

Kassel, Sarah: Hans Peter's daughter.

Papen, Heivert: bought 75 acres from Jacob Schumacher in 1693; charter member; committee-man; fence-viewer, recorder; subscriber to school; wife was Elisabeth Rittinghuysen; daughters were Styntje, Maria, Geertruyd, Margaret, Elisabeth; sold 50 acres (for £ 50) to the Friends, who built a stone meeting-house upon it in 1705.

Schumacher, Abraham: son of Georg and Sarah; aet. 19 in 1686.

Schumacher, Barbara: daughter of Georg and Sarah; aet. 20 in 1686.

Schumacher, Benjamin: son of Georg and Sarah; aet. 10 in 1686; ancestor of Benjamin Hallowell.

Schumacher, Elisabeth: daughter of Georg and Sarah; aet. 11 in 1686.

Schumacher, Frances: Peter's daughter.

Schumacher, Georg: son of Georg and Sarah; aet. 23 in 1686; married Sarah Wall, 1695;⁶³²*; "Georg Shoomaker" assessed, 1693, £ 80, taxed 6 s. 8 d; †(Geo. Shoemaker).

---

⁶³² Their marriage certificate is printed in the *Pennsylvania Magazine*, Vol. 16, pp. 461–2. In 1715, he removed with his wife, *Rebecca*, to Philadelphia, and received a certificate from Abington Monthly Meeting, dated 29th. of 6th. Month, 1715.

Schumacher, Gertrud: Peter's daughter.

Schumacher, Isaac: son of Georg and Sarah; aet. 17 in 1686; married Sarah, daughter of Gerhard Hendricks; sheriff, burgess; built prison and stocks (with Peter); subscribed to school;*; †(Isaac Shoemaker); died Feb. 12, 1732.

Schumacher, Jacob: Pastorius's indentured servant; "borne in ye Palatinate in Germany"[633] (originally from Mainz); sheriff;*; gave three perches of land (at Germantown Avenue and Coulter Street) to the Friends, who built a log meeting-house upon it; "Jacob Shoomaker with his wife Margaret, too sons Thomas and Jacob and daughter susanah" removed to Philadelphia and received a "certificate of clearance" from Abington Monthly Meeting, dated 28 of 12th 1714/5 (*Certificates Received,* Swarthmore College MSS., p. 95).[634]

Schumacher, Jacob, Jr.: †(Jacob Shoemaker).

Schumacher, Maria: Peter's daughter.

Schumacher, Peter (II): in Germantown, 1685; subscribed £ 4 to the Friends' Meeting-house, 1686; justice, burgess; collected money for the school;*; built prison and stocks (with Isaac); versus Keith; deed for his land written in Dutch.

Schumacher, Peter, Jr. (III): Peter's son; committee-man, burgess; collected for the school; wife was Margrit op den Graeff; †(Peter Shoemaker).

Schumacher, Sarah Hendricks: wife of Peter II.

Schumacher, Sarah: widow of Georg (who died apparently in Krisheim about 1684); cousin of Peter S.; in Germantown, March, 1686, with her four sons and three daughters.

Schumacher, Susanna: daughter of Georg and Sarah; aet. 13 in 1686; married Isaac Price, 1696.

(FROM WOLFSHEIM: KRISHEIM)

Kolb, Barbara: Mennonite, 1708.

Kolb, Henry: he and the three following were brothers; he removed to Bebber's Township, and died in 1730, leaving three sons (Peter, David and Thielman).

Kolb, Jacob: weaver; to Bebber's Township, 1709; married Sarah van Sintern, 1710.

Kolb, Johannes: weaver; to Bebber's Township, 1709.

Kolb, Martin: weaver; to Bebber's Township, 1709; first *wife* was living in 1707; second wife (1709) was Magdalena, daughter of Isaac van Sinteren of Hamburg; Mennonite preacher, 1708—.

---

[633] *Supra,* p. 181 (note 213).

[634] The certificate stated that Jacob and Margaret "are in unity with ffriends and have walked orderly and were seruiceable in theire place", and that their children were "clear from all Jngagements of marriage."

Strayer, Andrew: came in 1709, with three brothers; settled in Bebber's Township.

(FROM FLOMBORN: KRISHEIM)

Pannebecker (Pannebakkers), Hendrick; to Bebber's Township, 1702 (its real founder and "patroon").

V. FROM OTHER PLACES IN GERMANY

Altheim (Alsace): Frey, Heinrich: originally from Heilbron ? (see
      supra, p. 317); in America by 1681; in Pennsylvania
      before Penn (?); servant of Gerhard Hendricks: he is
      said to have come with Hendricks in October, 1685;
      but this would appear to be an error, unless he returned
      to Germany, perhaps to be married, and came to Amer-
      ica a second time.
Anhalt: Bidermann, Ludwig: wife was Maria Margaretha Zimmer-
      mann.
Bachersdorf (near Bruges): Kasselberg, Hendrick: †(Henry Kessle-
      berry).
      Kasselberg, Catherine: Mennonite, 1708.
Bietigheim (east of Pforzheim, in Würtemberg): John Jacob Zim-
      mermann's widow and four children (see Duisburg);
      Z. died in or after leaving Rotterdam, *en route* to Penn-
      sylvania.
Blomberg (Lippe-Detmold): Köster, Heinrich Bernhardt: to Ger-
      mantown, 1689; the first preacher in German, and
      English there.
Duisburg: Stork, Arnold: expected in Pennsylvania, in 1700; ac-
      quired some of Pastorius's land.
      Zimmermann, Maria Margaretha: widow of John Jacob
      Z; came with *two other* widows and their children, 1694;
      her children were: Maria Margaretha (married Ludwig
      Bidermann), Philip Christian, Matthaias, and Jacob
      Christoph (to Bebber's Township, 1708).
Fredrikstadt (Friedrichstadt): [Founded by Dutch emigrants, 1621;
      in Danish Holstein until 1866, when it became Prus-
      sian]:
      Muller, Georg: fined for betting that he could smoke
      more than 100 pipes in one day; unjustly acquired some
      of Pastorius's land.
Goch: Gottschalk (Gaetschalck), Jacob: in Germantown, 1702; a
      Mennonite teacher; wrote account of Germantown Men-
      nonites; *wife* a Mennonite member, 1708;*; †(Jacob
      Gaetschalck).
      Vandergach, Cornelis: †(Cornelius Vandergach).

Hamburg and Fendern: Berends, Klaas (Claes) : Brought his *family* in 1700, and his father-in-law, namely,

> Claessen, Cornelis: a Mennonite, 1700; Berends was also a Mennonite member, 1702.
> Claasen, Cornelia: daughter of Cornelis (?); wife of Isaac van Sintern.
> Harmens, Trijntje: a widow.
> Karsdorp (Casdorp), Harmen (Herman) : a Mennonite preacher, 1708– ; wife (Adriana van Vossen) and *children* with him; he and wife listed as Mennonite members, 1708.
> Roosen, Paul: he and his *wife* arrived, 1700.
> Sintern, Hendrick van: unmarried.
> Sintern, Isaac van: Mennonite deacon and overseer, 1708; wife was Cornelia Claessen of Hamburg;*.
> Sintern, Magdalena van: daughter of Isaac; married Martin Kolb, 1709.
> Sintern, Sarah van: married Jacob Kolb, 1710.

(From Fendern, near Hamburg, in Holstein) : Wolff (Wulf), Paul: a weaver; versus Keith; subscribed £ 6 to the Friends' Meeting-house, 1686; gave one acre for the Upper Grave-yard; subscribed to and collected for the school;*; jury foreman, clerk, burgess; 1704, received deed for Germantown lot signed by "Aret Klincken Bailiff, Hans Heinrich Meels, Peter and Isaac Schumacher, Dirck Janston, Thones Kunders, Barent Henderigcks, Anthony (his X mark) Gerkes, William Strepers", witnessed by Jacob Schumacher and Tho. Potts, "acknowledged in open Court of Record, certified by me Fr. Daniel Pastorius Cl Cur germ [Clerk of the Germantown Court]", recorded in Germantown Grund und Lager Buch, p. 209.

Heilbron: Frey, Peter: to Germantown, 1685, as indentured servant of Peter Schumacher; cf. *supra,* p. 318; cf. also Heinrich Frey, *supra,* pp. 316ff.

Lemgo (Lippe-Detmold) : Seelig, Johannes Gottfried, a former secretary of the Pietist Spener; book-binder and teacher; a "hermit of the Wissahickon"; he wrote a letter from Germantown, dated August 7, 1694, which was printed from the MS. (preserved in the archives of Halle) in 1695.

> Seelig, Godfried: a Germantown court witness.

Lübeck: Jauert, Johannes: attorney for the Frankfort Co.; recorder; †(John Javert).

Mülheim-an-der-Ruhr: Hoffen, Annecke in den.

> Hoffen, Evert in den: came in or before 1699, with *children;* †(Evert in Hoffee).

Hoffen, Gerhard in den: son of Evert; †(Gerhard in Hoffee); to Bebber's Township, 1706.

Hoffen, Herman in den: son of Evert; †(Herman in Hoffee); to Bebber's Township, 1706; married Anne op den Graeff.

Hoffen, Peter in den: son of Evert; †(Peter in Hoffee).

Klosterman, Ennecke (Annchen): wife of Francis Daniel Pastorius; born in Mülheim about 1658.

Levering, Gerhard: in Germantown, 1685.

Levering, Wigard (Wishert): in Germantown, 1685; died, 1744, aet. 109.

Lindeman, Jan: in Germantown, 1698.

Renberg, Dirck: son of Michael; to Bebber's Township, 1706.

Renberg, Michael: in Germantown, 1702.

Renberg, Willem: son of Michael; to Bebber's Township, 1706.

Trap, Hermann op de: naturalized in Germantown, 1691; drowned in Philadelphia, 1693.

Nürnberg: Jacquet, Jan: in Pennsylvania before 1683 (?).

"Saxony": Falckner, Daniel: born at Langenreinsdorf; to Germantown, 1694; agent for Frankfort Co. and for Benjamin Furly; versus Pastorius; bailiff; *children* as misdemeanents, he himself arrested.

Falckner, Justus: Daniel's brother; to Germantown, 1700; wife was Gerritje Hardick; agent for Furly; burgess; first Lutheran preacher in Pennsylvania, and the first Lutheran clergyman ordained in America.

Lehnmann (Lehenmann), Philip Theodor; one of Penn's private secretaries; in Germantown before 1710.

Schlegel (Slagle), Christopher: in Germantown, 1701.

Sommerhausen: Pastorius, Francis Daniel: subscribed £ 4 to the Friends' Meeting-house, 1686; married (in Germantown, 1688) Ennecke Klostermann; Germantown schoolmaster, 1702; †(ffrancis Daniel Pastorius).

Pastorius, Heinrich: son of Francis; born in Germantown, 1692; learned shoemaking; married Sarah Boutcher; two sons and three daughters.

Pastorius, Johann Samuel: son of Francis; born in Germantown, 1690; learned weaving with Paul Kästner, 1706; married, 1716, Jan Lukens's youngest daughter, Hannah; died 1722, leaving two sons.

VI. FROM UNSTATED PLACES IN HOLLAND OR GERMANY

Aderman, Ludwig: in Germantown before 1710.

Andreas, (Andrews), Sijmon (Simon): in Germantown, 1703; recorder.

Bacher (alias Rutters), Koenradt: with Pastorius, 1683.
Bartel, Henrij: son of Senwes; †(Henry Bartells).
Bartels, Senwes: †(Senwes Bartells).
Bartlesen, Sebastiaan: in Germantown, 1700.
Baumann, Wilhelm: *.
Baumstädt, Joseph: in Germantown before 1710.
Beer, Edward: to Bebber's Township, 1706.
Boekwolt (Buchholtz), Hendrick (Heinrich) : *wife* was Mary ———;
    in Germantown, 1685; fence-viewer; †(Henry Buc-
    holtz) ; called "Henry Pookeholes and Mary his wife"
    in the list of arrivals, 1682–87.
Bonij (Boney), Andreas: in Germantown before 1710.
Böter, Thomas: in Germantown before 1710.
Bowman, Wynant: *wife* was Ann ———; both Mennonite members,
    1708.
Brandt, Albertus: wife was Susanna Telner; recorder; fined for non-
    jury service; to Philadelphia.
Brown (Le Brun ?), Peter: Juryman, 1710.
Burklow, Reynier Hermans van: son-in-law of Peter Schumacher;
    appeal for naturalization, 1691; to Bohemia Manor,
    1704.
Carsten, Casper: in Germantown before 1710.
Carstens, Johan Heinrich: †(John Henry Kersten).
Casper (Gasper), Thomas: with Pastorius to Philadelphia, 1683.
Cotweis (Cod Weis), Conrad: in Germantown before 1710; bought
    Germantown land, 1701.
Cotweis, Johann Cornelis: in Germantown before 1710.
Cotweis (Codweis), Johann Cunrad: recorder, burgess;*; interpreter
    in New York after 1709.
Coulson, Joseph: court witness;*.
Delaplaine, James (Jacob) : a Walloon; subscribed £ 5 to the Friends'
    Meeting-house, 1686; wife was Hannah Cook of Long
    Island; subscribed to the school;*; gave land for market;
    coroner, bailiff; built prison and stocks, 1704 (with Her-
    man van Bon).
Delaplaine, Nicholaes: James' son.
Desmond, Daniel: to Bebber's Township, 1708.
Dewees, Johannes: in Germantown before 1710.
Doeden, Jan: burgess, committeeman, assessor;*; †(John Deeden).
Echelwich, Thomas: †(Thos. Echlewich).
Engell, Jacob: son of Paul; †(Jacob Engell).
Engell, Paul: naturalized, 1698; †(Paul Engell) ; attended evening
    school;*.
Frank, Mattheis: in Germantown, before 1710.
Geissler, Daniel: in Germantown, 1694.
Gorgas, Johannes: †(John Gorgaes).
Hapon, Heywart: in Germantown before 1710.

Harberdinck, Levin: subscribed to school; received Certificate of Removal.[635]

Hartzfelder, Andreas: attended evening school.

Hartzfelder, Jurian (Görg): deputy-sheriff under Andros (?); said to have taken up 350 acres on site north of later Philadelphia, in 1676.

Heggen, Goedschalk van der: son of Jacob; †(Gaetshalk Vander Heggen).

Heggen, Jacob: †(———— Vander Heggen).

Hermans, Reiner: juryman;*.

Hoedt, Casper: a tailor; wife was Elisabeth Delaplaine; versus Keith; recorder; †(Caspar Hoodt).

Houfer, Frank: naturalized, 1698.

Huberts, Margaret: Mennonite member, 1708.

Jacobs, Jan: to Bebber's Township, 1704.

Jacobs, Jurgen:*.

Jacobs, Jurgen Jacob: son of Jurgen (?).

Jerman, Edward: court witness, 1704.

Jerman (German), Johannes: in Germantown before 1710.

Kästner, Paul: a weaver; versus Keith; clerk;*.

Kästner, Samuel: attended evening school.

Kleinhoof, Casper: †(Casper Kleinhoof).

Klever, Peter: applied for citizenship; 1691; †(Peter Clever).

Klumpges, Jacob: in Germantown, 1688.

Klumpges, Jacob Jansen: son of Paul; †(Jno. Klumpges).

Klumpges, Paul: son of Jacob (?); †(Paul Klumpges).

---

[635] This certificate, illustrative of many others, is taken from the MS. book of Philadelphia Monthly Meeting's Certificates Received (p. 45), which is preserved in the Friends' Historical Library of Swarthmore College; it reads as follows:

"From our Monthly meeting of Dublin Township att ye house of Richard Worrell, this 22d day of ye 12th month 1702/3

"Whereas our aged Friend Levin Herberdink (who dwelled these many years in ye Germantownship) being resolved to leave his plantation & the harder work attending ye same, hath removed himself & family to the City of Philadelphia, in good hopes to live a more comfortable life, Did desire of our abovesd Meeting a Certificate in order to shew & produce it at the Monthly Meeting of Philadelphia aforesd. We hereby do Certify That the said Levin Herberdink hath been all the time he was in this province in full unity with Friends, and concerning his Conversation we (vpon Enquiry) cannot find anything justly to be objected as to let or hinder these psents, Therefore we were willing to set our hands hereunto And Do cōmit the sd our Friend to the further Leadings & Directions of gods holy & powerful grace In which we heartily salute you & remain yor. Frds & brethren . . . [Here follow the names of twenty-four Friends, among them being those of James Delaplaine, Arnold Clinken, Levart (Lenart) Arets, and Paul Woolf.]"

Kolk, Dirck van: in Germantown, 1689; committee-man.
Kramer, Andries (Andreas) : versus Keith; constable.
Krey, Helena: a Mennonite member, 1708.
Krey, Jan (Johannes) : to Bebber's Township, 1702; †(Jno. Krey).
Krey, Wilhelm: son of Paul; †(Willm. Krey).
Leer, Johannes van: in Germantown before 1710.
Loof, Anthonij: court-crier, clerk; subscribed to school;*.
Lorenz, Görg: to Germantown, 1694.
Lorenz, Heinrich: in Germantown, 1701; infant son died on voyage
    over.
Lutke (Lutkins), Daniel: to Germantown, 1694.
Marcus, Lorento: in Germantown before 1710.
Meels (Mehls), Hans Heinrich: burgess;*; bought Germantown land,
    1701, from Zytien de Wees.
Millan, Hans: fence-viewer, 1691.
Millan, Margaret: Hans's daughter; married Reyner Jansen's son.
Millan, Matteus: Hans's son; married Reyner Jansen's daughter
    Imity;*.
Nezelius, Mattheis: in Germantown before 1710.
Pedden, Jacob Isaac van: in Germantown before 1710.
Pelnes, Jacob: in Germantown before 1710.
Peters, Matthew: accused, 1701.
Peters, Reese: Monthly Meeting committee, 1699.
Peters, Reynier: juryman, 1701; fined.
Pettinger (Pottinger), Johannes: innkeeper, 1695; in legal difficulties.
Radwitzer, Johannes: in Germantown before 1710; †(John Rad-
    witzer).
Rebenstock, Altien: a Mennonite member, 1708.
Rebenstock, Johannes: German (?Dutch?) Reformed; †(Johannes
    Rebanstock).
Rittinghuysen, Henrick: in Germantown before 1710.
Rittinghuysen, Matthias: in Germantown before, 1710.
Rüttinghuysen, Paul: in Germantown before 1710.
Rutters, Thomas: pro Keith; bailiff.
Sanen, Weyntie van: married Jan Duplouvys.
Schaffer,[636] Isaac: weigh-master.
Scharbon, Peter: in Germantown before 1710.
Schmidt, Johannes: †(John Smith).
Scholl, Johannes: to Bebber's Township, 1708; †(Johannes Scholl).
Scholl, Peter: attended evening school; †(Peter Scholl).
Sentner, Gabriel: †(Gabriel Senter).
Silans, Johan: constable.
Souplis, Andries: sheriff.

---

[636] "Shepherd"; Low-Dutch =Scepers; Dutch= (Schaap) herder; German=
Schäfer; Latin =Pastor, Pastorius. Thus, the name of Francis Daniel Pastorius illustrates the migration of German words into the old world of Latin,
as he himself illustrates the migration of German people into the new world
of America.

Souplis, Margaret: married Peter Keyser.
Spiekerman, Marieke: in Germantown, 1702.
Stahls, Casper: †(Caspar Stalls).
Tamsen, Klas: subscribed to school.
Tibben (Tubben), Heindrick: juryman; †(Henry Tubben).
Timmerman, Christopher: a Mennonite member, 1708.
Tresse, Thomas: paper mill, 1690.
Tuynen, Harmen (Herman) : a Mennonite member, 1708; †(Herman
      Tuymen).
Tuynen, Marij: a Mennonite member, 1708.
Verbyman (Verbinnen), Peter: †(Peter Verbymen).
Vossen, Adriana van (de voss) : married Harmen Karsdorp.
Vossen, Arnold van: gave land to Mennonites, 1703; court witness;*.
Vossen, Civilia van: a Mennonite member, 1708.
Vossen, Maria van: a Mennonite member, 1708.
Warmer, Christian: in Germantown, 1694; bought 50 acres;*.
Wert, Johannes van der: in Germantown before 1710.
Willems, Gijsbert: died, 1692.
Wiseman, Thomas: to Bebber's Township, 1706.
Woestyne, Jan van de: in Germantown, 1693.*.

VII. FROM OTHER EUROPEAN COUNTRIES

Finland—Schaeffer, Pieter: with Johannes Kelpius, 1694.
Hungary—Soroschi, Isaac Ferdinand: to Germantown, 1695.
Silesia—Buylaert, Marijana van: came with the three following:
      Matern, Abigail: daughter of Johannes Matern.
      Matern, Rosijna Prache: widow of Johannes Matern;
      came as the wife of John Bringhurst.
      Prache, Barbara: widow of Hilarius Prache, mother of
      Rosijna and grandmother of Barbara.
Switzerland—Gottschalk (Gödschalk), Georg: from Lindau, Bodensee;
      †(George Gattschik).
      Wertmuller (Wertmüller), Joris (Georg) : from Berne;
      Pastorius' servant.
      Zimmermann, Emanuel: son of Heinrich.
      Zimmermann, Heinrich: came himself, 1698; brought
      his *family,* 1706; naturalized, 1709.
Transylvania—Kelpius, Johannes: from Denndorf; leader of "the
      forty" Pietist brethren to "the Ridge" on the Wis-
      sahickon, 1694; Society of "the Woman in the Wilder-
      ness" (*Das Weib in der Wüste*) : Revelation, 12:14.

VIII. FROM GREAT BRITAIN (?)

Armitage, Benjamin:*.
Griskum (Griscom ?), Andrew: drew lots for Germantown land, 1689.
Howe, Thomas: married Margaret, daughter of Abraham Isaacs op den
      Graeff.

Huggin, Richard:*.
James, Howell:*.
Miles, Griffith:*.
Morgan, Benjamin: arrived in Philadelphia, 1685;*.
Newberry, John: to Bebber's Township, 1706.
Paul, Joseph: in Germantown before 1710.
Potts, Jonas: sheriff, subscribed to school;*.
Potts, Thomas: juryman; married Martha, daughter of Peter and
          Elisabeth Keurlis;*.
Potts, Thomas, Jr.: sheriff, 1703.
Potts, William: †(William Puts).
Richardson, Samuel:*.
Simpson, Frances: a servant of Pastorius.
Townsend, Richard:*.
Witt, Christopher:*.

RECAPITULATION

This list sums up as follows:

From Holland: places stated (10) and unstated	58 names
From Krefeld and Kaldekerk	91 names
From Krisheim, Wolfsheim and Flomborn	38 names
From Germany: places stated (15) and unstated	49 names
From Holland *or* Germany (places not stated)	114 names
From other European countries (5)	11 names
From Great Britain	17 names

TOTAL—persons named 378

In addition to the persons named, there were:

wives referred to, but not named: Holland, 5;
    Krefeld, 5; Krisheim, 3; others, 6 ......}   19 persons

"children" referred to, some of them named,
    others not named in 57 families: counting
    as unnamed 1 1/3 child per family = 76 }   76 persons
    children ....

GRAND TOTAL—473 persons

GERMANTOWN RESIDENTS, 1692

A petition for the defeat of a tax-bill, addressed to the
Pennsylvania Assembly, the 10th of the 3rd Month, 1692,
was signed by 262 freemen of the Province, among whom
were the following 33 residents of Germantown:[637]

[637] *Pennsylvania Magazine,* Vol. 38 (1914), p. 495.

Albertus Brandt
Andrew Seeply (Andreas Souplis)
Claus Rittenhowes
Isaac Sheffers (Schäffers)
Jacob Isaac (van Bebber)
Leonard Arenes (Arents)
Peter Kearles (Keurlis)
John Luyken
Peter Clever
Walter Symans
Arent Clinken
John Duplovys
Thomas Rutter
Abraham Tunis
Harman Op, de Graves (op den Graef)
Jacob Shumaker
Jan Lensen

Cornelis Severs (Siverts)
Hanse Malan (Milan)
Thomas Shute
Francis Daniel Pastorius
Derick Keiser
Paul Kastner
Gerrit Hendricks
Derick Sall (Sellen)
Closs Tomson
John Douden (Doeden)
Arnold Cassel
Hans Peter Umstat
Daniel Van Beeck
Jan Willemse Huyseen (Rittinghuysen ?)
Thomas Kember
David Sherkis

GERMANTOWN RESIDENTS, 1693

On the 15th May 1693, the General Assembly passed the first law assessing and taxing the property of the inhabitants of Philadelphia County, which included 52 adult male residents of "German Town Pet[r] Knerless [Keurlis, Assessor]" as follows:[638]

	Assessed	Taxed			Assessed	Taxed	
Derick Up de Grave	£ 30	2 s.	6 d.	Claws Tamson	40	3	4
Thomas Rutter[639]	30	2	6	Hance Millan	80	6	8
Hermon Up de Grave	80	6	8	Henry Fry	30	2	6
Abraham Up de Grave	80	6	8	Aert Klinken	80	6	8
William Streipers	80	6	8	Arnold Wassell (Kassel)	—	6	—
Paul Woolf	30	2	6	John Silans	30	2	6
Daniel Pastorius	100	8	4	Dirick Keyser	60	5	—
Jacob Shoomaker	60	5	—	Geritt Henrix	50	4	2
Heyfert Papen	80	6	8	William Ruttinghuyson	50	4	2
Jacob Isaac & Isaac Jacobs	150	12	6	Andrew Souplis	50	4	2
Cornelius Siverts	80	6	8	John Doeden	40	3	4
Albertus Brant	120	10	—	Paul Castern (Kästner)	30	2	6

[638] *The Pennsylvania Magazine*, Vol. 8 (1884), pp. 98–100.

[639] Thomas Rutter was also assessed in Bristol Township £ 50, and taxed 4 s. 2 d.

	Assessed	Taxed			Assessed	Taxed	
Hermon Van Bon	50	4	2	Jacob Delaplain	30	2	6
Mary Henrix	50	4	2	David Scherkers	—	6	—
Abraham Tunes	50	4	2	Walter Simens	—	6	—
John Lucken	50	4	2	Peter Clever	—	6	—
Reinert Tisen	60	5	—	Johannis Pettinger	—	6	—
Lenert Artes	30	2	6	Hermon Op De Trap	—	—	—
John Lensen	30	2	6	John Van de			
Tunes Conders	50	4	2	Woestyne	—	6	—
Peter Kuerless	50	4	2	Anthony Loof	—	6	—
John Bleekers	50	4	2	Mathias Jackson			
Rineir Hermans	50	4	2	(Jansen)	—	6	—
Henry Sellen	50	4	2	Peter Shoomaker	—	6	—
Derick Sellen	30	2	6	Hance Peter Upstead			
Claws Rutting				(Umstad)	100	8	4
Heysen	—	6	—	Peter Shoomaker	80	6	8
Andrew Griscome	30	2	6				

From the above list of taxables,—the first that was made, —it is seen that with 52 tax-payers in Germantown, ten years after its first settlement, the assessed valuation of their property was £ 2,300 (about $57,500 in terms of our current money), on which they paid taxes amounting to £ 12—7 s. 6 d. (about $309.40 today).

GERMANTOWN RESIDENTS NATURALIZED, 1709 (AND 1691)

A Naturalization Petition, 1706: "At a Council held at Philadelphia, yᵉ 15th 3 mo., 1706.[640]

Present:

The Honble John Evans, Esq'r., Lieut. Govr.

Edward Shippen, John Guest, Samuel Carpenter, Thos. Story, Griffith Owen,	Esq'rs.	J. Logan, William Trent, Capt. Roche, Joseph Pidgeon.	Esq'rs.

"A Petition of Johannes Koster, and about 150 other high and low Germans, to the Govr. and Council was read, setting forth, that the Petrs., with many other aliens to the

---

[640] "Minutes of the Provincial Council of Pennsylvania", Phila., 1852 ("Colonial Archives", Vol. II, pp. 241–2).

Kingdom of England, by the Encouragement of the Propr.
had Transported themselves into this Province, & by their
Industry had changed the uncultivated Lands they had purchased into good settlemts., & for Twenty two years past
had behaved themselves as Liege & Loyal subjects of England, that above 60 of the said Ptrs. at one time, viz: the
7th of yᵉ 3 mo., 1691, had in open Court, promised allegiance
to K. William & Q. Mary, & fidelity to the Propr., besides
many others who had done the Like, &c., that such as have
not already obliged themselves are ready to do it when they
shall be admitted. They therefore request, that (seeing
they are not at present believed to be secure in their Estates,) for remedying the unhappiness they may be engaged
in, if they be still considered as foreigners, the assembly
may be convened with all Convenient speed, & a Bill recommended from this board for naturalizing all & every of the
said Ptrs., that they may have an undoubted right to hold,
enjoy, alienate, sell & dispose of any of their Lands, as the
natural born subjects of England may or can do in this
Province, & also that they may be capable of Electing &
being elected, to serve in Assembly & other Offices; also,
that some of the Petrs., being Mennists, who (with their
Predecessory [sic] for above 150 Years past,) could not
for Conscience sake take an Oath, the same provision may
be made for them by a law, as is made for those called
Quakers in this Province, and that the said Law may be sent
home with the rest, past by the late Assembly, in Order to
obtain the Queens Royal Approbation.

"Which Petition being argued and Considered, It is Resolved, that it is highly reasonable the Petrs., and all others
in their Circumstances, should be rendered Secure in their
Estates and Titles to their Lands in this Province, the value
of which is generally, but the effect of their own labours, and
in pursuance of some parts of the prayer of the said Petition leave is given to the sd. Petrs., to procure the attorney
Genl. to draw up a bill for that purpose, to be laid before
this Board, where it shall meet with all due Encouragement."

It was not until three and a half years later that we have

a record of the proposed naturalization bill being introduced and passed. This was as follows :[641]

"At a Council held at Philadia., the 29th. of Sepbr., 1709.

Present

The Honble Cha. Gookin, Esqr., Lt. Govr.

Edward Shippen,
Griffith Owen,   }Esq'rs.   Isaac Norris,
James Logan,   Samuel Preston,   }Esq'rs.

"The Govr. acquainted the board, that last night the Speaker attended with several members of the House, brought him the Bill for naturalizing the Germans, which he now desired to pass, and accordingly he was pleased to give his assent to the said bill, being Intituled an Act for the better Enabling of Divers Inhabitants of the Province of Pennsylvia., To Hold and Enjoy Lands, Tenemts. and Plantation in the same Province, by which are naturalized the persons following, vizt. [Here follow eighty-three names, "all of the County of Philadia.," except "Johannes Bleikers of the County of Bucks."] . . . which Act was Ordered to pass the Seal, when the persons concerned or any in their behalf should appear & pay the Charge, & then adjourned."

Meanwhile, nearly twenty years before, on the 7th. of 3rd. Month, 1691, Thomas Lloyd, Deputy Governor of Pennsylvania, had granted "naturalization" to sixty-two of the first settlers in Germantown, who were thereby made "freemen", a status which the law of England denied to foreigners. In return, they "solemnly promised faith and allegiance to William and Mary and fidelity and lawful obedience to William Penn as Proprietary".

The sixty-two naturalized in 1691 were as follows: Francis Daniel Pastorius,* Jacob Telner, Dirck Isaacs op de Graeff, Herman Isaacs op de Graeff, Tennis Conderts,* Abraham Isaacs op de Graeff, Jacob Jones, Johannes Cassels, Heivert Papen, Herman Bon, Albertus Brandt, Jacob Schumacker*, Dirck Keyser, Arnold Cassel, Dirck Keyser,

---

[641] "The Colonial Records of Pennsylvania", Philadelphia, 1852, Vol. 2., pp. 493–4.

Jr.,* Jan Lensen,* Jan Duplouvys, Peter Schumacker,*
Peter Schumacker, Jr.,* Isaac Dilbeck*, Jan Doeden*, Wal-
ter Simons*, Abraham Tunis*, Wm. Rittenhouse, Claus
Rittenhouse*, Johannes Kusters, Heinrick Buckholt*, Isaac
Jacobs, Matt. Jacobs*, Wiggert Levering, Isaac Schäffer,
Claus Jansen*, Hans Milan, Dirck Sellen, Heindrick Sellen*,
Paul Wolff, Lenart Arets*, Arents Klincken, Paul Kastner,
Wm. Striepers*, Johannes Bleickers*, Cornelius Siverts*,
Reiner Hermans, Andreas Souplis, Koenradt Backer, Viet
Scherkes, Hans Peter Umstadt, Anthony Duplouvys, Hen-
rich Kasselbergs*, Reinert Tissen*, Jan Lucken*, Peter
Klever*, Heinrich Frey, Hans Andreas Kramer, Jurgen
Schumacker*, Isaac Schumacker*, Peter Keurlis, Gerhard
Levering, Herman op de Trap, Herman Dirk op de Kolb,
Anthony Loof, Jan Williams.

Twenty-six of these survived to be re-naturalized in
1709,[642] and fifty-seven new names were added in the latter
year, as follows:[643] Jan Javert, Caspar Hoodt (Hoed),
Cunrad, Matthis and Jan Cunrads (Thones Kunders's three
sons), Jacobus Dilbeck (son of Isaac Dilbeck), Dirk Jansen,
Jr., Richard Vanderwerf and his son Jan Roelofs Vanderwerf, Jan Strepers Sr., Cornelis Vandergach, Georg Gatt-
schik, Paul Engell and his son Jacob Engell, Hans Nous,
Reiner Vander Sluys and his son Adrian Vander Sluys,
Jacob Gaetshalck, —— Vander Heggen and his son Gaet-
shalck Vander Heggen, Casper Kleinhoof, Herman Tuynen,
Paul Klumpges and his son Jno. Klumpges, Jan Neus and his
sons Matthis and Cornelis Neus, Caspar Stalls, Henry Tub-
ben, Willem Hendricks and his sons Hendrick and Laurens
Hendricks, Johannes Rebanstock, Peter Verbymen, John
Henry Kersten (Carstens), John Radwitzer, John Cunrads,
Sr., John Gorgaes, Senwes Bartells and his son Hendrik
Bartells, Jan Krey and his son Willem Krey, Cunrad Jan-
sen, Jan and Willem Jansen (sons of Claus Jansen), Evert
in Hoffee (in den Hoffen) and his sons Gerhard, Herman
and Peter, Peter Jansen, John Smith, Thomas Echelwich,
Johannes Scholl, Peter Scholl, Gabriel Senter, William
Puts (Potts), and Matthis Tysen.

---

[642] Namely, those marked above with *.
[643] "Colonial Records of Pennsylvania", Vol. 2, pp. 493–4.

APPENDIX D

Een attestatij voor Derick Isacks en Nöleken Vijten
aangaende haer L: heuwelijk

Dit dient om een Jegelijk die het soŭde Moogen aengaen
te Kennen te geŭen dat Derijck Isacks Jongman een gebohr-
en Bŭrgers Sohn in Kreŭel ende Nöleken Vijten Jonge
dochter gebohren tot Kampen te kennen hebben gegeven
aan het Volck Godts in kreŭell Qŭakers genaemt dat haer
L: Voornehem wäss om met malcanderen in den hŭwelijken
Staat te treden alsmede dat Sij L: vrij sijn van alle aendere
persoonen het welck dan ook also is aangetekent in het Boek
van die vergadering der Voorschreŭen volcks ende volgens
haar L: versoek om hetselŭe in een pŭblijqŭij vergadering
van voorschreven Volck te moogen pŭblicieren Soo is haer
sŭlcks geconsentirt om haer L. voornehmen in de pŭblijqŭe
vergadering te moogen pŭblicieren ende soo wanneer als
dan ook niet tot Belet verschijnen Soŭde haer voor Schreŭen
hŭwelijk ter Beqŭamer tit [sic] te Moogen Voltrecken
volgens de goede order die onder het voorschreŭen Volck is
beŭestigt welcke pŭblicatij geschiedt Sijnde in twee pŭblijqŭe vergaderinge de erste maell den 9 dag der 2 Maendt
en de 2 maell den 9 dag der 3 maendt 1681 So dat het
rŭgbaar en kennelick geworden is beide tot de Bŭrgerij als
ook tot de inwoenders van diese Staadt ende niet tot belet
verschijnenende [sic] so getŭigen wij ondergeschreŭenen
mits desen dat Sij L. Namemtlijk derick Isacks en Nöleken
Vijten in een pŭblijqŭe vergadering van het voorschreŭen
Volck tot dien Ende aangestelt Verschenen sijn ende hebben
aldaer in des heeren ende onser aller tegenwordigheijt haer
L. hŭwelijk beŭestigt op den 20 dag der 3 maendt 1681 in
kreŭell verklarende hij Derick Isack met diese Naerfolgende
worden Seggende Vrienden en Volck Naer dien het in de tijt

---

[644] For a translation of it in English, see *supra*, p. 207; for a photograph of
the original, see *supra*, the Frontispiece.

422

van 6 weeken hier ter plaetsen in onse pŭblijqŭe vergaderinge tot 2 maell toe bekent gemaekt iss dat ick D. I. ende
N. V. geresolvirt waeren om met Malcanderen in den
hŭwelijken Staet te treden en ons niets voor gekomen sijnde
tot belet van het selŭe so gedencken wij daer in Vort te gaen
om het selŭe godtlick en christelijk voor godt en die
Menschen te betŭigen en te beŭestigen gelijk dan medts
desen geschiedt In de tegenwordigheijt van den grooten Godt
de got abrahams Isacks en Jacobs [den] Godt die den hemell
de aarde de See en all wat daer op en daer in is geschaapen
ende gemaakt heeft en die het selve Noch dagelijks onder-
houdt door het wordt seiner kragt ick Segge vrienden in dessen tegenwordigheijt en in de tegenwordigheijt van ŭ allen
die hier vergadert sijt Nehme Ick Derick Isack ŭ Nöleken
Vijten tot mijn Echte vroŭ en Beloove in oprechtigheijt
getrouigheijt en in de vrese Godss ŭ bij te woonen en ŭ niet
te verlaeten tot dat het godt almagtig sall belieŭen onss door
den doodt van Malcanderen te Scheijden—Ende sij—Nöleken Vijten verklaerde segende—Vrienden op dese Beloften
en in de tegenwordigheijt van den leŭendige Godt den Godt
des hemels en der aarde en in de tegenwordigheijt van dese
vergadering Nehme ick (Nöleken Vijten) Derick Isacks voor
mijn Echte Man en Belove hem getroŭ te sijn in de vreese
Godts ende hem niet te verlaeten tot dat het den here sall
Believen onss door den doodt te Scheijden.—

Derick Isacks	nölken Vijtten
Herman Isacks	Greitijen peters
Abraham Isacks	Liesbet Isacks
Tunnes (?) Keŭnen	margrit Isacks
Herman Daŭrss	Jenneken (?) Jansen
henderijck Janssen	lijntijen teissen
Veit Scherkes	Judit preijers
Jan Siemes	mercken willems
Wolter Siemes	
Lenart Arents	
Johannes blijkers	

APPENDIX E

Inscriptions on the Pastorius Monument, in Krefeld, Prussia; erected, 1931. (Cf. *supra*, p. 259.)

At base, front:

ZUM ANDENKEN AN DIE NACH 74 TAEGIGER, AUF DEM SCHIFFE CONCORD ZURUECKGELEGTER SEEREISE, AM 6. OCTOBER DES JAHRES 1683 ERFOLGTEN LANDUNG DER GRUENDER VON GERMANTOWN, DER ERSTEN REINDEUTSCHEN NIEDERLASSUNG AUF AMERIKANISCHEM BODEN. SIE WURDEN EMPFANGEN VON DEM EDELGESINNTEN RECHTSGELEHRTEN

FRANZ DANIEL PASTORIUS
GEB. 1651 IN SOMMERHAUSEN
GEST. 1719 IN GERMANTOWN.

HERMANN, ABRAHAM, UND DIRK (DIETRICH) OP DEN GRAEFF, LEINERT (LEONHARD) ARETS, TÜNES (ANTON) KUNDERS, REINERT (REINHARDT) TISEN ODER THEISSEN, WILHELM STREPERS, JAN (JOHANNES) LENSEN, PETER KEURLIS ODER KUIRLIS, JAN SIEMENS, JOHANN BLEICKERS, ABRAHAM TÜNES, UND JAN LÜKEN ODER LUYKEN.

On left pylon, front:

GERMANTOWN, "DEUTSCHE STADT", JETZT EIN VORORT VON PHILADELPHIA, WURDE AM 24. OCTOBER 1683 UNTER DER LEITUNG VON FRANZ DANIEL PASTORIUS AUSGELEGT. DURCH UNERMUEDLICHEN FLEISS, BETRIEBSAMKEIT UND AUFRICHTIGEN, GENUEGSAMEN SINN, MACHTEN DIE BEWOHNER VON GERMANTOWN IHREN ORT ZUM VORBILD FUER ALLE ANDEREN NIEDERLASSUNGEN IN AMERIKA. HIER VERFASSTEN SIE AM 18. FEBRUAR 1688 EINEN SCHRIFTLICHEN PROTEST GEGEN DIE SKLAVEREI, DEN ERSTEN, WELCHER IN DER GANZEN WELT WIDER DIESE UNVUERDIGE EINRICHTUNG ERHOBEN WURDE. HIER DRUCKTE CHRISTOPH SAUER DIE ERSTEN IN AMERIKA MIT DEUTSCHEN LETTERN GESETZTEN BUECHER, HIER VEROEFFENTLICHTE ER AM 20. AUGUST, 1739 DIE ERSTE DEUTSCHAMERIKANISCHE ZEITUNG, UND HIER ERBLICKTE IM JAHRE 1748 DIE ERSTE, IN EUROPAEISCHER

424

SPRACHE AUF AMERIKANISCHEM BODEN GEDRUCKTE BIBEL—
EINE DEUTSCHE — DAS LICHT DER WELT. IN GERMANTOWN
ERSTAND FERNER DIE ERSTE PAPIERMUEHLE AMERIKAS, UND
HIER WURDE DER ERSTE BOTANISCHE GARTEN DER WESTLICHEN
ERDHAELFTE ANGELEGT.

On right pylon, front:

FRANZ DANIEL PASTORIUS, DER ERSTE BUERGERMEISTER VON
GERMANTOWN, EROEFFNETE DAS ERSTE GRUND UND LAGERBUCH
DES ORTES MIT FOLGENDEN WORTEN: SEID GEGRUESST NACH-
KOMMEN, IHR NACHKOMMEN IN GERMANOPOLIS ! UND ERFAHRET
ZUNAECHST, DASS EURE ELTERN UND VORFAHREN DEUTSCHLAND,
DAS HOLDE LAND, DAS SIE GEBOREN UND GENAEHRT, FREIWILLIG
VERLASSEN HABEN, — OH, IHR HEIMISCHEN HERDE, — UM IN
DIESEM WALDREICHEN PENNSYLVANIEN, INMITTEN WILDER
EINSAMKEIT DEN REST IHRES LEBENS MINDER SORGENVOLL IN
DEUTSCHER WEISE WIE BRUEDER MITEINANDER ZU VERBRINGEN.
ERFAHRT AUCH FERNER, WIE MUEHSELIG ES WAR, NACH UEBER-
SCHIFFEN DES ATLANTISCHEN MEERES IN DIESEM TEIL AMERIKAS
DEN DEUTSCHEN STAMM ZU GRUENDEN. UND IHR, GELIEBTE
ENKEL, WO WIR EIN VORBILD DES RECHTES WAREN, AHMT UNSER
BEISPIEL NACH, WO WIR ABER VON DEM SCHWIERIGEN PFAD
ABWICHEN, HABT NACHSICHT UND VERGEBT UNS. MOEGEN DIE
GEFAHREN, DIE ANDERE LIEFEN, EUCH VORSICHTIG MACHEN.
HEIL DIR NACHKOMMENSCHAFT! HEIL DIR DEUTSCHES BRUDER-
VOLK! HEIL DIR AUF IMMER !

On left pylon, back:[645]

UNTER DEM RUHMREICHEN BANNER DER VEREINIGTEN STAATEN
TRUGEN ZAHLLOSE AUS DEUTSCHLAND EINGEWANDERTE ODER
VON DEUTSCHEN ELTERN IN AMERIKA GEBORENE MAENNER UND
FRAUEN ZUR KULTURELLEN ENTWICKLUNG DER NEUEN WELT
IN AUSSERORDENTLICH HOHEM MASSE BEI. IN LANDWIRTSCHAFT,
HANDEL, INDUSTRIE, TECHNIK, KUENSTEN UND WISSENSCHAFTEN,

---

[645] In the center between these two inscriptions are the arms of the United States, the arms of Germantown (a clover leaf), and the arms of the *Nationalbund* (an acorn).

FEIERTEN SIE GROSSE, ALLGEMEIN ANERKANNTE TRIUMPFE. DURCH IHRE AUS DEM ALTEN VATERLANDE MITGEBRACHTE LIEBE ZU MUSIK UND GESANG FOERDERTEN SIE DIE LEBENS-FREUDE DES GESAMMTEN AMERIKANISCHEN VOLKES, UND DURCH DIE EINFUEHRUNG DER TURNEREI STAEHLTEN SIE SEINE KRAFT. IM OEFFENTLICHEN UND POLITISCHEN LEBEN BEFUERWORTETEN SIE STETS EHRLICHKEIT. ALS ECHTE VORKAEMPFER UND VERTEIDIGER WAHRER FREIHEIT, VERGOSSEN SIE IN TREUER HINGABE FUER IHRE ADOPTIVHEIMAT, SOWOHL AUF DEN SCHLACHTFELDERN DES UNABHAENGIGKEITSKRIEGES, WIE DES DER AUFRECHTERHALTUNG DER UNION GELTENDEN BUERGER-KRIEGES IHR BLUT. UND SO ERFUELLTEN SIE IN JEDER BEZIEH-UNG ALS TREUE BUERGER DER GROSSEN REPUBLIK IHR PFLICHT.

On right pylon, back:[645]

DES ALTEN VATERLANDES NIE VERGESSEND, STOLZ AUF SEINE JAHRTAUSENDE ALTE KULTUR UND SEINE WAEHREND DER NEUZEIT ERKAEMPFTEN, UNVERGLEICHLICHEN ERRUNGEN-SCHAFTEN, STETS EINGEDENK DER HERRLICHEN MITGABEN, DIE DAS DEUTSCHTUM DER VEREINIGTEN STAATEN DEM ALTEN VATERLANDE VERDANKT, WIDMET DER AM 6. OCTOBER DES JAHRES 1901 IN PHILADELPHIA GEGRUENDETE DEUTSCH-AMER-IKANISCHE NATIONALBUND DEM DEUTSCHEN VOLKE DIESES ERINNERUNGSZEICHEN, UND VERBINDET DAMIT DEN INNIGEN WUNSCH, DASS DIE TAUSENDFAELTIGEN BEZIEHUNGEN ZWISCHEN DEUTSCHLAND UND DEN VEREINIGTEN STAATEN WIE BISHER SO AUCH FUER ALLE KOMMENDEN ZEITEN DIE GLEICHEN HERZ-LICHEN UND FREUNDSCHAFTLICHEN BLEIBEN MOEGEN. IM HIN-BLICK AUF DIE TATSACHE, DASS DIE ERSTE REINDEUTSCHE NIEDERLASSUNG AUF AMERIKANISCHEM BODEN, GERMANTOWN, VON AUS CREFELD STAMMENDEN MENNONITEN GEGRUENDET WURDE, IST DIESES DEM GESAMMTEN DEUTSCHEN VOLKE GEWIDMETE ZEICHEN DANKBARER ERINNERUNG DER STADT CREFELD ZUR OBHUT UEBERGEBEN WORDEN.

---

[645] For this note, see p. 425.

INDEX

INDEX